THE TRAVEL BOOK

A JOURNEY THROUGH EVERY COUNTRY IN THE WORLD

MELBOURNE | OAKLAND | LONDON

THE STORY OF THE TRAVEL BOOK

Most travel journeys take in just a country or two, but the journey you're about to embark on incorporates every country on earth. In this book you'll find evocative glimpses of every single country in the world, from Afghanistan to Zimbabwe, from the postage-stamp-sized Vatican City to the epic expanse of the Russian Federation.

To actually visit all the countries in this book would require several passports and a suitcase of plane tickets, or it can be simulated with a turn of these pages. Highlighted by some of the finest photography in the world, the *Travel Book* offers a glimpse of each country's perks and quirks: when to go, what to see, how to eat it up and drink it in, and ways to immerse yourself in the life and the land. What results is a grand snapshot of our diverse and kaleidoscopic world rather than an encyclopedic reference. It's a book that unashamedly views the planet through the prism of the traveller, focusing on places for their beauty, charm or singularity, even if this does sometimes conflict with defined political or geographical borders.

THE COUNTRY CONUNDRUM

A country count can be an arbitrary thing. At its core we've used the UN's list of 192 member states. Every one of these countries features in the book, but we've also built on the list to include foreign dependencies, whether they be self-governing or not, that are popular traveller destinations. Thus you'll find Caribbean islands (Anguilla, Cayman Islands, Guadeloupe, Martinique, Puerto Rico, Turks & Caicos, Virgin Islands), Atlantic islands (Bermuda, Falkland Islands) and Pacific islands (Cook Islands, Guam & Northern Marianas, New Caledonia, Pitcairn Islands, Tahiti & French Polynesia). There are the two great land masses of Antarctica and Greenland, which are too large and fascinating to leave out of any true world guide. There are disputed lands such as Palestine, Kosovo, Tibet and Taiwan, and recognisably unique regions such as Hong Kong, Macau and French Guiana. We've also divided Great Britain into its

component parts – England, Scotland and Wales – to recognise their individual appeal and their rich and distinctive histories and cultures.

At the book's end you'll find an additional 11 places of interest, chosen by Lonely Planet's founder and chief frequent-flyer Tony Wheeler. These bonus destinations are small dependencies that still warrant great attraction, whether it be the smoking cigar of Montserrat or that little piece of Britannia on the Mediterranean – Gibraltar. In total, you can read about 229 countries and destinations. It's exhausting just to think about.

THE STRUCTURE

The *Travel Book* follows the most straightforward of formats – A to Z – rolling through the alphabet of nations. From a travellers' perspective, a country's might and power aren't necessarily relative to its fascination and appeal, and we've tried to capture that, giving equal weight to every country regardless of whether it has had 15 minutes or 15 centuries of world fame – the likes of Djibouti and Suriname are as noteworthy here as the superpowers of the US and China.

The book's guiding philosophy is to present a subjective view of the world from Lonely Planet's perspective, looking below the surface to show a slice of life from every country in the world. Entries evoke the spirit of each place by appealing to the senses – what you might see and feel, what kind of food and drink might flavour your visit, and which books, music or films will help prepare you for the experience. You'll find the events, objects and people that are central to each country's identity and you'll find curious, little known facts.

Photos are paramount to capturing and sharing the spirit of a place and its people, and images in this book have been chosen to weave stories of their own. Clichéd icons and picture-postcard views have been avoided in favour of photos that tell of life in its myriad forms – at work, at play, at worship, laughing, singing, relaxing, dancing or just surviving – in order to bring you countries not brochures.

You may never visit all the *Travel Book's* destinations, but if it's true, as Aldous Huxley once wrote, that 'to travel is to discover that everyone is wrong about other countries', then to read about them all is to find out if you are right.

We hope the *Travel Book* inspires a world of travel.

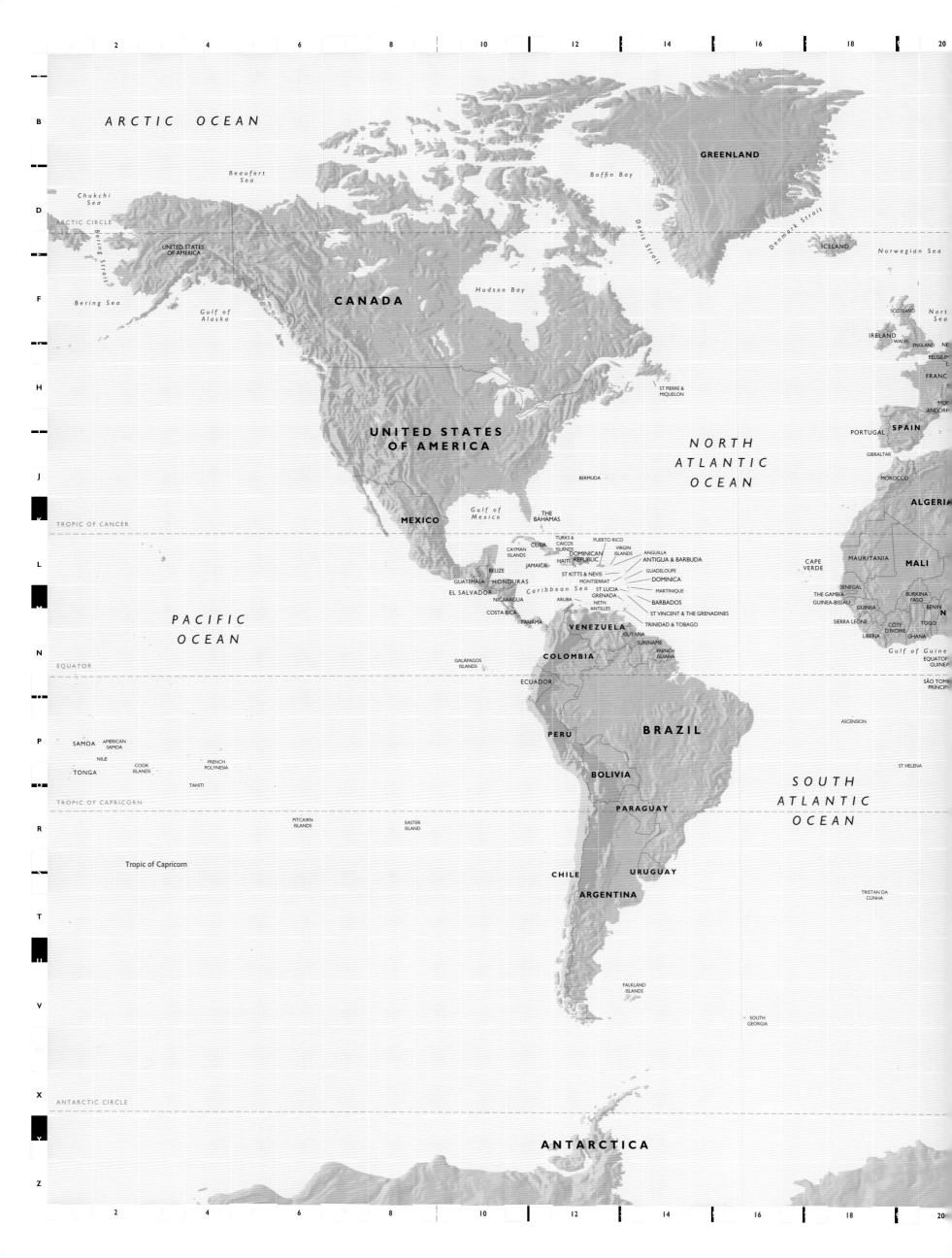

ARCTIC OCEAN

Chukchi Sea

Beaufort Sea

Baffin Bay

GREENLAND

Davis Strait

Denmark Strait

ARCTIC CIRCLE

ICELAND

Norwegian Sea

Bering Strait

Bering Sea

Gulf of Alaska

CANADA

Hudson Bay

SCOTLAND

North Sea

IRELAND

WALES

ENGLAND

NE

BELGIUM

UNITED STATES OF AMERICA

ST PIERRE & MIQUELON

FRANC

MON

ANDORR

PORTUGAL

SPAIN

NORTH ATLANTIC OCEAN

GIBRALTAR

UNITED STATES OF AMERICA

BERMUDA

MOROCCO

ALGERIA

TROPIC OF CANCER

MEXICO

Gulf of Mexico

THE BAHAMAS

TURKS & CAICOS ISLANDS

PUERTO RICO

CUBA

CAYMAN ISLANDS

DOMINICAN REPUBLIC

VIRGIN ISLANDS

ANGUILLA

ANTIGUA & BARBUDA

CAPE VERDE

MAURITANIA

MALI

HAITI

BELIZE

JAMAICA

ST KITTS & NEVIS

GUADELOUPE

SENEGAL

THE GAMBIA

BURKINA FASO

GUATEMALA

HONDURAS

MONTSERRAT

DOMINICA

GUINEA-BISSAU

BENIN

EL SALVADOR

Caribbean Sea

ST LUCIA

GRENADA

MARTINIQUE

GUINEA

N

NICARAGUA

ARUBA

NETH. ANTILLES

BARBADOS

SIERRA LEONE

CÔTE D'IVOIRE

TOGO

COSTA RICA

ST VINCENT & THE GRENADINES

LIBERIA

GHANA

PANAMA

TRINIDAD & TOBAGO

VENEZUELA

Gulf of Guine

PACIFIC OCEAN

GUYANA

SURINAME

EQUATOR

GALÁPAGOS ISLANDS

COLOMBIA

FRENCH GUIANA

EQUATOR

GUINEA

SÃO TOMÉ PRÍNCIPE

ECUADOR

SAMOA

AMERICAN SAMOA

ASCENSION

PERU

BRAZIL

NILE

FRENCH POLYNESIA

COOK ISLANDS

ST HELENA

TONGA

BOLIVIA

SOUTH ATLANTIC OCEAN

TAHITI

TROPIC OF CAPRICORN

PARAGUAY

PITCAIRN ISLANDS

EASTER ISLAND

R

Tropic of Capricorn

CHILE

URUGUAY

TRISTAN DA CUNHA

ARGENTINA

FALKLAND ISLANDS

SOUTH GEORGIA

ANTARCTIC CIRCLE

ANTARCTICA

2.

3.

1.

In another world, Afghanistan would be near the top of any list of must-see tourist destinations. The crossroads of Asia, it has blended cultural ingredients from the Indian subcontinent, Central Asia and Persia into something quite unique. Old Silk Road oases tell of a rich history of Buddhist and Islamic empires, while the Hindu Kush Mountains that bisect the country are as beautiful as Afghan hospitality is famously warm. Unfortunately, Afghanistan's recent troubled history is equally as famous, from the Soviet invasion to the continued trauma the country suffers following the Western intervention that ended Taliban rule. Afghan resilience and their desire for peace offer the ultimate key to the country's future.

BEST TIME TO VISIT
April to June and September to October – with all visits highly dependent on the political weather

TOP THINGS TO SEE
- The slow transformation of Kabul from war-ravaged capital to bustling Central Asian city
- The dizzying 800-year-old Minaret of Jam, adrift in the central mountains
- The skyline of Herat's medieval old city punctuated by its mighty citadel and thicket of minarets
- The blue domes of Mazar-e Sharif's Shrine of Hazrat Ali, Afghanistan's holiest pilgrimage site
- The Panjshir Valley, with its rushing river and neat villages and orchards

TOP THINGS TO DO
- Contemplate the ruins of the giant Buddha statues amid the serene Bamiyan Valley
- Trek with yaks across the High Pamir mountains in the Wakhan Corridor
- Dip your toes in the blue mineral waters of the Band-e Amir lakes
- Watch a thundering *buzkashi* match – Afghan polo played with a headless goat instead of a ball
- Haggle for Afghan carpets at their source with Pashtun, Uzbek and Turkmen traders

GETTING UNDER THE SKIN
Read Eric Newby's witty *A Short Walk in the Hindu Kush,* a genuine classic; Rory Stewart's *The Places In Between* makes an excellent post-Taliban travelogue

Watch *Osama*, directed by Siddiq Barmak, telling the story of a girl assuming a male identity to work in Taliban-era Kabul

Eat fat Kandahari pomegranates; sweet grapes from the Shomali Plain; and (according to Marco Polo) the best melons in the world

Drink *chai sabz* (green tea), drunk scaldingly hot at a traditional teahouse

IN A WORD
Salam aleikum (Peace be with you) – a ubiquitous greeting and blessing

TRADEMARKS
Bearded and turbaned men; veil-clad women; mountain views; tribal rugs; opium poppies; hospitality to guests

RANDOM FACT
The lapis lazuli in Tutankhamun's death mask were mined in northeastern Afghanistan

MAP REF J,27

1. Pilgrims arrive to pay their respects at the Shrine of Hazrat Ali, one of the country's most iconic sights
2. An Afghani man in Mazar-e Sharif sports an impressive beard typical of many locals
3. It's a good idea to find some shade in Kabul's warmer months
4. The remote and spectacular Minaret of Jam, rising 65m high, is Afghanistan's first World Heritage Site

1.

2.

3.

Albania may have been largely ignored by the rest of the world, but that doesn't seem to have bothered the Albanians. They've just got on with embracing life in a languid and chaotically post-communist way. Here, family and friends are most important and the gentle rhythms of rural life persist, as shepherds casually urge their flocks across major highways. In some regards, Albania is the wild frontier of Europe, little visited and little developed, but that is part of its charm. From its unforgiving northern mountains, to its unspoilt Adriatic and Ionian coastlines, from its vibrant markets to its picturesque museum towns, Albania unselfconsciously extends a warm welcome raising a weather-beaten fedora and a shot glass of raki in honour of visitors.

BEST TIME TO VISIT
April to October

TOP THINGS TO SEE
- Beautiful Berat, a preserved Ottoman town of whitewashed houses climbing up a hillside
- The serene ruins of ancient Butrint lost deep in the forest with a lakeside setting
- Bustling Tirana, a bizarre mix of state-of-the-art nightclubs, potholes, mosques, rainbow-coloured apartment buildings and communist-era architecture
- The 'Albanian gothic' of Gjirokastra, with its imposing views, looming citadel and grand architecture
- The castle of Kruja, with its *hamam* (Turkish bath) and dervish lodge

TOP THINGS TO DO
- Discover your own isolated beachside idyll on the little-visited Ionian coast
- Jump aboard the weekly ferry on Lake Koman for a trip into the mountainous interior
- Set out to explore the remote mountains and valleys of Thethi National Park
- Plunge into the bottomless, blue glassy depths of the Syr i Kalter spring
- Spend a night of grandeur in a restored Ottoman guesthouse in Gjirokastra

GETTING UNDER THE SKIN
Read *Chronicle in Stone* by Ismail Kadare, a boyhood tale set in Gjirokastra, and *Land of Eagles* by Robin Hanbury-Tenison, a horseback odyssey through modern Albania

Listen to the entwined vocal and instrumental parts of traditional southern Albanian polyphony

Watch Gjergj Xhuvani's *Slogan,* a wry and affectionate look at life in a mountain village during the communist era

Eat roast lamb in the mountains or freshly caught fish along the coast; *byrek* is the quintessential Albanian fast food: layered pastry filled with cheese, potato or minced meat

Drink raki (grape brandy, flavoured with aniseed) as an aperitif; or *konjak* (cognac) as an after-dinner tipple

IN A WORD
Tungjatjeta (Hello)

TRADEMARKS
Mountains; prickly minarets in mountain villages; the double-eagle flag; bunkers

RANDOM FACT
The Albanian language is unrelated to any other in Europe and is thought to derive from ancient Illyrian

MAP REF I,22

1. Three generations gather outside an old brick house, Peshkopi
2. Sticking close together: women looking after the cows in Peshkopi
3. A small brick church in the ancient Greek city of Apollonia is a reminder of the Middle Ages
4. Taxi drivers battle it out on the streets of Tirana

2.

3.

1.

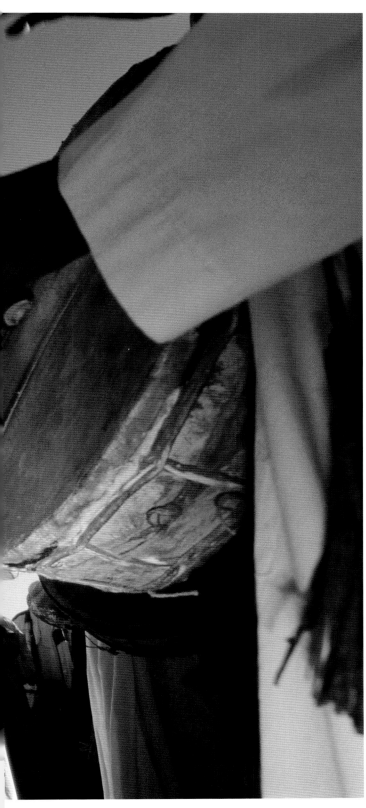

Until recently, Algeria was the great barrier to travel in North Africa, leaving a hole the size of Africa's second-largest country in the travellers' map of the continent. But after having been a byword for danger during the 1990s, Algeria has made a stunning return to peace. Not only is it safe to visit, but its catalogue of attractions – from wonderfully preserved Roman ruins in the north to the extraordinary Saharan landscapes and oasis towns of the south – may even surpass the better-known charms of Morocco, Tunisia and Libya. Best of all, with most travellers yet to realise that Algeria is open for business, you can enjoy all of these in the company of far more locals than tourists.

BEST TIME TO VISIT
November to April

TOP THINGS TO SEE
- The Casbah in Algiers, arguably North Africa's most intriguing medina
- Djemila's Roman ruins, beautifully sited in the Mediterranean's hinterland
- The stunning pastel-coloured oasis towns in the M'Zab Valley on the Sahara's northern fringe
- A spectacular sunrise from atop barren mountains deep in the Sahara at Assekrem
- Tassili N'Ajjer's open-air gallery of rock art from the time before the Sahara became a desert

TOP THINGS TO DO
- Sip a cafe au lait in Algiers' French-style sidewalk cafes then dive into the Casbah
- Dream of Algeria's Roman and Phoenician past at the charming old port of Tipaza
- Discover the hidden treasures of Tlemcen's extraordinary Arab-Islamic architecture
- Sleep amid the sand dunes of the Grand Erg Occidental
- Explore the Tassili du Hoggar, with some of the Sahara's most beautiful scenery

GETTING UNDER THE SKIN
Read *Between Sea and Sahara* by Eugene Fromentin, a classic of 19th-century travel literature; Jeremy Keenan's *Sahara Man: Travelling with the Tuareg*, which takes you deep into the Tuareg world

Listen to *King of Rai: The Best of Khaled*, for Algeria's best-loved musical (and most danceable) export

Watch Gillo Pontecorvo's *The Battle of Algiers*, a searing portrayal of the 1954–62 Algerian War of Independence, with Algiers' Casbah playing a starring role

Eat chickpea fritters, couscous and lamb tajine spiced with cinnamon

Drink three servings of strong tea around a Tuareg campfire

IN A WORD
Salaam aleikum (Peace be with you)

TRADEMARKS
The Sahara's biggest sand seas; the 'End of the World' (the literal translation of Assekrem); Tuareg nomads; Roman ruins along the Mediterranean Coast; civil war in the 1990s

RANDOM FACT
Some of France's most famous names were born in Algeria, including Edith Piaf, Albert Camus, Yves Saint-Laurent and Zinedine Zidane

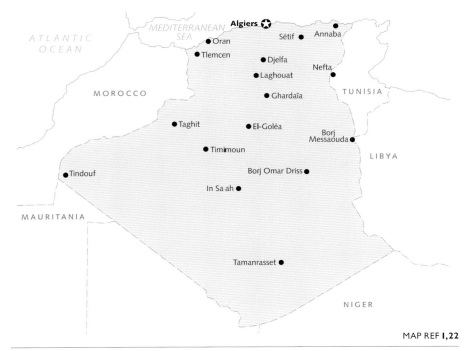

MAP REF I,22

1. Tuareg drummers defy the desert heat to put on a thumping performance, Tamanrasset
2. A rock climber's dream house? Traditional mudbrick buildings, complete with wooden spikes, are a common sight throughout Timimoun
3. A vehicle speeds through the lunar landscape of Tassili N'Ajjer, home to some incredible rock paintings
4. Giddy up! Camels race through the Sahara, Tuareg-style

1.

Racing down snowy pistes, nursing post-ski mulled wine and sleeping snug between ice-hotel walls is how most think of this principality in Europe, neatly wedged between France and Spain in the eastern Pyrenees. Fewer know about its history (that harks back to the 9th century), its people (Catalan-speaking Andorrans, staunchly Catholic and a minority in their own country), the cobbled old town that casts a summertime spell over the country's only town (Andorra la Vella) or its secret hoard of thermal spas that soothe skied-out limbs. Jet into Barcelona in neighbouring Spain, drive a couple of hours and dip into one of Western Europe's most intriguing mini-nations.

BEST TIME TO VISIT
Mid-December to early April during the ski season

TOP THINGS TO SEE
- The cobbled streets and hidden squares of Andorra la Vella's quaint historic quarter
- Andorra's three valleys – each justifies a one-day hike at least
- Grandvalira, the largest ski area in the Pyrenees
- The Musei del Tabac in Sant Julià de Lòria, a tobacco-factory-turned-museum devoted to the decadent pleasures of smoking and smuggling

TOP THINGS TO DO
- Ski the winter slopes of Grandvalira
- Wallow in toasty-warm mineral water at Europe's largest spa complex, Caldea in Andorra la Vella
- Join the dusk-time crowds on the rooftop of Plaça del Poble, Andorra la Vella, oohing and aahing over valley views
- Hike between tobacco fields and near-pristine meadows around the hamlet of Llorts
- Rip along downhill, cross-country and log-tree mountain-bike trails at the pulse-racing Vallnord Bike Park in La Massana

GETTING UNDER THE SKIN
Read the paperback reprint of *A Tramp in Spain: From Andalusia to Andorra,* a travelogue by Englishman Bart Kennedy who tramped, knapsack on back, to Andorra in 1904

Listen to something classical by the National Chamber Orchestra of Andorra directed by top Andorran violinist Gerard Claret – flip through its discography at www.onca.ad

Watch *Dies d'Hivern* (Days of Winter) directed by Andorran Josep Duran, about a band of young delinquents on a voyage of self-discovery

Eat hearty – think *trinxat* (bacon, potatoes and cabbage) or traditional *escudella* (a cockle-warming chicken, sausage and meatball stew)

Drink mulled red wine laced with lemon, apple, raisins, cinnamon and cognac after a day on the slopes

IN A WORD
Hola (Hello!)

TRADEMARKS
Skiing; shopping; smuggling; the Pyrenees

RANDOM FACT
Just 33% of people in Andorra are Andorran, making them a minority in their own country – Spaniards dominate

MAP REF **1,20**

1. In Arinsal, soar to dizzy heights for skiing in the winter and hiking in the summer

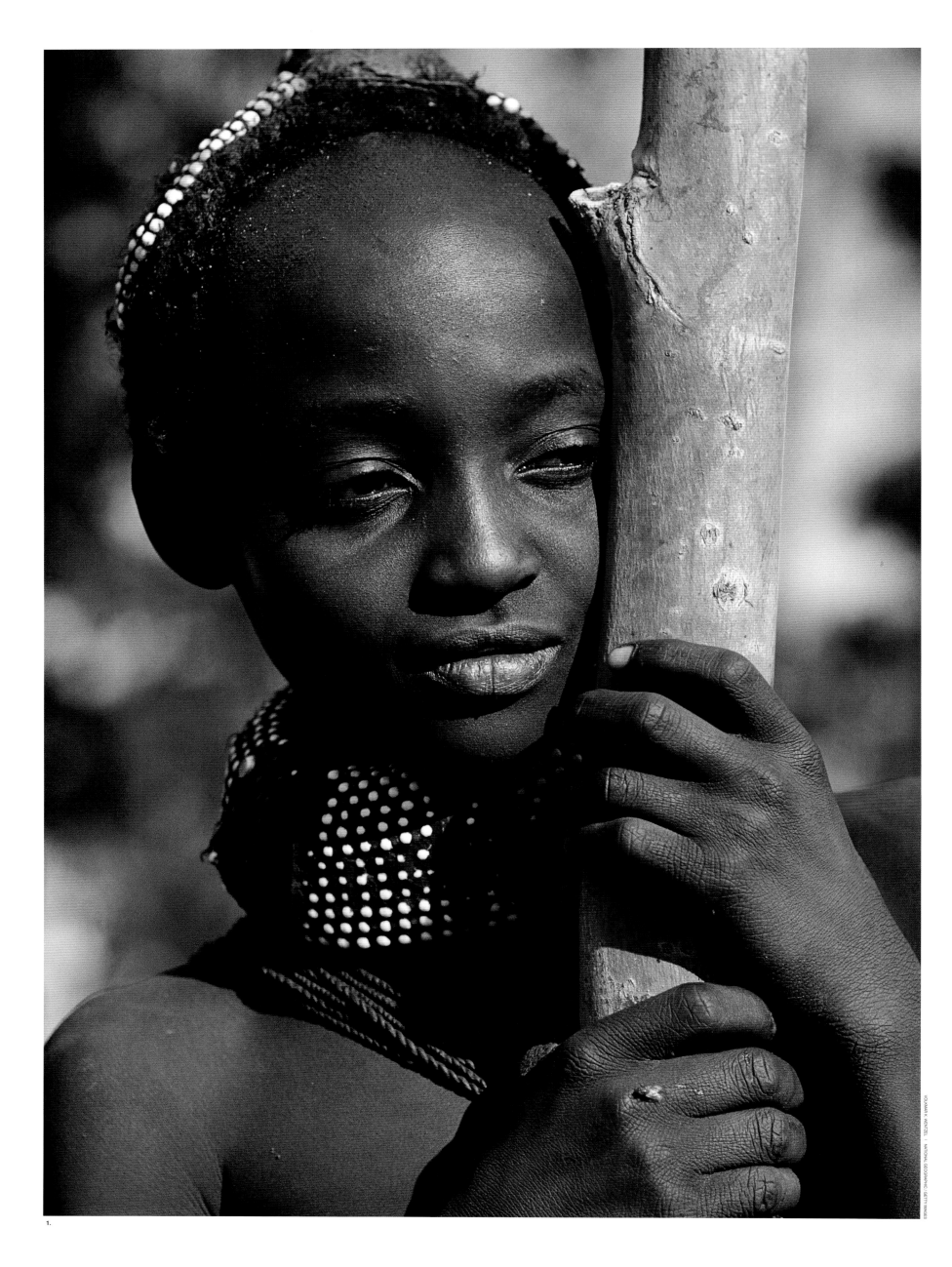

1.

2.

3.

Angolans are fighters – but they are lovers too. The latter fact has been lost on the world's press, who have long labelled this African nation a haven of havoc, broadcasting stories of its civil wars, blood diamonds, wasted oil revenues and starving people. For those who visit, however, it's the love that they'll remember. Whether it's an unquestioning love of God, an enthusiastic embrace of romance or an unwavering desire to dance like there is no tomorrow, the passion within the people of Angola is intoxicating to observe. Some may call it escapism to the nth degree – we call it resilience like no other.

BEST TIME TO VISIT
June to September during the cooler dry season

TOP THINGS TO SEE
- The crumbling art deco and neoclassical facades in the coastal town of Namibe
- Miradouro de Lua, a rusty-topped Martian-like rock formation that drops dramatically to the Atlantic
- The horizon-topping dunes of Parque Nacional do Iona
- The enigmatic Himba tribes that inhabit the nation's southern fringe
- The burgeoning wildlife of Parque Nacional da Kissama

TOP THINGS TO DO
- Join Cristo Rei, Angola's version of Rio's Cristo Rendentor, and stare down over the city of Lubango
- Get your hot hands on a surfboard and ride the cool Atlantic swells – they are some of Africa's best
- Be one of the first to ride the rejuvenated Benguela railway to the Congo's fringes
- Sink into the sands of a Luanda beach and soak up more than the sun – caipirinhas are a good start
- Try to keep your eyes open and your mouth shut at Luanda's mesmerising carnival

GETTING UNDER THE SKIN
Read *Angola: The Weight of History* by Patrick Chaba for an understanding of the social and political evolution since breaking free from Portuguese rule

Listen to anything with Carlos Vieira Dias, an acoustic guitarist who spread the influence of Angola's samba music

Watch *Rostov-Luanda*, a documentary hinged on a Mauritanian's journey to find an old friend in Angola

Eat *calulu de peixe* (fish stew)

Drink *galāos* (white coffee) – Angola has historically been one of the world's largest producers of the bean, and locals love it with milk

IN A WORD
Tudo bom (How's things?)

TRADEMARKS
Blood diamonds and *garimpeiros* (diamond diggers); oil; civil war; landmines; demining campaigns; staggering beaches; *kizomba* (a genre of dance and music that's full of romance and sensuality)

RANDOM FACT
It wasn't that long ago that Angola had more landmines than children

MAP REF **P,21**

4.

1. A Mwila girl is seemingly lost in thought
2. On the right track: three young friends walk the train line in Dondo
3. A church stands out upon the hill of Catumbela
4. A masked Chokwe man makes an imposing sight in front of a tree decorated with bones

17

2.

3.

1.

4.

The sun sets over the sea, leaving striations of orange amid the gently rippling azure waters. You lean back against the warm sands of a dune, letting an 'ahh' escape from your mouth as your back finds the perfect position. Artfully wrecked old wooden boats perch on the sand and soon you're hearing the ever-mellow strains of reggae, played by some of the Caribbean's most renowned musicians. It's just another evening on Anguilla, one of the region's smallest islands and one that takes every holiday cliché (perfect white sand, rum, reggae, turquoise waters et al) and distils them down to perfection. Visitors delight in a series of picture-perfect bays strung along the island's 10km length. Go for a stroll, chat to some locals, find your own beat.

BEST TIME TO VISIT
December to May are the best times to visit as hurricane threats and humidity levels are low

TOP THINGS TO SEE
° Shoal Bay, everything a Caribbean beach should be
° Prickly Pear is Anguilla distilled down to a milky white nub of sand amid the cyan sea
° Meads Bay, an idyllic mile-long crescent of blinding white sand
° Wallblake House and St Gerard's church, glimpses of 18th-century plantation life
° Sandy Ground is the appropriately named cluster of the island's languorous nightspots

TOP THINGS TO DO
° Sail the perfectly azure waters, it's the number one local sport
° Hide out in Junk's Hole, an especially intimate spot on an intimate island
° Carefully plan your day so that you do nothing at all; Anguilla means relaxation
° Dive the 1772 wreck of the *El Buen Consejo*
° Jam to the beat of the Dune Preserve, where local reggae legends play amid wrecked boats and, yes, dunes

GETTING UNDER THE SKIN
Read *Green Cane and Juicy Flotsam: Short Stories by Caribbean Women*

Listen to Bankie Banx, a celebrated Anguillan singer-songwriter known as a reggae pioneer

Watch one of the *Pirates of the Caribbean* movies to get in the mood

Eat the sweet, fresh local lobster and crayfish

Drink a Dune Shine (fresh ginger, pineapple juice, bitters and rum) at the Dune Preserve

IN A WORD
Limin' (Hanging out with friends, preferably on the beach)

TRADEMARKS
Beaches that are great even by Caribbean standards; wild goats running amok; ganja; sailing

RANDOM FACT
Anguilla was once part of St Kitts and Nevis but squabbles between pint-sized Anguilla and its more-populous neighbours caused a permanent split in 1967; it's taken shelter as a British overseas territory ever since

ATLANTIC OCEAN

Prickly Pear Cays

Sandy Island

CARIBBEAN SEA

Meads Bay

The Valley

Sandy Ground

Blowing Point

MAP REF **L,13**

1. A healthy catch: a spear fisherman reaps the rewards of a hard day's work
2. A musician concentrates on the absorbing beauty of the banjo
3. Sun, surf and church: a lovely stone church sits right on the beach
4. Lobster traps are unloaded amid stunning blue waters

1.

2.

3.

Snow, ice, water, rock, sky. The stark surroundings of Antarctica and the enormity of its ice shelves and mountain ranges make for an elemental beauty that can haunt you for the rest of your life. Nothing compares and nowhere else on earth can so heighten feelings of humanity's insignificance and nature's grandeur. The wildlife, including emperor penguins, leopard seals and minke whales, are not afraid of humans, allowing for spectacular and surreal close encounters. Governed by 29 nations, this continent/country is primarily dedicated to scientific research but it's also one of the planet's regions that's most visibly affected by global warming; as parts of the continent grow, others melt, leaving scientists to debate what it all actually means.

BEST TIME TO VISIT
November to February for 'summer'

TOP THINGS TO SEE
- Majestic icebergs and mountain reflections on the water at Paradise Harbour
- The true grit of Antarctic exploration icily preserved at Shackleton's expedition hut
- Dazzling blooms of violet, pink and white in the gardens on Campbell Island
- Three eerie ghost-filled explorer's huts on Ross Island
- A beautiful blue-eyed shag regurgitating a meal to its chick

TOP THINGS TO DO
- Glide on a zodiac under the morning's pink skies past basking Weddell seals and noisy gentoo penguins
- Sail inside the restless volcano at Deception Island
- Get startled by a loud 'fffff', then be bathed in a fish-scented mist as a whale surfaces next to your boat
- Experience the bluster of 'Home of the Blizzard', one of the windiest places on earth

GETTING UNDER THE SKIN
Read *Travelers' Tales Antarctica: Life on the Ice,* a collection of Antarctic tales from the goofy to the harrowing

Listen to Rothera Station's wintering rock band Nunatak – made up of two scientists, two engineers and a field assistant

Watch the beautifully restored footage of Shackleton's men and dogs working on the ice-beset ship *Endurance* in the 1998 film *South*

Eat an Antarctic barbecue, set up on deck or even on the ice

Drink an Antarctic Old Fashion: made from one fifth of 100-proof bourbon, seven packets of multiflavoured Life Savers sweets and just-melted snow

IN A WORD
The A-factor (The local term for the unexpected difficulties caused by the Antarctic environment)

TRADEMARKS
Icebergs; penguins; freezing cold; geologists; explorers; the South Pole; glaciers; seals; 24-hour sunlight, sled dogs; global warming

RANDOM FACT
Antarctica's ice sheets contain 90% of the world's ice – 28 million cu km – holding about 70% of the world's fresh water

MAP REF **Y,30**

1. You'll need a few layers of clothes to brave camping in the true wildnerness of Patriot Hills
2. The march of the king penguins spans the land as far as the eye can see, Lusitania Bay
3. Browning Peninsula resembles a bite taken from a giant ice-cream cake – and the aerial views are just as appetising
4. Roll on the ice like a local on the western Antarctic Peninsula

2.

3.

1.

Talk about opposites. Antigua is a bustling island that's home to many a commercial scheme including internet gambling plus a fair number of wintering celebrities, such as Eric Clapton, Ken Follet, Oprah and more. Island boosters push the notion that it has 365 beaches, one for every day of the year, but like wagers on the web, it's a tough claim to verify. No matter the number, the beaches are a sure bet, strung along the coasts like pearls on a necklace. Meanwhile Antigua's tiny sibling Barbuda has a fraction of the population, all scattered about a paradise of pink and white sand, much of it accessible only by boat.

BEST TIME TO VISIT
December to mid-April

TOP THINGS TO SEE
- Nelson's Dockyard on Antigua is an authentically preserved 18th-century British naval base
- Old hilltop forts guard serpentine coastal waters at English Harbour
- St John's, a slightly hardscrabble port town, has true-to-life markets and an energetic hubbub
- Flotsam, jetsam and shells of every shade and size fill the Nature of Things Museum
- The *Andes* is a coral-engulfed shipwreck easily reached by snorkellers

TOP THINGS TO DO
- Traverse Fig Tree Drive, some of the prettiest tropical scenery on Antigua
- Laze away on Hawksbill Bay, the best string of developed beaches
- Flock to Barbuda's rookery, Codrington Lagoon, the largest of its kind in the Caribbean
- Get in the pink strolling 17km of rose-hued sand on Barbuda's north side
- Hike with local history buffs on tours run by the Museum of Antigua and Barbuda

GETTING UNDER THE SKIN
Read Jamaica Kincaid's novel *Annie John*, which recounts growing up in Antigua

Listen to steel pan; calypso (with its roots in slave culture); ubiquitous reggae music; and zouk, the party music

Watch music videos shot on the islands by various big names in pop (many live on Antigua as tax exiles), such as Duran Duran

Eat *duckanoo* (a dessert made with cornmeal, coconut, spices and brown sugar); or black pineapple, sold along Fig Tree Drive

Drink the island's locally brewed rums – Cavalier or English Harbour

IN A WORD
Fire a grog (Drink rum)

TRADEMARKS
Cricket; countless pristine white-sand beaches on Antigua, and endless ones on Barbuda; internet gambling

RANDOM FACT
Most of Barbuda's 1100 people (2% of the country's population) share half a dozen surnames and can trace their lineage to a small group of slaves brought to the island in the late 1600s

MAP REF **L,13**

1. The picturesque site of Nelson's Dockyard, a restored 18th-century British naval base named after Lord Nelson, in English Harbour, is Antigua's most popular tourist attraction
2. Admire the colonial architecture of St John's Anglican Cathedral, Antigua's dominant landmark
3. Steel pan is the quintessential sound of Antigua and Barbuda
4. Showing her true colours: a woman celebrates Independence Day in Antigua

1.

2.

3.

Think big. The country boasting the highest Andean peak (Aconcagua) and the southernmost city (Ushuaia) can settle any other competing claims, true or not. In Argentina, engaging in life's everlasting debates – preferably over a steak and several bottles of wine – is part of the fun. Buenos Aires offers countless avenues to all-night revelry, but its rocket cab rides are only one route to adventure. Beyond the city limits, nature comes unabashed and boundless. The dry pastel hues of the desert in the north give way to the lush falls of Iguazú, the crisp skies of the lakes region and the glacier-clad south. Do as locals do. Slow down, accept time as fluid, and you will draw in all manner of encounters.

BEST TIME TO VISIT
March to May (spring) for Buenos Aires, December to March (summer) in Patagonia

TOP THINGS TO SEE
- A soaked and ear-shattering panorama of the spectacular Iguazú Falls
- The seductive steps of tango performed without a stage
- Endangered southern right whales in Reserva Faunística Península Valdés
- The kaleidoscopic colours of the desert valley of Quebrada de Humahuaca
- Stray cats and sculpted mausoleums in Recoleta Cemetery, the final stop for Buenos Aires' rich and famous

TOP THINGS TO DO
- Live it up till the sun comes up in Buenos Aires' bars and clubs
- Hear thunderous cracks watching the massive Glaciar Perito Moreno calve
- Test run various vintages on a *bodega* (winery) tour outside Mendoza
- Ride the windy range with *gauchos* (cowboys) at a Patagonian *estancia* (grazing establishment)
- Feast on steaks and every other part of a cow at a backyard *asado* (barbecue)

GETTING UNDER THE SKIN
Read Jorge Luis Borges' short story *The Gospel According to Mark*, a dark and witty allegory of admiration and misunderstanding between urban and rural folk

Listen to the wandering alt rhythms of Juana Molina, the folk-rock humor of Kevin Johansen, the tangos of Astor Piazzolla and gritty classic Argentine rock

Watch a young Che Guevara discover Latin America in *The Motorcycle Diaries*

Eat *empanadas* (pastries stuffed with savoury fillings), *alfajores* (a popular sweet) and *facturas* (sweet pastries)

Drink maté (pronounced mah-tay), a bitter tea served in a gourd with a metal straw and shared among friends and colleagues

IN A WORD
¡Andá! (Get out, I don't believe it!)

TRADEMARKS
Tango; maté rituals; Spanish colonial architecture; the Peróns; glaciers; the Andes; Patagonia; *gauchos;* grass-fed beef; Malbec wine

RANDOM FACT
At 70kg per capita, the yearly beef consumption in Argentina is the highest in the world

MAP REF **S,12**

1. Street art with a strong social message stands out in San Telmo, Buenos Aires
2. Tango dancers sweat it out in Plaza Dorrego, Buenos Aires
3. Argentinian cowboys await the call up at a rodeo in General Alvear, Buenos Aires Province
4. A hike in El Chaltén, Patagonia, will take you through some of the most spectacular scenery in the world

2.

3.

1.

4.

The high rocky plateau of Armenia is a redoubt of artistry and remote beauty. At the meeting point of Europe and the Middle East, an area noted for historical drama, the Armenians seem to have suffered more than their neighbours. Yet they have endured; seeking solace in their Christian faith, maintaining a fierce pride in their language, culture and homeland. Flaunting mountain passes, monasteries, walking trails, stonework architecture and lively Yerevan, Armenia offers an experience steeped in culture, outdoor adventure and the timeless pleasure of slowing down to the pace of the locals. Armenia is said to have its head in the West and its heart in the East: here you can experience a Mediterranean lifestyle beneath the Caucasus mountains.

BEST TIME TO VISIT
May to September

TOP THINGS TO SEE
- Yerevan, the cultural heart of the nation, with fabulous museums, galleries and buzzing Vernissage flea market
- Holy Echmiadzin, the seat of the Armenian Apostolic Church
- The artists' retreat of Dilijan, full of gingerbread-style houses and touted as the 'Switzerland of Armenia'
- Vayots Dzor, the southern province peppered with monasteries, walking trails, the Selim caravanserai and wine-growing Arpa Valley

TOP THINGS TO DO
- Slow down and tap into the fabulous street culture of Yerevan
- Clamber down to the snake pit once occupied by St Gregory the Illuminator, in Khor Virap Monastery
- Trundle the Debed Canyon, with forested valleys, quiet villages and monasteries
- Spend the day in Goris, home of potent fruit brandies and 5th-century cave houses

GETTING UNDER THE SKIN
Read *Visions of Ararat* by Christopher Walker, a compilation of writings by soldiers, anthropologists and poets; or *Armenia: Portraits of Survival and Hope* by Donald E Miller, snapshots of 1990s Armenian life

Listen to the mournful melodies of the *duduk* (traditional double-reed flute) played by *duduk* master Djivan Gasparyan

Watch the sumptuous, poetic *Colour of Pomegranates* by Sergei Paradjanov

Eat *khoravats* (skewered pork or lamb), so ubiquitous that lighting the barbecue is almost a daily ritual

Drink *soorch* (gritty and lusciously thick coffee); or *konyak* (cognac), the national liquor

IN A WORD
Genats (Cheers!)

TRADEMARKS
Intricate stonemasonry; medieval manuscripts; communal dining punctuated with raucous toasts

RANDOM FACT
Armenia was the first nation to accept Christianity as a state religion, converting en masse in AD 301

MAP REF I,24

1. A glowing atmosphere is created by worshippers lighting candles before Sunday Mass at the Mayr Tachar, Echmiadzin
2. A boy is carried by his faithful companion in rural Armenia
3. In Yerevan, a car boot provides transport for livestock
4. The 9th-century Tatev Monastery looks down over the Vorotan Canyon in southern Armenia

1.

2.

3.

Australia is as big as your imagination. Sure it's got deadly spiders, snakes and sharks, but they don't stop people from coming here, let alone living here. And for good reason. From endless sunbaked plains to dense tropical rainforest and wild southern beaches, Australia's biggest attraction is its natural beauty. Scattered along the coasts, its cities blend a European enthusiasm for art and food with a passionate love of sport and the outdoors. Visitors expecting to see an opera in Sydney one night and meet Crocodile Dundee the next day will have to rethink their geography; it is the sheer vastness that gives Australia – and its population – such immense character.

BEST TIME TO VISIT
Any time: when it's cold down south it's warm up north

TOP THINGS TO SEE
- The never-ending sunburnt horizons of the outback
- Kangaroos, koalas, platypuses and other near-alien, uniquely Australian critters
- A concert, dance or theatrical performance at the country's most recognisable icon, the Sydney Opera House
- The red hues of Uluru, an awe-inspiring place that is both ancient and sacred
- Broome, where the desert meets the sea in contrasting aquamarines, rust-reds and pearl whites

TOP THINGS TO DO
- Immerse yourself in the underwater world surrounding the only living structure visible from space, the Great Barrier Reef
- Discover Aboriginal culture, rock art and biological diversity at majestic Kakadu National Park
- Disappear into the wilderness along the Overland Track, Tasmania
- Breathe in the perfumes of bush and beach while driving the Great Ocean Road
- Sip on a well-balanced shiraz in the Barossa Valley

GETTING UNDER THE SKIN
Read *Cloudstreet,* Tim Winton's fascinating novel that chronicles the lives of two families thrown together in post-WWII Perth

Listen to Slim Dusty's 'Pub with No Beer', a classic Australian country tune; the soothing Aboriginal voice of Geoffrey Gurrumul Yunupingu on his album *Gurrumul*

Watch *Rabbit-Proof Fence,* a true story about three relocated Aboriginal girls who trek 2400km to return to their families

Eat fresh Sydney rock oysters; barely cooked purple-red kangaroo meat; Vegemite

Drink boutique beer; or any one of a huge selection of local wines

IN A WORD
G'day mate!

TRADEMARKS
Dangerous creatures; surfing; endless coastlines; outback pubs; barbecues; wildlife warriors; beer; Aussie Rules football; sunshine; Aboriginal art; convicts

RANDOM FACT
Great Australian inventions include the bionic ear, the black box flight recorder, the note pad and the wine cask

MAP REF **R,34**

1. Majestic hues characterise the outback scenery near Kookynie, Western Australia
2. One of Australia's iconic images: the Sydney Harbour Bridge sparkling over the harbour
3. A young Aboriginal dancer on Cape York Peninsula is marked with ceremonial paint
4. Hit by a freak cyclone in 1935, the shipwrecked *Maheno* still lies on Seventy Five Mile Beach, Fraser Island

2.

3.

1.

Austria is something of a film set, as lavish and decadent as a Viennese ball where old-society dames waltz, gallop and polka with new-millennium drag queens. Be it the jewel-box Habsburg palaces and coffee houses of Vienna, the baroque brilliance of Salzburg or the towering peaks that claw at the snowline above Innsbruck, the backdrop for travel in this predominantly German-speaking, landlocked Alpine country is phenomenal. Natural landscapes – a symphony of giddy mountain vistas, dazzling glaciers and jaw-dropping ravines – are as artful as a Mozart masterpiece or that romantic dance Strauss taught the world. Whether you're a culture vulture or a great-outdoors buff, Austria is one country in Europe where you'll have a real ball.

BEST TIME TO VISIT
Year-round

TOP THINGS TO SEE
- Vienna's Christkindlmarkt (Christmas market), mug of mulled wine in hand
- The opulent state apartments, prancing Lipizzaner stallions and jewels the size of golf balls in Vienna's palatial Hofburg
- Salzburg, the city where music, art and architecture achieve baroque perfection
- Innsbruck's medieval heart dwarfed by majestic snowcapped peaks
- Eisriesen, the world's largest accessible ice caves

TOP THINGS TO DO
- Revel in Vienna's extraordinary cultural extravaganza, climaxing with a performance at its celebrated opera house
- Catch a Sunday morning concert by the Vienna Boys' Choir, at the Burgkapelle
- Road-trip through the Hohe Tauern National Park along the overwhelmingly scenic Grossglockner road
- Dip into one lake after another in the glassy-blue Salzkammergut lake district
- Hurl yourself on skis down the spectacular Harakiri – Austria's steepest slope – in Mayrhofen, or hobnob with the jet-set ski crowd in upmarket Lech

GETTING UNDER THE SKIN
Read *The Piano Teacher* (also a film) by 2004 Nobel Laureate Elfriede Jelinek to acquaint yourself with one of the most provocative Austrian writers

Listen to Beethoven, Mozart, Haydn and Schubert

Watch Milos Forman's *Amadeus* for the tale of Mozart and composer Antonio Salieri

Eat a bowl of soup speckled with *Knödel* (dumplings), followed by a *Weiner schnitzel* (breaded veal or pork escalope) and sweet *Salzburger Nockerl* (fluffy soufflé)

Drink *Sturm* (semifermented Heuriger wine) in autumn; *Glühwein* (hot spiced red wine) in winter; and coffee in a *kaffeehaus* any time of year

IN A WORD
Grüss Gott (Hello)

TRADEMARKS
Julie Andrews and *The Sound of Music;* apple strudel; Strauss waltzes; edelweiss; Arnold Schwarzenegger; Freud; Mozart

RANDOM FACT
Vienna is the largest wine-growing city in the world

CAPITAL Vienna | **POPULATION** 8,210,281 | **AREA** 83,871 sq km | **OFFICIAL LANGUAGE** German (Slovene, Croat & Hungarian in southern states)

MAP REF **H,21**

1. Take a tram to the doorstep of the Staatsoper for a night at the opera, Vienna
2. The hills are alive with the sound of cow bells in the picturesque Alpine pastures of Tirol
3. Pop in for a bite at one of the atmospheric restaurants that line the streets of Grinzing, Vienna
4. Grab your toboggan and hit the slopes at Nauders, Tirol

1.

2.

3.

Legend has it that Azerbaijan was the site of the Garden of Eden. Tucked beneath the Caucasus Mountains and facing the Caspian Sea, it is where Central Asia edges into Europe, with a melange of Turkic, Persian and Russian influences contributing to its fabric. Little-visited Azerbaijan offers dramatic and untouched mountain vistas, the gritty reality of Caspian seashore oil rigs, ancient Zoroastrian temples, Bronze-Age petroglyphs and elegant caravanserais seemingly lifted straight out of the *Arabian Nights*. The modern Azeris, well versed in Turkic legend and Persian poetry, are a passionate and overwhelmingly hospitable people, who enjoy the timeless pleasures of a glass of *çay* (tea) with friends over a spirited game of *nard* (backgammon) and the lyrical intensity of local bards singing *muğam* (traditional musical style).

BEST TIME TO VISIT
May to June and September to November

TOP THINGS TO SEE
- Baku, the capital, a fabulous mix of belle époque mansions, Islamic architecture, modern nightspots and a medieval walled quarter
- Remote Xinaliq, tucked away in the high Caucasus, a village of stone houses untouched by modernity
- The rusty oil derricks emerging from the Caspian Sea off the Abşeron Peninsula
- The coppersmiths of Lahic, hammering away at the town's renowned artwork

TOP THINGS TO DO
- Horse trek in the Caucasus, following ancient mountain trails with a local guide
- Get lost in the atmosphere of Baku's Old City, wandering the narrow alleyways around the Palace of the Shirvanshahs
- Hold your nose as you visit the 'flatulent', sputtering mud volcanoes of Qobustan
- Climb to the peak of Beşbarmaq Dağ for the views and to kiss 'sacred' rocks

GETTING UNDER THE SKIN
Read *Ali & Nino,* Kurban Said's epic novel about a doomed love affair between an Azeri Muslim and a Georgian Christian, set in early-20th-century Baku

Listen to *muğam*, Azerbaijan's very own musical idiom, a traditional minstrel art form that's emotional and spine tingling

Watch Ayaz Salayev's award-winning *The Bat;* or Samil Aliyev's *The Accidental Meeting*

Eat flame-grilled *shashlyk* (lamb kebab); or the national speciality, *aş* (a local version of spicy pilaf laden with fruit, lamb and saffron)

Drink *çay* (tea) at a traditional teahouse, or just about anywhere else in the entire country

IN A WORD
Salam (Hello)

TRADEMARKS
Caspian caviar; traditional copperware and Turkic carpets; industrial detritus of the oil industry; the click-clack of *nard* (backgammon) tiles

RANDOM FACT
'Layla', Eric Clapton's classic rock song was inspired by the Azeri epic poem *Layla and Majnun*

MAP REF **1,25**

1. Furry hats are a sensible choice during winter in the Caucasus mountains
2. A game of backgammon is a popular way to spend a Sunday morning in Baku, the country's capital
3. The Soviet influence is clear in Baku
4. People displaced by the Nagorno-Karabakh conflict that ended in 1994 still reside in refugee camps

1.

3.

2.

GREG JOHNSTON | LONELY PLANET IMAGES

4.

GEORGE H H HUEY | CORBIS

If you visited an island a day, you'd have over eight years of perfect adventure in the Bahamas, where some 3100 dot the glistening blue waters like a king's ransom of diamonds spread across a velvet cloth. Hundreds are no bigger than a mere limestone poking above the swells and sheltering the odd sea bird. But others like Eleuthera are more than 150km in length: long linear playgrounds for sunseekers languidly seduced by the eternally balmy climate. Cities such as Nassau have a vibrant commercial beat that comes with a strong British accent. However, head out to the far and forgotten corners of the appropriately named Out Islands and the only accent you hear may well be your own.

BEST TIME TO VISIT
Year-round: December to February (winter) to escape northern cold, June to August (summer) for full-on tropical heat and humidity

TOP THINGS TO SEE
○ Nassau's pirate museums and seemingly endless shopping strips
○ Inagua National Park, roosting spot for untold thousands of pink flamingos
○ Harbour Island, where the sands – not the birds – are pink
○ Cat Island, a tradition-bound outpost untouched by modernity
○ Long Island with over 120km of empty beaches and pastel-hued villages

TOP THINGS TO DO
○ Kayak among dozens of tiny islands (cays) in the Exumas, camping when the mood strikes
○ Island-hop by mail boat, the traditional links to the nation's furthest reaches
○ Savour grilled lobster and conch at a beachside shack on Grand Bahama
○ Take the plunge at the divers haven of Small Hope Bay and explore the trademark tropical surrounds
○ Find and explore a perfect shipwreck (there's at least one or two for every island)

GETTING UNDER THE SKIN
Read Brian Antoni's *Paradise Overdose*, about the 1980s drug- and sex-addled Bahamian high life

Listen to Tony Mackay, alias Exuma, who was a performer and musical superhero from Cat Island; among his classic Caribbean-themed songs is 'The Obeah Man'

Watch James Bond in action in *For Your Eyes Only*, *The Spy Who Loved Me* and *Never Say Never Again* for the Bahamas backdrop

Eat conch (a mollusc served pounded, minced and frittered; marinated and grilled; or even raw as ceviche)

Drink Kalik (a light, sweet lager); or a goombay smash, a dangerously easy to quaff rum punch

IN A WORD
Hey man, what happ'nin'?

TRADEMARKS
Casinos; luxury yachts; golf courses; rum sun, sand and sin; deserted islands

RANDOM FACT
Many Bahamians practice obeah, a ritualistic form of magic with deep African roots

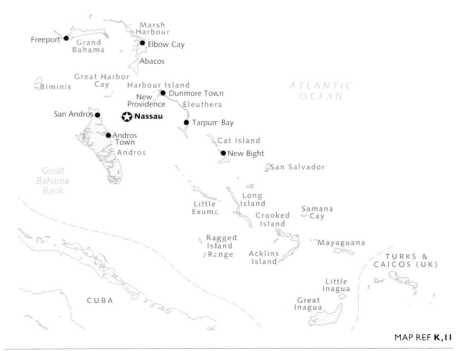

MAP REF **K,11**

1. Experience necessary: local sailors balance a boat while sailing the seas around the Bahamas
2. Even those living in paradise still have to go to school! Girls make their way along the white sands of one of the Bahama's many stunning beaches
3. Cycle the pleasant streets of Green Turtle Cay's New Plymouth, past weatherboards and picket fences
4. Refreshingly undeveloped for tourism, remote Cat Island has some superb diving and snorkelling

1.

2.

3.

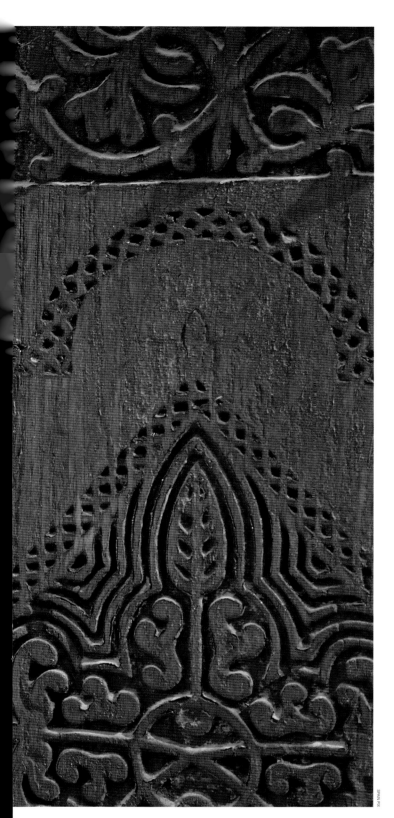

If you've never heard of Bahrain, don't be surprised – this tiny island state is the smallest of all Arab countries and rarely makes news. That's the way the locals like it, for this is Dubai without the glitz. It wasn't always thus. The one-time base for the ancient Dilmun Empire, Bahrain has been doubly blessed: not only is the country rich in oil, but in underwater pearls as well. And it packs into a small space plenty to keep you occupied, from improbable wildlife-watching opportunities to some of the region's best museums and archaeological sites. Best of all, this is one of the most easygoing of Persian (or Arabian) Gulf States and, as such, an ideal introduction to the region.

BEST TIME TO VISIT
November to March

TOP THINGS TO SEE
° 5000 years of history under one roof at Bahrain National Museum
° The Portuguese-era Bahrain Fort built atop fascinating archaeological ruins
° A'Ali with Dilmun burial mounds, pottery workshops and modern art
° King Fahd Causeway, an extraordinary feat of modern engineering connecting Bahrain to Saudi Arabia
° Al-Areen Wildlife Park and Reserve, where you can see 240 bird species and Arabian oryx

TOP THINGS TO DO
° Dive for pearls then visit the Museum of Pearl Diving to learn all about Bahrain's most exotic industry
° Get up close and personal with dolphins in the calm waters of the Gulf
° Wander amid the traditional wind towers, sandstone architecture and Manama's modern jewels of Beit al-Quran and Al-Fatih Mosque
° Explore modern Bahrain's alter ego in the old-style architecture of Muharraq Island
° Spot flamingos and cormorants en masse on the Hawar Islands

GETTING UNDER THE SKIN
Read Geoffrey Bibby's *Looking for Dilmun*, a story of archaeological treasure-hunting and a window onto 1950s and '60s Bahrain

Listen to *Desert Beat* by Hashim al-Alawi

Watch *Al-Hajiz* (The Barrier), *Za'er* (Visitor) or *A Bahraini Tale*, all directed by Bassam Al Thawadi – they're the only three films ever made in Bahrain

Eat *nekheh*, *bajelah* and *loobah* (a trio of spicy bean soups); *makboos* (rice and spices served with chicken, lamb or fish); *khabees* (a date-laden dessert)

Drink fresh fruit juices; cardamom-infused Arabic-style coffee

IN A WORD
Al-hamdu lillah (Thanks to God)

TRADEMARKS
Ancient Dilmun Empire; pearl diving and natural pearls for sale; Gulf Air; some of the Arab world's most sought-after dates

RANDOM FACT
The creative interpretation of ancient texts has led some historians to conclude that Bahrain is the true Garden of Eden of biblical fame…

MAP REF **K,25**

1. Open-door policy: a hospitable local holds open a traditional carved door in Muharraq
2. A special occasion: a young Bahraini girl is resplendent in traditional gold jewellery
3. The Al-Fatih Mosque was lovingly constructed with marble from Italy, glass from Austria and teak wood from India
4. Musicians drum up a festive spirit in the lively city of Manama

2.

3.

1.

4.

For years the Bangladesh tourist board used the slogan 'See Bangladesh before the tourists come', but the anticipated flood of tourists never materialised. Don't worry – the lack of tourist infrastructure is half the appeal of this fascinating Asian backwater, where rivers function as main roads and the Muslim call to prayer rings out across the paddy fields. Before 1947, Bangladesh was the eastern half of Indian Bengal; then from 1947 to 1971 it was East Pakistan. Even today, the world's most crowded nation is struggling to forge its own identity in the face of floods, cyclones and political turmoil. Nevertheless, visitors love Bangladesh for the way it seems to float forever in a vanished monsoon summer from the 1970s.

BEST TIME TO VISIT
October to February

TOP THINGS TO SEE
- The unbelievable crowds at the Sadarghat docks in Dhaka
- The domes and arches of the Shait Gumbad Mosque in Bagerhat
- A Royal Bengal tiger (if you get lucky) in the Sundarbans National Park
- Time-worn temple ruins at Paharpur and Kantanagar
- Ocean waves breaking on the beach on tiny St Martin's Island

TOP THINGS TO DO
- Ride the *Rocket* – the paddle-wheel ferry that trundles from Dhaka to Khulna
- Feel the liberation of wearing a *lungi* (sarong) for the day
- Drop in on the Buddhist tribal villages cotted around serene Kaptai Lake
- Stroll barefoot along the world's longest beach at Inani near Cox's Bazaar
- Experience the surreal phenomenon of a rickshaw traffic jam

GETTING UNDER THE SKIN
Read the blogs and polemic poetry of Maqsoodul Haque, Bangladesh's 'poet of impropriety', at http://tpoi.blogspot.com

Listen to the rousing poems of Bangladesh's national poet Kari Nazrul Islam – dozens of different recordings of his works are available in Dhaka

Watch Satyarjit Ray's Bengali classic *Apu Trilogy;* or hunt down Tareque Masud's *Matir Moina* to appreciate the growing maturity of the Dallywood (Dhaka) film industry

Eat *ilish macher paturi* (a classic Bengali dish of *hilsa* fish steamed inside banana leaves)

Drink *sharbat* (chilled yoghurt with chilli, coriander, cumin and mint) – the perfect accompaniment to a fiery curry

IN A WORD
Tik aache (No problem)

TRADEMARKS
Endless rice fields; monsoon-swollen rivers; rickshaw traffic jams; men in *lungis*; tea plantations; swaying coconut palms; Buddhist hill tribes; tigers in the Sundarbans; the political legacy of the 1971 Bangladesh Liberation War

RANDOM FACT
The national game of Bangladesh is *hadudu,* a group version of tag where players must evade the opposing team while holding a single breath of air

MAP REF **K,29**

1. Escape the heat and chaos of the cities to unwind in the peaceful tea plantations of Srimangal
2. No need to prebook train tickets in Bangladesh – unless you want a seat that is!
3. You'll come across plenty of colour, friendly faces and memories in the hectic streets of Old Dhaka
4. In a country that's 90% Muslim, Hindu Street in Old Dhaka is a fascinating point of difference

You can drive almost all day on Barbados and never see a beach. Is that heresy in the sandy-shore-obsessed Caribbean? Not really, as this pork-chop-shaped island has a deep interior traversed by narrow, winding roads that pass through colonial backwaters, atmospheric old plantations and tiny villages where the unscrewing of a rum bottle cap is the highlight of the day. And beach bums take heart – all roads eventually lead to the coast, which is ringed with strands of white sand, each with a distinct personality. Find wave-tossed surfer havens in the east; palm-fringed bays with resorts great and small in the west. Across this tidy island nation you can enjoy one of the Caribbean's most genteel cultures.

BEST TIME TO VISIT
February to May

TOP THINGS TO SEE
- Barclay's Park with miles of walks along a seashore ripe for beachcombing
- St Nicholas Abbey combines the beauty of a plantation estate with revelations about the horrors of the slavery
- Andromeda Gardens, one of several lushly flowered botanical gardens
- Lavishly restored George Washington House, the great man's home in 1751
- Nidhe Israel Museum attests to the richly multicultural heritage of Barbados

TOP THINGS TO DO
- Cheer madly for your team at a raucous cricket match
- Surf the legendary Soup Bowl on the east coast
- Get in the groove of Bridgetown, the island's capital and home to dockside cafes, appealing shops and thriving markets
- Flit across the waves at southern windsurfing havens like Silver Sands
- Explore the tiny coastal road to Fustic, where ages-old fishing enclaves snooze amid riots of flowers

GETTING UNDER THE SKIN
Read the acclaimed 1953 novel *The Castle of My Skin* by Bajan author George Lamming, in which he tells what it was like growing up black in colonial Barbados

Listen to calypso artist the Mighty Gabby and Rupee, a soca artist

Watch *The Tamarind Seed* starring Omar Sharif and Julie Andrews, a romance-cum-spy thriller

Eat a range of dishes with African roots adapted to local produce, such as *cou-cou* (a creamy cornmeal and okra mash, often served with saltfish) and *jug-jug* (a mix of cornmeal, peas and salted meat)

Drink world-renowned Mount Gay rum

IN A WORD
Workin' up (dancing)

TRADEMARKS
Cricket fanatics; elderly women in prim hats; calypso music; flying fish sandwiches

RANDOM FACT
Barbados boasts more world-class cricket players on a per capita basis than any other nation

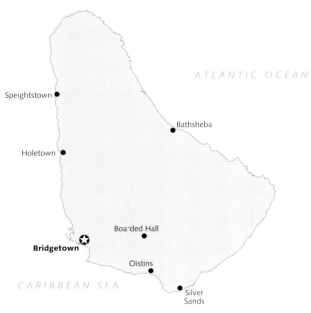

ATLANTIC OCEAN

Speightstown

Bathsheba

Holetown

Boarded Hall

Bridgetown

Oistins

CARIBBEAN SEA

Silver Sands

MAP REF **M,13**

1. Party time in Barbados! Crop-Over Festival, a must for calypso lovers, is a three-week event celebrating the end of the sugar-cane harvest
2. Share a joke with the locals
3. The sun sets over another day in paradise
4. Leave coconut fetching to the experts as you relax on stunning beaches

4.

2.

3.

1.

Widely hailed as 'the last dictatorship in Europe', Belarus is at first glance a country deeply in touch with the USSR circa 1974. This is the land of Soviet-style architecture, state-run media and a centralised economy that ensures every supermarket carries the same bland assortment of goods. Despite the hardships, Belarusians still find cause for animation: traditional folk singing and dancing features prominently on the calendar, and the performing arts remain a national treasure. Belarusians are also among the most generous and warm-hearted of people and relish life's simple pleasures: weekends spent at the *dacha* (summer country house); mushroom picking among birch groves; steaming away at the *banya* (bathhouse); or lingering over memorable, all-day feasts at a friend's home.

BEST TIME TO VISIT
May to September

TOP THINGS TO SEE
- Minsk with its mix of Soviet-era glower, clubs and top-notch theatre and dance
- Wild bison (and 55 other mammal species) plus 600-year-old oak trees at Belavezhskaja Pushcha National Park, the oldest wildlife refuge in Europe
- The stunning Brest Fortress, a Soviet WWII memorial that commemorates Soviet resistance against the German invasion
- Dudutki, a reconstructed 19th-century Belarusian village with craft-making exhibits, horse riding and local delicacies, including *samagon* (moonshine)

TOP THINGS TO DO
- Follow the masochistic recipe for good health at a Belarusian bathhouse: sit in a steam room, beat yourself with damp twigs, dunk yourself in icy water, repeat
- Wander the atmospheric old neighbourhoods of Vitsebsk, birthplace of native son Marc Chagall, one of the great masters of 20th-century art
- Explore the vast swath of marshes, swampland and floodplains of the seemingly haunted Pripyatsky National Park

GETTING UNDER THE SKIN
Read *Home Fires: Stories by Writers from Byelorussia*, edited by Elvina Moroz, a collection of short stories by some of the country's finest prose stylists

Listen to the vaguely apocalyptic improvisations of Knyaz Myshkin, a Minsk-based band

Watch Viktar Dashuk's *Report From the Rabbit Hutch*, an investigation into the disappearance of President Lukashenko critics

Eat *solyanka* (meat, potato and pickled vegetable soup); and *draniki* (potato pancakes)

Drink *kvass* (an elixir made of malt, flour, sugar, mint and fruit)

IN A WORD
Vitayu (Hello)

TRADEMARKS
Onion-domed churches; mountain villages; potatoes; snow; fur hats; monasteries; radioactive countryside (near Chornobyl)

RANDOM FACT
Many Belarusian folk-remedies involve vodka: gargle with it to cure a sore throat, wash your hair with it to alleviate dandruff and pour it in your ear to treat an earache

LATVIA

RUSSIA

LITHUANIA

Polatsk

Vitsebsk

Orsha

Maladzechna · Khatyn

✪ Minsk

Hrodna

Njasvizh · Babrujsk

Baranavichy

POLAND

Salihorsk

Homel

Brest

UKRAINE

MAP REF **G,23**

---

1. A big drill makes ice fishing that little bit easier
2. A Belarusian man enjoys a cigarette
3. In Homel devout worshippers pray in a church decorated with images of Jesus
4. Sunbathing is a serious business in Minsk

2.

3.

4.

There are few places that feel more in the heart of Europe than this, a multilingual country smack-bang in the middle of Western Europe that Dutch-speaking Flemish in the north call België, and French-speaking Walloons in the south call La Belgique. Indeed, it's this north–south, cultural and linguistic divide that makes this unusually intimate country with such dreary wet weather so unexpectedly fascinating. Amble in the shade of sensual art-nouveau architecture in its capital; give a nod to the EU headquarters; surrender to the sweet seduction of Europe's finest chocolate; have a ball in Antwerp's avant-garde fashion and dance clubs; down a fine local beer or three; and know this is what Belgians north and south call the good life.

BEST TIME TO VISIT
May to September

TOP THINGS TO SEE
° Brussels' guildhalls of medieval craftsmen on Grand Place
° Galeries St Hubert, the grande dame of 19th-century shopping arcades, and nearby rue des Bouchers with its barking hawkers and bevy of dining addresses
° Medieval Bruges
° Go-slow Ghent – explore it by bike
° In Antwerp, Belgium's largest Gothic cathedral Onze Lieve Vrouwekathedraal and the four paintings by Rubens inside

TOP THINGS TO DO
° Meet the art-nouveau movement at the Musée Horta, Brussels
° Get gooey over expensive and extraordinary pralines and truffles by prized chocolate-maker Pierre Marcolini
° Shop for fashion by local designers, fine dine and dance until dawn in Antwerp
° Chill in the French-speaking town of La Roche-en-Ardenne
° Join beer pilgrims in In de Vrede – the Westvleteren trio brewed is Belgium's best

GETTING UNDER THE SKIN
Read two hilarity-packed chapters on Belgium by Bill Bryson in *Neither Here nor There*

Listen to harmonica virtuoso Toots Thielemans blast the best of Belgian jazz with *Hard to Say Goodbye – The Very Best of Toots Thielemans*

Watch *Le Silence de Lorna* (Lorna's Silence) – the grim tale of an Albanian girl growing up in Belgium – by Belgian film-making brothers Jean-Pierre and Luc Dardenne

Eat a steaming cauldron of mussels cooked in white wine with a mountain of *frieten/frites* (fries or chips)

Drink Trappist beer brewed by monks in Rochefort

IN A WORD
Dag/Bonjour (Hello in Dutch/French)

TRADEMARKS
Chocolate; beer; cafe culture; comic-strip hero Tintin; the EU; Battle of Waterloo; 1960s *chansonnier* Jacques Brel; art-nouveau architecture

RANDOM FACT
Belgium's real-time linguistic divide was carved in stone in 1962 when the official line was drawn between Dutch-speaking Flanders and French-speaking Wallonia

MAP REF **G,20**

1. The Cathedral of St Bavon makes for a great landmark when you've been out on the town in Ghent
2. Explore the old town of Ghent for character-filled bars and Belgian beer
3. Get into the festive spirit at the Carnival of Binche
4. Whimsical colours accent the beautiful architecture in the popular Flemish city of Bruges

1.

2.

3.

Could you be loved? Belize's answer to Bob Marley is yes. Reggae and the barefoot lifestyle rule this pocket-sized English-speaking nation, creating an ambience more-precisely Caribbean than Central American. Long the haunt of pirates, its modern treasures include wide sandy beaches, turquoise waters and the second-biggest coral reef in the world. Paradise does have its flaws. Belize still struggles to recover its image from smugglers and street crime. Yet most find it open to respectful newcomers and to be decidedly laid-back. Over half a million visitors flock here yearly – but be assured that most arrive via cruise ship and sail off just as quickly, leaving the rest for you.

BEST TIME TO VISIT
January to June (when there is less rain)

TOP THINGS TO SEE
- Northern Cayes, the world's second-largest coral reef
- Black howler monkeys at the Community Baboon Sanctuary
- Caracol, a vast Mayan city whose population once rivalled today's Belize, now tucked into matted jungle
- A rousing cricket match in the MCC grounds of Belize City
- Belmopan, the world's smallest capital city

TOP THINGS TO DO
- Groove to live Punta rock, which fuses Garífuna drum beats, soca and reggae
- Sail the cayes with rod and flippers ready
- Explore the narrow passages of Barton Creek Cave amid archaeological remnants
- Snorkel the warm Caribbean waters with sharks and sea horses
- Look for Big Bird – the 5ft-tall jaberoo stork common to Crooked Tree Lagoon

GETTING UNDER THE SKIN
Read *The Last Flight of the Scarlet Macaw,* Bruce Barcott's account of one activist making a difference in Belize

Listen to the Garífuna rhythms, culture and politics of Andy Palacio's *Til Da Mawnin*

Watch Harrison Ford face jungle fever in *The Mosquito Coast,* filmed in the Belize interior, though the setting is neighbouring Honduras

Eat the Belizean menu staples of rice and beans, perfect with a dash of Marie Sharp's famous hot sauce

Drink the sweet water of green coconuts split open by machete; traditional cashew wine at the Cashew Festival in Crooked Tree

IN A WORD
Arright? (You alright? – the ubiquitous greeting)

TRADEMARKS
Mayan ruins; beach resorts; reef diving; reefers

RANDOM FACT
As a solution to the overpopulation of the red lionfish, whose poisonous spines make it all but invincible, Belize wants to commercialise this invasive Pacific species as fine cuisine – and some top chefs are biting

MAP REF **L,10**

1. Kids have a ball in the steets of Belize City
2. Make friends with laid-back locals in Belize City
3. Move your hips to the rhythm of Punta rock
4. Track the elusive jaguar in the jungles of Belize

2.

3.

1.

CHRISTOPHER HERWIG | LONELY PLANET IMAGES

4.

PHOTOLIBRARY

Small it may be, but Benin punches above its weight both for historical significance and for an extraordinary array of sights. Benin is the birthplace of voodoo, was the last place many Africans saw as they were shipped off to slavery, and Abomey still has evocative remnants of the fabled and bloodthirsty kingdom of Dahomey. But for all its tumultuous past, Benin is an African success story. Ecotourism initiatives abound, its people are among Africa's friendliest and it is known as a beacon of stability in a tough neighbourhood. Whether you're picking your way through clamorous markets, lying back on a tropical beach or watching wildlife in the north, you'll find it easy to fall in love with Benin.

BEST TIME TO VISIT
November to February (the dry season)

TOP THINGS TO SEE
○ The enduring monument to the kings of Dahomey in Abomey
○ The Point of No Return for countless African slaves at Ouidah, plus its voodoo centre and Afro-Brazilian cultural outpost
○ Grand Popo, the loveliest palm-fringed corner of Benin's Gulf of Guinea coast
○ The tranquil capital, Porto Novo, with shady streets and colonial buildings
○ Dassa Zoumé, Benin's most striking terrain with rocky outcrops and lush hills

TOP THINGS TO DO
○ Track lions, cheetahs and elephants in the Parc National de la Pendjari
○ Hike through the rugged northern Atakora region with a local ecotourism association
○ Get an insight into local culture by learning traditional fishing at Lake Ahémé
○ Dance deep into the night in Ouidah on 10 January, Benin's Voodoo Day
○ Take a slow pirogue journey to the traditional bamboo stilt houses of Ganvié

GETTING UNDER THE SKIN
Read Bruce Chatwin's *The Viceroy of Ouidah,* which tells the story of a 17th-century Brazilian trader stranded on the 'Slave Coast'; while Annie Caulfield's taxi journey around Benin is wittily told in *Show Me the Magic*

Listen to anything by Angelique Kidjo, Gangbe Brass Band or Orchestre Poly-Rythmo

Watch *Angelique Kidjo: World Music Portraits*, a fascinating biopic of one of Africa's biggest stars on the international stage

Eat *igname pilé* (pounded yam served with vegetables and meat) and *gombo* (okra)

Drink Benin's national beer, La Béninoise

IN A WORD
Neh àh dèh gbò (How are you?)

TRADEMARKS
Voodoo; fishing villages on stilts; an emerging ecotourism scene; singing sensation Angelique Kidjo; Oscar-nominated actor Djimon Hounsou (*Gladiator* and *Blood Diamond*)

RANDOM FACT
Almost a quarter of Benin's land area has been set aside as national parks or reserves, easily the highest proportion in West Africa

MAP REF **M,20**

1. A mud-hut village surrounded by cornfields, Koutagou
2. Stop and chat to the kids in Benin's largest city, Cotonou
3. Taneka man takes a break, Benin-style
4. A woman runs chores beneath the stilt houses of Lake Nokoué

Like a vision rising above the otherwise landless central Atlantic, Bermuda is a temperate haven borrowing traditions from distant British and American shores. Truly isolated (the Caribbean is 1600km south), this ink blot of an island group has a culture perfectly encapsulated by the namesake shorts: casual comfort with an overlay of formality. Traditions seem little changed from the time of Queen Victoria, yet there's a commercial buzz more fitting of a New World boomtown. The legendary pink sands never fail to amaze and offer beach delights for those tuckered out after sessions of croquette, lawn tennis or golf. Tea beckons at the proper afternoon time; at night however, starchy creases are wrinkled away to booming Bermuda musical beats.

BEST TIME TO VISIT
Year-round

TOP THINGS TO SEE
- Pink-sand beaches that bring a smile to the face of even the most stressed visitor
- The same huge rubber trees in Par-la-ville Park that entranced Mark Twain
- Echoes of the lash at the richly historic Royal Naval Dockyard
- St George with its pastel houses, stoic churches and meandering lanes
- The harbour rhythms of Victorian Hamilton

TOP THINGS TO DO
- Dive the world's greatest concentration of shipwrecks – those not lost forever in the Bermuda Triangle
- Spot whales beyond the reefs of South Shore during March and April
- Play tennis on grass, just like a group of New Yorkers did in 1874 and then brought the sport to America
- Tuck into a traditional Sunday codfish breakfast (codfish, eggs, boiled Irish potatoes, bananas and avocado, with a sauce of onions and tomatoes)
- Swim your cares away in the pristine waters of Horseshoe Bay

GETTING UNDER THE SKIN
Read *Bermuda's Story* by Terry Tucker, the island's most highly regarded historian

Listen to reggae, calypso and Bermuda's own *gombey*, which features groups of wildly clad men dancing in manic fashion to music that blends African and Caribbean rhythms

Watch *The Deep*, an underwater thriller of drug lords and treasure; *You Only Live Twice*, a 1967 Bond film with Sean Connery

Eat fish chowder (flavoured with local black rum and sherry peppers sauce)

Drink Gosling's Black Seal Rum (a dark rum); or dark 'n' stormy (a two-to-one mix of carbonated ginger beer with Black Seal Rum)

IN A WORD
Yo Ace Boy! (Hello good friend!)

TRADEMARKS
Bermuda shorts; tidy pastel cottages; pink-sand beaches; namesake 'triangle' sucking in hapless ships and planes

RANDOM FACT
Bermuda's stunning natural beauty was protected by the world's first environmental laws (dating back to the 1600s)

ATLANTIC OCEAN

Town of St George
St David's
Bailey's Bay
Castle Harbor
Nonsuch Island
Tucker's Town
Harrington Sound
South Channel
Flatts Village
Hamilton
Somerset Village
Great Sound
Little Sound

MAP REF J,13

1. Bermuda's Scottish heritage is kept alive during a festival in Fort Hamilton

1.

2.

3.

If Shangri La exists in the modern world, it must look an awful lot like Bhutan. With a pristine mountain environment, fairy-tale clifftop monasteries and a famous preference for Gross National Happiness over Gross National Product, the last Himalayan kingdom has admirably managed to conserve its unique Buddhist identity. Yet change is slowly afoot. Hand over the substantial wad of dollars it takes to travel here and you'll see noblemen in 15th-century traditional robes chatting on their mobile phones and saffron-robed monks paying their respects to bloodthirsty demons while discussing the recent elections. It's all part of the charm of a country that offers travellers an alternative vision of what 'development' truly means.

BEST TIME TO VISIT
March to May, October to November

TOP THINGS TO SEE
- Taktshang Goemba (Tiger's Nest) attached to the cliff-face by the hairs of angels
- The monastic buildings of Paro Dzong and the nearby National Museum
- The weekend market, museums and bars of Thimphu, Bhutan's only real town
- Punakha Dzong, Bhutan's most beautiful building, set at the junction of the Mo (Mother) and Po (Father) rivers
- Bumthang Valley, a circuit of ancient 7th-century temples, sacred sites and hikes through rhododendron forests

TOP THINGS TO DO
- Trek along Himalayan trade routes to the sacred peak of Jhomolhari bordering Tibet
- Take in the banter and the boasting of an archery tournament in Thimphu
- Spot rare black-necked cranes in the glacier-carved Phobjikha Valley
- Watch snow lions dance and monks pacify demons during one of the country's colourful *tsechu* (religious festivals)

GETTING UNDER THE SKIN
Read *Beyond the Sky and Earth* by Jamie Zeppa or *Buttertea at Sunrise: A Year in the Bhutan Himalaya* by Britte Das, for insights into Bhutanese culture from two women who lived there

Listen to *Endless Songs from Bhutan* by Jigme Drukpa, a timeless collection of traditional Bhutanese folk songs accompanied by lute and flute

Watch *Travellers and Magicians*, a stylish 'film within a film', directed by the reincarnated lama Khyentse Norbu

Eat mouth-melting *ema datse* (green chillies and cheese) with Bhutanese pink rice

Drink Red Panda beer, a delicious wheat beer brewed in the Bumthang valley

IN A WORD
Kuzuzangbo la (Hello)

TRADEMARKS
Gross National Happiness; Shangri La; national dress; argyle socks; *dzongs* (monasteries); rhododendrons; expensive daily fees; archery; prayer flags; monks

RANDOM FACT
Buying cigarettes is illegal in Bhutan (as is selling plastic bags and watching MTV)

MAP REF **K,29**

1. The show must go on: Buddhist monks defy the rain to participate in a tsechu festival, Tamshing
2. Masters of disguise: merry pranksters fool around at Wangdue Phodrang
3. Tibetan prayer flags flap in the breeze in front of the precariously positioned Taktshang Goemba
4. A woman and a novice monk rest beside a giant prayer wheel at Dechen Phodrang monastery

2.

3.

1.

MICHAEL TAYLOR | LONELY PLANET IMAGES

4.

WOODS WHEATCROFT | LONELY PLANET IMAGES

At the heart of South America, Bolivia is the highest and most isolated country on the continent. This land of dramatic extremes encompasses Andean peaks soaring to over 6000m, high-altitude deserts, surreal salt flats, Amazonian rainforest and the wildlife-filled savannahs of the Pantanal. Despite its mineral riches, Bolivia remains one of the poorest countries in Latin America – a fact that its large Amerindian population is eager to redress. Today the Quechua, Aymara and other indigenous groups are playing an increasingly important role in the country and have even elected the nation's first indigenous president.

BEST TIME TO VISIT
May to October

TOP THINGS TO SEE
- Isla del Sol: the mystical island and legendary Inca creation site found on Lake Titicaca
- The Salar de Uyuni, the blindingly white salt deserts complete with bubbling geysers and aquamarine lagoons
- The dizzying city of La Paz, dramatically set deep in a canyon and fringed by snow-covered mountains
- The astounding range of wildlife in Bolivia's Amazonian rainforest

TOP THINGS TO DO
- Trek through the giddying heights of the Cordillera Real along ancient Inca routes
- Feel the adrenaline rush on a mountain-biking trek along what was once known as 'the world's most dangerous road'
- Overnight it in the Chalalan Ecolodge in a wildlife-rich area up the Río Tuichi
- Go horseback riding in the dramatic mountain scenery of the Cordillera de Chichas
- Exploring the remarkably diverse Parque Nacional Madidi, home to 6000m Andean glaciers, steamy rainforests and over 1000 bird species

GETTING UNDER THE SKIN
Read *The Fat Man from La Paz: Contemporary Fiction from Bolivia*, edited by Rosario Santos. It contains 20 short stories illustrating the struggles and beauty of life in Bolivia

Listen to Charango masters Celestino Campos, Ernesto Cavour and Mauro Nunez

Watch *The Devil's Miner*, Kief Davidson and Richard Ladkani's award-winning documentary that follows the hardship and hope of two brothers working in one of South America's most harrowing mines

Eat *saltena* (a meat and vegetable empanada); *surubi* (catfish)

Drink the favourite alcoholic drink *chicha cochabambina*, made from fermented corn; *mate de coca* (coca leaf tea) helps ease altitude sickness

IN A WORD
Que tal? (How are you?)

TRADEMARKS
Bowler hats; llamas; Andean peaks; Lake Titicaca; hand-woven shawls and blankets

RANDOM FACT
Many of the riches of Spain flowed from Cerro Rico above Potosí, where an estimated 45,000 tons of pure silver was mined between 1550 and 1780

CAPITAL La Paz (administrative) and Sucre (judicial) | **POPULATION** 9,775,246 | **AREA** 1,098,581 sq km | **OFFICIAL LANGUAGE** Spanish

MAP REF **Q,12**

1. The stunning peak of Huayna Potosí stands guard over a village near La Paz
2. A child clutches on for support while making feathered friends in Plaza Murillo, La Paz
3. One fine example of colonial architecture is the ochre-coloured Iglesia de La Merced, in the World Heritage–listed town of Potosí
4. A leisurely row is by far the best way to enjoy Lake Titicaca, South America's largest lake

1.

2.

3.

CAPITAL Sarajevo | POPULATION 4,613,414 | AREA 51,197 sq km | OFFICIAL LANGUAGES Bosnian, Croatian & Serbian

Bosnia may be considered a byword for urban warzones and factional strife, but the Bosnians themselves described theirs as a 'heart-shaped land'. Such a description may not be wide of the mark geographically, and over centuries it has been the scene of intense commingling of peoples, traditions and cultures. Political tensions still linger after the fratricidal wars of the 1990s, but Bosnians of all stripes look to a brighter future. And in all pursuits, Bosnians display a spirit and vitality heightened by the difficulties of the recent past, from the students and chain-smoking bohemians of Sarajevo, to the hardy villagers of outlying mountain hamlets and burghers of regional cities that display neat configurations of mosques, Orthodox domes and Catholic bel towers.

BEST TIME TO VISIT
April to September

TOP THINGS TO SEE
- Daredevils plunging from Mostar's bridge into the racing green waters below
- Sarajevo, the 'Jerusalem of the Balkans', a fabulous, vibrant, riverside city with cultural events and nightlife aplenty
- The castle and Ottoman-era architecture of Travnik
- The 12,000-year-old 'pyramid' of Visoko
- Secluded attractions like the petite village of Vranduk, the craggy castle of Srebrenik or ecovillage of Zelenkovac

TOP THINGS TO DO
- Wander the cobbled alleys, coppersmith workshops and artisanal stalls of Baščaršija in Sarajevo
- Join the pilgrims as they wait for an apparition of Mary in Medugorje, or nod at Sufi tombs in the *tekija* (dervish lodge) in Blagaj
- Plummet down the Vrbas or Buna rivers on a raft or in your own kayak
- Skip up the cobbled streets of Počitelj to look out over domes, minarets, slate roofs and the Neretva River

GETTING UNDER THE SKIN
Read *Sarajevo Marlboro* by Miljenko Jergovic, tales set during the siege of Sarajevo, or *People of the Book*, Geraldine Brooks' fictionalised tale about the Sarajevo Haggadah

Listen to *sevdah* music, Bosnia's folk music, an excursion in harmonious melancholy

Watch Danis Tanovic's *No Man's Land* or *Grbavica: Land of my Dreams*, by Jasmila Zbanic, both poignant reflections on the Bosnian war

Eat *zeljanica* (tasty spinach pastry); or *Bosanski lonac* (meat stew with cabbage)

Drink the local dry red wine, Blatina; or *sljivovica* (plum brandy)

IN A WORD
Zijveli (Cheers)

TRADEMARKS
Copper coffee pots; rugged hillsides; mountain villages; the siege of Sarajevo; juxtaposed mosques and churches; rafting on emerald rivers

RANDOM FACT
Bosnia was long home to the Sarajevo Haggadah, an illuminated Jewish manuscript that was saved from the Nazis by local Muslims

MAP REF **H,21**

1. Stari Most (Old Bridge) arcs across the Neretva River in the ancient, picturesque town of Mostar
2. Locals pass the time of day outside Gazi-Husrevbey Mosque, Sarajevo
3. The Moorish-style Austro-Hungarian National Library in Sarajevo was badly damaged during the conflict in 1992, with restoration continuing today
4. Stars and crescents feature prominently in the Islamic architecture of Sarajevo

2.

3.

1.

4.

Diamonds are forever. If only. Their discovery in Botswana – thanks to the efforts of industrious termites (yes, really) – in the late 1960s turned one of the world's poorest countries into an international player overnight. Although the billions in revenues have been rightfully spent on healthcare, education and infrastructure, all is not well – HIV/AIDS has gripped a quarter of the population, and their proverbial cash cow (diamond mines) will run dry in a few decades. However, with vast tracts of unparalleled wilderness, incredible wildlife and no shortage of charming, peace-loving citizens, tourism will undoubtedly have an increased role to play in Botswana's future.

BEST TIME TO VISIT
May to September (dry season) for classic safaris; November to April (wet season) for birds

TOP THINGS TO SEE
- A procession of trunks crossing the Chobe River, each a lifeline to the elephant lurking in the depths below
- The grasses of the Central Kalahari Game Reserve coming to life with the rains
- Africa's forgotten great migration, which brings thousands of zebra into Makgadikgadi Pans National Park
- The sandstone landscape of the Tuli Block being set alight by the setting sun
- San rock paintings that date back millennia – the natural gallery in the remote Tsodilo Hills is equally riveting

TOP THINGS TO DO
- Wake to sunrise on the blank, bleached canvas that is Makgadikgadi Pan
- Skirt between the reeds that line the Okavango Delta's myriad channels in a *mokoro* (traditional canoe)
- Rise before dawn to share your morning with the vast amount of wildlife in Moremi Wildlife Reserve
- Spend time understanding San culture in D'kar

GETTING UNDER THE SKIN
Read *Serowe: Village of the Rain Wind* by Bessie Head for an understanding of Tswana culture and village life

Listen to Franco and Afro Musica, a 12-piece *kwasa kwasa* band

Watch *The Gods Must Be Crazy; The No 1 Ladies' Detective Agency*

Eat *leputshe* (wild pumpkin) atop *bogobe* (sorghum porridge)

Drink the stiff concoction from fermented marula fruit

IN A WORD
Dumela ('Hello' in Tswana) – extra marks if it's done with a 'special' handshake (place your left hand on your elbow while shaking)

TRADEMARKS
The Kalahari; San (aka Bushmen); the world's largest inland delta; luxurious safari camps; diamonds; HIV/AIDS

RANDOM FACT
As a percentage of GDP, Botswana's education budget is the world's 10th largest, outranking Sweden (21), Switzerland (45), UK (47) and USA (57)

MAP REF **Q,22**

1. Get up close and personal with wildlife in the Okavango Delta
2. Teeming life follows the floodplains in the Okavango Delta
3. Ever get the feeling you're being watched? A pack of curious African Wild Dogs are watchful observers in the Central Kalahari Game Reserve
4. San people convene for a ceremonial get-together in the Central Kalahari Game Reserve

1.

2.

3.

South America's largest and arguably most seductive country continues to turn heads – and not merely for its breathtaking beaches and hedonistic festivals. Today, energy-independent Brazil basks in the glow of a surging economy and some notable successes combating social problems – not to mention their winning bid for the 2016 Olympic Games. Football remains a big source of pride (Brazil has won more World Cup titles than any other nation), as is the country's incredible biodiversity. Brazil is, after all, home to the greatest assortment of plant and animal life on earth. It's no wonder locals claim '*Deus e brasileiro*' (God is Brazilian).

BEST TIME TO VISIT
November to April on the coast, and May to September in the Amazon and the Pantanal

TOP THINGS TO SEE
○ Ipanema Beach, Rio's loveliest and most fabled stretch of coastline
○ The enchanting colonial centre of Salvador, the Afro-Brazilian soul of the country
○ The thunderous Iguaçu Falls surrounded by Atlantic rainforest
○ A football match at Maracanã stadium in Rio, Brazil's great temple to their national addiction
○ The spectacular island of Fernando de Noronha, with gorgeous beaches and world-class diving

TOP THINGS TO DO
○ Go wildlife-watching in the Pantanal, home to the greatest concentration of fauna in the New World
○ Peer out over the world's most famous rainforest from a canopy tower in the Amazon
○ Dance to samba at an old-school dance hall in Rio's fabled Lapa district
○ Join the mayhem of Brazil's biggest street party at carnaval in Rio, Salvador or Olinda
○ Hike amid dramatic mountain scenery in the Chapada Diamantina

GETTING UNDER THE SKIN
Read *Gabriela, Clove and Cinnamon* by Brazil's most famous writer, Jorge Amado, for a colourful portrait of early 20th-century Bahia

Listen to the addictive Afro-Brazilian rhythms of Jorge Benjor, or the classic bossa nova grooves of Joao Gilberto

Watch The poignant *Central do Brasil* (Central Station), Walter Salles' Academy Award–winning film set in Rio and the northeast

Eat *feijoada* (a black bean and pork stew); or *moqueca* (a rich Bahian fish stew with coconut milk)

Drink *acai* (a juice made from an Amazonian berry) and *caipirinhas* made with *cachaca* (a sugar-cane alcohol), crushed limes and sugar

IN A WORD
Tudo bem? (All's well?)

TRADEMARKS
Carnaval; football; bossa nova; samba; beaches; the Amazon; *favelas* (shanty towns)

RANDOM FACT
Brazilian ethanol, made from sugar cane (eight times more efficient than fuel made from US corn) provides 40% of the country's fuel

MAP REF **P,14**

1. Sunset casts a pink glow over the bay as Pão de Açúcar looms in the background, Rio de Janeiro
2. Take your pick: from spectating on the balcony, to full participation on the floor dancing to the groove of samba music, Rio de Janeiro
3. No one knows how to dress for a party better than Brazilians...Salgueiro comes alive during Carnaval
4. A Mebengokre elder wears a headdress made of macaw and stork feathers in Amazonas

1.

Hemmed in by the jungles of Malaysian Borneo, Brunei is a nation built around a single personality – the enigmatic Sultan Hassana Bolkiah. Famous for his addiction to sports cars, the sultan presides over one of the richest nations in Asia, thanks to the vast oil fields beneath the South China Sea. Officially known as Negara Brunei Darussalam (Brunei - the Abode of Peace), this tropical sultanate is best known for its glittering mosques, its keen observance of Islam and for the traditional stilt villages surrounding the capital, Bandar Seri Begawan. Less well known are the steamy rainforest reserves in the interior. However, don't expect pulsing nightlife – all bars and nightclubs were closed down when alcohol was banned in 1991.

BEST TIME TO VISIT
March to April for dry, warm days

TOP THINGS TO SEE
o The gleaming dome of the Omar Ali Saifuddien Mosque
o Islamic treasures and displays on the discovery of oil in the Brunei Museum
o Exotic fruit and local delicacies at the Tamu Kianggeh food market
o A chariot fit for a sultan at the Royal Regalia Museum
o Istana Nurul Iman, the world's largest palace, and private home of the sultan

TOP THINGS TO DO
o Take a water taxi through the atmospheric stilt villages of Kampung Ayer
o Search for proboscis monkeys in the dense jungles of Ulu Temburong National Park
o Spend a night in an Iban longhouse in Batang Duri
o Stroll barefoot on the sand at Pantai Muara and Pantai Seri Kerangan
o Hike along the lichen-covered boardwalk through Peradayan Forest Reserve

GETTING UNDER THE SKIN
Read *Time and the River*, an autobiography by Prince Mohammed Bolkiah, the sultan's youngest brother

Listen to the popular classical concerts arranged by the Brunei Music Society

Watch local dancers performing the *adai-adai*, based on the traditional work-songs of native fishermen

Eat *ambuyat* (a thick soup made from sago), often described as 'edible glue'

Drink anything but alcohol, unless you bring it with you – non-Muslims are allowed to import a limited amount of alcohol for personal consumption

IN A WORD
Panas (Hot)

TRADEMARKS
Golden mosques; oilfields; jungles; stilt houses; the extravagant lifestyle of the sultan; the playboy antics of Prince Jefri, the sultan's brother

RANDOM FACTS
As well as owning more than 3000 cars, the sultan of Brunei has his own Airbus 340 jet, kitted out as a flying palace with gold-plated bathrooms

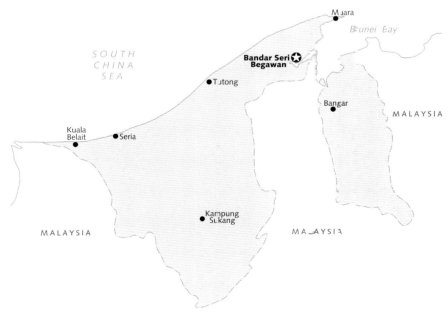

MAP REF **N,32**

1. Named after the 28th sultan of Brunei, the Omar Ali Saifuddien Mosque was built in 1958 at a cost of about US$5 million.

1.

2.

3.

Surrounded by more famous neighbours – Greeks, Turks, even Romanians have their Transylvania myths – Bulgaria is the last Eastern European country on a top-to-bottom trip across the region, and well worth some investigation. Its snowcapped mountains offer cheap ski slopes, its Black Sea beaches (at spots) some of the most isolated beaches in Europe, and villages' 19th-century revival-era architecture the most atmospheric bases. Now part of the EU, Bulgaria still half looks back to traditions like sheep yoghurt stands, traditional music (on TV nightly, sometimes on every channel), ancient Thracian and Roman sites, and around 160 Bulgarian Orthodox monasteries, many of which survived 800 years living under the 'yoke' of Ottoman rule.

BEST TIME TO VISIT
May and June, September and October

TOP THINGS TO SEE
- The hilltop Tsarevets Fortress in Veliko Târnovo
- Jagged rocks sticking above the walled Kaleto Fortress in Belogradchik
- The 2000-year-old Roman amphitheatre in the heart of Old Plovdiv
- The bluff-top ruins looking over the Black Sea at Kaliakra Cape
- Mountain-framed Rila Monastery

TOP THINGS TO DO
- Sip Melnik's unique 'hangover-free wine' from Shestaka, the six-fingered man
- Explore Thracian ruins, like the mountain-top site at Perperikon
- Eat a 'Bulgarian breakfast': an espresso, a *banitsa* (cheese pastry) and (usually) a cigarette
- Learn Cyrillic – it's a Bulgarian invention
- Search out undeveloped (or less developed) Black Sea beaches like those south of Sinemorets

GETTING UNDER THE SKIN
Read about Paul Theroux's problems with eating in Sofia in his classic *Great Railway Bazaar;* Ivan Ilchev's *The Rose of the Balkans,* a recent historical overview

Listen to traditional music with the *gaida* (Bulgarian bagpipe) or the polarising Serbian-style disco *chalga*

Watch *Under the Same Sky*, an award-winning film of the Sofia International Film Festival about a 15-year-old girl who goes in search of her father

Eat cool *tarator* (yoghurt soup with cucumber) to beat summer temperatures; or hearty *kavarma* stews to warm up in winter

Drink local wines that utilise local grapes like the mavrud or rubin in the birthplace of the god of wine (Dionysus)

IN A WORD
Oshte bira molya (Another beer please)

TRADEMARKS
Yoghurt; Cyrillic alphabet; Black Sea beaches; budget ski slopes; shaking your head 'yes' and nodding it 'no'; *kâshta* (traditional) taverns; pizzas with ketchup

RANDOM FACT
Bulgaria is a leading exporter of rose oil and the world's fifth-largest exporter of wine

MAP REF I,22

1. Belogradchik rock formations make the perfect setting for the Kaleto Fortress, built by the Romans in the 1st century BC
2. Who says chess isn't a spectator sport? Witness a tense battle in Sofia, Bulgaria's capital
3. Often bypassed by tourists, Sofia contains many gems for travellers to discover
4. Medieval churches have earned the rocky island town of Nesebâr a World Heritage listing

2.

3.

1.

PHOTOGRAPHY

4.

ARMOINE VAN ZANDBERGEN | LONELY PLANET IMAGES

Once named Upper Volta and forever far from the world's consciousness, Burkina Faso nonetheless ends up being many travellers' favourite West African country. Burkina may lack famous attractions, but the vibrant (and evocatively named) cities, thriving arts milieu, stunning traditional architecture, surprising wildlife-watching opportunities and stirring landscapes will all turn your head. And yet, it's the friendliness of the people and their sheer diversity that wins most plaudits. In the Sahel, the Thursday market in Gorom-Gorom is like a who's who of the Sahel's peoples, Ouagadougou has its share of signposts to the once-powerful Mossi Empire, and the Lobi and Gourounsi peoples of the south rank among the most intriguing yet accessible traditional cultures in the region.

BEST TIME TO VISIT
November to February

TOP THINGS TO SEE
- Bobo-Dioulasso with tree-lined streets, live music and a lovely mosque
- Fespaco, Africa's premier film festival from February to March in Ouagadougou in odd-numbered years
- The colourfully painted, fortress-like houses in the heart of Gourounsi country, Tiébélé
- Ouagadougou, with great restaurants, dance bars and arts scene
- The small village of Bani with seven exceptional mud-brick mosques

TOP THINGS TO DO
- Get close to elephants with scarcely another tourist in sight at Ranch de Nazinga
- Trek amid the bizarre rock formations of the Sindou Peaks
- Sleep in the dunes near Oursi or Markoyé after a morning at Gorom-Gorom market
- Explore Lobi Country, a fascinating outpost of animist culture
- Attend the Moro-Naba Ceremony, a throwback to the Mossi's golden age in Ouagadougou

GETTING UNDER THE SKIN
Read *Un voyage interieur au Burkina Faso*, a stunning photographical journey through the country by Antoine Périgot

Listen to *Kanou* or *Nemako* by Farafina; the eponymous *Victor Démé*, which emerged from Bobo-Dioulasso's thriving live music scene; reggae by Black So Man

Watch the prize-winning *Tilä* by Idrissa Ouédraogo or *Buud Yam* by Gaston Kaboré, two of Burkina's most celebrated directors

Eat *riz sauce* (rice with sauce) – the sauce could be *arachide* (groundnut) or *graine* (a hot sauce made with palm oil nuts)

Drink Brakina and So.b.bra (pronounced *so-bay-bra*), two locally produced beers

IN A WORD
La fee bay may? (How are you?)

TRADEMARKS
Fespaco, the prestigious film festival; Thomas Sankara, Africa's Che Guevara

RANDOM FACT
Burkina Faso's national parks and wildlife reserves are home to West Africa's largest elephant population

MAP REF **M,20**

1. Bobo-Dioulasso boasts the unique spiny Sahel-style wooden mosque
2. Girls work diligently in a typical thatched, mudbrick village near Sindou
3. A baobab tree dwarfs children in Burkina Faso's distinctive savannah landscape
4. Interact with curious locals in the little village of Bani

A pint-sized country with a world's worth of pain, Burundi is slowly emerging from the fog of its devastating civil war. While similar Hutu–Tutsi conflicts have been soothed in Rwanda by removing historical tribal labels, Burundi has chosen a different path, one of open dialogue and good-hearted debate. If this approach brings stability, travellers will have the first opportunity in a generation to explore this diverse nation. Its jungle-clad volcanoes offer lung-busting escapades tracking chimpanzees, while its less frenzied Lake Tanganyika beaches are perfect for soothing your soul. Encounters with Burundians are rewarding lessons in life – they prove that where there are lows, there still can be highs.

BEST TIME TO VISIT
June to September, when the skies are their driest

TOP THINGS TO SEE
- The mountain-top spring at Mt Kikizi, the southernmost source of the mighty Nile
- La Pierre de Livingstone et Stanley, the supposed site of Africa's most infamous historical uttering – 'Dr Livingstone, I presume?'
- Chutes de la Kagera during the wet season, when torrents tumble from this waterfall
- Hungry hippos and crocs sharing the shoreline in Parc National de la Rusizi
- Lasting peace

TOP THINGS TO DO
- Experience Bujumbura's legendary nightlife in 3D – dining, drinking and dancing
- Realise first hand that some of the world's best beaches are nowhere near a coast
- Look forward to the day when the depths of Parc National de la Kibira's chimp-laden rainforest are once again open to the travelling public
- Sink your teeth into East Africa's finest croissants at an authentic patisserie in Bujumbura
- Take to Lake Tanganyika's waters and cruise the classic Bujumbura–Kigoma route south to Tanzania

GETTING UNDER THE SKIN
Read *Strength in What Remains: A Journey of Remembrance and Forgiveness*, Tracy Kidder's Pulitzer Prize–winning novel about one man's survival of the Burundi civil war

Listen to *Les Tambourinaires du Burundi: Live at Real World*, an amazing performance

Watch *Gito, l'ingrat*, a story of an African intellectual's troubled return to his homeland with his French girlfriend

Eat *impeke* (a cereal made from corn, soybeans and sorghum)

Drink a cold bottle of Primus beer, one of the many churned out of the national brewery

IN A WORD
Bwa ('Hello' in Kirundi)

TRADEMARKS
'Dr Livingstone, I presume?'; ethnic conflict; Les Tambourinaires; languid lakeside villages; superb inland beaches; forest-clad mountains

RANDOM FACT
The government of Burundi banned the use of real Christmas trees in 2005 – deforestation was its main concern

RWANDA

Kirund

Muyinga

Kayanza

DEMOCRATIC
REPUBLIC
OF CONGO
(ZAÏRE)

Muramvya

Cankuzo

Bujumbura

Gitega

Lake
Tanganyika

TANZANIA

Bururi

Makamba

MAP REF O,23

1. The famous Burundi drummers will set your head spinning

1.

2.

3.

One of the last travel frontiers, Cambodia is slowly being rehabilitated as a key destination on the Asia overland trail. Although the legacy of Pol Pot and the Khmer Rouge remains imprinted on the landscape, a can-do spirit is sweeping across the country and aspiration rather than desperation is the new watchword for the nation. The attractions of Cambodia are the same as they ever were – the awe-inspiring temples of Angkor, the swirling yellow waters of the Mekong, monks in saffron robes, beaches on the Gulf of Thailand, hill tribes and steamy jungles, motorcycle traffic jams and chaotic markets in Phnom Penh. Bring your pith helmet and push back some travel boundaries.

BEST TIME TO VISIT
November to January (the dry season)

TOP THINGS TO SEE
- Astonishing temples consumed by the jungle at Angkor
- Irrawaddy dolphins splashing in the Mekong at Kratie
- Rarely-seen Angkor-era temples in remote Preah Vihear Province
- Mist swirling around the ruins of the French hill station in Bokor National Park
- The heart-rending displays at Tuol Sleng and Choeung Ek in Phnom Penh

TOP THINGS TO DO
- Feel the pulse of Phnom Penh from the back of a motorcycle taxi
- Ride the Mekong ferry through stunning scenery between Siem Reap and Battambang
- Cheer on the racing boat crews during the annual Water Festival
- Trek through uncharted jungles in Virachay National Park
- Let the surf tickle your toes on a beach at Sihanoukville

GETTING UNDER THE SKIN
Read harrowing accounts of the Khmer Rouge years in Pin Yathay's *Stay Alive, My Son;* and Loung Ung's *First They Killed My Father*

Listen to a *pinpeat* orchestra playing tunes that were composed for the kings of Angkor

Watch Roland Joffé's *The Killing Fields*, still the most powerful portrayal of the Khmer Rouge revolution

Eat *pleah* (hot and sour beef salad) or *kyteow* (rice-noodle soup) – or bite into a deep-fried tarantula

Drink the thick and delicious fruit smoothies known as *tukalok*

IN A WORD
Niak teuv naa? (Where are you going?) – something visitors are asked all the time by inquisitive Khmers

TRADEMARKS
Angkor Wat; the mighty Mekong; Pol Pot; the Khmer Rouge; monks on bikes; maniacal motorcycle taxi drivers; fried spiders; landmines; easily available drugs and tough penalties

RANDOM FACTS
Pol Pot formulated his radical Marxist ideas while studying for an electronics degree in Paris

MAP REF **M,31**

1. Get your head around the exotic fortified city of Angkor Thom, Siem Reap
2. Easy does it: a delicate load wends its way through the busy streets of Phnom Penh
3. Gleaming eyes and a cheeky grin light up a Cambodian face
4. Buddhist monks take a short-cut through a lily pond in Bavel

Cameroon is often described as all of Africa contained within a single country and, whichever way you look at it, that cliché rings true. Here at the crossroads of West and Central Africa, the natural world spans the full spectrum of signature African landscapes: from the steamy tropical beaches of the south; and even steamier rainforests of the interior; to the semi-deserts of the Sahelian north. Its human geography is similarly diverse: a remarkable 263 ethnic groups call Cameroon home and a wealth of traditional kingdoms continue to hold sway. Even Cameroon's history gets in on the act: Cameroon is the only African country to have been colonised by three European powers. The result is an extraordinary deep-immersion African experience.

BEST TIME TO VISIT
November to February

TOP THINGS TO SEE
- Korup National Park, the oldest rainforest in Africa and one of its most accessible
- Ebodje, which has an even more beautiful beach than more-famous Kribi with nesting sea turtles
- The fascinating Sahelian town of Maroua with its colourful market
- Yaoundé, arrayed across seven hills and brimful of life
- The traditional Islamic kingdom of Foumban with a royal palace and strong artistic heritage

TOP THINGS TO DO
- Climb to the summit of Mt Cameroon (4095m), West Africa's highest peak
- Get so far off the beaten track that there scarcely is one in the traditional kingdoms of the Ring Road
- Commune with elephants, giraffe, hippo and lion in the Parc National du Waza
- Hike into the rocky outcrops and traditional villages of the Mandara Mountains
- Take the train from the Sahel to the tropics, passing through dense rainforest en route

GETTING UNDER THE SKIN
Read *The Poor Christ of Bomba*, renowned Cameroonian novelist Mongo Beti's masterful account of a missionary's failures in a small village; *Cameroon with Egbert* by Dervla Murphy; Gerald Durrell's *A Zoo in My Luggage* and *The Bafut Beagles*

Listen to Manu Dibango's *Soul Makossa*, one of Africa's most influential albums

Watch *Afrique, Je Te Plumerai* (Africa, I Will Fleece You) by Jean-Marie Teno, an outstanding documentary about modern Cameroon

Eat *fufu* (mashed yam, corn or plantain) with *ndole* (a bitter-leaf-and-smoked-fish sauce), or *suya* (beef cooked on outdoor grills)

Drink Castel and 33 (beers), Guinness and milky-white palm wine

IN A WORD
No ngoolu daa (Hello)

TRADEMARKS
Rainforest; logging; pygmies; gorillas; sea turtles; *makossa* music created and made famous by Manu Dibango

RANDOM FACT
Around 45% of Cameroon is covered by forest, down from almost 53% in 1990

MAP REF **N,21**

1. Masks of the incredible beaded clothing of the Bamiléké dancers often represent elephants and leopards.
2. A Kapsikis medicine man considers a case
3. Volcanic plugs jut out of the landscape near Rhumsiki
4. Reliable transportation carries its passenger to the Palais du Lamido, Maroua

73

1.

2.

3.

You can literally lose yourself almost anywhere in Canada. The world's second-largest country has more gorgeous and remote corners than you can ever count or visit. From the glaciers of Kluane National Park in the Yukon to Nova Scotia's Cape Breton Highlands, the natural wonders never cease. When you're ready for civilisation, you'll find cities that are among the world's most genteel and pleasurable. Although most people live within 100km of the US border, Canada boasts a multicultural society that combines elements of Britain, France, Asia and almost every other world culture. It's an intoxicating melange found no place else. The nation's indigenous cultures have rich pasts that enrich the entire nation today. First Nations art honours both the glories of nature and aeons-old traditions.

BEST TIME TO VISIT
March to November, except in the north where winter comes early (October) and leaves late (April)

TOP THINGS TO SEE
° Black bears, grizzly bears, moose and more in the wilds across the country
° Québec City's Old Town, a Unesco World Heritage site exuding historical romance
° The Queen Charlotte Islands, where the rich Haida culture is thriving again
° Toronto, with superb food, drink and shopping
° Newfoundland's Northern Peninsula which blends icebergs, craggy cliffs and the odd Viking artefact

TOP THINGS TO DO
° Relive the Klondike Gold Rush by hiking and canoeing across the Yukon to Dawson
° Brave the far north for stark Arctic beauty enlivened by polar bears
° Sail the whale- and dolphin-filled Inside Passage along British Columbia
° Cracking shells at a glorious Prince Edward Island lobster feast
° Booming Vancouver, where Asia meets North America and the outdoors looms

GETTING UNDER THE SKIN
Read Margaret Atwood's Booker Prize–winning *Blind Assassin*, and Michael Ondaatje's *In the Skin of a Lion,* both set in 1930s Canada

Listen to Leonard Cohen, Neil Young, Broken Social Scene and the Cowboy Junkies

Watch Douglas Coupland's *Everything's Gone Green*, a hard-edged comic work about modern Canadian life

Eat seafood from the coasts; maple syrup from the trees

Drink many superb wines from the Okanagan Valley in southern British Columbia

IN A WORD
Eh? (bilingual and all-purpose, eg 'Nice day, eh?')

TRADEMARKS
Moose; bears; the Rockies; Bryan Adams; maple trees; Mounties

RANDOM FACT
French-speaking Québec has not quite a quarter of Canada's population but wields great power nationally: English-speakers usually also speak French while the obverse is less true

MAP REF **G,9**

1. The sheer power and ferocity of the grizzly bear is on display at Grouse Mountain, Vancouver
2. Elaborate feathered decorations appear at a powwow of the Oji-Cree people, Ottawa
3. Street sculpture points out the talent of Montréal's art scene
4. Be completely humbled while canoeing the turquoise waters of Moraine Lake in Banff National Park, Alberta

4.

3.

2.

1.

Rising up from the Atlantic depths some 500km off the coast of West Africa, the islands of Cape Verde are at once unmistakeably African and a world away from the continent. Wherever you are in the archipelago it's easy to be overwhelmed by the raw power of nature – active volcanoes, canyons, desert plains and beaches all vie for space in this astonishing place that is brushed with Atlantic breezes and Saharan trade winds. With these winds has come a complicated cultural mix that blends Portuguese and African influences in the islands' food, architecture and the world-famous music which is in turns melancholy and uplifting. The overall effect is like nowhere else on earth.

BEST TIME TO VISIT
October to August

TOP THINGS TO SEE
- Mindelo, Cape Verde's prettiest city with a moon-shaped bay, stark mountains and a lovely old quarter
- São Filipe, a gorgeous town, set high on the cliffs and with colonial architecture
- Porto Do Sol, one of the wildest and most beautiful coastlines in Africa
- The Unesco World Heritage–listed remnants of West Africa's first European settlement, Cidade Velha
- The sandy beaches, desert plains and verdant mountainous interior of Santiago

TOP THINGS TO DO
- Windsurf the giant waves off the islands of Sal and Boa Vista
- Trek alongside the precipitous cliffs and green valleys of Santa Antão
- Dive into the famous Mardi Gras festivities on Mindelo
- Climb to Cape Verde's highest point, the active volcano of Mt Fogo (2829m)
- Take up residence in a smoky bar to hear Cape Verde's unmistakeable *mornas* (mournful old-style music)

GETTING UNDER THE SKIN

Read poet Jorge Barbosa's *Arquipélago*, which is laden with melancholic reflections on the sea; or Basil Davidson's *The Fortunate Isles*

Listen to Cape Verde's barefoot diva, Cesária Évora, and her heartbreaking *mornas* and *coladeiras* (sentimental love songs)

Watch *Fintar o Destino* (Dribbling Fate) by Fernando Vendrel, a very African tale of a young footballer torn between dreams of Europe and his home in the islands

Eat the national dish *cachupa* (a tasty stew of beans, corn and meat or fish)

Drink Ceris (the local beer); *grogue* (the local sugar-cane spirit); and white or róse wines from Fogo

IN A WORD
Ta bon (I'm fine)

TRADEMARKS
Afro-Portuguese cultural mix; one of the stars of African economic development; Cesária Évora and other Cape Verdean music; wild volcanic beauty

RANDOM FACT
Cape Verde has the highest adult literacy (83.8%) and life expectancy (71.1 years) of any West African country

MAP REF **L,17**

1. The boats of São Pedro village on São Vicente are stranded like flotsam on the beach
2. A Ponta do Sol local chews meditatively on a pipe
3. A Pedra Lume church, built for the town's salt workers, seems more part of the sky than the earth
4. The village of Fontainhas clings precariously – but picturesquely – to a mountain on Santo Antão

1.

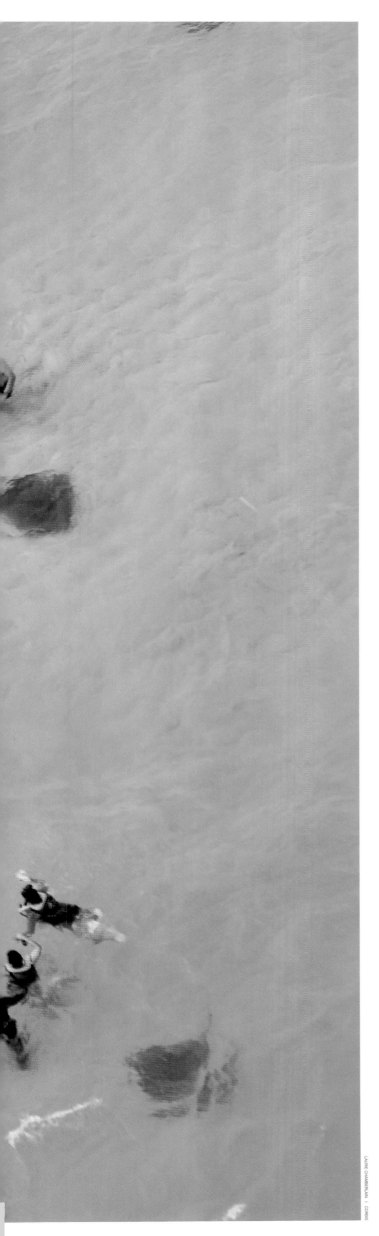

The three Cayman Islands are like a mother hen and two chicks (fitting given the huge range of birds that nest here). Grand Cayman lives up to its name and is home to most of the population, development and resorts. Seven-Mile Beach is a holiday haven, a collection of resorts and condos where the well-heeled cash in on the good life. Worlds away are the tiny offspring: Cayman Brac and Little Cayman. The former is an untrammelled sliver of tropical charm, with large areas of preserved natural beauty on land and underwater plus a few tidy villages of pastel-wood houses. The latter has barely 100 souls, who are vastly outnumbered by birds, iguanas and large fish.

BEST TIME TO VISIT
Weather is beautifully balmy year-round except during the sticky months of July and August

TOP THINGS TO SEE
º Wedge-shaped Cayman Brac has sweeping views and enervating hikes from its namesake bluff
º Rare original-growth tropical trees on the Mastic Trail
º Pedro St James, an 18th-century grand plantation house that cast off its slavery heritage by serving as the site of abolition in 1835
º Emerald green parrots at the Cayman Brac's National Trust Parrot Preserve
º Red-footed boobies and imposing frigate birds at Booby Pond Nature Reserve on Little Cayman

TOP THINGS TO DO
º Commune with iguanas and parrots while sniffing the orchids at Queen Elizabeth II Botanic Park
º Savour some of the world's best wall diving at Bloody Bay off Little Cayman
º Take several lazy days to explore the length of spectacular Seven-Mile Beach on Grand Cayman
º Hope to discover pirate booty in the labyrinth caves on Cayman Brac
º Feed the languid and mellow stingrays at Stingray City

GETTING UNDER THE SKIN
Read *The Cayman Islands: The Beach and Beyond* by former beach bunny Martha K Smith

Listen to West Indian soca, calypso and reggae

Watch *The Firm* (from the John Grisham book); and *Into the Blue* (with Josh Brolin et al)

Eat local specialties that all seem to use conch in one form or another

Drink 'jelly ice' (chilled coconut juice sucked out of the shell)

IN A WORD
Brac (actually a Gaelic word meaning bluff, refers to the most rural of the islands)

TRADEMARKS
Shipwrecks; pirate history; condos; snorkelling and diving; tax shelters

RANDOM FACT
The Caymans have close to 600 banks, although only a few are recognisable as such (with lobbies, tellers, ATMs etc); most are secretive institutions with little more than a brass plaque above an office building mail drop

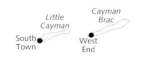

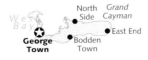

MAP REF **L,11**

1. Strange bedfellows: people flock to feed the stingrays at Stingray City, Grand Cayman

1.

2.

3.

It's a study in chaos. And not of the mathematical variety. First, the republic's sophisticated society, which had been several thousand years in the making, was shattered by the slave trade. The desperate remnants were then catapulted into the harsh yoke of French colonial rule, only to be subsequently subjected to agonisingly egocentric governments after independence. The lack of development has left large swathes of lush rainforest, which still teem with wildlife, including thousands of gorillas and elephants. Travellers can float along wild rivers into an Africa that the world thought no longer existed. As rich life looms in its darkest jungles, warmth, generosity and pride steadfastly survive in the hearts of its people. CAR is Africa at its most raw.

BEST TIME TO VISIT
November to April, during the dry season

TOP THINGS TO SEE
- Western lowland gorillas – the pristine rainforests of the Dzanga-Sangha Reserve are home to a few thousand of them
- Chutes de Boali, a 50m-high waterfall that bursts to life in the rainy season
- Nature's artwork, painted brilliantly on the wings of countless butterfly species
- The ruined palace of former 'Emperor' Bokassa at Berengo
- Megalithic stone monuments that dot the landscape around Bouar

TOP THINGS TO DO
- Wade through the murky waters beneath the Congo Basin's tree canopy to find rare forest elephants
- Watch BaAka (pygmies) summon forest spirits as they hunt *mboloko* (blue duiker)
- Skirt the fringes of the Democratic Republic of Congo as you float atop the tea-coloured waters of the Oubangui River
- Drink a little palm wine and join locals in dancing the *gbadoumba* and *lououdou*

GETTING UNDER THE SKIN
Read *The Central African Republic: The Continent's Hidden Heart* by Thomas E O'Toole, which delves into the nation's social history

Listen to *African Rhythms* by Aka Pygmies and Pierre-Laurent Aimard

Eat plenty of manioc – *ngunza* (manioc leaf salad) and *gozo* (manioc paste) are particular local favourites

Drink locally brewed banana or palm wine

IN A WORD
Bara ala kwe (Hello, in Sango)

TRADEMARKS
Post-colonial chaos; western lowland gorillas; butterflies; forest elephants; BaAka (pygmies); big game trophy hunting by the French; corruption; uranium; diamonds; lush tropical rainforests

RANDOM FACT
Jean-Bédel Bokassa wasn't happy with just being president of the country, so in 1976 he converted the Central African Republic into the Central African Empire; most of the bill for the $20 million coronation to make him emperor was footed by France

PIERRE MERIMÉ | CORBIS

GIACOMO PIROZZI | PANOS

CHAD

Birao

SUDAN

Gounda

Ndélé
Ouadda

Banmingui

CAMEROON

Paoua
Batangafo
Kaga Bandoro
Yalinga

Bossangoa
Dékoa

Baoro
Bambari
Bakouma
Obo

Bossembélé
Rafai

Carnot
Damara
Mobaye

Bangui ✪

Nola
Mongoumba

DEMOCRATIC
REPUBLIC OF
CONGO (ZAÏRE)

CONGO

MAP REF **M,22**

1. Aka people cut a path through the heart of Africa
2. A Bayanga local
3. Locals celebrate a traditional festival in Bayanga
4. Turning on, tuning in: the radio accompanies the day's activities

4.

2.

3.

4.

Bullet vs ballot. Christian vs Muslim. These battles define modern Chad. Tragically, the only thing uniting the north's Muslims with the south's Christians is abject poverty. Without obvious natural resources Chad was virtually ignored during French colonial rule, leaving it teetering towards political turmoil upon independence. And what tragic turmoil it has been. Devoid of pity, the Sahara has continued its march south, leaving its beautiful but bleak calling card – visitors can pluck stunning parched aquatic shells from the desert floor or climb the Sahara's highest peak to absorb a horizon-curving expanse like no other. Meanwhile, beyond the desert's grip life abounds in Central African splendour. Chad, like its people, provides glimpses of surreal beauty with harsh doses of reality.

BEST TIME TO VISIT
December to mid-February

TOP THINGS TO SEE
- The nation's feel good story, the elephants, giraffes and lions of Zakouma National Park
- Elegant, perfectly preserved shells of aquatic molluscs poking from the powdery sands of the Sahara
- Hundreds of camels (and a few crocodiles) sharing the cooling waters of the dramatic Guelta d'Archei
- Emi Koussi and its cratered summit standing high above the desert it dominates

TOP THINGS TO DO
- Journey into the transcendent Tibesti Mountains on a Saharan expedition of a lifetime
- Toast to hippos bobbing in the Chari River while enjoying a sunset drink in N'Djaména
- Head south from the Sahel to the peaceful riverside village of Sarh for a true taste of Central Africa
- Wander between the mud-brick houses of the Sao people in the village of Gaoui

GETTING UNDER THE SKIN
Read *Le Commandant Chaka*, a work denouncing military dictatorships, by Baba Moustapha; *Chad: A Nation in Search of its Future* by Mario J Azevedo and Emmanuel U Nnadozie for an indepth overview of the nation

Listen to anything by Tibesti, a group who popularised the rhythmic 'sai' sound

Watch *Abouna*, a gripping story following two boys' misguided search for their father

Eat *nachif* (finely minced meat in sauce); *salanga* and *banda* (sun-dried/smoked fish)

Drink a bottle of Gala beer, straight from the brewery in Moundou

IN A WORD
Lale (A warm greeting in southern Chad)

TRADEMARKS
Harmattan (the Saharan trade wind); coups; assassinations; conflicts with Libya and Sudan; surprising wildlife

RANDOM FACT
Lake Chad, the inspiration for the nation's name, is falling victim to the Sahara and is receding northwards each year – it may soon not even be in Chad!

LIBYA
NIGER
Aouzou
Bardai
Zouar
Gouro
Faya (Largeau)
Fada
Oum-Chalouba
Koub Olanga
Lake Chad
Biltine
SUDAN
Adré
Massakori Ati
Gos Beïda
⊕ N'Djaména
NIGERIA
Melfi Am Timan
Bongor
Pala Sarh
Goré
CAMEROON CENTRAL AFRICAN REPUBLIC (CAR)

MAP REF **L,22**

1. Quenching a long, hard thirst, camels take a much needed break in a jaw-dropping gorge
2. A stern-faced army commander and his wife pose in a colourful Bardai home
3. Shepherds of the Sahara tend to a flock of goats
4. A refugee from Darfur makes a temporary home in the Bahai refugee camp

2.

3.

1.

4.

Long and slim, Chile spans half the length of South America, from the earth's driest desert to the largest glacial fields outside the poles. Surrounded by the Pacific Ocean and the Andes, the country's long-time isolation has forged a national character that is by turns hospitable, patient and persevering. When an enormous 8.8 earthquake rocked south-central Chile and triggered devastating tsunamis in 2010, the country kept on plugging. It's this work ethic, and huge copper reserves, that has made Chile a Latin American leader. Yet where some see business potential, others just see raw potential: this is Mother Nature's magnificent playground. Visitors should embrace the outdoors. Seek out the mysteries of Easter Island, the craggy Andean summits or the lush forests of the south. Surf, paddle or sail the seemingly endless coast.

BEST TIME TO VISIT

Year-round in the north, November to April in the south, June to August for skiing

TOP THINGS TO SEE

° Steep hills, stairways and street art in the port of Valparaíso
° The alerce, an endangered hardwood native to temperate Valdivian rainforest with specimens over 3000 years old
° Santiago's glittering skyline from the powder-clad ski slopes above it
° The thousands of islands that comprise the solitary Strait of Magellan
° Rano Raraku, the mountain quarry of mammoth Easter Island statues

TOP THINGS TO DO

° Sip your way through the vineyards of the Central Valley
° Trek under the sharp spires of Torres del Paine, South America's premiere national park
° Feast on fresh oysters and mythical lore on the archipelago of Chiloé
° Drink in the wild starscape above the Atacama Desert
° Mosey with pack horses through the lush river valleys of northern Patagonia

GETTING UNDER THE SKIN

Read aloud from Pablo Neruda's *Twenty Love Poems and a Song of Despair*

Listen to wind roaring across the Patagonian steppe

Watch Andres Wood's *Machuca*, about growing up on the cusp of the military coup

Eat the ocean's bounty with conger eel soup, garlic mussels and crab casserole

Drink a tart pisco sour (grape brandy shaken with fresh lime and powdered sugar)

IN A WORD

¿Que onda? (What's up?)

TRADEMARKS

Seismic shocks; volcanoes; cowboys; the great Andean condor; Carmenere wine; Nobel prize–winning poets; Patagonia and the legacy of Pinochet

RANDOM FACT

Chileans love their tubers. Evidence of potato consumption in southern Chile dates as far back as 14,000 years ago. Today, 99% of European potatoes can be traced to the island of Chiloé

MAP REF **S,12**

1. An imposing dune that surrounds the city provides a magnificent vantage point over Iquique
2. Easter Island's most famous residents are the mysterious *moai*
3. Rising above the Patagonian steppe, Los Cuemos mountains are a giant feature of the Parque Nacional Torres del Paine
4. Vivid blue body paint is used by the Rapa Nui people during ceremonies in Valparaíso, Easter Island

1.

2.

3.

Secretive and reclusive for much of the 20th century, China is cutting an ever bigger figure on the world stage, as you might expect from a nation that is home to one in six human beings on the planet. The guiding light of modern China is not Chairman Mao but the yuan – consumerism is the new religion and vast swathes of the country are being concreted over to provide space for new shopping centres and apartment buildings. Nevertheless, China's captivating culture and history still manage to shine through. For every new skyscraper there is a thousand-year-old pagoda, and for every fast-food franchise, there is a teahouse serving hand-pulled noodles and steamed buns.

BEST TIME TO VISIT
March to May and September to November

TOP THINGS TO SEE
- The Great Wall – you can't actually see it from space, but it's just as impressive close up
- Lavish palaces in the Forbidden City and tiny courtyard homes in Beijing's *hutongs* (narrow alleyways)
- The six thousand sculpted faces of Xi'an's terracotta warriors
- Silk Road relics and sifting sands in the empty wilds of Xinjiang
- T'ai chi practitioners moving silently in unison in parks across China

TOP THINGS TO DO
- Take a 'hard class' train journey across China to grasp the scale of this enormous country
- Climb a karst mountain in the scenic traveller hangout of Yangshuo
- Eat a banquet fit for an emperor on one of Beijing's 'food streets'
- Stroll past the kite flyers and colonial office buildings on Shanghai's Bund

GETTING UNDER THE SKIN
Read *Wild Swans* by Jung Chang and *The Search for Modern China* by Jonathan Spence for insights into China's tumultuous last century

Listen to the dissonant melodies of Chinese opera – skip the touristy shows in Beijing for the real deal in Chengdu

Watch Zhang Zimou's *Raise the Red Lantern* or Fei Mu's *Spring in a Small Town* and marvel at the wistful beauty of Chinese film-making

Eat the fiery cuisine of Sichuan – flavoured with 'flower pepper', an incendiary spice unrelated to chillies or black pepper

Drink *chá* (tea) at a traditional teahouse – leaves are rolled, brewed and roasted to create an astonishing variety of brews

IN A WORD
Chi fanle ma? (Have you eaten yet?)

TRADEMARKS
Chopsticks; calligraphy; the Cultural Revolution; t'ai chi; green tea; acupuncture; state censors; the Olympic Games; unchecked development; the ghosts of Tiananmen and Tibet

RANDOM FACT
Among other things, the Chinese invented paper, printing, gunpowder, the compass and the umbrella

MAP REF **J,30**

1. Snaking up and down misty hills, the Great Wall of China is justifiably one of the world's most famous sights
2. Long Horn Miao girls in traditional dress celebrate the Flower Dance Festival in Guizhou
3. The exquisite Temple of Heaven in Beijing symbolises the connection between heaven and earth
4. Plate-spinning Chinese acrobats will leave you gobsmacked

2.

3.

1.

Once typecast as the bad boy of South America, Colombia is one of the continent's most remarkable success stories. A decades-long civil war has been largely relegated to the past, and Colombians and foreign travellers alike are rediscovering this captivating country. Colombia's trump card is its diverse geography, which includes Andean peaks, rainforests and savannahs, supporting an astounding 14% of the world's biodiversity. Riding on the wave of newfound optimism, Colombian cities are also experiencing a dramatic rebirth, with a flurry of urban renewal projects underway. The country's greatest asset may be its people – a mix of indigenous, African and European ancestry – who are famed for their hospitality.

BEST TIME TO VISIT
January to March (the dry season)

TOP THINGS TO SEE
- The cobbled lanes of Cartagena, Colombia's most romantic colonial city
- Zona Cafetera, the coffee-growing region set against a backdrop of volcanoes
- The rebirth of Bogotá, a vibrant and style-conscious city with a burgeoning arts scene
- Laid-back Capurgana and Sapzurro, two blissfully old-fashioned settlements ringed by rainforest on the Caribbean coast
- The hauntingly beautiful subterranean salt cathedral in Zipaquirá

TOP THINGS TO DO
- Head to San Gil, a mecca for adventure lovers with incredible rafting, caving, horseback riding and mountain biking
- Journey to Colombia's Amazonian wilderness at the Reserva Natural Zacambú
- Trek through rainforest and mountains to the ruins of the Ciudad Perdida
- Explore the archaeological sites hidden in the rolling hills around San Agustín
- Take a mud bath inside the crater of the diminutive Volcán de Lodo El Totumo

GETTING UNDER THE SKIN
Read *Love in the Time of Cholera,* the fantastical love story by Nobel prize–winning author Gabriel García Márquez

Listen to pop vocalists Carlos Vives and Shakira, or the Afro-Caribbean beats of *Toto La Momposina*

Watch *Maria Full of Grace*, Joshua Marston's complex film about a pregnant drug mule seeking a new life in the US

Eat satisfying *arepas* (corn cakes served with cheese, pork and many other toppings); *sancocho* (a hearty soup made with meat, yucca and other vegetables)

Drink probably the world's best coffee; order a *tinto* (black, espresso size), *pintado* (small milk coffee) or *cafe con leche* (latte-size with more milk than coffee)

IN A WORD
Que hubo? (What's up?)

TRADEMARKS
Coffee; Gabriel García Márquez; emeralds; lost cities; Shakira; football; cocaine

RANDOM FACT
Avianca, Colombia's flagship airline, was the first commercial airline founded in the Americas

MAP REF **N,12**

1. Musicians jam on the streets of Bogotá
2. A performer is dressed to impress at the November Independence festivities in Cartagena
3. Colonial houses line the cobblestone streets of the World Heritage–listed city of Cartagena
4. Straight out of a fairy tale, the imposing Santuario de las Lajas stands over the Guaitara River

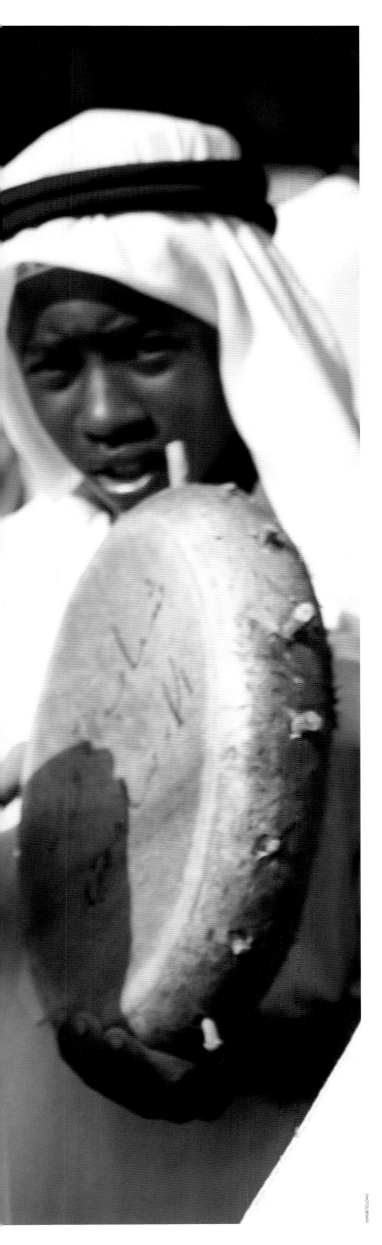

CO||OROS & ||AYOTTE

CAPITAL Moroni (C), Mamoudzou (M) | POPULATION 752,438 (C), 223,765 (M) | AREA 2235 sq km (C), 374 sq km (M) | OFFICIAL LANGUAGES Arabic & French (C), French (M)

Born of fire, these Indian Ocean islands have seldom come off the boil. Discontent, intrigue and ambition, much like the omnipresent lava lurking beneath this archipelago, have all erupted habitually, resulting in numerous coups and civilian riots. However, for visitors, the melange of Polynesian, Swahili and Arabic cultures is as intoxicating as the fragrant fields of ylang-ylang, jasmine, cassis and orange flowers. Also rooted in the islands' fertile volcanic soils are virgin rainforests, which host everything from giant bats to rare lemurs. Surrounding it all is a coast blessed with turquoise waters, colourful sand beaches and ports laden with historical architecture.

BEST TIME TO VISIT
May to October (the dry season)

TOP THINGS TO SEE
- The entirety of this Indian Ocean archipelago spread out below you from the lofty summit of Mt Ntingui
- A mere fraction of the 600 colourful species of fish inhabiting the mammoth coral reef that surrounds the island of Mayotte
- The faultless sandy beaches fringing the islets of Parc Marin de Mohéli
- Locals transfixed by the ancient African game of *bao*
- Your sails filled while cruising one of the world's largest lagoons

TOP THINGS TO DO
- Trek up to Lac Dzialaoutsounga and Lac Dzialandzé, peaceful crater lakes on the flank of Mt Ntingui
- Swim with sea turtles off the Sazilé Peninsula
- Spend a few sweaty hours reeling in a marlin – replenish your fluids while chilling on a gloriously empty beach
- Meander through shadows and past intricately carved Swahili doors in the crooked alleys of Moroni's ancient medina
- Inhale the sweet fragrance wafting from the ylang-ylang distillery in Bamboa

GETTING UNDER THE SKIN
Read *The Comoros Islands: Struggle Against Dependency in the Indian Ocean*, Malyn Newitt's outline of the region's turbulent, coup-riddled modern history

Listen to Mohammed Hassan singing *twarab*, a Comoran version of Swahili music accompanied by a *gabusi* (short-necked lute) and a *ndzendze* (box-shaped zither)

Eat your first ever inexpensive lobster, and you'll remember more than the petite price tag – *langouste à la vanille* is particularly divine

Drink tea spiced with lemon grass and ginger

IN A WORD
Salama (Hello, in Comoran)

TRADEMARKS
Azure waters lapping on long beaches; plantations of ylang-ylang, jasmine and cassis; incredible seafood; volcanic eruptions; tumultuous politics; countless coups

RANDOM FACT
A wedding, or *grande marriage* as it's known in the Comoros, can last up to nine days – the groom is expected to fund the *toirab* (celebration) that caters for the entire village

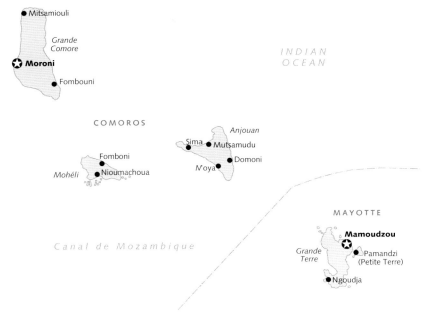

MAP REF **P,24**

PHOTOGRAPHY

1. A group of musicians contribute to the festivities at a wedding on the island of Anjouan

2.

3.

1.

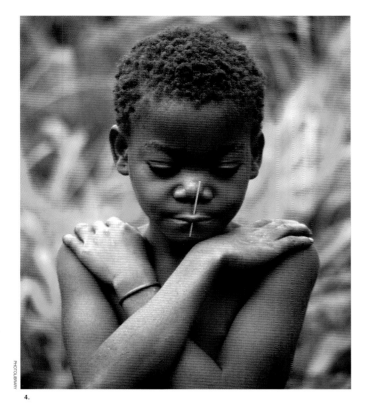

PHOTOLIBRARY

4.

TEUN VOETEN | PANOS

Never was so much sacrificed by so many for so few. Sadly, the suffering people of the Democratic Republic of Congo haven't had much say in the matter. Intrepid travellers, unlike the nation's successive kleptocrats, aren't concerned with the mineral wealth beneath the soil – instead, they long for things that are more valuable: compelling conversations with locals in cities and remote villages; exhilarating interactions with silverbacks and elephants in impenetrable forests; and beckoning rivers offering a serpentine path into the truly unknown. While continued insecurity and a lack of development puts much of the DRC out of reach, the country remains an adventurer's dream.

BEST TIME TO VISIT
December to February (north of equator). May to October (south of equator)

TOP THINGS TO SEE
- Bonobos and forest elephants in the untouched wilds of Parc National de la Salonga
- The footwork of the fishermen working above the torrents at Wagenia Falls
- A flood in a 347m freefall from the top of Lofoi Falls, Parc National de Kundelungu
- Lava spewing skyward from the crater of Mt Nyiragongo, one of the world's most active volcanoes

TOP THINGS TO DO
- Throw out your watch (and calendar) and journey by barge up the Congo River from Kinshasa to Kisangani
- Spend the best hour of your life sharing glances with mountain gorillas in Parc National des Virunga
- Bathe in the chaotic symphony that is Kinshasa
- Brave the wet and reward yourself with a trek into the Rwenzoris, the 'Mountains of the Moon'

GETTING UNDER THE SKIN
Read *King Leopold's Ghost* by Adam Hochschild; and *In the Footsteps of Mr Kurtz*, Michaela Wrong's compelling look into President Mobutu's regime

Listen to the kings of *soukous* (African rumba), Franco Luambo and Papa Wemba, Africa's equiavalent of James Brown and Elvis Presley

Watch *Lumumba*, a gripping story of the political upheaval surrounding Patrice Lumumba's life and death

Eat *liboke* (fish stewed in manioc leaves) with the omnipresent *fufu* (manioc porridge)

Drink a Primus beer, or Turbo King if you prefer darker brews

IN A WORD
Sángo níni? (How are you? in Lingala)

TRADEMARKS
Zaïre; The Rumble in the Jungle; *Heart of Darkness*; blood diamonds; kleptocracy; war; UN peacekeeping soldiers

RANDOM FACT
While the country (then Zaïre) was receiving billions in international aid, President Mobutu was chartering Concordes for shopping trips to Paris; by 1984 Mobutu was believed to have about US$4 billion – an amount equivalent to the country's national debt – in his personal Swiss bank account

MAP REF O,22

1. Traditional dancers in leopard-skin motif prepare for a ceremonial performance in Goma
2. Plantains get the thumbs-up recommendation in a market
3. Kickin' back in a dugout canoe on the Congo River, Yangambi
4. A pygmy girl at the Gungu festival

93

2.

3.

4.

Do you like your emotions shaken or stirred? The Republic of Congo has the power to do both. Its wild jungles, which blanket vast sections of the north, continue to be home to pygmies and countless species of wildlife, including Africa's largest population of lowland gorillas and chimpanzees – the intense travel experiences here are as unforgettable as they are uncomfortable. Equally indelible, but at the other end of the spectrum, are the devastating stories of the latest civil war, which was based more on tribal conflicts than political ones. However, the Congolese look positively toward their future, and they continue to ensure there is one thing reverberating within them more than thoughts of their past: laughter.

BEST TIME TO VISIT
December to February (north of equator). May to September (south of equator)

TOP THINGS TO SEE
- Congolese navigating the shifting currents of the Congo River in their pirogues
- The inconceivable concentration of the nation's wealth in Pointe-Noir
- Herds of forest elephants congregating in Wali Bai, a natural clearing in Parc National Nouabalé-Ndoki
- The joyous celebrations when you've been narrowly beaten by a local youth in babyfoot (table football)
- Rusty, tendril-like ridges of rock snaking through the rainforest in Diosso Gorge

TOP THINGS TO DO
- Drift through Parc National d'Odzala's waters in search of gorillas and elephants
- Peruse Brazzaville's fragrant markets for a treasure to call your own
- Explore the protected marine areas of Parc National Conkouati-Douli, home to sea turtles and rare West African manatees
- Sip a cappuccino on a terrace in Brazzaville and watch Africans, Arabs, Europeans and Asians peacefully going about their daily life

GETTING UNDER THE SKIN
Read *Congo Journey*, Redmond O'Hanlon's captivating travelogue that delves into the nation's superstitions and cultures

Listen to anything by Congo's jazz king, Jean Serge Essous

Watch *Congo*, Frank Marshall's adaptation of the novel of the same name by the late Michael Crichton

Eat fresh fish with fried bananas

Drink palm wine, the ubiquitous beverage of the Congo

IN A WORD
Losáko (Hello, in Lingala)

TRADEMARKS
Congo River; untamed rainforests; lowland gorillas; candlelit night markets; oil; civil war; Marxist revolution and 'scientific socialism'

RANDOM FACT
On the Congo River's northern bank, Brazzaville sits across from Kinshasa in the Democratic Republic of Congo; it's the only place in the world where two national capitals are situated on the opposite banks of a river within sight of each other

MAP REF O,21

1. Looking sharp: a village chief displays a necklace of large animal teeth and a feathered headdress
2. A Brazzaville resident watches life on the street
3. Congolese children glide skilfully through the water on their way to school
4. An imperious silverback western lowland gorilla stalks across Odzala National Park

1.

2.

3.

NICHOLAS DEVORE / STONE /GETTY IMAGES

Smack in the centre of the Pacific, the Cook Islands are 15 flecks of land spread over an oceanic space about the size of India. Named after the great explorer Captain James Cook, these dazzling tropical morsels have long been a refuge for runaways, hermits and wannabe Robinson Crusoes. And who can blame them? With the heady mix of South Seas air, pristine beaches, cerulean lagoons, and fish and fruit a-plenty, the Cook Islands are practically the definition of a remote island paradise. To get a fix of civilisation, head to the capital Avarua for an enticing mix of modern fine restaurants, boutique shopping and a thriving Polynesian culture.

BEST TIME TO VISIT
April to November is the driest season but any time of year is warm and sunny

TOP THINGS TO SEE
○ Ancient *marae* (temples) and gardens at the Highland Paradise Cultural Centre
○ Humpback whales skimming the clear-water reefs
○ Green turtles eating the guts of local fishermen's morning catch at Avarua Landing, Mangaia
○ The view over the sapphire Aitutaki lagoon from Maungapu peak

TOP THINGS TO DO
○ Traverse Rarotonga on foot via the lush, tropical wonderland of the cross-island trail
○ Snorkel the fish-filled *ra'ui* (traditional conservation areas) around Rarotonga
○ Island hop throughout the impossibly blue Aitutaki lagoon
○ Explore the jungle-clad burial caves on 'Aitu and Mangaia Islands
○ Stuff your face and enjoy the dancing, singing, fire-juggling and whatever else is on at an Island Nights extravaganza

GETTING UNDER THE SKIN
Read *An Island to Oneself,* the classic desert-island read by Tom Neale, who lived on Suwarrow Atoll in the 1950s and '60s

Listen to anything by Tyson, who has had Pacific-wide success with his modern, hip-hop Polynesian hits

Watch *The Other Side of Heaven*, a delightful coming-of-age tale that was mostly filmed on Rarotonga

Eat *ika mata* (raw fish in coconut milk); or *anga kuru akaki ia* (stuffed breadfruit)

Drink at a *tumunu* (bush beer-drinking club), the Cook Islands equivalent of a kava ceremony but with a lethal orange homebrew

IN A WORD
Kia orana! (May you live long!)

TRADEMARKS
Saucy traditional dancing; pandanus-thatched roofs; Maori culture; black pearls; deserted atolls; breadfruit

RANDOM FACT
Residents of Palmerston can trace their lineage back to one man, William Masters, who arrived on the atoll with a handful of Polynesian wives in 1863. Today these islanders still speak English with a Gloucestershire accent

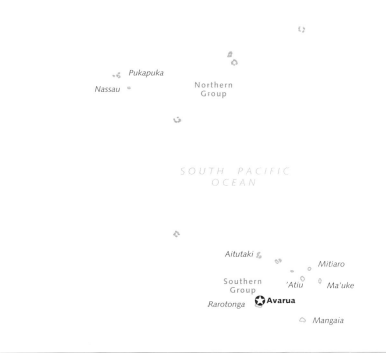

Pukapuka
Nassau
Northern Group

SOUTH PACIFIC OCEAN

Aitutaki
Mitiaro
Southern Group
'Atiu
Ma'uke
Rarotonga ✪ Avarua
Mangaia

MAP REF **Q,3**

1. The carved wooden sign of Matavera's church in Rarotonga stands sentry
2. Steady aim and lightning reflexes reward these spear-fishermen with a plentiful catch in Aitutaki
3. Gorgeous gigglers crowned with floral leis take a fast ride on the water
4. Boo! A threatening stone carving wards off evil spirits in Avarua, Rarotonga

2.

3.

1.

A calm oasis in a region of strong political riptides, Costa Rica has blossomed into tourism gold. For starters, it's hard to beat the Disneyesque cast of creatures – from morpho butterflies to monkeys – traipsing the numerous parks. The waves are prime, the beauty is staggering and the sluggish pace seductive. Of course, playing paradise to a world audience has its consequences. With the tourism boom came US retirees and real estate speculators. Now two-thirds of the coast is foreign-owned and development often outpaces sustainability. Lucky for Costa Rica that its do-gooder fans, ranging from ecologists to proud Ticos (Costa Ricans), are vocal and vigilant. Nature here may suffer its blows, but at least it is taken seriously.

BEST TIME TO VISIT
December to April (the dry season)

TOP THINGS TO SEE
- Parque Nacional Corcovado, among the most biodiverse places on earth
- The windswept wilderness beaches at the end of the Nicoya Peninsula
- Misbehaving monkeys staging a guerrilla raid on picnics in Parque Nacional Manuel Antonio
- Leatherback sea turtles making their millennial migration to Playa Grande
- Masked devils schooling the colonial Spanish in the Fiesta de los Diablitos

TOP THINGS TO DO
- Whiz across the cloud forest on a canopy zip line in Monteverde
- Take a night time trek out to Arenal Volcano to see luminescent lava flows and soak in nearby hot springs
- Study hard in surf school and ride your first wave at Witch's Rock
- Soak up the calypso beats of Cahuita on the steamy Caribbean coast
- Paddle a maze of jungle canals thick with wildlife in Parque Nacional Tortuguero

GETTING UNDER THE SKIN
Read *Costa Rica: A Traveler's Literary Companion*, 26 short stories that capture the soul of the county

Listen to *Costa Rica: Calypso*, fun Caribbean sound from rootsy trad to pop

Watch *Caribe*, directed by Esteban Ramírez, a drama where environmentalist meets US oil company, with forbidden love interest

Eat *casado* (a plate of meat, beans, rice and fried plantain)

Drink palm wine, the preferred fire water of rural farmers; coffee at any local lunch counter

IN A WORD
Pura vida (Pure life – for thumbs up or a salutation)

TRADEMARKS
Dripping rainforests; surf bums; active volcanoes; La Negrita (or the Black Madonna); soccer (football) fans; foaming waterfalls

RANDOM FACT
Costa Rica tops world rankings of happiest nations; its citizens also outlive their North American counterparts

MAP REF **M,11**

1. Dense tropical rainforest surrounds the awe-inspiring crater and sulphurous lagoon of Poás Volcano
2. A resplendent male quetzal flashes his electric-blue plumage in the rainforests near Puntarenas
3. A farmer and his oxen toil in the fields in Playa Camaronal
4. Learn the ropes from an experienced Costa Rican *gaucho* (cowboy) at Hacienda Guachipelin

1.

2.

3.

After almost a decade of making headlines for all the wrong reasons, Côte d'Ivoire is making a tentative comeback. Once lauded as West Africa's success story – the country was a magnet for workers from all across the region, not to mention travellers drawn by idyllic beaches and intriguing cultural traditions – Côte d'Ivoire's descent into civil war was especially tragic. But with a fragile peace taking root, travellers are beginning to return, albeit at a trickle. Aside from the country's many stand-out attractions, Côte d'Ivoire's appeal resides – as it always has – in its ability to project modern Africa in microcosm, from the confidence and sophistication of muscular Abidjan to the deeply traditional Dan and Baoulé peoples of the rural interior.

BEST TIME TO VISIT
November to March

TOP THINGS TO SEE
- Abidjan's skyscrapers and roiling nightlife in the brash powerhouse of West Africa
- The languid coastal town of Grand Bassam with its decaying colonial buildings
- Yamoussoukro, the village-turned-capital with the tallest basilica in Christendom
- Sassandra's deserted, postcard-perfect beaches, especially at Niega
- The stunning mountain region of Man, with mask ceremonies and stilt dancers

TOP THINGS TO DO
- Surf the Atlantic breakers at Assinie, arguably Côte d'Ivoire's loveliest beach
- Set off in search of nut-cracking chimps in the rainforest of Parc National de Taï
- Hike to the summit of Mt Tonkoui (1223m), near Man, for a view of three countries
- Haggle for the famous Korhogo cloth in the rust-red city of the same name in northern Côte d'Ivoire
- Take a slow pirogue ride close to Assirie

GETTING UNDER THE SKIN
Read the magic-realist tale *Waiting for the Wild Beasts to Vote* by Côte d'Ivoirean novelist Amadou Kourouma

Listen to Alpha Blondy, the king of West African reggae, or the *coupé decalé* (cut and run) dance sensation

Watch Henri Duparc's acclaimed *Bal Poussière* (Dancing in the Dust), which tackles traditional polygamy; or Désiré Ecaré's *Visages des Femmes* (Faces of Women)

Eat *poisson braisé* (grilled fish) with *attiéké* (grated cassava); or *kedjenou* (chicken or guinea-fowl simmered with vegetables in a mild sauce)

Drink Flag or Tuborg beers; or *bandji* (palm wine)

IN A WORD
I-ni-cheh. I-kah-kéné (Hello. How are you? in Dioula, the market language)

TRADEMARKS
Yamoussoukro basilica; Korhogo cloth and Dan masks; eating out in *maquis* (rustic open-air restaurants); reggae and *coupé decalé* music; former economic powerhouse; postponed elections

RANDOM FACT
Despite (or perhaps because of) a name that translates as 'Ivory Coast', less than 300 elephants are thought to survive in Côte d'Ivoire

MAP REF **N,19**

1. Masterful village musicians sound out a powerful rhythm on balafons
2. Young children make their journey home, skilfully balancing basins of food on their heads
3. Girls in Zala, preparing for an acrobatic performance, make an impact with striking headdresses and face paint
4. Pungent chillies are arranged for sale at Adjema market in Abidjan

2.

3.

1.

4.

Croatia is back! It may have disappeared from the radar for a while, but its idyllic stretch of Adriatic bays, beaches and rocky islets is well and truly buzzing with visitors again, and with good reason. Here the Mediterranean lifestyle and mindset is exemplified in the gentle chugging of water taxis, harbour-side promenades, siestas behind shuttered windows and a willingness to stop for gossip and coffee at any hour. There's more to Croatia than glamour and hedonism, too: Croatian culture has been informed by manifold influences – Venetian merchants, Slavic folklore, rugged geography, devout Catholicism and maritime adventurism – all of which contribute to this sun-drenched country of warm stone architecture where oleanders seem to bloom year-round and the water is implausibly clear.

BEST TIME TO VISIT
April to June and September to October

TOP THINGS TO SEE
° Dubrovnik, the 'pearl of the Adriatic', the limestone-walled city jutting into the sea
° The sparkling lakes, waterfalls and walkways at Plitvice Lakes National Park
° Diocletian's Palace in Split, now full of cafes, plazas and boutique shops
° Zagreb's galleries, churches, museums and kickin' nightlife
° Untouched forests and hidden coves on Cres Island

TOP THINGS TO DO
° Sail, catch a ferry, or paddle a canoe, but you must cruise the Adriatic coast, a sublime stretch of land and sea
° Hunt truffles or just enjoy a slow-food banquet in Istria, Croatia's ecotourism capital
° Get your gear off and plunge into the sea in your birthday suit on the islands off Hvar, and plenty of other spots besides
° Straighten your collar, nod and smile at passers-by during the *corso*, the communal, early-evening promenade that happens in every Croatian town

GETTING UNDER THE SKIN
Read *Black Lamb and Grey Falcon* by Rebecca West, a classic Balkan travelogue; and noted Croatian journalist Slavenka Drakulic's *Cafe Europa*

Listen to traditional *tamburica* (lute) music, or modern pop from Gibonni and Severina

Watch *Armin* directed by Ognjen Svilicic, a poignant observation of father-son relationships on the road to Zagreb; or *Libertas*, a biopic about 16th-century poet from Dubrovnik, Marin Drzic

Eat *cevapcici* (skinless sausages) with hot bread and raw onions; or *pasticada* (beef stewed in wine and spices)

Drink Ozusko or Karlovacko, the two most popular beers; wine from Kvarner or Baranja

IN A WORD
Zdravo (Hello)

TRADEMARKS
Azure seas; Dubrovnik's city walls; baroque cathedrals; terracotta roofs; yachties

RANDOM FACT
Fine weather is so reliable in Hvar that some hoteliers offer free accommodation if it snows

MAP REF **H,21**

1. Lovrjenac Fort provides a spectacular view of the stronghold of Dubrovnik
2. Folk dancers in traditional dress are a blur of motion as they perform at Diocletian's Palace in Split
3. Sea and sky fuse into one in Rovinj, where fishermen make preparations at the waterfront
4. Immerse yourself in the aquamarine waters of Krka waterfalls, near the town of Skradin

1.

2.

3.

Cuba might just be a synonym for drama. The largest body of land in the Caribbean has been at the centre of intrigue for centuries, from the late 1800s when the US flexed its colonial muscles to its iconic revolution in 1959. Years of isolation have preserved ancient architecture from destruction even as it crumbles. But this intoxicating nation is no snoozy time warp: it's a raucous stew of African, Caribbean and Latin culture with manic and melodic rhythms that lure fans from around the globe. Change, when it inevitably comes, will forever alter this bizarre, beautiful and beguiling nation. In the meantime Cuba is unlike any other nation, from its hulking colonial relics to its shambolic cities and its palm-backed beaches.

BEST TIME TO VISIT
November to May, to avoid the heat and hurricanes

TOP THINGS TO SEE
- Havana, the steaming, bubbling centre of the nation
- Santiago de Cuba, an often-overlooked city with rich traditions as old as colonialism and as recent as the revolution
- Las Parrandas, Remedios, year-round street party nights and languid beach days
- Habana Vieja, Havana's Unesco-recognised ancient quarter, the largest and best-preserved in the Caribbean
- Classic American cars that collectors would kill for

TOP THINGS TO DO
- Smoking one of the fabled local cigars, accessories to local luminaries
- Strolling the impromptu street festival that is Havana's waterfront Malecón
- Cheering on your team of choice at a baseball game rich with talent
- Hike, climb and explore the soaring limestone cliffs and quiet forests of Viñales
- Immerse yourself with giant lobsters and manatees at Punta Frances on Isla de la Juventud, an unspoiled wonderland rich with life

GETTING UNDER THE SKIN
Read *Trading with the Enemy: A Yankee Travels Through Castro's Cuba* by Tom Miller, a rich feast of Cuban lore

Listen to Cuban takes on reggaeton, the combo of hip hop, dance-hall and reggae

Watch everyone's favourite, *Fresa y Chocolate*, 1995's hit Havana comedy directed by Tomás Gutiérrez and Juan Carlos Tabío

Eat homecooked *ajiaco* stew, featuring potatoes, meat, plantains, corn and old beer

Drink a minty, sweet rum mojito

IN A WORD
Queué bolá assure? (What's up, brother?)

TRADEMARKS
Cigars; communists; rum; salsa; Fidel Castro; poverty; sex; ancient American sedans; *The Buena Vista Social Club*

RANDOM FACT
Baseball was introduced by American dockworkers in the late 1800s and remains the national sport. Games at stadiums across the nation are, like the country itself, passionate, raucous affairs

MAP REF **L,II**

1. Cruise by Havana's elegant Spanish colonial buildings in a hot 1950s American ride
2. Nimble fingers pluck at a double bass at a restaurant in the Vieja district, Havana
3. Revolutionary books are as bright and bold as flags in Plaza de Armas, Havana
4. A couple of cool cats are dressed to the nines in Havana's Plaza de la Catedral

2.

3.

1.

4.

Basking in balmy seas at the sunny end of the Mediterranean, Cyprus is an island with a split personality. After a failed invasion attempt in 1974, this sleepy isle was split into two countries, separated by a few hundred yards, but worlds apart. The southern, Greek-speaking half of the island bustles with beach resorts, attracting hordes of holidaymakers in search of sunshine and sand. Across the Green Line, the politically isolated Turkish republic is all empty stone towns, orange groves and dust. Yet the two sides of Cyprus have more in common than they care to admit: fine beaches, pine-forested mountains, terracotta-tiled villages, a unique Greek-meets-Turkish culture and more historic ruins than you can shake an amphora at.

BEST TIME TO VISIT
April to May and September to October

TOP THINGS TO SEE
- Frescoes of sword-wielding angels in the Byzantine churches at Pedoulas and Kakopetria
- Amazing mosaics in the Greco-Roman cities of Salamis, Kourion and Pafos
- Mile after mile of untouched golden sand in the remote Karpas Peninsula
- Ten thousand years of treasures in the museums of Nicosia (Lefkosia)
- The view from the slopes of mighty Mt Olympus

TOP THINGS TO DO
- Sip mountain wine in the pine-scented Troodos Mountains
- Feast on a Cypriot meze in the crescent-shaped harbour at Kyrenia (Girne)
- See the Green Line from both sides in the maze-like backstreets of Nicosia
- Swim with turtles in the Karpas and Akamas peninsulas
- Storm the Crusader castles at St Hilarion, Kolossi and Kantara

GETTING UNDER THE SKIN
Read *Journey Into Cyprus* by Colin Thubron or *Bitter Lemons of Cyprus* by Lawrence Durrell for evocative descriptions of pre-partition Cyprus

Listen to Pelagia Kyriakou's *Paralimnitika* recordings, a superb collection of Cypriot demotic songs

Watch *Attila 74*, directed by Michael Cacoyannis, or *The Slaughter of the Cock*, directed by Andreas Pantazis, for insights into the Turkish invasion of 1974

Eat the classic Cypriot *mezedes* – a pick-and-mix of savoury bites, from fried halloumi cheese to *seftalia* (pork crepinettes)

Drink the local firewater, distilled from fermented grape skins – Greek Cypriots call it *zivania*, Turkish Cypriots call it *raki*

IN A WORD
Avrio (Tomorrow) – the best time to do anything on this laid-back island

TRADEMARKS
Turkish coffee; fried halloumi; orange groves; Aphrodite; Roman relics; army bases; turtle beaches; the Green Line; DJ bars and hangovers in Agia Napa and Lemesos

RANDOM FACT
Around 3% of the island is officially part of Great Britain thanks to the sovereign army bases at Akrotiri and Dekelia

MAP REF **J,23**

1. Locals take their icons out for a walk in an Orthodox procession, Agros
2. The small church of the Stavrovouni Monastery is the earliest documented monastery on the island
3. Kick back with an ice cream while your shoes receive the star treatment in Nicosia
4. Enveloped by a field of mustard flowers beside the Church of the Archangel Michael in Kato Lefkara, a girl carries a basket of perfectly ripe oranges

1.

2.

3.

For many, the Czech Republic is all about Prague. There's no denying the beauty of the capital, from the cobbled streets of Staré Město to the architectural majesty of the castle district, but Prague is just one of the country's numerous gracious cities. The Renaissance and baroque elegance of Olomouc, Český Krumlov and Telč are manifestations of the artistic heights achieved by the Czechs, a people with a penchant for hot spas and a genius for brewing beer. The Czech Republic is home to the original Bohemians, after all, and who else but the Czechs would elect a playwright as their first president? So head first to Prague, by all means, but be sure to see the rest of the country as well.

BEST TIME TO VISIT
April to June

TOP THINGS TO SEE
- The changing of the guard at Prague Castle
- The Renaissance facades and Gothic arcades of the old town square in Telč
- Rippling sandstone stratifications at Adrspach-Teplice Rocks
- The charm of Olomouc, with its astronomical clock and religious architecture
- Elegant Česky Krumlov on the serpentine bends of the Vltava River

TOP THINGS TO DO
- Stride out across Prague's iconic Charles Bridge without the tourists, either at first light, late at night or in the depth of winter
- Savour a quiet ale at the storied breweries of Plzeň, home of the original pilsner, and České Budějovice
- Ponder the sad fate of European Jewish communities in the cemetery of Josefov
- Explore the richly forested hills of Šumava on foot or mountain bike
- Take a spa treatment, and mix with B-list celebrities, at Karlovy Vary

GETTING UNDER THE SKIN
Read *The Book of Laughter and Forgetting* by Milan Kundera, a wry and sometimes hilarious look at life in communist Czechoslavakia; or Myla Goldberg's keen-eyed musing on Prague, *Time's Magpie*

Listen to Antonin Dvorak's *Slavonic Dances*, or his religious masterpiece *Stabat Mater*

Watch *Kolya*, Jan Sverak's Academy Award–winning tale of a Prague musician left to look after a small Russian boy during the Velvet Revolution; or *Česky Sen* a documentary about the launch of a hoax department store

Eat *knedlícky* (dumplings) and *svícková na smetaně* (roast beef with sour cream and cranberries)

Drink *pivo* (beer) at countless breweries and raffish pubs throughout the county

IN A WORD
Dobry den (Good day)

TRADEMARKS
Elegant architecture of Prague; Good King Wenceslas; spa towns; prickly castles; breweries and beer-inspired revelry

RANDOM FACT
The sugar cube was invented in the former Czechoslavakia

MAP REF **G,21**

1. Glorious autumnal foliage frames a view of Prague Castle and St Vitus Cathedral from Petřín Hill, Prague
2. Figures on the Astronomical Clock in the Old Town Square in Prague date from the 15th century
3. Flags swirl and drumsticks twirl as men in Italian Renaissance dress perform during the Gold Trail Festival in Prachatice
4. Knights of Malta Order are decked out in their ceremonial robes at a procession in Prague

4.

2.

3.

1.

It's heart-warming to know there's still a country where the term 'fairy tale' can be used freely – from its most enduring literary legacy to its textbook castles. In a nutshell, Denmark gets it right: old-fashioned charm embraces the most avowedly forward-looking design and social developments, and wins it a regular chart-topping place on lists of both the most-liveable *and* the happiest nations on earth. Its egalitarian spirit embraces visitors too – you won't have to search hard to find some much-prized *hygge*. This means social nirvana in Denmark: a sense of cosiness, camaraderie and contentment. Sure, Denmark may not have the stop-you-in-your-tracks natural grandeur of its neighbours, but after one visit (and a taste of *hygge*) you may start plotting to move here for good.

BEST TIME TO VISIT
May to September

TOP THINGS TO SEE
- The world in miniature at plastic-fantastic Legoland
- Charming cobblestoned streets in Ribe, Denmark's oldest town
- Danish style personified in the streets, stores and eateries of Copenhagen
- Viking history up close and personal at Roskilde's Viking Ship Museum
- The gleaming white chalk cliffs of Møns Klint

TOP THINGS TO DO
- Escape to the beaches and bike lanes of the island of Bornholm
- Stand with one foot in the Skagerrak (North Sea), the other in the Kattegat (Baltic Sea), at postcard-pretty Skagen
- Join 80,000 others at the Roskilde Festival, northern Europe's biggest rock event
- Dine in one of Copenhagen's foodie hot spots – restaurants here have as many Michelin stars as Madrid or Rome

GETTING UNDER THE SKIN
Read *Miss Smilla's Feeling for Snow* by Peter Hoeg; Karen Blixen's *Out of Africa* (written under the pen-name Isak Dinesen); or, for a change of pace, Kierkegaard's philosophical works or Hans Christian Andersen's fairy tales

Listen to old-school Euro-rock from D-A-D; indie rockers Veto; or chanteuse Aura

Watch Academy Award winners *Babette's Feast* and *Pelle the Conqueror*; *After the Wedding*; anything directed by *enfant terrible* Lars von Trier

Eat *smørrebrød* (open-faced sandwich); *frikadeller* (Danish meatballs); *sild* (pickled herring); and of course Danish pastries, known locally as *wienerbrød* (Vienna bread)

Drink *øl* (beer – the biggies are Carlsberg and Tuborg); or *akvavit* (schnapps)

IN A WORD
Det var hyggeligt! (That was cosy!)

TRADEMARKS
Beer; furniture design from the likes of Arne Jacobsen and Hans Wegner; Hans Christian Andersen fairy tales; Lego; the Little Mermaid; Vikings

RANDOM FACT
Scandinavia may be prime Winter Olympics territory, but Denmark has no downhill skiing – its highest point is a trifling 173m

MAP REF **G,21**

1. A youngster steps out for a stroll in Snogebæk, Bornholm
2. Cafe crowds line Copenhagen's Nyhavn Canal
3. With clockwork precision, royal guards patrol the Amalienborg Palace in Copenhagen
4. Beautiful in form and function: clean white lines house a Hasle fishery's smokehouse in Bornholm

1.

2.

3.

All good things come to an end. Although few endings will be as epic a show as Djibouti's. Straddling the meeting point of three diverging tectonic plates, Djibouti is currently being ripped apart by Mother Nature: fumaroles spew steam from the earth's insides; lava pokes through ever-thinning crust; and its dramatic, lunar-like deserts are collapsing. In geological terms, it is occurring at breakneck pace. In human terms, it is in spectacularly slow motion – a reason to make travel plans, not to cancel them! The intoxicating culture, dominated by Somali and Afar peoples, is peppered with influences from Arabia, India and Europe. Meanwhile, setting the speed of life to 'unhurried' is *qat*, a mild narcotic herb that's a national obsession.

BEST TIME TO VISIT
November to mid-April, when temperatures are tolerable

TOP THINGS TO SEE
- Afar tribesmen gathering gleaming salt crystals from the blinding floor of Lac Assal
- Whale sharks swimming silently past you in the Gulf of Tadjoura
- French legionnaires rubbing shoulders with traditionally robed tribesmen in the streets of Djibouti City
- The ancient juniper forests in the national park of Fôret du Day, one of Djibouti's rare spectacles of green

TOP THINGS TO DO
- Search for heaven-sent shadows in the otherworldly landscape that is Lac Abbé
- Absorb the Arabic atmosphere of Tadjoura, a coastal town fringed with palms
- Remember to breathe while floating among an armada of manta rays in the Ghoubbet al-Kharab
- Stand on the 'bridge of lava', perhaps the thinnest piece of the earth's crust
- Follow in the footsteps of Afar nomads along the ancient salt route

GETTING UNDER THE SKIN
Read *Le Pays Sans Ombre*, a series of short stories by Djiboutian Abdourahman Waberi – non-French speakers can pick up Jeanne Garane's English translation, *The Land Without Shadows*

Listen to the solo guitar of Aïdarous, Djibouti's leader of modern music

Watch *Total Eclipse*, a film – partly shot in Djibouti – that follows the tumultuous life of French poet Arthur Rimbaud

Eat *cabri farci* (stuffed kid) roasted on a spit; or *poisson yéménite* (fish suppers served in newspaper)

Drink black coffee; or tea with lemon

IN A WORD
Tasharrafna (Pleased to meet you)

TRADEMARKS
Salt lakes; fumaroles; *qat*; $5 cucumbers; whale sharks; French and American military presence

RANDOM FACT
It has been estimated that 40% of an average family's expenditure is spent on *qat*, and over two months of productivity is lost per worker per year due to its effects

MAP REF **M,24**

1. A force to be reckoned with – draped in dazzling costumes, women from the Sultanate of Tadjoura display the curved daggers of their men
2. The Afar people make up more than a third of the population of Djibouti
3. Lac Abbé's apocalyptic terrain sprouts limestone chimneys up to 50m high
4. An Afar girl tends to one of her family's goats

Rare among Caribbean islands, tear-drop shaped Dominica is *not* known for bleached white beaches. Rather, the colour here is green, the overwhelming colour of its lush jungles that cover much of this mountainous island. Amid these dense interior forests, you're never far from the roar of a waterfall. Walk just a short distance and you'll pass dozens of species of tropical trees, vines and flowers. Twisting, narrow dirt roads and scattered tiny villages create a mood of isolation that's an escapist's fantasy. Geologic oddities abound, including lakes that boil from lava vents and offshore reefs that bubble with subterranean gases. Nominally English in language and tradition, locals have a strong French Creole accent that flavours everything from speech to food.

BEST TIME TO VISIT
Mild trade winds keep Dominica beautifully pleasant year-round

TOP THINGS TO SEE
- Cabrits National Park, which encompasses 18th-century British Fort Shirley, swamps on land and coral reefs offshore
- Roseau, a thriving Caribbean port town for 300 years
- Emerald Pool, a crystalline jungle pool at the base of a waterfall
- Scotts Head, a minnow-sized fishing village on dramatic Soufrière Bay
- The Macoucherie Distillery, which is uncommercial in inverse proportion to the perfection of its rum

TOP THINGS TO DO
- Plunge into jungles so verdant they could be a cliché at Morne Trois Pitons National Park
- Wonder at the natural fizz of the waters below the surface while diving at Champagne Beach
- Traverse deep canyons on a trek to Trafalgar Falls
- Percolate in eponymously named Boiling Lake, a large body thought to lie directly above a lava-filled crack in the earth's crust
- Serenely glide along with whales aboard a sailboat

GETTING UNDER THE SKIN
Read *Voyage in the Dark* by Jean Rhys; or Dominica's other noted novelist, Phyllis Shand Allfrey, who is best known for *The Orchid House*

Listen to African *soukous*, Louisiana zydeco and a variety of local bands at the World Creole Music Festival in Roseau

Watch the second and third *Pirates of the Caribbean* movies for scenes shot in Dominica

Eat *callaloo* soup (a creamy concoction made with dasheen leaves)

Drink fruit punch made with fresh fruit and Macoucherie rum

IN A WORD
Irie (Hi, bye, cool)

TRADEMARKS
Diving; Rasta colours; rainforests; cricket; Creole culture; undiscovered areas

RANDOM FACT
Dominica's national bird, the Sisserou parrot, is the largest of all the Amazon parrots and thrives in trees along the island's 200 rivers

MAP REF **L,13**

1. Two Carib girls take a break in the lush surrounds of their village

115

1.

Dominicans will tell you that it's no accident their country is one of the most popular tourist destinations in the Caribbean. What's not to like they'd ask, pulling you out for a night soaked in rum and merengue dancing. It's a hard argument to fight against. Santo Domingo holds colonial architecture dating back to the time of Columbus, the coast is fringed with white beaches and scuba diving sites, while the more energetic can delve into the lush green interior to trek along mountain trails. All those sugar plantations give the country a buzz, and it takes its fun seriously, listing baseball diamonds alongside churches as hallowed ground, and having not one but two annual carnival celebrations.

BEST TIME TO VISIT
December to July (to avoid the hurricane season)

TOP THINGS TO SEE
- Santo Domingo's Zona Colonial, Spain s original stepping stone into the New World
- Humpback whales, who gather every January to March to mate and give birth at Península de Samaná
- The white sand and turquoise waters cf Playa Rincón, one of the Caribbean's finest beaches
- Carnival, celebrated most raucously in Santo Domingo, Santiago and La Vega
- Damajagua, a cascade of 27 waterfalls tumbling into glorious limestone pools

TOP THINGS TO DO
- Dive beneath the waves to explore the coast's myriad reefs and wrecks
- Pick up the Atlantic breeze at the kite-surfing heaven of Cabarete beach
- Go for the home run at a baseball match, the DR's (other) national religion
- Put on your dancing shoes to the heady rhythms of the merengue clubs
- Buzz from the adrenaline rush of white-water rafting on the Río Yaque del Norte

GETTING UNDER THE SKIN
Read *Dead Man in Paradise* by JB Mackinnon for travelogue-meets-murder mystery; or *Feast of the Goat* by Mario Vargas Llosa, about the Trujillo regime

Listen to merengue legends Johnny Venture and Coco Band; or *bachata* (popular guitar music based on bolero rhythms) stars Raulín Rodriguez and Juan Luís Guerra

Watch *Sugar* by Anna Boden and Ryan Fleck, about a Dominican baseball player going to the USA to play in the minor leagues

Eat *la bandera* ('the flag') – red beans, white rice and green plantain with meat stew

Drink beer – a cold glass of Presidente at a sidewalk bar is a quintessentially Dominican experience

IN A WORD
¡Que chulo! (Great!)

TRADEMARKS
Palm-lined beaches; plantains; merengue; rum; cigars that are better than but not as famous as those from Cuba; Sammy Sosa

RANDOM FACT
The foundation stone of Santo Domingo s Catedral Primada de América was laid in 1514, making it the oldest cathedral in the Americas

MAP REF **L,12**

1. The bell tower of the historic Catedral Primada de América in Santo Domingo has aged gracefully
2. With his cart piled high with fresh produce, a vendor pedals through the streets of Santo Domingo
3. La Romana boasts an idyllic palm-lined beach and bright-white sands
4. Men prepare for a fishing trip in Laguna Gri Gri the tangled roots and vines beside Río San Juan

1.

2.

3.

East Timor enjoyed its status as the 'world's newest country' after it gained independence from Indonesia in 1999. Although the first years of freedom were tumultuous, this impoverished nation now seems intent on tackling its myriad problems. All-but-undiscovered natural wonders, from mist-shrouded mountain peaks to horizon-stretching white-sand beaches, await those ready to challenge the lack of infrastructure and most other visitor comforts. Roads to important cities vanish without a trace in the lush countryside where people live as they have for centuries. Dive spots, as pristine as any in the hemisphere, include many not yet named. Everywhere you go, you'll meet locals, especially children, utterly amazed, and amused, to encounter strangers in this tiny nation.

BEST TIME TO VISIT
It is equatorial hot year-round but May to November has the least rain

TOP THINGS TO SEE
- Unpopulated Jaco Island at the west end of East Timor is a sacred spot with the purest white-sand beaches in the Pacific
- Atauro Island, a starkly beautiful and almost barren island offshore, where a few beach huts welcome the intrepid
- Traditional architecture, including the iconic stilted Fataluku houses in the east
- Sudden swarms of children who surprise visitors in even the most remote outposts

TOP THINGS TO DO
- Dive the untarnished blue waters that ring the coast, starting with the reefs right off Dili
- Understand East Timor's tortuous history that has scarred virtually every citizen
- Name your own beach: they come with the regularity of waves along the barely populated coast
- Escape the heat in misty and mountainous Maubisse, home to an old colonial inn

GETTING UNDER THE SKIN
Read Luis Cardoso's *Crossing: A Story of East Timor,* a memoir of growing up under Portuguese and Indonesian rule

Listen for *tebe,* the festive folk music heard at any celebration

Watch *Death of a Nation: The Timor Conspiracy*, John Pilger's exploration of the international abandonment of the tiny nation

Eat excellent fresh seafood available in Dili

Drink rich Arabica coffee grown in the hills above Dili; or *sopi,* a potent brew distilled from the pandanus plant

IN A WORD
Olá (Hello)

TRADEMARKS
Xanana Gusmão; José Ramos-Horta; UN troops; freedom fighters; colourful woven lengths of *tais* (traditional cloth)

RANDOM FACT
A small patch of East Timor (the Oecussi Enclave) sits nearly 100km removed from the rest of the country, sharing all its land borders with Indonesian West Timor

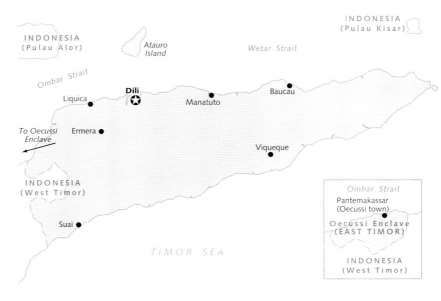

MAP REF **P,33**

1. Travellers perched atop a vehicle have a spectacular view of the mountainous coastal fringe east of Dili
2. The waters in Dili bubble over with excited children helping each other bring in a fishing canoe
3. A congregation in its Sunday best flocks to the Ainaro village church in the mountains south of Dili
4. A Timorese woman adorned with a feathered headdress performs a traditional dance

4.

2.

3.

1.

4.

ECUADOR & THE GALÁPAGOS ISLANDS

This Andean nation may be South America's second-smallest country, but it towers above most other places when it comes to natural and cultural wonders. Home to Amazonian rainforest, 5000m-high volcanoes and the awe-inspiring Galápagos Islands, Ecuador remains one of the world's most extraordinary wildlife-watching spots. Its cultural diversity is as varied as its geography, with a dozen different indigenous groups, a sizeable Afro-Ecuadorian population and a more recent influx of immigrants from Asia, each offering a unique take on the quintessential Ecuadorian experience. There are highland towns renowned for the colourful textiles and haunting folk music; laid-back fishing villages that move to the galloping beat of cumbia; and vibrant cities that hold a captivating blend of old and new.

BEST TIME TO VISIT
May to December on the mainland, or January to April for the Galápagos

TOP THINGS TO SEE
° The splendid colonial centres of Quito and Cuenca, Unesco World Heritage sites with foundations dating back to the 16th century
° Ecuador's Amazon rainforest, a vast region of unsurpassed biodiversity
° The 5897m-high Volcán Cotopaxi, best seen from atop a horse or from the windows of a 400-year-old hacienda on the mountain's slopes
° Cloud forests near Mindo, where over 400 bird species have been recorded

TOP THINGS TO DO
° Go wildlife watching in the Galápagos Islands and see giant tortoises, water-loving iguanas and extremely approachable sea lions
° Hike the Andes, overnighting in peaceful villages amid the spectacular scenery of the Quilotoa Loop
° Browse for handicrafts in Otavalo, one of Latin America's largest craft markets
° Feel the adrenaline rush while white-water rafting on the jungle-lined Río Napo

GETTING UNDER THE SKIN
Read *Huasipungo* (The Villagers), by Jorge Icaza, a powerful depiction of indigenous villagers in the early 20th century

Listen to Esto Es Eso, a US-Ecuadorian duo that blend traditional Ecuadorian sounds with hip hop and rock

Watch Tania Hermida's *Que Tan Lejos?* (How Much Further?), a road movie about two young women on an unplanned journey of self-discovery in the highlands

Eat *encocado* (Afro-Ecuadorian seafood stew cooked with coconut milk and spices)

Drink *canelazo*, a warming drink of hot *aguardiente* (sugar-cane alcohol) served with cinnamon, sugar and citrus

IN A WORD
Hola (Hello)

TRADEMARKS
The Galapagos Islands; Panama hats; pan pipes; the Andes; roasted guinea pig

RANDOM FACT
Tiny Ecuador is home to some 300 mammal species and over 1600 bird species – more than Europe and North America combined

MAP REF O,11

1. Piercing the clouds, the snowy cone of Volcán Cotopaxi reaches a height of 5897m
2. Bullfighters in Quito get psyched up to enter the ring for a display of style, technique and courage
3. A lava lizard clings to a spiky marine iguana at Punta Espinoza, both of them blending into their rocky surrounds
4. The sky-blue domes of Cuenca's Catedral de la Inmaculada Concepción glow in gentle light

1.

2.

3.

Egypt is a colossus and a crossroads of continents. Its history reads like a grand epic and the country is rich in signposts to this story, from the peerless glories of Ancient Egypt to the jewels of Islamic Cairo where the call to prayer will transport you back centuries. Even Egypt's geography has the quality of a myth, from the Sahara and its mythical Cave of Swimmers or the Nile, that great river of legend, to the rich marine life of the Red Sea coast. But Egypt is above all an assault on the senses, a place where many worlds – Middle Eastern, African and Mediterranean – collide, often at breakneck speed. The impact can be overwhelming, but is utterly unforgettable.

BEST TIME TO VISIT
October to May to avoid the heat

TOP THINGS TO SEE
- Pyramids of Giza, the last intact Ancient Wonder of the World, and don't forget the Sphinx
- Ancient Egypt's heartland, Luxor, from the Valley of the Kings to the sublime Karnak Temple
- Cairo, the clamorous 'Mother of the World', with mosques, mausoleums and the Egyptian Museum
- Abu Simbel, arguably the singlemost beautiful landmark from Ancient Egypt
- Siwa, one of the Sahara's most beguiling oasis towns rich in ancient myths

TOP THINGS TO DO
- Dive or snorkel in the Red Sea, an unbelievable world beneath the water
- Climb to the summit and watch the sunrise from Mount Sinai
- Spend days drifting down the Nile aboard a felucca (traditional sailing boat)
- Drive out into the White Desert from the western oasis of Farafra
- Go on a camel safari with the Bedouin in Sinai

GETTING UNDER THE SKIN
Read Naguib Mahfouz's *The Cairo Trilogy;* and either *In the Eye of the Sun* or *The Map of Love* by Ahdaf Soueif, for deep insights into Egyptian culture

Listen to Umm Kolthum, forever Egypt's diva

Watch *The Yacoubian Building* by Marwan Hamed, and the landmark *Baby Doll Night* by Adel Adeeb, which are windows on modern Egypt

Eat *fuul* (salty fava bean paste); *taamia* (falafel); or *kushari* (noodles, rice, black lentils and dried onions, served with a fiery tomato sauce)

Drink fresh fruit juices, mint tea and Turkish coffee

IN A WORD
Inshallah (God willing)

TRADEMARKS
Pyramids and pharaohs; King Tut and Cleopatra; Nile journeys and camels into the desert; world-class diving; tacky souvenirs; incessant honking

RANDOM FACT
Don't pack your brolly – Egypt is the driest country in Africa with average annual rainfall of less than 51mm

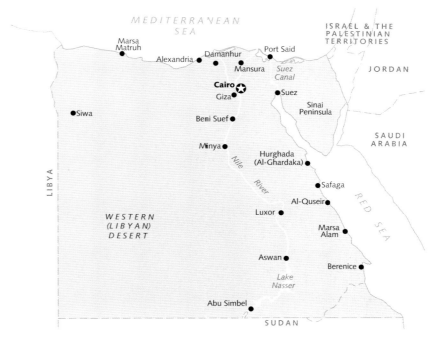

MAP REF **K,23**

1. A sunrise balloon ride over Luxor is an exhilarating way to start the day
2. Ships of the desert await tourist flocks at the Pyramids of Giza, above the hazy Cairo cityscape
3. Mounds of piping-hot Egyptian bread spill out of the oven
4. Feluccas sail at sunset along the Nile

2.

3.

1.

PHOTOLIBRARY

4.

CHRISTOPHER PILLITZ | THE IMAGE BANK / GETTY IMAGES

Resilient, real and sometimes raw, El Salvador is strong coffee for the senses. Ambivalent about its hardships and the not-so-distant civil war, most travellers have kept their distance. But there is no reconciling the old reputation with today's goodwill. El Salvador is something of a puzzle. Contrast the frank talk of war survivors with artists' whimsical folk carvings and the recycled US school buses done up as psychedelic chariots. This is a place to absorb and unravel. While the smallest nation in Central America does not boast abundant wildlife or primary forest, El Salvador does have countless volcanoes, mountains, swimming holes and a wild Pacific coast. But the best benefit may be the opportunity to forge a human connection long untapped.

BEST TIME TO VISIT
November to April (the dry season)

TOP THINGS TO SEE
° Hot springs and highland coffee farms on the Ruta de las Flores
° Surfistas hitting serious swells on the Balsam Coast
° The hours' quiet passage in Alegría, the country's mountain-top flower capital
° Rugged ridges and mountain grandeur in Parque Nacional El Imposible
° The little pink houses of the Naïve art birthplace of remote La Palma

TOP THINGS TO DO
° Conquer the longest break in Central America at Punta Roca
° Sample marinated rabbit or grilled frog at colonial Juayúa's popular weekend fair
° Strike up a conversation with an ex-guerrilla guide at the Museo de la Revolución Salvadoreña in Perquín
° Shop for *sorpresas* (intricate folk scenes carved in ceramic shells), or their naughty version called *pícara*
° Help release thousands of Olive Ridley turtles hatching in Barra de Santiago

GETTING UNDER THE SKIN
Read The bold erotic poems of Claudia Lars; *Salvador* by Joan Didion, a moving account of the early days of the Civil War

Listen to pre-Hispanic fusion, Cumbia and new-wave ska in San Salvador's progressive music scene

Watch *Salvador*, the story of a war correspondent directed by Oliver Stone, for Hollywood's insights into the civil war; *Romero* with Raul Julia, a true story about the high price of opposing tyrannical leadership

Eat *pupusas* (cornmeal pockets filled with farmer's cheese, refried beans or pork rinds) topped with *curtido* (pickled cabbage and vegetables)

Drink *refrescos de ensalada* (juices with chunks of fresh fruit)

IN A WORD
Que chivo (How cool)

TRADEMARKS
Hot surf spots; guns; ex-guerrillas; remittances from US-based relatives

RANDOM FACT
Over a third of El Salvadorans live and work abroad, sending US$3billion home yearly in remittances to support their families

MAP REF **M,10**

1. A vision in white – the final touches are made to a bride's veil before her big day in Anamorós Village
2. Suchitoto's Iglesia Santa Lucía, seen from Parque Centenario, is blindingly white in the sun
3. Local taste sensations fill a street-food store in Calle San Antonio Abad, San Salvador
4. Panchimalco school children in crisp checked uniforms crowd together to face the camera

1.

2.

3.

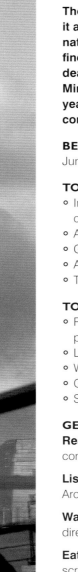

The British Empire spread English culture around the globe, but this is where it all started, from the cricket bats to the bowler hats. The largest of the four nations that make up the United Kingdom, England is famous for football and fine art, film makers and fashionistas, real ale and roast beef, live bands and dead playwrights, a nice cup of tea and the BBC, the Ministry of Sound and the Ministry of Silly Walks, Queen, the Queen, pearly kings and queens, and 4000 years of history. Thanks to the cooking talents of England's diverse immigrant communities, you might even be pleasantly surprised by the food.

BEST TIME TO VISIT
June to September

TOP THINGS TO SEE
- In London, make time for St Paul's, the Tate Modern, the British Museum and a bar crawl through Shoreditch and Soho
- A gig by the 'next big thing' at the Leadmill or the Boardwalk in Sheffield
- Giddy views over the Lake District from the top of Scafell Pike
- A home game at Arsenal, Chelsea or Manchester United Football Club
- The gorgeous gothic cathedrals at York, Durham and Lincoln

TOP THINGS TO DO
- Relive Spinal Tap's finest hour at Stonehenge, England's most iconic prehistoric monument
- Laze away a sunny afternoon drinking bitter beer at an English country pub
- Wash away your worries by taking a bath in the Roman baths at Bath
- Go crazy for curry in Birmingham's 'Balti Triangle'
- Slurp on a stick of seaside rock on Brighton pier

GETTING UNDER THE SKIN
Read Charles Dickens for historical context; and *The English* by Jeremy Paxman for a contemporary exploration of the English psyche

Listen to the English take on England by adding the Kinks, Squeeze, Pulp and the Arctic Monkeys to your MP3 playlist

Watch *The Madness of King George*, directed by Nicholas Hytner, and *This is England*, directed by Shane Meadows, for contrasting explorations of English culture

Eat a pickled egg, munch some dry-roasted peanuts and nibble on a bag of pork scratchings for the full English pub experience

Drink a hearty pint of real ale – look out for anything from Crouch Vale Brewery or the Dark Star Brewing Company

IN A WORD
Cheers!

TRADEMARKS
The weather; the white cliffs of Dover; ageing rockers; the Royal Family; fish and chips; page-three lovelies; warm beer; cool Britannia; period dramas; binge-drinking; the full English breakfast; Wimbledon, Wembley and Lords

RANDOM FACT
The closest language to English is Frisian, spoken by 500,000 people in Germany, Denmark and the Netherlands

MAP REF **G,19**

1. The iconic dome of St Paul's Cathedral in London rises behind the Millennium Bridge
2. Classical striped deck chairs entice weary beach bods at St Ives, Cornwall
3. A sunset ride above the city skyline on the London Eye is the perfect way to end the day
4. Water jets cool down a young crowd in Piccadilly Gardens

1.

2.

3.

4.

A country of two worlds, Equatorial Guinea is a nation divided not only by sea but also by oil. Large reserves of black gold were discovered beneath the ocean's floor off the coast of Bioko Island in the mid-1990s, and the subsequent industrial development forever changed the island's landscape, economy and culture. The country's mainland (Rio Muni), however, is much the same as it has been for centuries. For those who don't mind being treated like they're a potential foreign mercenary, Rio Muni's wild jungles, remote villages and pristine beaches are an authentic adventure into the Africa of old.

BEST TIME TO VISIT

December to February, for Bioko Island; May to September for Rio Muni

TOP THINGS TO SEE

- ° Hâkâ, the lengthy sandbar that snakes into the dark depths of the Atlantic from Isla Corisco's palm-dotted southeastern shore
- ° The seemingly irrepressible wave of westernisation rolling back each evening as streets of Bata come alive with Equatoguineans
- ° The tug of war between natural beauty and the oil industry off Bioko's coast
- ° Plaza de España and the colonial cathedral in the heart of Malabo

TOP THINGS TO DO

- ° Push your way through the jungle's undergrowth in Parque Naciónal de Monte Alen while on a quest for gorillas, chimpanzees and forest elephants
- ° Step gently into a pirogue and explore the wild fringes of the Estuario del Muni near Gabon's frontier
- ° Settle into the bleached sands and soak up what the peaceful heavens have to offer on Isla Corisco's deserted beaches
- ° Trek through the fern-tree forests on the volcanic slopes near Moka

GETTING UNDER THE SKIN

Read The Wonga Coup: Guns, Thugs and a Ruthless Determination to Create Mayhem in an Oil-Rich Corner of Africa by Adam Roberts – the title says it all

Listen to the lyrics of Eyi Moan Ndong and his chorus, accompanied by drums and the mvet (a cross between a zither and harp)

Eat seafood plucked from the ocean that very day

Drink osang (local tea); or malamba, brewed from sugar cane

IN A WORD

Mbôlo (Hello)

TRADEMARKS

An unbridled oil industry; corrupt officials; attempted coups; continental rainforests; gorillas; Eric Moussambani (aka 'Eric the Eel', for his heroically slow 100m freestyle at the Sydney 2000 Olympic Games)

RANDOM FACT

Former British Prime Minister Margaret Thatcher's son, Sir Mark, was one of those accused of plotting to overthrow Equatorial Guinea's government in 2004 – unlike other conspirators, he avoided jail time, receiving a four-year suspended sentence and $500,000 fine

MAP REF N,21

1. The Ole River rushes through the dense verdant forest of Gran Caldera on Bioko Island
2. Curious children peek over a village fence in Evinayong
3. Acrobat of the trees on Bioko Island, Pennant's red colobus monkey ranks among the most endangered primates in Central West Africa
4. Villagers gather on the steps of a colonial-style Catholic church in Ebebiyín

2.

3.

1.

ROBERT CAPUTO | AURORA | GETTY IMAGES

4.

PHOTOLIBRARY

Part Fellini film set, part Ottoman Empire, 100% Africa – Eritrea is a country like no other. The apocalyptic, volcanic desert of Dankalia sits at one end of its colourful spectrum, while the life thriving on the coral reefs of the Red Sea bookends the other. Wedged between the two, in what is a mere sliver on the Horn of Africa, is a wealth of culture, history and beauty for travellers to experience. Relics of ancient African civilisations, early Arab traders, Ottoman rulers and Italian colonialism abound. The fight for sovereignty and continuing conflicts with Ethiopia have brought hard times to Eritreans, but they remain proud, clinging to their strong sense of identity and independence.

BEST TIME TO VISIT
October to May, when temperatures have settled down

TOP THINGS TO SEE
- Inspired examples of art deco, expressionist, cubist and neoclassical Italian architecture in Asmara, the 'Piccolo Roma'
- The Temple of Mariam Wakiro, one of the ancient archaeological ruins in Qohaito
- Debre Libanos, an extraordinary 6th-century monastery embedded into a lofty cliff face
- *Passeggiata*, an evening ritual when the people of Asmara take to the streets to stroll

TOP THINGS TO DO
- Get cosy with corals while diving the depths of the Dahlak Archipelago
- Depart earth for the stark wonders of planet Dankalia
- Inhale the aromas (and a macchiato or two) in the many classic art deco cafes on Asmara's Harnet Ave
- Wend through the whitewashed buildings, porticoes and arcades of Massawa, an island with an engaging, Arab appeal

GETTING UNDER THE SKIN
Read *I Didn't Do it for You: How the World Used and Abused a Small African Nation* by Michela Wrong, an entertaining and angering portrayal of Eritrea's heart and soul

Listen to *Greatest Hits* by Atewebrhan Segid, Eritrea's leading traditional musician and singer

Watch *Heart of Fire*, a film based on the real life of a young female soldier who came of age during Eritrea's civil war

Eat *legamat* (deep-fried dough balls sold hot in newspaper cones)

Drink a piping-hot macchiato

IN A WORD
Selam (Hello, in Tigrinya)

TRADEMARKS
Infallible politeness; classic art deco architecture; marvellous macchiatos; conflict with Ethiopia

RANDOM FACT
Having successfully fought together as friends to finally defeat the Derg in 1991, Eritrea's President Isaias and Ethiopia's Prime Minister Zenawi soon waged war against each other – the trigger of the falling-out was Eritrea's decision to introduce its own currency (the nakfa) to replace the Ethiopian birr

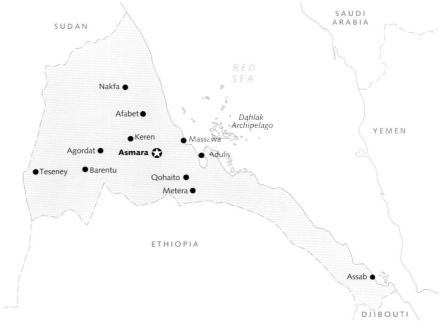

MAP REF **L,24**

1. Prayer time takes place at a mosque in Asmara
2. A goatherd is dressed in deep yellow robes near Sittona
3. Relics of Italian colonial days, yellow Fiat taxis cruise the streets of Asmara
4. Children pull a container of water past ornate architecture in Massawa

1.

2.

3.

You can't help but admire this diminutive country for shaking off the yoke of the Soviet era and embracing change with gusto. And in return, the world is tuning in to Estonia's understated charms, an irresistible mix of Eastern European and Nordic flavours. Soaking up Tallinn's long white nights and medieval history, or exploring the country's coastline, are joys to be savoured. National parks provide plenty of elbow room, quaint villages evoke a timeless sense of history, and uplifting song festivals celebrate age-old traditions. You can experience unspoilt seaside or windswept island solitude, while still enjoying the comforts of a thoroughly modern, e-savvy country that's hell-bent on catching up with its Nordic neighbours in the quality-of-life stakes.

BEST TIME TO VISIT
May to September

TOP THINGS TO SEE
- The chocolate-box confection of Tallinn's medieval Old Town
- How inhabitants of the capital unwind in the bucolic splendour of Lahemaa National Park
- Live music at the hugely popular Viljandi Folk Music Festival
- The futuristic, award-winning KUMU art museum in Tallinn's Kadriorg Park

TOP THINGS TO DO
- Island-hop along the west coast, ensuring a visit to both Saaremaa and Hiiumaa
- Go bog-shoe-walking and canoeing in the wetlands of Soomaa National Park
- Do a spot of cross-country skiing in the picturesque countryside around Otepää
- Get sand in your shorts at Pärnu, the country's summertime mecca
- Down a beer among students in the university town of Tartu

GETTING UNDER THE SKIN
Read *The Czar's Madman* by Jaan Kross Estonia's most internationally acclaimed author; *Between Each Breath* by Adam Thorpe, in which Tallinn and the Estonian islands provide the setting for an Englishman's midlife crisis

Listen to the austere music of composer Arvo Pärt; rock from Ultima Thule, Genialistid and Smilers, all among the country's longest-running and most loved bands

Watch *Sügisball* (Autumn Ball), based on a 1979 novel portraying six residents of a drab high-rise apartment in Soviet-era Tallinn

Eat *verivorst* (blood sausages), if you're feeling bloodthirsty; pork and potatoes (it's on every menu); smoked fish; fresh summer berries

Drink Vana Tallinnn – no one knows what this syrupy liqueur is made from, but it's sweet and strong and best served in coffee, or over ice with milk

IN A WORD
Terviseks! (Cheers!)

TRADEMARKS
an e-savvy populace; Finnish day-trippers; folk tales; the sport of *kiiking*; software development and Skype (it was invented here); saunas; song festivals; Vana Tallinn

RANDOM FACT
Estonians invented the weird and wonderful sport of *kiiking*, whereby competitors stand on a swing and attempt to complete a 360-degree loop around the top bar

MAP REF **F,22**

1. Wander past Tallinn's old-town Gothic spires and Kiek in de Kõk, the most powerful cannon tower in Baltic Europe
2. Like giant blue onions, the bulbous domes of Alexander Nevsky Cathedral float above Toompea Hill
3. A fishing boat is tucked away in the reeds in Treimani, near Pärnu
4. A gentleman and his hat are all set for a Baltic winter in Harju County

2.

3.

1.

ETHIOPIA

CAPITAL Addis Ababa | POPULATION 85,237,338 | AREA 1,104,300 sq km | OFFICIAL LANGUAGES Amharic, Oromiga, Tigrinya, Somali, Guaragigna, Sidama & Hadiyigna

Ethiopia proudly blurs the line between present and past. As the oldest sovereign state in Africa, and having successfully routed Italian armies seeking colonisation, it is understandable that Ethiopians embrace their ancient rituals and all the relics associated with their 2000-year-old civilisation. Ornate, rock-hewn churches dating back to the first millennium AD are not simply showpieces of past grandeur for tourists – they are active places of daily worship, hosting age-old ceremonies for locals. The historical treasures pepper a dramatic, mountainous landscape where dozens of animal species seen nowhere else on earth play. For the traveller, entering this unique world, with its own culture, language, script, calendar, timekeeping and wildlife, is as exciting as it is enlightening.

BEST TIME TO VISIT
October to January, when the watered highlands are blooming marvellous

TOP THINGS TO SEE
- Endemic walia ibex butting heads on a dramatic Abyssinian precipice in the Simien Mountains
- The vibrant tribes of the Omo Valley
- Africa's Camelot and its emperors' 17th-century castles in Gonder
- Hyena feeding outside the fabled gates of the walled city of Harar
- Lake Chamo's crocodile market – be careful, the reptiles are the ones shopping

TOP THINGS TO DO
- Flirt with gravity when climbing to reach Tigray's most precariously positioned church, Abuna Yemata Guh
- Take an expedition to Erta Ale's lava lake in the Danakil Depression
- Step into the medieval shadows to see Lalibela's light, its 11 rock-hewn churches
- Soak up the ambience during a traditional coffee ceremony
- Emerge from Aksumite tombs and stare skyward at the ancient civilisation's stelae

GETTING UNDER THE SKIN
Read *Wax & Gold* by Donald N Levine, which offers an insightful look into Amharic culture

Listen to *The Very Best of the Éthiopiques* a compilation of evocative Ethiopian jazz

Watch Mary Olive Smith's documentary *A Walk to Beautiful*, the telling journey of five outcast women rebuilding their lives

Eat *injera* (rubbery, sponge-like flatbread of national importance) laden with *berbere*-spiced beef and *gomen* (minced spinach)

Drink coffee (Ethiopia is at its origins)

IN A WORD
Ishee (OK, Hello, Goodbye – or with a smile it's a gesture of friendliness and goodwill)

TRADEMARKS
Ethiopian Orthodox Church; rock-hewn churches; African castles; stelae; the coffee ceremony; 'bleeding heart' baboons; Abyssinia; middle- and long-distance runners

RANDOM FACT
When the Ethiopian People's Revolutionary Democratic Front tanks rolled into Addis Ababa in 1991, they were navigating with the map in Lonely Planet's *Africa on a Shoestring*

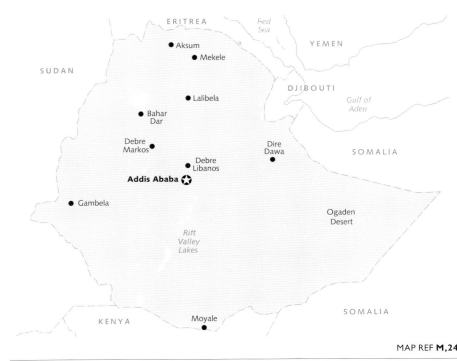

MAP REF **M,24**

1. Hamer tribespeople are exquisitely adorned
2. A priest holds a cross in Bet Meskel, an excavated chapel in the courtyard of Bet Maryam, Lalibela
3. Holding hands across the plains, Hamer girls frame the landscape in southwest Ethiopia
4. Pilgrims wearing *gabi* (traditional white shawls) gather near the rock-hewn monolithic church of Bet Giyorgis

135

1.

2.

3.

On a windswept chain of islands 500km off the coast of Argentina, 'the Falklands' are a curious slice of Great Britain plonked down in the South Atlantic. Afternoon tea and cake, English pubs and Anglican steeples remind visitors who is in charge (a detail still disputed by Argentina), while the majority of its tiny population claim British descent. Step outside of Stanley, the capital, however, and another world awaits – one where large herds of sheep roam the rugged countryside, and penguins, seals and sea lions are regularly sighted at chilly beaches across the islands. Despite the isolation, most 'islanders' couldn't imagine living anywhere else.

BEST TIME TO VISIT
October to March

TOP THINGS TO SEE
- Stanley, a colourful seaside town with a ramshackle assemblage of buildings and distinctly English pubs
- Saunders Island, a birdwatching wonderland, home to five species of penguin, plus black-browed albatross and cormorants
- The white sands of Bertha's Beach, to spot dolphins and gentoo penguins
- Goose Green and nearby Darwin, where some of the fiercest fighting occurred in the Falklands War

TOP THINGS TO DO
- Hike to the summit of Mt Usborne, offering expansive views over Cape Dolphin and the Berkeley Sound
- Feast on fresh local seafood, including snow crab, oysters and Atlantic rock cod
- Photograph sea lions and elephant seals on the aptly named Sea Lion Island
- Commune with the King Penguin colony at Volunteer Point
- Take a scenic stroll around Gypsy Cove, taking in views over Yorke Bay and Mt Lowe

GETTING UNDER THE SKIN
Read *A Falkland Islander Till I Die* by Terrence Severine Betts, a fascinating portrait of life on the islands from the 1950s to the 1982 invasion and up to the present

Listen Ian Strange's evocative collection of animal calls on *South Atlantic Islands: A Portrait of Falkland Islands Wildlife*

Watch *An Ungentlemanly Act*, an eye-opening film describing behind-the-scenes events leading up to the Falklands War

Eat fantastic seafood; and organic, locally raised lamb and free-range beef

Drink a cup of tea during a regular smoko (traditional tea break)

IN A WORD
Hi there

TRADEMARKS
British-Argentine battlefield; penguin mating grounds; snow-covered islands; near dark winters; sheep; rain; snow and plenty of it

RANDOM FACT
Anywhere outside of Stanley is known as 'camp', from the Spanish word *campo*, countryside. With over 500,000 sheep scattered across the islands, ruminants outnumber humans by 160 to one

SOUTH ATLANTIC OCEAN

Jason Islands

Saunders Island

Pebble Island

Port Louis

Johnson's Harbour

Port Howard

Berkeley Sound

West Falkland

Stanley

King George Bay

Weddell Island

Goose Green

Weddell Settlement

Fox Bay West

East Falkland

Choiseul Sound

Falkland Sound

Port Stephens

Albermarle

Bay of Harbours

George Island

Sea Lion Island

MAP REF **V,13**

1. The carcass of a ship remains marooned off Carcass Island
2. A southern elephant seal pup basks in the pale sun on Sea Lion Island
3. All fluffed up with no place to go – black-browed albatross chicks watch the world from the safety of their nests
4. Built in 1855, the distinctive lighthouse at Cape Pembroke is a human mark on the wild landscape

1.

2.

3.

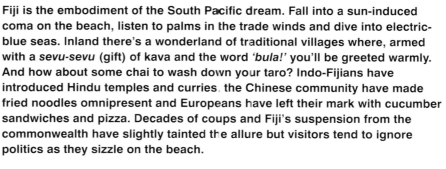

PETER SOLNESS | LONELY PLANET IMAGES

Fiji is the embodiment of the South Pacific dream. Fall into a sun-induced coma on the beach, listen to palms in the trade winds and dive into electric-blue seas. Inland there's a wonderland of traditional villages where, armed with a *sevu-sevu* (gift) of kava and the word *'bula!'* you'll be greeted warmly. And how about some chai to wash down your taro? Indo-Fijians have introduced Hindu temples and curries, the Chinese community have made fried noodles omnipresent and Europeans have left their mark with cucumber sandwiches and pizza. Decades of coups and Fiji's suspension from the commonwealth have slightly tainted the allure but visitors tend to ignore politics as they sizzle on the beach.

BEST TIME TO VISIT
May to October when rainfall and humidity are lower

TOP THINGS TO SEE
○ Navala, Fiji's most picturesque traditional village
○ Indo-Fijians walking across glowing coals at the South Indian fire-walking festival
○ Suva's Municipal Market, a photo-heaven of tropical fruit
○ The immense windswept Sigatoka Sand Dunes on Viti Levu
○ Orchids, walking tracks and lily ponds at the Garden of the Sleeping Giant

TOP THINGS TO DO
○ Dive with 4m-long tiger sharks and barrel-chested bull sharks near Pacific Harbour
○ Island hop through the Mamanuca and Yasawa islands, bask on beaches, snorkel and lap up local culture
○ Swim through the ethereal Sawa-i-Lau caves made famous by Brooke Shields in *The Blue Lagoon*
○ Birdwatch and trek through prehistoric rainforest to lofty Des Voeux Peak
○ Surf the world-class wave, Cloudbreak off Tavarua

GETTING UNDER THE SKIN
Read *Kava in the Blood* by Peter Thompson, an autobiography of a white Fijian imprisoned during the 1987 coup

Listen to the harmonies of choral music at Sunday service – a major part of the Fiji experience

Watch *Pear Ta Ma'on Maf (The Land Has Eyes)*, the tale of a girl's struggle with poverty and the strength she finds in her traditional mythology

Eat a Fijian pit-cooked *lovo* (traditional feast) one day, Indian curries and roti the next and Chinese specialties the next

Drink a bowl of traditional *yaqona* (kava) to numb your mind and your lips

IN A WORD
Bula (Health, happiness, cheers and 'bless you' if you sneeze)

TRADEMARKS
Kava; *The Blue Lagoon*; *Cast Away*; surfing; coral reefs; Melanesian smiles; white-sand beaches

RANDOM FACT
Europeans adopted 'Fiji' which is actually the Tongan name of these islands. The inhabitants formerly called their home Viti

CAPITAL Suva (Viti Levu) | POPULATION 861,000 | AREA 18,300 sq km | OFFICIAL LANGUAGES English & Fijian

DAVID WALL | LONELY PLANET IMAGES

SOUTH PACIFIC OCEAN

Labasa
Vanua Levu
Savusavu
Yasawa Group
Taveuni
Nanuku Passage
Mamanuca Group
Ba
Lautoka
Lomaiviti Group
Nadi
Levuka
Viti Levu
Lau Group
Sigatoka
Suva
KORO SEA
SOUTH PACIFIC OCEAN
Kadavu Group
Moala Group

MAP REF **Q,38**

1. Some mean tackles pack a punch at a rugby match in Albert Park, Suva
2. A historic church stands strong in the Western Division
3. Churchgoers spill over into the balcony at a Catholic cathedral in Suva
4. Iridescent waters lap around the shores of the Mamanuca Islands

4.

2.

3.

1.

FRANS LEMMENS | PHOTOGRAPHER'S CHOICE | GETTY IMAGES

4.

VERONICA GARBUTT | LONELY PLANET IMAGES

Nordic stillness in a lakeside cottage, lingering summer sunshine on convivial beer terraces, avant-garde Helsinki design and cafes warm with cinnamon aromas are just the beginning of Suomi seduction. Finland has long been regarded as the least prominent, and the most quirky and enigmatic, of the Nordic countries. It is, for the most part, a land of tranquillity: a vast expanse of forests and lakes – there's something pure in the Finnish air and spirit that draws you out of doors all year round. Then afterwards it's to the sauna, one of the most essential elements of Finnish culture. Share a sauna with locals and you're on your way to discovering the true meaning of life, Suomi-style.

BEST TIME TO VISIT
May to September to avoid the dark and cold, or December to February for snow, Santa and the northern lights

TOP THINGS TO SEE
- Summer beer terraces sprouting all over Helsinki at the first hint of summer
- The mesmerising aurora borealis (northern lights) flit across the winter sky
- Opera performances at the Savonlinna Castle during the July opera festival
- Christmas commercialism at the Santa Claus Village, north of Rovaniemi

TOP THINGS TO DO
- Join in one of the off-beat festivals like the wife-carrying or air-guitar world championships
- Sweat it out in the world's largest smoke sauna in Kuopio, interspersed with dips in the lake
- Get pulled through the snow by a team of huskies (or reindeer) in Lapland
- Poke around Helsinki's harbourside *kauopatori* (marketplace) in search of local delicacies

GETTING UNDER THE SKIN
Read the Moomin children's books by Tove Jansson – stories of a family of lovable trolls that resemble hippopotamuses

Listen to the classical music of revered composer Jean Sibelius; or for a change of pace, the hard rock of Eurovision-winning Lordi

Watch Aki Kaurismäki's *Man Without a Past* or *Leningrad Cowboys Go America!*; *Sauna*, a horror film set in the 16th century

Eat fish (herring, whitefish); reindeer stew; Lapland cloudberries and lingonberries

Drink coffee (Finns are the world's biggest coffee drinkers), or *salmiakkikossu* – a handmade spirit combining dissolved liquorice sweets with vodka

IN A WORD
Onko sauna lämmin? (Is your sauna warm?)

TRADEMARKS
Architect and designer Alvar Aalto; Formula One racing drivers; Marimekko designs; Moomintrolls; Nokia; reindeers; Sami; Santa Claus village; saunas

RANDOM FACT
Finns are renowned for being quiet – there's an old joke that they invented text messaging so they wouldn't have to speak to each other

NORWAY
- Kaamanen
- Karesuvanto
- Kolari
RUSSIA
- Rovaniemi
SWEDEN
- Kemi
Gulf of Bothnia
- Oulu
- Raahe
- Kajaani
- Kokkola
- Iisalmi
- Vaasa
- Seinäjoki
- Kuopio
- Jyväskylä
- Varkaus
- Pori
- Tampere
- Rauma
- Hämeenlinna
- Imatra
Baltic Sea
- Turku
- Helsinki ✪
- Kotka

MAP REF E,22

1. Traditional wooden dwellings line the banks of the river in medieval Porvoo
2. Marching to their own beat, much like the city itself, musicians move ceremoniously through Helsinki's streets
3. Even the reindeer is dressed up in all its finery
4. Finland is something of a sanctuary for around a thousand rare European brown bears

1.

CAROL ANN WILEY / LONELY PLANET IMAGES

2.

JEAN-PIERRE LESCOURRET / LONELY PLANET IMAGES

3.

A stubborn conviction that they live in the best place on the planet is what makes most French tick – which accounts for an awful lot of those zesty stereotypes showered on this Gallic goliath: arrogant, snooty, officious, opinionated, sexy and super-stylish are accolades and insults bestowed upon this cultured set who have some of the world's greatest philosophers, artists, musicians and literati in their gene set. No surprise then to find France is a timeless land of deep-rooted tradition and modern innovation, a fabled feast of fine food and wine, a place which has unfaltering romance woven into every second footstep, a cinematic trip from opulent Renaissance chateau to Parisian jazz bar to electric-blue seascape.

BEST TIME TO VISIT
April to June, September and October

TOP THINGS TO SEE
° The mindblowing glacial panorama atop Aiguille du Midi (3842m), a cable-car ride from the mountaineering mecca of Chamonix in the French Alps
° How French kings and queens lived at France's grandest chateau in Versailles
° Capital art in Paris: *Mona Lisa* at the Louvre, *The Kiss* at Musée du Rodin and cutting-edge contemporary at the Pompidou
° The garden Monet painted at his home in Giverny
° Europe's highest sand dune (Dune du Pilat) overlooking views of amazing surf

TOP THINGS TO DO
° Taste champagne in ancient cellars in Reims and Épernay
° Walk barefoot across kilometres of wave-rippled sand to Mont St-Michel
° Pedal through vineyards, cherry orchards and lavender fields in rural Provence
° Tuck into French gastronomic *art de vivre* in gourmet Bordeaux
° Motor the mythical corniches (coast roads) on the French Riviera

GETTING UNDER THE SKIN
Read *Sixty Million Frenchmen Can't be Wrong: What Makes the French so French* by Jean-Benoît Nadeau and Julie Barlow for a witty insight into the French

Listen to Serge Gainsbourg's breathless *Je t'aime…moi non plus* and feel your soul turn Francophile

Watch *La Fabuleux Destin d'Amélie Poulain* and feel like a Parisian in Montmartre

Eat Breton crêpes in a traditional long house encircled by a *cromlech* (prehistoric megalith) in Brittany

Drink cider in Normandy, pastis in Provence and well-aged red in Burgundy

IN A WORD
Salut! (Hi!)

TRADEMARKS
Baguettes; cheese; cafe society; red wine; designer fashion; cabaret; Tour de France

RANDOM FACT
Among other things, the French invented the first digital calculator, the hot-air balloon, Braille and margarine

MAP REF **H,20**

1. The sight of the Mont Blanc massif towering above pristine Lac Blanc is awe-inspiring
2. François I used Château de Chambord in the Loire Valley as his rather beautiful, rather big hunting lodge
3. Even rush hour looks special under the shimmering Christmas lights of the Champs-Élysées
4. Buskers contribute to the colour and life of the Latin Quarter in Paris

2.

3.

1.

Technically not a country at all (but rather an Overseas Department of France), French Guiana, with its impenetrable rainforests, Caribbean rhythms and unique pre- and post-colonial history, could never be confused with Old Europe. South America's smallest and least populous 'nation' is a surprising melange of Europeans, Creole-speaking Haitians, Buddhist Hmong refugees from Laos, Maroons (descendants from escaped African slaves) and Amerindian tribes. Funds pouring in from France keep Europe's premier space centre in operation, while also providing one of South America's highest standards of living. With over 90% of its rainforests intact and incredible biodiversity, French Guiana has emerged in recent years as one of the continent's most highly touted ecotourism destinations.

BEST TIME TO VISIT
July to December, or during carnaval (February or March)

TOP THINGS TO SEE
- Îles du Salut, peaceful tropical islands with the ruins of South America's most notorious penal colony
- The Centre Spatial Guyanais (Guianese Space Center), one of the world's busiest satellite launchers (about nine per year)
- The village of Cacao, with its sparkling rivers, Hmong residents and colourful market days is a surreal piece of Laos in South America
- Jaw-dropping numbers of giant leatherback turtles swimming ashore to lay their eggs (April to July) at Awala-Yalimopo

TOP THINGS TO DO
- Journey into the rainforest on a two-day trek along the Sentier Molokoi de Cacao
- Stroll the colourful streets of Cayenne, taking in the vibrant markets, ethnic diversity, colonial architecture and tasty Creole fare
- Photograph nature's finery in the virgin rainforest of the Trésor Nature Reserve
- Travel by boat up the Maroni River en route to Amerindian settlements

GETTING UNDER THE SKIN
Read *Papillon,* by Henri Charriere, the remarkable first-person account of the infamous penal colony on Devil's Island

Listen to the Caribbean-style dance grooves of *bigi pokoe*, a rhythmic style common in western French Guiana

Watch the legendary film *Papillon* starring Steve McQueen and Dustin Hoffman

Eat the so-called *jamais goute* (never eaten), a delicious fish native to the country

Drink *ti' punch*, a rum-based drink with lime and sugar that's served as an aperitif

IN A WORD
Bonjour (Good day)

TRADEMARKS
Penal settlements (particularly Devil's Island); French colonial architecture; European space rockets; Francophiles; sea turtles

RANDOM FACT
Plage les Hattes contains the highest density of leatherback-turtle nesting sites found anywhere in the world

MAP REF **N,14**

1. These children, from the village of Antecum Pata, are descendants of Wayana Indians
2. The village of Cacao, populated mostly by Hmong farmers, is a little slice of Laos in French Guiana
3. Preparations for Carnaval inspire a riot of colourful costumes, at once beautiful and eerie
4. In Roura, a pretty church catches the light under a brooding sky

1.

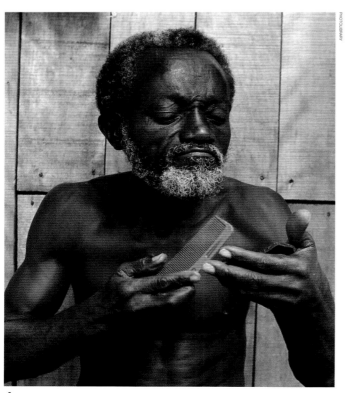

2.

3.

Gabon is Africa's last Eden. And for the traveller, it may just be ecotourism heaven. Prior to 1999, the profound splendour of its natural environment wasn't known to the outside world – it wasn't even known to the man who'd been ruling Gabon for over three decades! However, after President Bongo observed the results of the historic Megatransect project, which revealed Gabon's many fragile treasures, he promptly created 13 national parks. That bold move ensured gorillas, chimpanzees, elephants, mandrils and more continue to populate the jungle floors. Tourism is still finding its feet, but the lush rewards of this ecoindustry are unprecedented. It's hoped Bongo's son, elected president after his father's death, will also embrace the environment.

BEST TIME TO VISIT
May to August (the dry season)

TOP THINGS TO SEE
- Hippos surfing in the Atlantic swells breaking onto Parc National du Petit Loango's shores
- Cirque de Léconi, the Bateke Plateau's spectacular red-rock abyss
- Turtles nesting on the beaches of Parc National de Mayumba while humpback whales breach in the distance
- Fire dancers lighting up the night in a traditional Bwiti initiation ceremony
- Yourself shaking your bootie on a dance floor in Libreville's Quartier Louis

TOP THINGS TO DO
- Drop your jaw while gazing down over gorillas and forest elephants from Langoué Bai's observation platform in Parc National de l'Ivindo
- Learn how to track chimpanzees in the jungle of Parc National de la Lopé
- Stroll along Mayumba's gloriously deserted beach
- Roll through dense jungles and dramatic landscapes on the Transgabonais railway
- Meander along the scenic Rive Droite (right bank) in Lambaréné to Albert Schweitzer's landmark hospital

GETTING UNDER THE SKIN
Read Michael Fay's Megatransect expedition reports from his 3000km, 15-month walk across Gabon and other parts of Central Africa

Listen to *Best of Oliver N'Goma*, the greatest hits of Gabon's most popular singer

Watch *The Great White Man of Lambaréné*, a docudrama revealing the disturbing cultural chasm between Albert Schweitzer and the Gabonese he was there to help

Eat smoked fish with rice and *nyembwe* (a sauce of pulped palm nuts)

Drink a Régab – beer from the Sobraga brewery in Libreville

IN A WORD
Mbôlo (Hello, in Fang)

TRADEMARKS
El Hadj Omar Bongo Ondimba; surfing hippos and beach-bathing elephants; national parks; ecotourism; oil

RANDOM FACT
High on nature – Gabon's forest elephants are particularly fond of iboga, a shrub known for its strong hallucinogenic properties

CAMEROON
EQUATORIAL GUINEA
Bitam
Oyem
Bélinga
Cocobeach
Makokou
Libreville
Bocué
Equator
Ndjolé
Port-Gentil
Lambaréné
Lastoursville
Iguéla
Franceville
Mouila
CONGO
ATLANTIC OCEAN
Tchibanga

MAP REF O,21

1. The business of feeding and caring for others is a constant occupation for many women in Gabon
2. It takes effort to look this good: a Libreville man gets ready to face the day
3. Gabon's plains and jungles are rich in wildlife, such as these forest buffalo
4. A Baka child journeys along the river the way his forebears have for thousands of years

147

1.

2.

3.

CHRIS MELLOR | LONELY PLANET IMAGES

4.

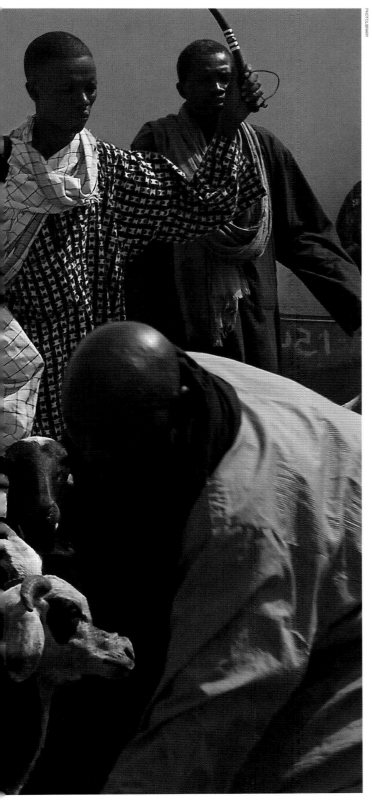
PHOTOLIBRARY

Size does matter in Gambia. This tiny sliver of land – Gambia is the smallest country in mainland Africa – packs a lot into a small space. Its beaches and the adjacent resorts long ago became famous among sun-starved Europeans. Among birdwatchers, Gambia is revered as one of Africa's best and most accessible birding destinations – it lies on the main migratory path between Europe and Africa and more than 560 bird species have been sighted here. Beyond these two big-ticket reasons to visit, however, you'll find a host of smaller-scale attractions, including thriving traditional music and ecotourism scenes, landmarks to the slaving past and the chance to take a slow wooden pirogue up the river that gives Gambia its name.

BEST TIME TO VISIT
November to April (dry season)

TOP THINGS TO SEE
º The Atlantic Coast Resorts, where lovely beaches are lined with party resorts and fishing villages
º Kartong, the pretty town that has become the centre of Gambia's ecotourism projects
º James Island, the focal point for treading gently through Africa's slaving past
º Georgetown (Janjangbureh), the historic inland Gambian town with islands and a bird-call soundtrack
º Banjul, one of the quietest capital cities in Africa with a fine market

TOP THINGS TO DO
º Learn to play the traditional *kora* (21-stringed harp-like musical instrument) from a famous griot family in Brikama
º Take a pirogue ride through the mangroves or walk through the sacred jungle of Makasutu Culture Forest
º Go birdwatching and spot Nile crocodiles and monkeys in Abuko Nature Reserve
º Track down chimpanzees reintroduced into the wild in the Gambia River National Park
º Learn African dance, drumming, batik or yoga in Serekunda

GETTING UNDER THE SKIN
Read *Chaff on the Wind* by Gambian author Ebou Dibba, which follows two rural boys seeking a new life in the city

Listen to Jali Nyama Suso, Tata Dindin, Pa Jobarteh and Jaliba Kuyateh *kora* masters from the birthplace of the instrument

Watch *Roots* by Alex Haley, who traced his origins to Jufureh, a village on the lower Gambia River

Eat *domodah* (peanut stew) or *benechin* (rice baked in a sauce of fish and vegetables)

Drink *bissap* (hibiscus juice), *bouyi* (baobab juice) or JulBrew, the refreshing local beer

IN A WORD
I be ñaading (Hello)

TRADEMARKS
Birdwatching and beaches; a tiny Anglophone island in an ocean of French

RANDOM FACT
Gambia may be famous for its beaches, but it has the second-shortest coastline in Africa (80km), after Democratic Republic of Congo (37km)

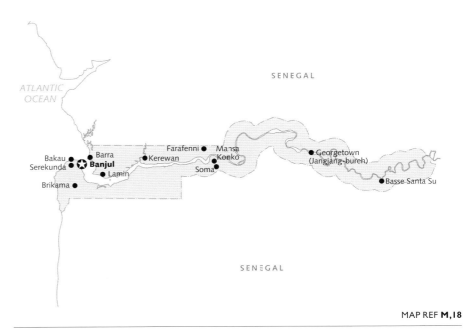

SENEGAL

ATLANTIC OCEAN

Bakau
Serekunda
Barra
Banjul
Lamin
Brikama
Kerewan
Farafenni
Soma
Mansa Konko
Georgetown (Jangjang-bureh)
Basse Santa Su

SENEGAL

MAP REF **M,18**

1. Goats are an important part of the agricultural economy in Gambia
2. These Gambian schoolgirls are dressed for success
3. A Wassu stone circle, a burial site dating from as early as AD500, makes an atmospheric arena
4. Calabash fruit are crafted into musical instruments similar to harps, lyres, flutes and percussive instruments

1.

Georgians are prone to extravagant claims: that they are the original Europeans; that they invented wine; that theirs is the most beautiful country in the world. Extravagant, perhaps, but they could all well be true. But why be weighed down by facts in a country of such natural splendour, such lively cultures, where the welcome is spontaneous and always genuine. In Georgia dramatic mountains rise, wolves, bears and hyenas lurk, rivers race through steep gorges, mountain folk bedeck stone shrines with sacrificed goats' heads, and everybody crosses themselves three times when they pass a church. From cultured Tbilisi, to the arid lowlands and subtropical Adjara, Georgians live life to the fullest, believing t is far better to do things with 'heart', and extravagance be damned…

BEST TIME TO VISIT
April to October

TOP THINGS TO SEE
- The hilltop silhouette of Tsminda Sameba Church in front of Mt Kazbek
- Tbilisi, a city of ramshackle elegance, balcoried mansions, markets, a gallery-filled old town and thumping nightlife
- The wild, beautiful border provinces of Svaneti, Tusheti and Khevsureti, so remote that pagan traditions persist
- The imposing churches of Mtskheta, Georgia's spiritual heart since Christianity was introduced in AD 327
- The wine region of Kakheti, including Italianate hilltop Sighnaghi

TOP THINGS TO DO
- Raise your glass with the locals for an alcohol-laden dinner and singalong
- Head for the hills and take advantage of almost limitless opportunities for trekking
- Ponder the ascetic life in the secluded cave monasteries of Davit Gareja and Vardzia
- Sweat it up amid belle époque architecture and subtropical greenery in Batumi, Georgia's 'summer capital' on the steamy Black Sea coast

GETTING UNDER THE SKIN
Read *Bread & Ashes*, Tony Anderson's wonderful account of walks in the Caucasus; and *Georgia: in the Mountains of Poetry* by Peter Nasmyth

Listen to table songs, sung during wine-drinking sessions, including toasts to life, love and fatherland

Watch Julie Bertucelli's *Since Otar Left*, a clever tale about life in modern Georgia

Eat *khachapuri* (cheese pie), a national institution; delicious meats and stews always cleverly spiced and flavoured with walnut paste

Drink sublime Saperavi and Tsinandali wines, or, if you dare, *chacha*, the local firewater

IN A WORD
Gaumarjos (Cheers)

TRADEMARKS
Snow-topped mountains; Joseph Stalin; lofty churches; fabulous trekking

RANDOM FACT
Georgia is thought to be named after St George, however the Georgians themselves call their country Sakartvelo, translated as 'land of the descendants of Kartlos'

MAP REF I,24

1. The dramatic setting of Tsminda Sameba Church in Kazbegi inspires a reverence all of its own

2.

3.

1.

German wine is surprisingly good. For a country justifiably known around the world for its beers, the products of its beautifully terraced vineyards are a treat – albeit an often sweet one. And that's a perfect metaphor for the rest of this proud nation that is the heart of Europe in more ways than one. Two decades after the prosperous west and downtrodden east were reunified, the marriage is finally bedding down. Opinions about this densely populated country are only equalled by the number of surprises. The land of sausages excels at organic foods, people renowned for their order have the wildest clubs, and life today really does overshadow the event-strewn past. And yes, the wine is often better than the beer.

BEST TIME TO VISIT
June to August (summer) for beer gardens at their best; March to May (spring) and September to November (autumn) for fewer crowds and mostly mild weather

TOP THINGS TO SEE
- Berlin, which continues to reinvent itself ever as the past still haunts
- The soaring – and ever-surviving – spires of Cologne's centuries old cathedral
- The inhuman horrors of Holocaust sites, such as Dachau and Buchenwald
- Dresden's atmospheric old backstreets where modernity is missing but hedonism lurks
- Munich with its Alpine accents, gregarious locals and fully realised good life

TOP THINGS TO DO
- Get lost in perfect little small towns, such as Bamberg or Weimar
- Join the tourist mobs sailing along the impossibly clichéd sites of the Rhine River
- Drink your way to nirvana finding your favourite Bavarian beer hall or garden
- Hike the meadows and forests of the Alps
- Explore the tiny hamlets nestled amid the Harz Mountains

GETTING UNDER THE SKIN
Read Goethe's *Faust*, which tells of the classic deal with the devil

Listen to classics by Bach or Beethoven, then jump forward a few centuries to Berlin-style punk symbol Nina Hagen, Kraftwerk's '80s techno and hugely popular Wir sind Helden

Watch *The Lives of Others*, an award-winning examination of the compromises demanded by life in the old Communist east

Eat any of hundreds of types of sausage

Drink any of hundreds of types of beer, as varied as the variety of sausages

IN A WORD
Wie gehts? (How's it going?)

TRADEMARKS
Cuckoo clocks; dark memories of WWII; no speed limits; Oktoberfest; the Berlin Wall; timely fast trains; BMW, Volkswagen, Mercedes, Audi and Porsche

RANDOM FACT
More than 5000 varieties of beer are sold in Germany, most made by small, local brewers and most being quite similar lagers known for their natural ingredients and crisp taste

MAP REF **G,21**

1. Beer tastes better when imbibed alongside revellers in the atmospheric Oktoberfest 'tents' in Munich
2. The glistening glass dome of Berlin's Reichstag was built to symbolise Germany's reunification
3. A farmer moves his heavy burden of hay across snow-swept fields
4. A thousand years of history live on in Nördlingen, still surrounded by its intact, 14th-century city wall

2.

3.

1.

Ghana has always been West Africa's golden child. It was from here that the pre-colonial Asante Empire ruled the region and gave birth to gold-laden legends of fabulous wealth; Asante artefacts remain as prized by collectors of African art as Asante history is beloved by historians. Centuries later, it shrugged off the shackles of colonialism long before other West African countries dared and has since become a poster child for stability and democracy. But this is only half the story. Ghana has the signature African attractions of beautiful beaches, poignant slaving castles and large herds of elephants in its fine national parks. Perhaps best of all, travelling in Ghana couldn't be easier because you can do it all in English.

BEST TIME TO VISIT
November to March, when the weather is cooler and drier

TOP THINGS TO SEE
- Cape Coast and Elmina, two of many former colonial (and slaving) forts overlooking the Atlantic
- Kumasi's Kejetia Market (West Africa's largest) and monuments of the ancient Asante capital
- Accra's busy markets, restaurants and a sprinkling of historic buildings
- The mud-brick mosques of Wa and a nearby hippo sanctuary in the far northwest
- Akosombo's fine hilltop views over Lake Volta, the world's largest artificial lake

TOP THINGS TO DO
- Set off on Africa's cheapest safaris in search of elephants in Mole National Park
- Learn how to play the balafon (West African xylophone) by the beach at Kokrobite
- Go surfing at Busua or laze on the beach at nearby Akwidaa, Ghana's most beautiful beach
- Walk high through the rainforest canopy in Kakum National Park
- Trek along the Gambarga Escarpment and into villages time forgot

GETTING UNDER THE SKIN
Read *The Beautiful Ones Are Not Yet Born* by Ghanaian novelist Ayi Kwei Armah, or *African Market Women: Seven Life Stories from Ghana* by Gracia Clark

Listen to guitar-heavy highlife music, or the edgier sounds of its heir, hip-life

Watch *Heritage Africa* by Ghanaian director Kwaw P Ansah, an exploration of colonialism in Ghana

Eat *fufu* (pounded cassava, plantain or yam) with a fiery sauce; groundnut stew; jollof rice; *omo tuo* (rice balls served in fish or meat soup)

Drink *pito* (millet beer) in the north, palm wine in the north

IN A WORD
Hani wodzo (Let's dance)

TRADEMARKS
Highlife and hip-life, the soundtrack of a nation; formidable coastal forts with a slaving past; beautiful beaches; a rich Asante (Ashanti) past

RANDOM FACT
Ghana produces one-fifth of the world's cocoa beans, making it the world's second-largest producer

MAP REF **N,19**

1. Fishing boats hold clouds of green nets that will bring in the day's catch for the town of Elmina
2. The jars this woman is painstakingly moulding will become essential vessels for fellow Ghanaians
3. How thoughtful: the Palace of Paga Pio has ready-made seats, perfect for a rest in the sun
4. A woman sails across Lake Volta, the world's largest artificial lake

1.

2.

3.

Ulysses lingered 10 years before coming home; Byron fell in love with the land and people; Lawrence Durrell wrote lyrically of island life: Greece seems to inspire all who come here. While it is commonly associated with blue seascapes and white-washed villages, Greece, with a rugged Balkan hinterland, architecture from classical to modern periods and islands dotted across three seas, exhibits stunning diversity. There are olive groves in flower, Chios' mastic villages, sprawling Athens, crimson poppies every April, hirsute priests, old men sitting for hours over a single coffee and ferries nudging into rickety piers. Many visitors come seeking sun and sea, but are smitten by the hospitality of the Greeks and find they are as captivated as all who went before.

BEST TIME TO VISIT
Easter until June

TOP THINGS TO SEE
- The imposing white columns of the Parthenon, on a hill lording it over Athens
- Spectacular sunsets from Oia village at the northern tip of Santorini
- The monasteries of Meteora astride rocky pillars on the plain of Thessaly
- Greek Easter in Corfu: priests in glorious vestments, candlelit midnight church services, sweet breads, coloured eggs
- The Knights Quarter and Turkish relics of Rhodes' walled old town

TOP THINGS TO DO
- Hop a ferry in Piraeus and cruise between countless Greek islands, each with their own distinctive character and attractions
- Settle in at a harbourside restaurant or village taverna and dine on what is surely the world's most underrated cuisine
- Keep an eye out for centaurs, satyrs or stray Greek gods as you trek up Mt Olympus
- Wander the mountain hamlets of the Zagorohoria, and trek the Vikos Gorge

GETTING UNDER THE SKIN
Read *The Hill of Kronos* by Peter Levi, a record of a lifetime exploring Greece; and *The Little Infamies* by Panos Karnezis, tales from the backwoods

Listen to melancholy and passionate *rebetiko*, sometimes called the Greek blues

Watch the films of Theodoros Angelopoulos, including *Ulysses' Gaze* and *Eternity and a Day*

Eat *saganaki* (fried cheese); *gemistes* (stuffed peppers); *spanokopita* (spinach pastry); *soutzoukakia* (meatballs); grilled octopus; roast lamb and more

Drink *ouzo* (grape brandy with anise); *retsina* (wine with resin); Greek coffee

IN A WORD
Yamas (Cheers)

TRADEMARKS
The Acropolis; Kalamata olives; old women in black; Zorba the Greek; white-washed villages; Homer; myths and fables of classical antiquity

RANDOM FACT
Around 500 BC Thepsis is said to have improvised during a religious choral performance, thus becoming the first 'thespian', ie theatre performer

MAP REF I,22

1. Dramatic views from the Holy Monastery of Rousanou, Meteora, encourage contemplation
2. The dome and bell tower of the Orthodox Church at Fira dazzle in shades of sapphire and white
3. The caryatids of the Erechtheion bear their load serenely, focussing their eternal gaze out over Athens
4. Suitably serious soldiers perform the changing of the guards ceremony at Greece's Parliament, Syntagma Square

4.

2.

3.

1.

It's said that once a traveller has seen the rest of the world, there's always Greenland. But with climate change undoubtedly stirring things up in this part of the world, we don't think you should wait that long. Nature, at its most raw and powerful, calls the shots here: the world's biggest noncontinental island is actually more than 80% icecap, leading to the world's sparsest population. Adventurers have the unique freedom to wander at will, on foot, by ski or by dogsled. With virtually no roads, transport is thanks to helicopter and boat rides (expensive, yes, but worth every penny). These whisk you over awe-inspiring mountainscapes and glaciers, or through some of the planet's most spectacular, iceberg-littered fjords.

BEST TIME TO VISIT
April for dogsledding and skiing tours, or July to mid-September during the thaw

TOP THINGS TO SEE
- Fly or sail into the gloriously scenic island of Uummannaq
- The awesome force of Ilulissat, one of the most active glaciers on the planet
- Norse ruins around Qassiarsuk, and a reconstructed longhouse built and furnished to a 10th-century Viking design
- The picture-perfect old town of Nanortalik, like a film-set New England fishing village given a pantomime mountain backdrop

TOP THINGS TO DO
- Dogsled under the midnight sun on the fabulously named Disko Island
- Kayak the ice-choked fjords around Tasiilaq village, surrounded by an outdoor adventurer's dream landscape
- Sail through south Greenland's magnificent fjordland scenery from Aappilattoq
- Savour gourmet Arctic gastronomy at Restaurant Nipisa in Nuuk

GETTING UNDER THE SKIN
Read *Last Places – A Journey in the North* by Lawrence Millman; *This Cold Heaven: Seven Seasons in Greenland* by Gretel Ehrlich

Listen to the beloved 'old man' of Greenlandic pop, Rasmus Lyberth; rock band Chilly Friday; hip hop from Nuuk Posse

Watch the Oscar-nominated 1950s classic *Qivitoq*, set in Greenland

Eat whale meat – traditional fare, and regulated by strict quota; seal meat; caribou; fish; summer blueberries and crowberries

Drink the symbolic cocktail *Kalaallit Kaffiat* (Greenland Coffee), made from Kahlua, whisky and fresh coffee. Whipped cream is added, as metaphorical ice, then flaming Grand Marnier, representing the northern lights

IN A WORD
Haluu (Hello)

TRADEMARKS
Dog sleds; glaciers; icebergs; Inuit people; kayaks (the word comes from the Inuit *qajaq*); seal hunting; seasonally affected depression (SAD syndrome); whale steak

RANDOM FACT
Numbers in Greenlandic only go up to 12 – after 12 there is only *amerlasoorpassuit* (many). From 12 onwards you have to use Danish numbers

MAP REF **C,15**

1. Sled dogs huddle together for warmth by icy Disko Bay
2. Greenland's population, tiny for the size of the land, is predominantly Inuit
3. The majestic Nordenskjold Glacier slides ever so slowly through Northeast Greenland National Park, the largest national park in the world
4. An Atlantic walrus surveys his surrounds, solemn and dignified

1.

2.

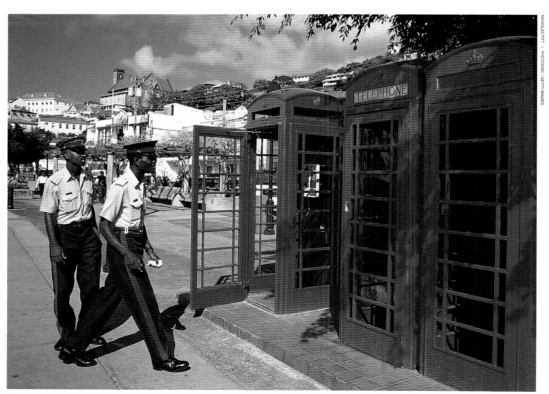

3.

In an ocean of beautiful islands ringed by dazzling white-sand beaches, Grenada is an underrated star. Its beaches are indeed white but the sand is so pure it seems to have an inner radiance; and diving in the requisite turquoise waters is appropriately sublime, although here you'll likely have only your partner and some sea turtles for company. The towns are like visions from Gauguin, with their bright tropical colours accenting lush, green hillsides. Besides the country's main namesake island, there are two tiny charmers: Carriacou and Petit Martinique, which are idyllic, isolated and intoxicating. And forget anything you heard about invasions or hurricanes, it's all ancient history.

BEST TIME TO VISIT
The weather is warm throughout the year January to April are the driest months

TOP THINGS TO SEE
- St George's: a vision of hillside colonial heritage and rainbow of Caribbean colours
- Carriacou: the coconut-sized sibling of the big island with all the charms distilled down to a rich essence
- Petit Martinique: the smallest of the Grenada troika and the ultimate hideaway
- La Sagesse Nature Centre, which preserves and explains the local fauna, all on the estate of a relative of British royalty
- Grenville is Grenada's untouristed town away from the glitz but with a community of nutmeg growers and a rum distillery

TOP THINGS TO DO
- Pound the crystalline sands at Grand Anse beach, Grenada's trademark beauty
- Dive into the underwater art gallery at Molinere Bay, where coral and statues combine to create masterpieces
- Join the sea turtles at Anse La Roche, a hidden beach on isolated Carriacou
- Hike amid mahogany trees and dew-dropping ferns in the Grand Etang rainforest
- Build the best sandcastle ever on unvisited Bathways Beach

GETTING UNDER THE SKIN
Read native Grenadian Jean Buffong's *Under the Silk Cotton Tree*

Listen to reggae master David Emmanuel and Mighty Sparrow, a world-famous calypsonian

Watch the documentary *Grenada: The Future Coming Towards Us*

Eat the national dish 'oil down', which combines vegetables and meat in a coconut-flavoured stew

Drink the nonalcoholic fruit juice *mauby* (a bittersweet drink made from the bark of the rhamnaceous tree)

IN A WORD
Sa ki fé'w? (What's happening?)

TRADEMARKS
'The Spice Islands'; Grand Anse beach; the *Bianca C* shipwreck

RANDOM FACT
Grenada produces one third of the world's nutmeg, the kernel is the odd-looking yellow blob on the left side of the Grenada flag

MAP REF **M,13**

1. A ball of sand sparks an impromptu game on Grand Anse beach
2. A Grenadian woman proudly displays her wares at a Saturday market
3. Local colour: police officers' smart uniforms coordinate with their surroundings
4. This boat's home at Sandy Island, Carriacou, appears almost too idyllic to be real

2.

3.

1.

Think of Guadeloupe as a butterfly: the two main islands, Grand-Terre and Basse-Terre, look like wings and are joined by a swamp. Here lingua Franca rules and there's a strong French accent to all aspects of life, from the simple island bakeries turning out baguettes to preference for Gitanes and Pernod at the dozens of tiny beachside cafes. South of the main island pair is a cluster of archipelagos called Îles des Saintes with seven small inhabited islands and a spray of tiny, people-free ones. Linked by useful ferries, these islands are a step back to a condo-free time. Terre-de-Haut never had slavery and locals here are descended from Norman and Breton colonists. It's a vision of old France, albeit one scented by hibiscus.

BEST TIME TO VISIT
December to May are the driest and busiest months

TOP THINGS TO SEE
- Remote beaches that reward after pushing through the cane fields of northern Grand-Terre
- Deshaies, a luxe port stop for yachties sailing the globe
- The tiny island of Terre-de-Haut and its 19th-century Fort Napoleon
- La Désirade and Marie-Galante, two natural island gems
- Terre-de-Bas, the Caribbean at its untouristed best – a tiny island of coffee plantations and traditional villages

TOP THINGS TO DO
- Try to avoid exhaustion at Grand-Terre, which has surfing, diving and general frolicking
- Tackle the summit of La Soufrière, a 1467m-high active volcano
- Stroke Jacques Cousteau underwater at the aquatic preserve that bears his name (and memorial statue)
- Hike the orchid- and ginger-lined trails of Parc National de la Guadaloupe in the green hills of Basse-Terre
- Doing nothing at all on La Désirade, the archipelago's least-visited island (but still one with silky sands and alluring waters)

GETTING UNDER THE SKIN
Read *Anabase* by local poet Alexis Léger (translated by TS Eliot)

Listen to local *zouk* group Malavoi; or Gwo-ka drum master Guy Konket

Watch *Sucre Amer* directed by Christian Lara; *Speed 2: Cruise Control*, the film where the series ran aground

Eat *crabes farci* (spicy stuffed land crabs) or *colombo cabri* (curried goat)

Drink *ti-punch* (white rum, cane sugar and fresh lime, mixed to your own proportions)

IN A WORD
Bonjour (Hello, used at every interaction)

TRADEMARKS
Underwater preserves; butterfly-shaped island; fishing villages; Creole food

RANDOM FACT
Guadeloupe is an overseas department of France, which means it has representation in the French parliament and is technically part of the EU

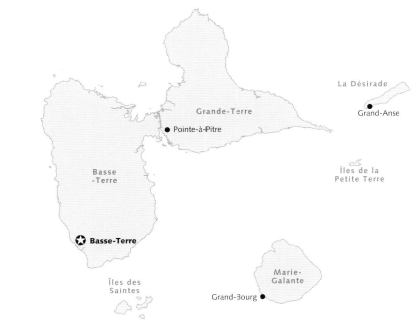

MAP REF **L,13**

1. Spectators cheer on their favourite teams in a bull-and-cart race in St-François
2. Rainbow scarfs, bright jewellery and crisp white cotton are the local style
3. Carnival time in Pointe-à-Pitre provides a good excuse to don magical costumes and make merry
4. An old windmill rises from a sea of harvested sugarcane

1.

GUAM & NORTHERN MARIANAS

CAPITAL Agana (Hagatna, G); Saipan (Garapan, NM) | **POPULATION** 178,000 (G), 80,362 (NM) | **AREA** 549 sq km (G), 477 sq km (NM) | **OFFICIAL LANGUAGES** English & Chamorro

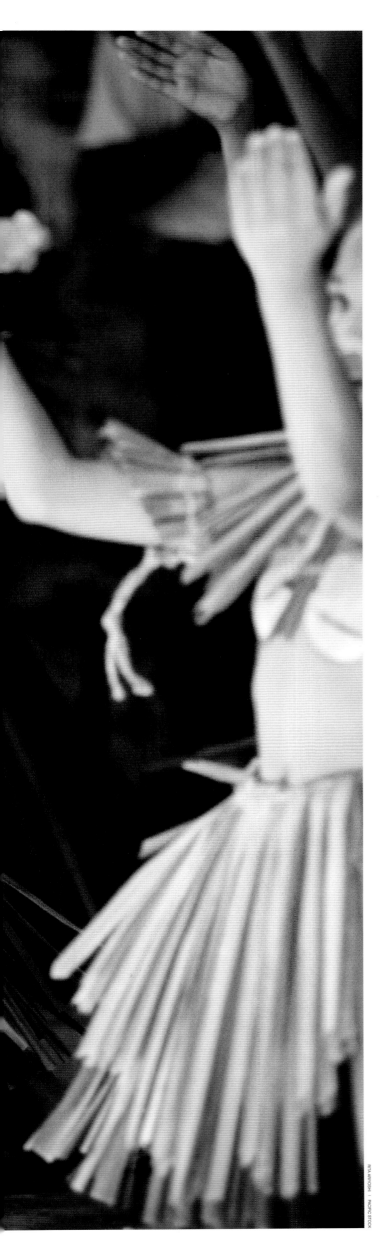

Floating in American accents, Japanese tourists and convenience stores, Guam and the Northern Marianas capital of Saipan, are package-tour favourites. Get beyond the two main islands and you'll find a less-cluttered version of paradise where turquoise waters and white beaches are livened up by an upsurging Chamorro culture. When caught at the right angle, all the islands offer poignant experiences: flame trees in bloom, melancholy historical sights, outrageous diving and tiered waterfalls. Watch out for typhoons (this area is called 'Typhoon Alley'), put on your WWII history caps and plunge into deep thought about the Mariana Trench; then head to the two capitals for poker and duty-free shopping.

BEST TIME TO VISIT
December to March (the dry season), October and November are the most probable months for typhoons

TOP THINGS TO SEE
- Towering latte stones thought to be ancient house pillars on Guam
- Boiling pools of sulphur, Micronesian megapodes (birds that use volcanic heat to incubate their eggs) and rare beaked whales at the Mariana Trench Marine National Monument
- Talofofo Falls from the wooden swinging bridge
- The jagged Banzai Cliff where hundreds of Japanese jumped to their deaths during the 1944 American invasion

TOP THINGS TO DO
- Feast and party local-style at Chamorro Village Night Market
- Escape to the pristine beaches and azure waters of Ritidian Point
- Dive at Southern Guam or the underwater passageways of the Grotto in Saipan
- Relax and loaf on idyllic Tinian
- Commune with the beaked ones at the teeming bird sanctuary on Rota

GETTING UNDER THE SKIN
Read *The Chorito Hog Leg, Book 1: A Novel of Guam in Time of War* by Pat Hickey set in WWII Guam

Listen to funky Chamorro *It's Party Time in the Marianas* by the Castro Boyz

Watch the award-winning 2009 documentary *Under the American Sun* about Filipino-American immigrants on Guam post-WWII

Eat *finadene*, a hot sauce made with red peppers, soy sauce, lemon juice and onions that turns a dish into a real Chamorro meal

Drink *tuba*, made from the fermented sap of a young coconut tree

IN A WORD
Inafa'maolek (Interdependence, a key value in Chamorro culture)

TRADEMARKS
Chamorro culture; Mariana Trench; American military; Japanese tourists; Spanish colonial influences; the garment industry; latte stones; Battle of Guam

RANDOM FACT
The B-29s that dropped atomic bombs on Japan in WWII flew from Tinian in the Northern Mariana Islands

Farallon de Pajaros
Maug Islands
Asuncion
PHILIPPINE SEA
Agrihan
Pagan
NORTHERN MARIANA ISLANDS (USA)
Alamagan
Guguar
Sarigan
Anatahan
Farallon de Medinilla
Saipan
Aguijan — Tinian
NORTH PACIFIC OCEAN
GUAM (USA)
Rota
Agana
Mariana Trench

MAP REF **M,35**

1. Dancers in Inarajan lift their arms skyward, graceful in their swinging grass skirts

2.

3.

1.

DIEGO LEZAMA | LONELY PLANET IMAGES

4.

PAUL KENNEDY | LONELY PLANET IMAGES

Intricate and patient, Guatemala resonates like the fine designs of its Mayan textiles. This is a place of strong impressions. Speaking 20 separate languages, Mayas comprise over 60% of the population, making this Central America's most indigenous nation. Although long on tradition, the modern political face of Guatemala has been one of corruption, violence and injustice. Yet despite generations of hardship, citizens remain mostly open and accessible to visitors. Immersion in this fascinating world starts with a visit to its world-class markets. Landscapes are diverse and evocative, from coffee estates and colonial towns to magnificent Mayan ruins, rumbling volcanoes and empty surf breaks.

BEST TIME TO VISIT
November through to May (the dry season)

TOP THINGS TO SEE
- Lost temples above the jungle canopy at Tikal, the country's foremost Mayan ruin
- The chic city of Antigua, with its Spanish-era convents, ruins and sushi bars
- Sunrise from atop Volcán Tajumulco, the highest point in Central America
- Quema del Diablo, where lapping bonfires and fireworks psychically purge the year's trash
- The rugged route from Huehuetenango to Cobán, which teeters through highland coffee plantations

TOP THINGS TO DO
- Barter for Mayan textiles at the Chichicastenango market
- Boat the lush Río Dulce to the Garífuna settlement of Lívingston
- Finesse your bar talk by studying at a Spanish language school in Antigua
- Soak in the cool emerald pools of Semuc Champey
- Board the breaks at Sipacate, the country's largely undiscovered surf capital

GETTING UNDER THE SKIN
Read *Hombres De Maíz* by Miguel Ángel Asturias, the Nobel Prize–winning author and long-time exile who combines Mayan mysticism and social consciousness to deliver an indictment of dictatorial rule

Listen to *Guatemala: Celebrated Marimbas;* Paco Pérez's 'Luna de Xelaju' is the best-known composition for marimbas

Watch *What Sebastian Dreamt,* part documentary, part narrative, this rare Guatemalan film offers the rainforests as primary suspect in a murder/mystery thriller

Eat a hearty Chapín breakfast of eggs, corn tortillas, beans, fried plantain and coffee

Drink the velvety hot chocolate and Zacapa rum

IN A WORD
De huevos (Cool)

TRADEMARKS
Old Mayan gods and ruins; wild masks and bright textiles; the quetzal; brooding volcanoes; rainforests; corn fields; Mayan trouble dolls; ornate iron crucifixes

RANDOM FACT
For the Maya, the night sky was the theatre of all supernatural doings. The seasonal movement of constellations was a narrative of gods and places

MEXICO

- Naranjo
- Bethel
- Flores

BELIZE

Gulf of Honduras

- Lívingston
- Puerto Barrios

Lago de Izabal

- Huehuetenango
- Cobán

- Quetzaltenango
- Chichicastenango
- Zacapa

HONDURAS

- Panajachel
- Antigua Guatemala
- ✪ Guatemala City
- Esquipulas

- Retalhuleu
- Champerico
- Santa Lucía Cotzumalguapa

PACIFIC OCEAN

EL SALVADOR

MAP REF **M,10**

1. Pale and stately, Iglesia del Hermano Pedro church watches over Sacatepéquez
2. Many hands make light work of shepherding a wooden float through a procession in the village of Santa María de Jesús
3. Access to plentiful, safe drinking water remains an issue in Guatemala
4. The natural bridge and waterfalls of Semuc Champey form pools that make perfect swimming holes

1.

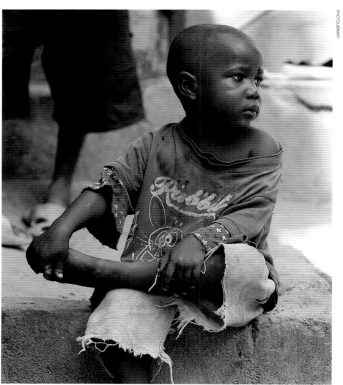

2.

3.

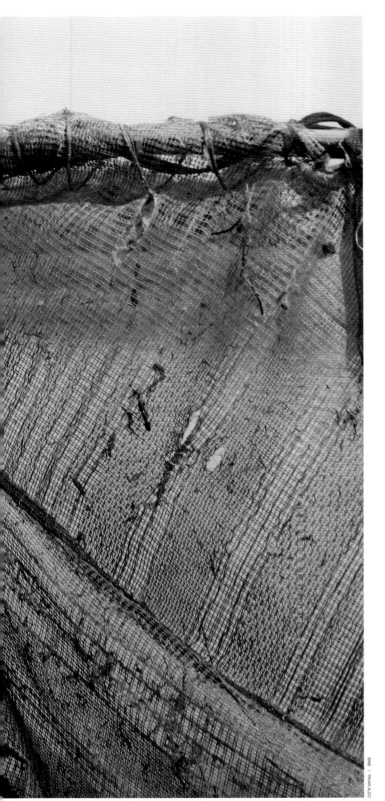

Guinea could be a West African paradise. With a strong self-reliant streak that saw it defy France to claim independence and with almost half of the world's bauxite reserves, post-colonial Guinea had all the ingredients for success. As a traveller destination, its future looked similarly assured with a vibrant capital, world-class musical scene and stunningly beautiful scenery in the interior. Sadly it hasn't quite worked out that way. Decades of dictatorial rule, followed by a seemingly perpetual stand-off between an unruly army and restless population, have left Guinea's long-suffering people still dreaming of a prosperous future that should have begun decades ago. Neglected infrastructure makes travelling here a challenge, but for all the country's travails, it's almost always worth it.

BEST TIME TO VISIT
November to February (the dry season). Otherwise, Guinea is one of the wettest countries in the world

TOP THINGS TO SEE
○ Îles de Los' palm beaches that are a world (or pirogue-ride) away from the capital
○ Conakry, with its clamour and chaos, and a world-class live music scene
○ Bel Air's lovely golden stretch of sand
○ The source of the Niger River – the trickle that becomes one of Africa's greatest rivers
○ The fascinating Sahelian town of Kankan, spiritual home of the Malinké people

TOP THINGS TO DO
○ Hike from Mali-Yemberem up La Dame du Mali with its womanly shape and sweeping views
○ Learn the kora (21-stringed instrument) or acrobatics from the Conakry experts
○ Climb Mt Nimba where Guinea intersects with Côte d'Ivoire and Liberia
○ Chase some of West Africa's last chimps through the forest in remote Bossou
○ Look for forest elephants in the Tabala Conservation Zone

GETTING UNDER THE SKIN
Read Camara Laye's *The African Child* (also called *The Dark Child*), first published in 1954 and one of the most widely printed works by an African

Listen to Sekouba Bambino Diabaté and Ba Cissoko as a primer for seeing them live in the clubs of Conakry, or the big-band sound of Bembeya Jazz National

Watch the ground-breaking *Dakan*, by Mohamed Camara, one of the first African movies to address homosexuality

Eat *kulikuli* (peanut balls cooked with onion and cayenne pepper); grilled fish

Drink cafe noir; or the beers Skol, Guiluxe and Flag

IN A WORD
Bonne soirée (Have a good evening)

TRADEMARKS
Traditional music and dance; Fouta Djalon Highlands; political instability

RANDOM FACT
At least 22 West African rivers begin in the Guinean highlands, including the Niger, Senegal and Gambia Rivers

MAP REF M,18

1. Fishing the river in Douné requires perfect balance
2. A serious moment overtakes this young thinker
3. A smile and a handshake are the universal language of greeting
4. The busy, colourful marketplace is a gathering point in Kankan

2.

3.

1.

One of Africa's most forgotten corners, Guinea-Bissau is also one of its most beautiful and diverse. Wildlife-rich rainforests and decaying colonial-era towns dominate the mainland, and there are 23 different ethnic groups. But it's the offshore Arquipélago dos Bijagós, among the world's prettiest (and least-visited) island chains, that will really take your breath away. The peace and tranquillity of the archipelago's secluded coves stands in stark contrast to the turmoil that has blighted the country for decades. A brutal war of liberation was the precursor to Guinea-Bissau's extremely late independence from Portugal in 1980, and peace and prosperity have proved just as elusive ever since. Not that you'd know it, however, as Guinea-Bissau's people are some of Africa's friendliest.

BEST TIME TO VISIT
Late November to February, when it's dry and relatively cool

TOP THINGS TO SEE
- The capital's decadent old colonial quarter, Bissau Velho
- Ilha de Bolama, an island charmingly frozen in time from its days as the colonial capital
- Ilha de Bubaque, the most accessible of the islands with luxury accommodation
- Kere, the most beautiful island in the Arquipélago dos Bijagós
- Bafatá, a lovely riverside town with the eerie tranquillity of a ghost town

TOP THINGS TO DO
- Take a week-long minicruise around the Arquipélago dos Bijagós
- Search for rare saltwater hippos and crocodiles in Orango Islands National Park
- Commune with endangered sea turtles on the near-perfect beaches of the João Vieira Poilão National Marine Park
- Laze on the gorgeous beaches of mainland Varela
- Discover elephants and Africa's westernmost chimps in the Parque National de Cantanhez

GETTING UNDER THE SKIN
Read Susan Lowerre's *Under the Neem Tree*, which recounts a Peace Corps volunteer's experiences

Listen to the classic band Super Mama Djombo; and modern singers Dulce Maria Neves of Manecas Costa (*Paraiso di Gumbe*)

Watch *The Blue Eyes of Yonta,* by Flora Gomes, about dreams and revolution

Eat *chabeu* (deep-fried fish served in a thick, palm-oil sauce with rice)

Drink *cajeu* (a sickly sweet and dangerously strong cashew liquor)

IN A WORD
Pode mostrar-me (no mapa)? – Can you show me (on the map)?

TRADEMARKS
Arquipélago dos Bijagós; Portuguese colonialism; saltwater hippos; forest elephants

RANDOM FACT
Guinea-Bissau's proportion of land under forest (73.7%) is the second-highest in Africa after Gabon

MAP REF **M,18**

1. In the matriarchal society of the Arquipélago dos Bijagós, men perform ritual dances in an effort to attract wives
2. The Ilha de Bolama's ornate colonial architecture evokes the charm of another era
3. Take some time to chill out by the water in Ilha de Soga
4. Hair-braiding requires dexterity, patience and lots of practice

1.

2.

3.

4.

Like neighbouring Suriname to the east, Guyana has an eclectic cultural heritage, owing to its colonial past. The present population is descended largely from African slaves and indentured immigrants brought from East India, while scattered Amerindian settlements dot the interior. Guyana's rough-and-tumble capital, Georgetown, has a frontier aspect to it, though tensions tend to dissolve when the national cricket team takes the field. Beneath the headlines of corruption, power outages and economic troubles, is a joyful mix of people who are turning Guyana into a top wildlife-watching and adventure destination. The pristine forests and incredible biodiversity within them are increasingly seen as Guyana's greatest assets.

BEST TIME TO VISIT
Mid-October to mid-May

TOP THINGS TO SEE
- Iwokrama, a virgin rainforest with incredible biodiversity
- The Rupununi savannahs, African-like plains sprinkled with indigenous villages, pockets of jungle and exceptional wildlife
- Georgetown, with its ramshackle 19th-century architecture, bird-filled botanical gardens and classic colonial inns
- The Amerindian village of Santa Mission, a favourite destination for Guyanese who want to appreciate Carib and Arawak customs

TOP THINGS TO DO
- Take the five-day trek through rainforest to see the spectacular Kaieteur Falls
- Head off the beaten path on a cattle drive with local *vaqueros* (cowboys) in the remote Kanuku Mountains
- Travel by boat from Charity to Shell Beach, a pristine stretch of coastline, sprinkled with small Amerindian settlements and packed with wildlife
- Climb to the top of Surama mountain, followed by a visit to the indigenous Makushi village of Surama

GETTING UNDER THE SKIN
Read *Peacocks Dancing* by Guyana-born Sharon Maas, an enthralling coming-of-age story set in both Guyana and India

Listen *Is We Ting*, containing works by some of Guyana's best-loved musicians

Watch *Guiana 1838,* Rohit Jagessar's riveting story about the struggles against empire following the abolition of slavery and the ensuing arrival of labourers from East India

Eat pepperpot (a spicy stew cooked with different meats and a fermented juice made from cassava); or East Indian curry

Drink refreshing Banks beer; 15-year-old El Dorado, one of the world's best rums

IN A WORD
Howdy (How are you?)

TRADEMARKS
Sugar cane; the Jim Jones tragedy; legendary cricketer Clive Lloyd

RANDOM FACT
An estimated 500,000 Guyanese live abroad – an astounding figure given the country's small population (772,298)

MAP REF **N,13**

1. The Kaieteur Falls thunder over a precipice, drumming up a wall of mist from the Potaro River below
2. The capable hands of this boat handler frame a friendly face
3. An Anglican cathedral in Georgetown is fringed with delicate balustrading
4. Children relax beside the Kamuni River, part of Guyana's extensive system of walkways.

1.

2.

3.

4.

CAPITAL Port-au-Prince | **POPULATION** 9,035,500 | **AREA** 27,750 sq km | **OFFICIAL LANGUAGES** French & Creole

It's fair to say that the currents of history haven't been generous to Haiti since its slave rebellion proclaimed the world's first black republic over two centuries ago. Lasting political stability has often seemed just out of grasp, an unfair situation for a Haitian population struggling amid urban and environmental chaos and the aftermath of the devastating January 2010 earthquake. Yet Haiti has a proudly singular culture – the closest of all Caribbean countries to its African roots, with a rich artistic tradition and a deep spiritualty drawing on its mixed Vodou and Christian heritage. While infrastructure remains rough, and the path to reconstruction is rocky, Haitians welcome visitors and the opportunity to show them a country removed from the media headlines.

BEST TIME TO VISIT
December to July (to avoid hurricane season)

TOP THINGS TO SEE
- The Citadelle fortress built to defend Haiti against Napoleonic invasion
- The fancy 'gingerbread' houses of Victorian-era Port-au-Prince
- Haiti's Museé National, housing King Christophe's suicide pistol and the anchor salvaged from Columbus' *Santa Maria*
- Congregations of the Vodou faithful at the great celebrations at Saut d'Eau, Souvenance and Soukri
- The scrap metal turned cyberpunk Vodou sculpture of Port-au-Prince's Grand Rue artists' collective

TOP THINGS TO DO
- Catch a brightly painted *tap tap* (local bus) across Port-au-Prince
- Party at Jacmel Carnival, one of the Caribbean's liveliest carnivals
- Pay your respects at a Vodou ceremony, to get a new insight into this unfairly maligned religion
- Hike through the pine forests of Parc National La Visite
- Trek by horse to the cobalt-blue waterfalls and pools of Bassins Bleu

GETTING UNDER THE SKIN
Read travelogue *Bonjour Blanc* by Ian Thomson; and Graham Greene's scathingly satirical novel, *The Comedians*

Listen to the Vodou rock 'n' roots band RAM

Watch Jonathan Demme's *The Agronomist*, about the life of Haitian journalist and activist Jean Dominque

Eat *griyo* and *bannan peze* (fried pork and plantain) with *ti malice* (chilli) sauce

Drink rum (preferably Barbancourt), the only drink that matters

IN A WORD
M pa pli mal (No worse than before) – the standard answer to 'How are you?'

TRADEMARKS
Vodou; Wyclef Jean; rum; Toussaint Louverture and slave history; political instability

RANDOM FACT
Vodou is a blend of West African and Catholic beliefs – the spelling 'voodoo' is avoided due to lurid associations with Western popular culture

MAP REF **L,12**

1. The streets of Port-au-Prince hum with the energy and din of its three million inhabitants
2. The cult band RAM plays its famous Vodou rhythms at Hôtel Oloffson in Port-au-Prince
3. The palace of Sans Souci, built for Henri Christophe, is known as the Versailles of Haiti
4. A well-made hat is essential in the sunny Hiatian climate

1.

2.

3.

Columbus may have discovered it on his final voyage, but Honduras remains a little-explored world where opportunity has not knocked. The 2009 army coup proved that politics are all but settled. Little by little, the countryside is emptied as residents emigrate to the capital or abroad. It's little wonder that few know Honduras' unpolished gems. The Copán ruins are festooned with the finest sculptures of Mesoamerica. The brilliant wonders of the Bay Islands range from tiny seahorses to whale sharks. And bumpy roads whiz from remote cloud forests to colonial towns, wetlands and lagoons. The *catracho* (Honduran) welcome becomes warmer the further afar you probe. After all, discovery is just a state of mind.

BEST TIME TO VISIT
May to June for the festivals

TOP THINGS TO SEE
- The extraordinary and intricate temples of Copán Ruinas
- Rare whale sharks trolling the Caribbean from May to September
- The dozy cloud forest hamlet of Gracias, once a colonial capital of Central America
- Muddy jaguar prints in the wilderness Río Plátano Biosphere Reserve
- Neighbourly goodwill at Guancasco, an annual Lenca ceremony promoting peace and friendship

TOP THINGS TO DO
- Get scuba certified, affordably, in the gemstone waters around Roatán
- Spot some of the 400 bird species that teem Lago de Yojoa
- Find the Virgin de Suyapa in the former men's room of a Teguchigalpa dive
- Set out in the spectacular cloud forest of Parque Nacional Celaque
- Glide down jungle rivers to find guzzling tapirs along the banks

GETTING UNDER THE SKIN
Read *El Gran Hotel* by Guillermo Yuscarán, one of Honduras' most celebrated writers; or *The Soccer War* by Ryszard Kapuscinski, about the 100-hour war between Honduras and El Salvador

Listen to Garífuna band Los Menudos

Watch *Sin Nombre* (Nameless), directed by Cary Fukunaga, about gangs and US migration; and *El Espiritu de mi Mama* (Spirit of my Mother), directed by Ali Allie, about a young Garífuna woman

Eat coconut bread or *casabe* (a crispy flat bread common throughout the Caribbean)

Drink ice-cold Port Royal or Salva Vida beer

IN A WORD
Todo cheque (It's all cool)

TRADEMARKS
The 2009 coup and deposed President Zelaya; the Mosquito Coast; quetzals; howler monkeys; Copán Ruinas; cheap diving

RANDOM FACT
Honduras is experiencing the most rapid urbanisation in Central America, currently 48% of the population lives in cities

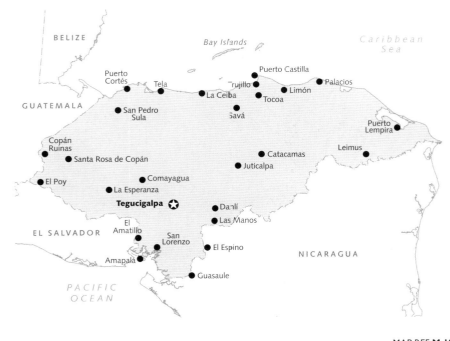

MAP REF **M,10**

1. The stony faces of the Acropolis, Copán Ruinas, have seen more than a thousand years of history
2. Cowboys from Ojojona hold onto their trusty steed
3. *Laveros* (shrimp-larvae harvesters) concentrate on collecting larvae from the swamp, to sell to shrimp farmers
4. The common iguana looks anything but common as he shows off his fierce crest

2.

3.

1.

GREG ELMS | LONELY PLANET IMAGES

4.

GREG ELMS | LONELY PLANET IMAGES

As British as dim sum and joss sticks, the former colony of Hong Kong was always the Asian tiger with the biggest teeth, and little has changed under Chinese rule. Bankers still trade fortunes on the Hong Kong stock exchange, skyscrapers still blast their light across Victoria Harbour and the streets still teem with some of the most entrepreneurial individuals in Asia. Despite the unmistakably Chinese atmosphere, Hong Kong's outlook is distinctly European, a major draw for travellers breaking the trip to Australasia. As ever, the action is centred on Kowloon and Hong Kong Island, with their bustling shopping streets and sky-piercing towers, but peaceful beaches and jungle trails await in the outlying islands of the New Territories.

BEST TIME TO VISIT
October to December (to avoid the rains)

TOP THINGS TO SEE
- Agreeable commercial chaos at Stanley Market
- The curious, labour-saving street escalators of the Mid-Levels
- Sweeping island views from the swaying cable car at Ocean Park
- The house-sized Tian Tan Buddha statue on Lantau Island
- Disco-style light effects at the Symphony of Light show on Hong Kong Island

TOP THINGS TO DO
- Rumble up to Victoria Peak on the Peak Tram
- Tuck into a dim sum feast at a banquet restaurant in Kowloon
- Mingle with the crowds on the crammed Star Ferry across Victoria Harbour
- Escape the bustle on a jungle hike across Lantau Island or Sai Kung Country Park
- Sip a sundowner overlooking the Hong Kong skyline from a rooftop bar in Kowloon

GETTING UNDER THE SKIN
Read James Clavell's unashamedly populist *Tai-Pan*; or *The Piano Teacher* by Janice YK Lee

Listen to the Canto-pop warblings of the Four Heavenly Kings (Jacky Cheung, Andy Lau, Aaron Kwok and Leon Lai)

Watch John Woo's *A Better Tomorrow*; Andrew Lau and Alan Mak's *Infernal Affairs*; or Jackie Chan's *Police Story* – essential Hong Kong viewing

Eat dim sum – weekend mornings are the best time to enjoy this steamed dumpling feast

Drink green tea, bubble tea with tapioca 'pearls' or *yuanyang* (half tea, half coffee)

IN A WORD
Yum cha (Drinking tea – the act of feasting on dim sum)

TRADEMARKS
Skyscrapers; double-decker buses; shopping sprees; that skyline; the Peak Tram; Jackie Chan; Chinese New Year; dim sum banquets

RANDOM FACT
In Hong Kong, wives are legally allowed to kill adulterous husbands, so long as they only use their bare hands

MAP REF **K,32**

1. Glow-in-the-dark Hong Kong lights up the waters of Victoria Harbour
2. All the drama of opera comes alive in the theatrical dress of this seasoned performer
3. A rickshaw puller takes a break from taxiing people around Star Ferry pier
4. Foodies rejoice: spectacular feasts await in the restaurants of Hong Kong

1.

2.

3.

Hungary lies in the Carpathian basin, slap bang in the middle of Europe, and the Hungarians themselves will tell you that theirs is a Central (not Eastern) European nation – even though they trace their ancestry to beyond the Ural Mountains. A flat land dominated by the *puszta* (great plain), Hungary's culture is anything but featureless. With a predilection for zesty paprika-infused cuisine and thermal baths (even during chilly winter days), traditions of horseback cowboy acrobatics and heel-clicking folk songs, back-to-front surname-first monikers and an inscrutable language, the Hungarians remain entirely distinct from any of their neighbours. From Budapest, to the sandy beaches of Lake Balaton, Turkish-influenced Pécs and Kiskunság National Park, Hungary is elegant, romantic and a land of adventure.

BEST TIME TO VISIT
April to June and September to October

TOP THINGS TO SEE
- Fabulous views of Budapest's Parliament building and Danube River frontage from the Fisherman's Bastion on Castle Hill
- The whip-cracking performances of *csikos* (cowboys) astride bareback horses
- Almond trees in blossom and ceramics, embroidery and other folk arts in Tihany
- The galleries, museums, mosques, beautifully preserved synagogue and Ottoman-era baths of Pécs
- Week-long Sziget music festival, Europe's biggest, on a leafy island in the middle of the Danube

TOP THINGS TO DO
- Plunge in for a hot soak and rub down with the locals in the steamy surrounds of Budapest's elegant thermal baths
- Wet your whistle sampling feisty local wines in Eger's Valley of Beautiful Women
- Cruise the Danube on a ferry from Budapest to Szentendre, a former artists' colony
- Dip your toes in the northern shore of Lake Balaton, Hungary's freshwater 'riviera'

GETTING UNDER THE SKIN
Read Nobel Prize–winner Imre Kertesz' semiautobiographical novel *Fateless* about a teenage Jewish boy sent to the Nazi death camps

Listen to the *Hungarian Rhapsodies* of Franz Liszt or the haunting Hungarian folk music of Marta Sebestyen, as heard in the soundtrack to *The English Patient*

Watch *Kontroll,* a comedy-thriller involving ticket inspectors and an elusive killer on the Budapest metro

Eat *paprikas csirke* (paprika chicken); or *gulyás* (goulash), full of beefy goodness

Drink Tokaji Azsú, a sweeter-than-sweet dessert wine; or Egri Bikavér, a full-bodied red knows as bull's blood

IN A WORD
Egesegere (Cheers!)

TRADEMARKS
Paprika; Tokaj Azsú; goulash; Rubik's Cube; thermal baths; home-grown cowboys

RANDOM FACT
The ballpoint pen was invented by Hungarian Laszlo Biro

ROBERTO SONCIN GEROMETTA | LONELY PLANET IMAGES

DAVID RYAN | LONELY PLANET IMAGES

MAP REF **H,22**

1. Horses and their riders in Kalocsa showcase bravura displays of riding prowess
2. The Danube sweeps by Budapest's magnificent Parliament building, near the Széchenyi Chain Bridge
3. Trips to communal baths like the Gellért Baths in Budapest are a feature of daily life for many Hungarians
4. A cadet parades in uniform on St Stephen's Day, commemorating the patron saint of Hungary

4.

2.

3.

1.

Iceland is a country in the making, a vast volcanic laboratory where mighty forces shape the land and shrink you to an awestruck speck. See it in the gushing geysers, glooping mud pools and slow, grinding glaciers. Experience it first hand, bathing in turquoise-coloured hot springs, kayaking through a fjord or crunching across a dazzling-white icecap. The landscape is infectious: hidden energy and a desire to shape the world are Icelandic traits. Compact capital Reykjavík may just contain the world's highest concentration of dreamers, authors, poets and musicians. They all love a party – join them on the *runtur*, a weekend-long pub crawl like no other, to see the unexpected side of local life.

BEST TIME TO VISIT
May to September to avoid the dark and cold, or December to February to see Iceland at its iciest

TOP THINGS TO SEE
- A breaching whale and curious dolphins on a whale-watching cruise from Húsavik
- The smouldering volcanic wastelands of Krafla
- The peaks and glaciers (and waterfalls and twisted birch woods) of Skaftafell
- Thousands of puffin chicks taking flight every August from Vestmannaeyjar

TOP THINGS TO DO
- Cavort with crowds of partygoers on the drunken Reykjavík *runtur*
- Breathe cool, pure air while luxuriating in hot water at the Blue Lagoon
- Explore the fjords on a kayaking trip under the midnight sun
- Wait for water to shoot up at Geysir, the original hot-water spout after which all other geysers are named

GETTING UNDER THE SKIN
Read *Independent People* and other novels by Nobel Prize–winner Halldór Laxness; crime fiction from Arnaldur Indriðason; the sagas of the late 12th and 13th centuries

Listen to the genre-defying works of Björk; pop/folk singer-songwriter Emilíana Torrini; the ethereal sounds of Sigur Rós

Watch *101 Reykjavík*, based on Hallgrimur Helgason's book of the same name – a painful, funny tale of a Reykjavík dropout's fling with his mother's lesbian lover

Eat some challenging local dishes: putrefied shark meat, puffin meat or singed sheep's head complete with eyeballs

Drink *brennivín* ('burnt wine'); schnapps made from potatoes and caraway seeds with the foreboding nickname *svarti dauði* (black death)

IN A WORD
Skál! (Cheers!)

TRADEMARKS
Björk; the Blue Lagoon; economic meltdown; geysers; Icelandic horses; puffins; sagas; volcanoes; whale-watching; whaling

RANDOM FACT
Due to the unique way in which surnames are formed (girls add the suffix *-dóttir*, daughter, to their father's first name; boys add the suffix *-son*), telephone directories in Iceland are alphabetised by first name

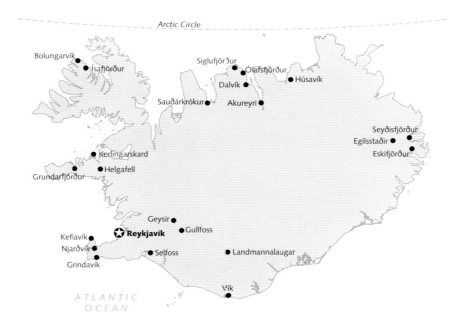

MAP REF **E,18**

1. The steeple of Hallgrímskirkja in Reykjavík soars heavenward
2. A waterfall tumbles over the green cliffs at Skógar, dwarfing its spectators
3. In Kollsvik, puffins catch up on the day's events
4. The Strokkur hot spring erupts in an almighty column, roaring towards the sky

1.

2.

3.

CAPITAL New Delhi | **POPULATION** 1,166,079,217 | **AREA** 3,287,263 sq km | **OFFICIAL LANGUAGES** Hindi, English, Bengali, Telugu, Marathi, Tamil, Urdu, Gujarati, Malayalam, Kannada, Oriya, Punjabi, Assamese, Kashmiri, Sindhi & Sanskrit

Crowned by the Himalaya, crossed by sacred rivers, coveted by empires from the Persians to the British Raj, India is vast and unfathomable, a kaleidoscope of cultures and the birthplace of at least two of the world's great religions. Countless civilisations have risen and fallen among the paddy fields and palms, but India still endures. Overcrowding, poverty and bureaucracy are daily challenges, but for every rush-hour crush there is a moment of utter serenity – dawn breaking over a sacred pool, or a monk chanting to the music of the spheres. Besides, the frenetic energy is part of the appeal. After India, other countries feel like they have the sound turned down.

BEST TIME TO VISIT
November to March in the plains; July to September for the Himalaya

TOP THINGS TO SEE
- The white marble magnificence of the Taj Mahal
- Pilgrims crowding the banks of the Ganges River in the sacred city of Varanasi
- The astounding crush of humanity in Mumbai and Kolkata
- Mountain views and relics of the Raj in Shimla, the quintessential Indian hill station
- The Himalaya, up close and personal, on a trek through rugged Ladakh

TOP THINGS TO DO
- Embark on a camel safari through the desert dunes of Rajasthan
- Scan the jungle for tigers in one of India's glorious national parks
- Kick back on the palm-brushed beaches of Goa
- Bend your body into shapes you never thought possible in Rishikesh, India's yoga capital
- Rumble across India by sleeper train – it's the most atmospheric way to explore the subcontinent

GETTING UNDER THE SKIN
Read Salman Rushdie's *Midnight's Children*; Vikram Seth's *A Suitable Boy;* or Kiran Desai's *The Inheritance of Loss*

Listen to the myriad *filmi* (movie soundtracks) recordings of Allah Rakha Rahman

Watch Ramesh Sippy's Bollywood classic *Sholay;* or Satyarjit Ray's haunting *Pather Panchali*

Eat delicious *thalis* (rice, curries, chapatis, pappadams and condiments, served on a metal platter or banana leaf)

Drink *lassi* (sweet or salty yoghurt shakes); or *chai* (sweet Indian tea)

IN A WORD
Jai hind! (Long live India!)

TRADEMARKS
Maharajas; holy cows; Gandhi; the Taj Mahal; hill stations; the Himalaya; towering temples; bottomless slums; Bollywood; the outsourcing revolution

RANDOM FACT
There is no such thing as curry in India – the Southern Indian word *kari* simply means 'fried' or 'sauce'

MAP REF **L,28**

1. The everyday and the extraordinary: vegetable sellers carry their wares to market past Agra's Taj Mahal
2. A Kathakali dancer's face is transformed by performance make-up
3. Tea plantation workers pick their way homewards, the day's harvest carried on their heads, in Kerala
4. In a swirl of red, a young dancer and a musician entertain at Jaipur's City Palace

1.

2.

3.

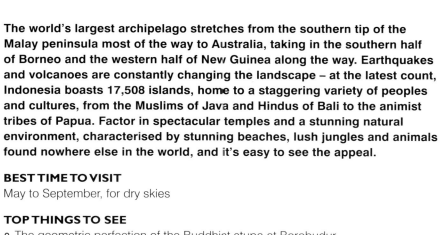

The world's largest archipelago stretches from the southern tip of the Malay peninsula most of the way to Australia, taking in the southern half of Borneo and the western half of New Guinea along the way. Earthquakes and volcanoes are constantly changing the landscape – at the latest count, Indonesia boasts 17,508 islands, home to a staggering variety of peoples and cultures, from the Muslims of Java and Hindus of Bali to the animist tribes of Papua. Factor in spectacular temples and a stunning natural environment, characterised by stunning beaches, lush jungles and animals found nowhere else in the world, and it's easy to see the appeal.

BEST TIME TO VISIT
May to September, for dry skies

TOP THINGS TO SEE
- The geometric perfection of the Buddhist stupa at Borobudur
- Shadow puppetry, batik dying and other ancient arts in Yogyakarta
- Death rituals straight out of Indiana Jones in other-worldly Tana Toraja
- Beach bums, rice terraces and tiered temples on touristy but sublime Bali
- Views over a primordial landscape of steaming volcanoes from the top of Gunung Bromo

TOP THINGS TO DO
- Soak up the tropical vibe on the gorgeous Gili Islands
- Catch the perfect wave at Ulu Watu, Bali's surfing mecca
- Descend into a kaleidoscope of colour at dive sites throughout the islands
- Trek to timeless Dani villages in Papua's Baliem Valley
- Meet the old man of the forest – the enigmatic orangutan – in Tanjung Puting National Park

GETTING UNDER THE SKIN
Read Ayu Utami's *Saman*, a novel of gender taboos, political repression and religious intolerance

Listen to the unmistakable sound of gamelan – the traditional orchestra of Java, Bali and Lombok

Watch arthouse cinema, Indonesian-style, in the layered films of Garin Nugroho

Eat the ubiquitous *nasi goreng* (fried rice); or rich and spicy *rendang* (beef cooked slowly with roasted coconut and lemongrass)

Drink *kopi* (coffee) or, if you feel brave, 'civet coffee' made from beans retrieved from the droppings of civet cats

IN A WORD
Tidak apa-apa (No problem)

TRADEMARKS
Coffee beans; palm plantations; Suharto; blissful island beaches; active volcanoes; legendary surf breaks; gamelan orchestras; Komodo dragons; shadow puppets

RANDOM FACT
The Komodo dragon of Komodo Island is the largest lizard on earth and an occasional maneater – even a bite can prove fatal because of the virulent bacteria in the dragons' saliva

MAP REF **O,32**

1. A puncture in the earth's surface: the crater lake of Gunung Rinjani
2. A pretty Balinese smile
3. Dani men in ceremonial dress welcome visitors to their Baliem Valley village
4. Locals take to the water at Tampaksiring's Spring Water Temple

2.

3.

1.

IRAN

All is not what it seems in Iran. The simple stereotype is of an oil-addled desert land flush with scowling mullahs and anti-Western feeling. Oh, and nice carpets. Don't be fooled! The reality is far more complex and far more diverse. Iran boasts a sophisticated culture where poetry is valued over dogma and hospitality trumps austerity. Visitors are more likely to be welcomed by men cycling the wrong way down four-lane highways than they are to encounter suspicion or slogans. Islam retains an important place but is not overwhelming, and the Iranians, despite the trials of a long history and modern politics, are upbeat and genuinely interested in meeting travellers. Like those famous carpets, Iran is textured, subtle and richly coloured.

BEST TIME TO VISIT
April to June and September to November

TOP THINGS TO SEE
- The arched market arcades and beautiful mosques of Imam Square in Esfahan
- Winding lanes and wind towers in the mud-brick old town of Yazd
- The tea terraces and hills surrounding Masuleh on the Caspian Sea littoral
- Magnificent Persepolis, now in ruins, but an awe-inspiring reminder of the might of the ancient Persian Empire
- The domes and minarets of the Holy Shrine of Imam Reza in Mashhad

TOP THINGS TO DO
- Settle in for an afternoon of banter, bluffing and tea while haggling for a carpet
- Listen to the silence amid the date palms of Garmeh oasis
- Accept an invitation to someone's home for dinner – you are sure to receive one – to experience first-hand Iranian hospitality
- Escape the smog and rumble of Tehran on the walking trails of Darband in the foothills of the Alborz Mountains

GETTING UNDER THE SKIN
Read *The Way of the World* by Nicolas Bouvier, a rollicking tale of a 1950s road trip; and *Mirrors of the Unseen* by Jason Elliot, an observation of modern Iran

Listen to the sombre melodies of Persian epic poetry sung to traditional accompaniment

Watch *Gabbeh,* directed by Mohsen Makhmalbaf, a colourful evocation of nomadic life; or *the Lizard*, by Kamal Tabrizi, a comedy box-office smash

Eat mouthwatering *mirza ghasemi* (mashed aubergine with garlic, egg and tomato); or *kababs* in all sorts of varieties

Drink *chay* (tea) at a *chaykhane* (traditional teahouse); or 'Islamic' – ie no-alcohol – beer

IN A WORD
Khosh amadin (Welcome!)

TRADEMARKS
Turbanned mullahs; chadors; carpets; bazaars desert citadels; oil refineries; poetry; the Islamic regime

RANDOM FACT
Iranians use Arabic script, but their language, Persian, entirely unrelated to Arabic, is related to European languages

MAP REF **J,25**

CAPITAL Tehran | POPULATION 66,429,284 | AREA 1,648,195 sq km | OFFICIAL LANGUAGES Persian, Azari & Kurdish

1. Awe-inspiring: the mosaic interior of the Sheikh Lotfollah Mosque, Esfahan
2. Top of the class: a student reads aloud in her Tehran school
3. An avenue of fountains leads to the imposing Azadi (Freedom) Tower, Tehran
4. Friends gather for tea and a chat in a teahouse in Imam Khomeini Square, Esfahan

1.

2.

3.

Welcome to one of the most dangerous places on earth. Things may be improving slowly, but it will be a long time before you'd choose to spend your annual holidays in Iraq. When peace finally does return, Iraq's ancient history will quickly drown out the tragedy of the more recent past, at least for those who didn't have to live through the dark years of war. Iraq, or Mesopotamia as it was once known, played host to many of the great civilisations of the ancient world, while a fascinating religious and cultural mix plays out in the largely peaceful north of the country, in Iraqi Kurdistan. In the meantime, Iraqis pray for peace...

BEST TIME TO VISIT
April to September, and when peace returns

TOP THINGS TO SEE
- Erbil, one of the oldest cities on earth and a symbol of peace in Iraqi Kurdistan
- The breathtakingly located village of Amadiya in the mountains of Iraqi Kurdistan
- The hillside town of Akre and the former Jewish signposts in the country's north
- Ur, with one of the world's best-preserved ziggurats and the possible birthplace of Abraham
- Peace in our time

TOP THINGS TO DO
- Don your flak jacket, keep your head down and try to picture Baghdad the Beautiful amid the dangers of war
- Dive into the infectiously optimistic cultural scene in Sulaymaniyah in Iraqi Kurdistan
- Drive the unrelentingly scenic Hamilton Road in northeastern Iraqi Kurdistan
- Try to imagine the glory days of Babylon in this now-humble, one-time colossus of the ancient world
- Hike the high country around Ahmadawa

GETTING UNDER THE SKIN
Read the fantastical tales of *Thousand and One Nights* to see what Baghdad once was; or *The Occupation of Iraq* by Ali A Allawi to see what it has become

Listen to Kazem (Kadim) al-Saher, an Iraqi musical megastar; or the more sedate, haunting oud (lute) of Naseer Shama on *Le Luth de Baghdad*

Watch *Kilomètre Zero* by Hiner Saleem, which debuted at the Cannes Festival in 2005 and is a searing portrait of life under Saddam

Eat *masgouf* (skewered Tigris River fish barbecued on an outdoor grill)

Drink thick black coffee and dark sweet tea

IN A WORD
Salaam aleikum (Peace be with you)

TRADEMARKS
One of the world's flashpoints and most dangerous places; long-suffering people; the cradle of civilisation

RANDOM FACT
The Bible's Garden of Eden is believed by some archaeologists and amateur historians to have been in Iraq

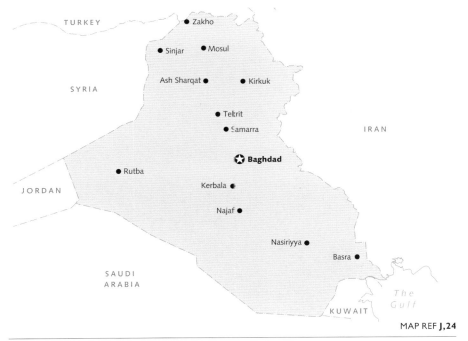

MAP REF J,24

1. Shiite Muslims offer up prayers at the Al-Imam Al-Adham mosque in Baghdad
2. The spiral minaret of Samarra twirls into the sky
3. Fires are often lit to celebrate Newroz (Kurdish New Year)
4. The lap of learning: a boy sits on the statue of Mubarek Ahmed Sharafaddin at the entrance to the Citadel of Erbil

1.

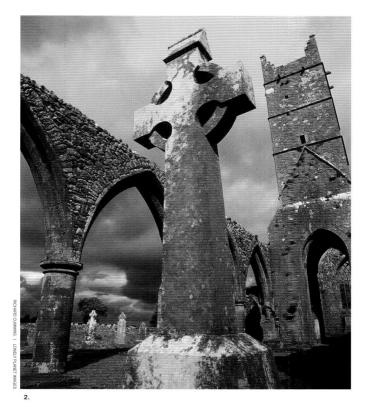

2.

3.

4.

Thanks to worldwide economic troubles and the death of the Irish tiger economy, Ireland's efforts to improve its dire roads have been dealt a setback. Good. If you could scoot along as you do in other First World countries, you'd reach one end of Ireland almost before you left the other. But like a properly poured Guinness (or a simple exchange of pleasantries), the Emerald Isle is best enjoyed slowly. That's when the haunting Celtic notes of the traditional music, the lilt to everyday discourse and the intricacies of the minutely featured countryside can be appreciated. At its best, Ireland encourages you to stop altogether and become part of the merriment (or *craic*), beguiled by seemingly nothing at all.

BEST TIME TO VISIT
May to September, when the weather is warmer and the days are longer

TOP THINGS TO SEE
- The Dingle Peninsula combines classic craggy Irish coastal scenery with beautiful villages
- Impossibly quaint and photogenic lanes through green fields freshened by bracing ocean winds in Donegal
- The soaring, royal castle ruins of the Rock of Cashel
- Bobbing boats, narrow lanes and seaside walks in the precincts of Kinsale
- Dark tunnels and ancient wonders at Neolithic Bru na Boinne

TOP THINGS TO DO
- Shed your preconceptions and misconceptions in the Irish metropolis of Dublin
- Bounce from one venue to the next in rollicking Galway
- Find your own authentic musical moment in a hidden County Clare pub
- Hike the wondrous 16km from Carrick-a-Rede to the Giant's Causeway in Counties Derry and Antrim
- Get lost and hope not to be found on confounding and beguiling rural backroads

GETTING UNDER THE SKIN
Read *Angela's Ashes* to understand why Ireland's biggest export for centuries was people; plough through James Joyce to understand the Irish gift for words

Listen to U2 for sounds bigger than the island; or the Chieftains for sounds *of* the island

Watch Roddy Doyle's words come to life in *The Commitments*, a melodic lark; and *The Snapper*, with the comedic travails of modern life

Eat hearty bacon and cabbage; seafood chowder; or smoked salmon and soda bread

Drink Guinness, possibly chased by a shot of boggy, smoky whisky

IN A WORD
What's the *craic*? (What's happening?)

TRADEMARKS
Potatoes; harps; shamrocks; Guinness; leprechauns; shillelaghs; the Troubles; everything green; simple questions that turn into 20-minute conversations

RANDOM FACT
Until the 19th century the national colour of the Emerald Isle was blue, as the flag of St Patrick featured a gold harp on a blue background

MAP REF **G,19**

1. Somewhere over the rainbow: St Colman's Cathedral, Cobh
2. The remnants of the Franciscan-built Claregalway Abbey stand tall against a stony sky
3. A busker provides a city soundtrack on the streets of Dublin
4. A site of immeasurable cultural importance – a traditional Irish pub

1.

2.

3.

ISRAEL

CAPITAL Jerusalem | POPULATION 7,233,701 | AREA 22,072 sq km | OFFICIAL LANGUAGE Hebrew

Israel's reputation precedes it. Ever since the modern state of Israel was created in 1948, this has been one of the most contested terrains on earth. Israel is rich in sacred reference points for Jews, Christians and Muslims, and both Israelis and Palestinians consider it to be their homeland. Against this backdrop of more than six decades of tension and outright conflict, Israel is also, remarkably, a vibrant modern country that combines deeply traditional religious life, a multicultural melting pot of peoples from all over the world and a liberal oasis in an often conservative region. Its attractions – holy sites, natural beauty and glorious beaches – aside, discovering Israel behind the headlines is the most rewarding aspect of any visit here.

BEST TIME TO VISIT
Year-round, although travelling here can be difficult during major Jewish holidays, when transport and accommodation are overbooked

TOP THINGS TO SEE
- Jerusalem's Old City, with the Western (Wailing) Wall, Temple Mount, the Church of the Holy Sepulchre and so much more
- Jerusalem's Mount of Olives, among the holiest of all Christian sites and with terrific views
- Tel Aviv, the secular city that never sleeps and modern Israel writ large
- Caesarea's Roman ruins and a Crusader castle
- The charming Unesco World Heritage-listed old town, Akko

TOP THINGS TO DO
- Float atop the waters of the Dead Sea
- Follow Jesus' footsteps through Galilee, Tiberias and the Sea of Galilee
- Hike through the beautiful nature reserves of the disputed Golan Heights
- Explore the desert wilderness of the Negev and climb Maktesh Ramon Crater
- Climb Mt Tsfahot for sunrise views of the Red Sea, Jordan, Egypt and Saudi Arabia

GETTING UNDER THE SKIN
Read anything by Amos Oz, considered by many to be the most eloquent voice of modern Israel

Listen to *The Idan Raichel Project*, a blend of Israeli love songs, Ethiopian instruments, Jamaican rhythms and Yemeni vocals

Watch *The Band's Visit*, directed by Edan Kolirin, a tragi-comic tale of an Egyptian police band that becomes lost while touring Israel

Eat *hummus*, a national obsession

Drink award-winning Israeli wines from the country's burgeoning boutique wineries

IN A WORD
Shalom (Hello; peace)

TRADEMARKS
Jerusalem and Tel Aviv, the two sides to Israel's split personality; thriving arts and cultural scene; robust political debates; international kids on kibbutzim; Holy Land

RANDOM FACT
Israeli films have received more Oscar nominations (six) for Best Foreign-Language Film than any other Middle Eastern country

MAP REF **J,23**

1. By the book: prayers at the Western (Wailing) Wall in Jerusalem's Old City
2. No added salt: a woman rinses away the remnants of a therapeutic Dead Sea dip
3. Palestinians play the world game in East Jerusalem
4. The gold Dome of the Rock is a bright beacon in the city of Jerusalem

2.

3.

1.

As exquisite as a finely staged opera, as exuberant as the best street carnival, as earthy as a mucky white truffle snouted fresh from the ground by a dog – Italy spares no expense when it comes to the traveller experience. It is Europe's iconic land of effortless style, easy living, insatiable passion and ubercool chic. It's where history's ancient glories harmoniously fuse with third-millennium sophistication to create a beautiful love affair that never dies. From Rome's magnificent monuments to the masterpiece of Renaissance Florence and Venetian romance, from the in-your-face drama of the Amalfi Coast to the remote flamboyance of southern Italy's mountains, this is one country where the passion never dulls.

BEST TIME TO VISIT
April, June, September

TOP THINGS TO SEE
- Ancient Rome – the Colosseum, Forum, Palatine Hill and Panetheon
- Priceless masterpieces in Florence's Uffizi and *David* at the Galleria dell'Accademia
- Verona of Shakespearian *Romeo and Juliet* romance
- Venice's Piazza di San Marco, bewitched by the spangled spires of Basilica di San Marco
- What's left of Pompeii, a thriving commercial town until Mt Vesuvius erupted in AD 79

TOP THINGS TO DO
- Walk and get lost in Rome – the city that has swept artists and lovers off their feet since time began
- Party between baroque architecture in Lecce, Puglia's hip capital slap-bang on Italy's boot heel
- Be an adrenalin junkie: ski the Alps, hike the Dolomites, dive Sardinia's golden coast or play with Sicilian volcanic fire
- Savour a night at the opera at Milan's La Scala
- Lounge over an *aperitivo* (aperitif) and banquet of sumptuous antipasto in one of Turin's historic cafe-bars

GETTING UNDER THE SKIN
Read Peter Moore's *Vroom by The Sea: The Sunny Parts of Italy on a Bright Orange Vespa* if you want a brilliantly written Italy travelogue
Listen to Andrea Bocelli's renditions of popular Italian classics
Watch Fellini's classic, *La Dolce Vita*
Eat *trippa alla Romana* (tripe with potatoes, tomato and pecorino cheese) in Rome; *bistecca alla fiorentina* (T-bone steak) in Florence; and pizza in Naples
Drink a fine red Brunello di Montalcino n Tuscany; or Barolo in Piedmont

IN A WORD
Ciao bella! (Hi/Bye beautiful!)

TRADEMARKS
Renaissance art; ancient ruins; pizza, pasta and olive oil; espresso; Pavarotti; mad drivers; Vespas; world's best ice cream

RANDOM FACT
On average €3000 a day is tossed into the Fontana di Trevi, Rome's lucky fountain that promises a return trip to the capital in exchange for a coin

CAPITAL Rome | **POPULATION** 58,126,212 | **AREA** 301,340 sq km | **OFFICIAL LANGUAGE** Italian

MAP REF **1,21**

1. The heart-stopping Il Palio of Siena is won by the first-placed horse, with or without its jockey intact
2. Gothic pinnacles pierce the sky above Milan's cathedral, the magnificent Duomo
3. A *pizzaiolo* (pizza maker) produces mouth-watering examples of Naples' beloved export
4. A gondola plies the serene waters of Venice

1.

2.

3.

Beginning in the 16th century, Jamaica was the nexus of the brutal Caribbean economy that saw slaves from Africa producing sugar and rum for Europe and America. First a colony of Spain and later Britain, today's Jamaica is the result of this grim past. No Caribbean country has greater links to Africa, whether food, culture or politics. The ubiquitous sound of the island, reggae, is drawn from African folk music and is the nation's greatest export (the studios of Kingston churn out 500 tunes a month). And tunes blasting are just one of the cacophonous features of this heavily populated island where wildly popular, and often hedonistic, resorts mix with urban life in all its raucous, ganja-scented glory.

BEST TIME TO VISIT
The weather is beautiful year-round but high season is December to April

TOP THINGS TO SEE
○ Sunset from the 11km stretch of beach bars and fun at Long Bay on Negril
○ The museum dedicated to Bob Marley – having heard his music the world over, now see his home and studio while learning about his life
○ The red (sand), white (surf-perfect breaks) and blue (waters) at Long Bay
○ Port Royal, the collapsing former pirate capital of the Caribbean
○ Rocklands, where thousands of buzzing hummingbirds delight in nectar-rich flowers

TOP THINGS TO DO
○ Climb 2256m Blue Mountain Peak, which rises from lush, dense forest preserves
○ Not caress a crocodile in the swampy, remote and ominously named Black River Great Morass
○ Balance on limestone ledges at Dunn's River Falls, which cascade down to a beach
○ Get jammin' to the trademark beat of Jamaica: reggae
○ Dive in the marine parks on Montego Bay and Negril

GETTING UNDER THE SKIN
Read Jean Rhys' *Wide Sargasso Sea*, a tale of post-emancipation Jamaica; Herbert de Lisser's classic *White Witch of Rose Hall*

Listen to Bob Marley in his homeland and forget the clichés

Watch the original James Bond, *Dr No*, which shows a sultry, colonial Jamaica in the early 1960s

Eat *jerk* (meat smothered in tongue-searing marinade and barbecued in an outdoor pit)

Drink the famous Blue Mountain coffee; or the region's greatest variety of rums, including mind-numbing 'overproof'

IN A WORD
Evert'ing cool, mon? (A common greeting much like 'how are you?')

TRADEMARKS
Reggae, reefers and rum; Bob Marley; Rastafarianism; Kingston; palm-fringed beaches; anything-goes couples resorts

RANDOM FACT
Once the major celebration on the slave calendar, Jonkanoo is a Christmas party in which masked revellers parade through the streets

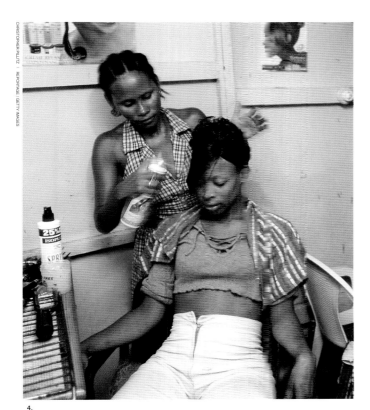

MAP REF **L,11**

1. A fisherman is ready to cast off into pristine Caribbean waters
2. The dreadlocked hair and mellow smile are unmistakably Jamaican
3. The beat of the street: dancers get down in Kingston
4. A Kingston hairdresser is doin' the 'do

2.

3.

1.

Japan is one of those places that both conforms to and confounds your expectations. All the clichés – Zen gardens, sumo wrestlers, bullet trains, geishas – are easy to find, but what blows travellers away is the way that Japan consistently delivers the unexpected. For every Shinto shrine and space-age city, there is a beach-fringed tropical island or a forest trail climbing the slopes of a snowcapped mountain. Then there's the famous Japanese quirkiness – this is a nation where vending machines sell underpants and neckties and where dressing up as a manga character is as commonplace as celebrating the arrival of the cherry blossom every spring.

BEST TIME TO VISIT

March to May, to avoid winter snow and summer rain

TOP THINGS TO SEE

- The unbelievable crush of humanity in Tokyo
- Zen gardens, Shinto shrines and geishas in historic Kyoto
- Ancient mausoleums scattered through the forest in Nikko National Park
- World Heritage–listed wonders in Nara, ancient capital of Japan
- The colours of the *sakura* (cherry blossom), best observed at Yoshinoyama

TOP THINGS TO DO

- Slurp down a bowl of ramen noodles in Fukuoka
- Soak away your worries in the historic Dogo Onsen in Matsuyama
- Hike through an otherworldly forest of Japanese cedars on Yakushima Island
- Be humbled by the lessons of history at Hiroshima and Nagasaki
- Scuba dive, scramble through the jungle or just bask on the beach on tropical Iriomote-jima

GETTING UNDER THE SKIN

Read Natsume Soseki's satirical *I am a Cat*; or Shikibu Murasaki's *The Tale of Genji*, written around AD 1000

Listen to the curious hybrid sound of Japanese heavy metal, such as Murasaki or X Japan; for Japanese punk rock, try the Stalin, or Blue Hearts

Watch Akira Kurosawa's epic *Seven Samurai*; Katsuhiro Otomo's classic anime *Akira*; or Hideo Nakata's chilling *Ringu*

Eat raw fish, preferably as *sashimi* – wafer-thin slices served with soy, wasabi and preserved daikon radish

Drink *shochu*, the national spirit of Japan; or sake, Japanese rice wine – served hot it infuses the senses

IN A WORD

Sugoi (The universal exclamation, used whenever something is terrific, or terrible or just worth shouting about)

TRADEMARKS

Mt Fuji; ninjas; sumo; sushi; geishas in kimonos; paper walls; bowing; Cosplay; anime and manga; cherry blossoms; earthquakes; the legacy of WWII

RANDOM FACTS

Saying 'no' is considered confrontational in Japan – most Japanese use the word *tabun*, meaning 'maybe', instead

MAP REF **J,34**

1. The striking Fuji Sengen Jinja Shrine watches over the gentle slopes of Mt Fuji
2. A geisha embodies perfection in grooming and gesture
3. Pedestrians are like fish on a neon reef in Tokyo's Shinjuku district
4. Young sumo wrestlers take a break from training

1.

2.

3.

Buffeted on all sides by the conflicts in Iraq and Israel and the Palestinian Territories, Jordan could be forgiven for cursing its luck. And yet, this remarkable oasis of stability in the toughest of neighbourhoods has seen it all before. Biblical stories, mysterious lost cities and Lawrence of Arabia – all these and so much more have always placed Jordan at the centre of great historical events, and signposts to an epic past still provide the centrepiece for Jordan's many attractions, including Petra, Wadi Rum and the Dead Sea. But it's the warmth and gracious hospitality – perfected down through centuries of watching the world pass through – of ordinary Jordanians that you'll remember most from a visit here.

BEST TIME TO VISIT
April to May or September to October

TOP THINGS TO SEE
- Petra's rose-red, rock-hewn Nabataean city
- Jerash's stunning Roman ruins that would be the star of the show were it not for Petra
- Crusader castles, the formidable, evocative bastions in Karak and Shobak
- Madaba's Byzantine-era mosaics, and Mt Nebo, where Moses looked out upon the Promised Land
- Remote Desert Castles dating back to Umayyad times

TOP THINGS TO DO
- Listen for the echo of Lawrence of Arabia and camp with the Bedouin in Wadi Rum
- Dive or snorkel through some of the Red Sea's most beautiful underwater scenery
- Giggle in disbelief as you float in the salty waters of the Dead Sea
- Hike the stunning Dana Nature Reserve, the Middle East's most impressive ecotourism project
- Dive into Amman, one of the Arab world's most hip and sophisticated cities

GETTING UNDER THE SKIN
Read *Seven Pillars of Wisdom* by TE Lawrence; or *Petra: Lost City of the Ancient World* by Christian Augé and Jean-Marie Dentzer

Listen to Sakher Hattar, revered as the Arab world's finest oud (lute) player

Watch *Lawrence of Arabia* or *Indiana Jones and the Last Crusade* for stunning climactic scenes filmed in Petra

Eat *mensaf* (a Bedouin specialty of spit-roasted lamb basted with spices and served on a platter of rice and pine nuts)

Drink tea, that symbol of Jordanian hospitality

IN A WORD
Ahlan wa sahlan (Welcome)

TRADEMARKS
Petra and Wadi Rum; Bedouins and Palestinians in *keffiyah* (head robes); hospitality; peace and stability while wars rage all around

RANDOM FACT
Bethany Beyond the Jordan is where Jesus is believed to have been baptised – it was authenticated by the Pope in 2000

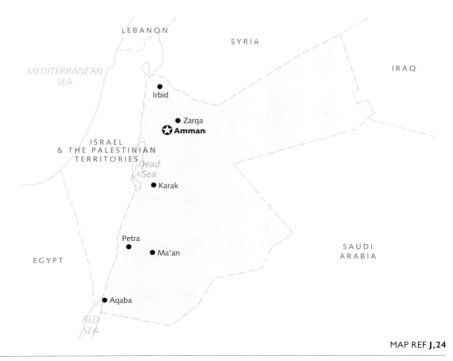

MAP REF J,24

1. Twilight creeps across a desert camp in Wadi Rum
2. Happiness is a contented flock
3. Cream-coloured metropolis: Amman at sunset
4. A Bedouin boy is on top of the world at Petra's Al-Deir (Monastery)

2.

3.

1.

4.

Sacha Baron Cohen may have briefly raised the profile of the world's ninth-largest country, but most travellers have yet to realise that there's more to Kazakhstan than *Borat*. The big draws are definitely the superb Altai and Tian Shan mountains bordering China, but the bleak, bewildering steppe also beckons with surreal, surprising secrets ranging from Soviet-era cosmodromes and underground mosques to the rusting ruins of the Aral Sea. After years of collectivisation, the former horsemen of the Golden Horde are now getting rich on petro-dollars, while trying to deal with the legacy of serving as the Soviet Union's favourite dumping grounds. Today the Eurasian steppe offers one of the last great undiscovered frontiers of travel.

BEST TIME TO VISIT
May to September

TOP THINGS TO SEE
- The glittering blue domes and 15th-century Timurid tilework of the Yasaui Mausoleum in Turkistan
- Kazakhstan's futuristic new capital Astana, which boasts the world's largest tent
- Cosmopolitan Almaty, with Orthodox cathedrals and engaging museums
- Fishing boats marooned in the desert sand of Aralsk, miles from the nearest waters of the Aral Sea

TOP THINGS TO DO
- Ride to Shambhala on a horse trek to the base of Mt Belukha in the magnificent Altai Mountains
- Hike to the three Köl-Say Lakes in the southeastern Zailiysky Alatau mountains
- Glide around Medeu's giant ice rink or snowboard nearby Chimbulak ski resort
- Spot flamingos in their most northerly habitat at Korgalzhyn Nature Reserve
- Buy some birch twigs and give yourself a good thrashing at Almaty's Arasan Baths

GETTING UNDER THE SKIN
Read *Apples are from Kazakhstan: The Land that Disappeared* by Christopher Robbins, a witty and engaging travelogue that blends history with modern insight

Listen to *The Silk Road: A Musical Caravan*, a collection of traditional music from across inner Asia, including several tracks from Kazakhstan

Watch Kazakh hordes battle the Dzungarian armies in Sergei Bodrov's *Nomad*, Kazakhstan's US$40-million blockbuster

Eat *qazy* (smoked horsemeat sausage) – the ultimate nomad snack

Drink *shubat* (fermented camel's milk), washed down by *kumys* (fermented mare's milk); or play it safe with a cold Tian-Shansky beer

IN A WORD
Salemetsiz be (Hello/How are you?)

TRADEMARKS
Steppe; *Borat;* Aral Sea; oil; Tian Shan mountains; Baikonur Cosmodrome; Semipalatinsk nuclear site; horses

RANDOM FACT
Kazakhstan sits atop an estimated 100 billion barrels of oil, most of it underneath the Caspian Sea

MAP REF **H,27**

1. Feathered and hooved friends aid Kazakh men on a traditional hunting expedition
2. Kazakh women wear traditional red and gold to celebrate Republic Day
3. A monumental occasion: hot-air balloons add grandeur to Independence Day celebrations in Almaty
4. The fabulous confection of Zenkov Cathedral, Almaty, is part wedding cake, part Christmas tree

1.

2.

3.

Picture the scene: a Maasai warrior leans on his spear, watching a train of wildebeest snaking across the savannah, while a flock of ibis takes wing from the acacia trees, casting curved silhouettes against the sky. That's Kenya. Long regarded as one of Africa's success stories, the original 'sun, sand and safari' destination has been through a few political ups and downs, but the sun still beams, the ocean still laps the beaches of the Swahili coast and the lions, elephants and rhinos still charge across the plains. Indeed, there are few countries in the world that offer such a richness of wildlife, such a diversity of tribal culture – and such a challenging capital city as Nairobi.

BEST TIME TO VISIT
January to February

TOP THINGS TO SEE
- The annual migration of the wildebeest across the Masai Mara
- Traditional tribal culture in the arid badlands around Lake Turkana
- Epic views across the Rift Valley from the Nairobi–Naivasha road
- The pink ribbon of greater flamingos around the edge of Lake Nakuru
- The summit of Mt Kenya – you'll appreciate it even more after the gruelling five-day trek to get there

TOP THINGS TO DO
- Sip a cold Tusker beer and bop to a live band in one of Nairobi's surprisingly laid-back pubs
- Ride the rails in colonial comfort on the night train from Nairobi to Mombasa
- Dream under canvas on a luxury tented safari
- Float over the savannah in a hot-air balloon
- Splash around on the drifting beaches of lovely Lamu island

GETTING UNDER THE SKIN
Read *The Man-Eaters of Tsavo* by John Henry Patterson; or *The Lunatic Express* by Charles Miller for the tragic, gripping story of the Mombasa–Uganda railway

Listen to *benga*, the upbeat, popular dance music of the nation – best exemplified by the songs of Extra Golden, Okatch Biggy and Dola Kabarry

Watch Robert Redford and Meryl Streep earning their Oscars in Sydney Pollack's *Out of Africa*, based on the famous novel by Isak Dinesen

Eat *nyama choma* (Kenyan-style roasted meat), a perfect accompaniment to cold beer

Drink milk mixed with cow's blood at a Maasai celebration – if you dare!

IN A WORD
Hakuna matata (No worries)

TRADEMARKS
The Big Five (lions, elephants, rhinos, buffaloes and leopards); the Rift Valley; leaping Maasai warriors; shoes made from tyres; tribal beads; lean marathon runners; gin-soaked colonials; Nairobbery

RANDOM FACT
Kenya is the third-largest exporter of tea after India and China

MAP REF **N,24**

1. Bold and brilliant, Samburu women participate in a traditional dance
2. A pair of leggy cheetahs are on the alert in the Masai Mara National Reserve
3. A cyclist makes his way from A to B in Mombasa's Old Town
4. In a frozen moment, a Samburu warrior seems to take flight

207

2.

3.

1.

Kiribati (pronounce 'Kiribas'), with its aqua lagoons and splendid sunsets, is as beautiful for its real-world simplicity. Hidden by ocean and untainted by tourism, the country is made up of 33 low-lying islands and atolls flung across the equator. The sound and sight of the sea dominates here, fish are the staple and boats are the major form of transport. Locals might not understand why you've come to visit, but with a friendly attitude you'll be greeted with sun-scorched smiles and invited in. Explore densely populated and increasingly modern Tarawa, or get completely back to island roots on the outer islands. Wherever you go, don't expect schedules or luxury, just go with the warm but basic Gilbertese flow.

BEST TIME TO VISIT
March to October, the dry season

TOP THINGS TO SEE
- A traditional dance performance – then get up to boogie yourself
- An abundance of seabirds, crabs and turtles at the isolated Phoenix Islands Protected Area, the largest marine protected area on the planet
- Rusted tanks, ships and airplanes, all remains from the WWII Battle of Tarawa, visible on the reef at low tide
- Kiribati crafts from the outer islands including *te wii ni bakua* (hand-smocked tops) and conical woven pandanus fishermen's hats

TOP THINGS TO DO
- Saltwater fly-fish for famously rough-fighting bone fish
- Perfect surf – lonely reef breaks off Fanning Island
- Dive or snorkel the sublimely clear waters
- Salt or smoke your catch and learn to be self-sufficient in the outer islands
- Relax with a cold coconut at one of North Tarawa's homestays

GETTING UNDER THE SKIN
Read *A Pattern of Islands* by Arthur Grimbal who loved the islands; *The Sex Lives of Cannibals* by J Maarten Troost who grew to sort of like them

Listen to beautiful singing emanating from *maneaba* (traditional meeting houses) across the country

Watch documentaries produced by the Tarawa nonprofit film company, Tabera Ni Kai

Eat fresh fish, breadfruit and rice

Drink *kaokioki*, also called sour toddy, a local brew made from fermented coconut palm sap

IN A WORD
Mauri-i-Matang! (Hello stranger!)

TRADEMARKS
Far-flung coral atolls; deep-blue ocean; bonefish; birdwatching, WWII Battle of Tarawa; Kiritimati (Christmas) Island; hydrogen-bomb testing

RANDOM FACT
Kiribati is spread over 3.55 million sq km of ocean, giving it the largest ocean-to-land ratio in the world

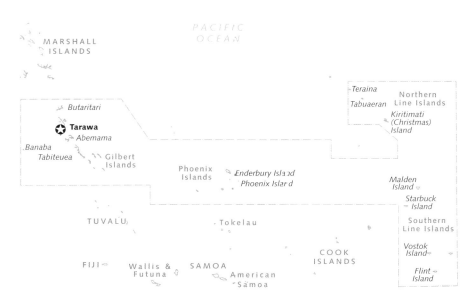

MAP REF O,38

1. Out in the 'fields': a man works his seaweed farm on Tabiteuea
2. A decorated dancer on Kiritimati (Christmas) Island
3. A fish trap on Marakei Island snares the unwitting
4. A good haul: a Tarawa woman sells skipjack tuna caught earlier in the day

1.

2.

3.

Secretive only just describes North Korea, the insular northern half of the Korean peninsula, which closed its doors to the world at the end of the Korean War and, even today, only opens them to visitors on strictly regimented tours. Most people form their opinions of this so-called 'rogue state' from news reports and James Bond movies, but there's more to the Democratic People's Republic than military parades and stand-offs with the UN. With official minders, you can roam to mountain resorts and ancient capitals, though the main attractions remain the bombastic iconography of the North Korean regime and the surreal existence of ordinary people in this troubled, autocratic state.

BEST TIME TO VISIT
May, for the staggering crowd spectacles of the Arirang Mass Games

TOP THINGS TO SEE
○ Blissful mountain scenery at the hill resort of Kumgangsan
○ Volcanic springs and revolutionary relics at Baekdu Mountain
○ Children engaged in patriotic activities at Mangyongdae Children's Palace
○ Sacred Paekdusan – the mountain birthplace of Hwanung, the founder of the first Korean kingdom
○ Pyongyang's Juche Tower, a three-dimensional embodiment of the Korean principle of self-reliance

TOP THINGS TO DO
○ Watch locals picnicking on peaceful Moran Hill
○ Step back into Korea's history at Kaesong, the ancient capital of the Goryeo kings
○ Enjoy the freedom of shopping without minders at Department Store No 1
○ See Kim Il-sung in the (embalmed) flesh at the Kumsusan Memorial Palace
○ Pay your respects to Kim Il-sung at the Mansudae Grand Monument

GETTING UNDER THE SKIN
Read *Under the Loving Care of the Fatherly Leader* by Bradley Martin; or *North Korea: Another Country* by Bruce Cumings

Listen to the rousing patriotic anthems played continuously on the Pyongyang metro

Watch Daniel Gordon's *A State of Mind*, a surprising documentary about the lives of two young North Korean gymnasts

Eat *naengmyeon* (cold kudzu-flour or buckwheat noodles)

Drink *soju* (local vodka); or Taedonggang, the national beer of North Korea

IN A WORD
Juche (The national policy of 'Self Reliance')

TRADEMARKS
The Great Leader (Kim Il-sung); the Great Leader (Kim Jong-il, aka the Dear Leader); weapons of mass destruction; political sabre-rattling; vast military parades; the Mass Games; the 38th parallel; 1.2 million landmines in the Demilitarized Zone (DMZ)

RANDOM FACT
The Great Leader, Kim Jong-il, has only uttered six words in public – 'Glory to the heroic soldiers of the People's Army!'

KOREA, NORTH

CAPITAL Pyongyang | POPULATION 22,665,345 | AREA 120,538 sq km | OFFICIAL LANGUAGE Korean

CHINA

Onsong
Hoeryong
Chongjin
Hyesan
Manpo
Kilju
Kanggye
Pukchong
Sinuiju
Hyangsan
East Sea (Sea of Japan)
Gulf of West Korea
Wonsan
⊕ **Pyongyang**
Nampo
Kumgang
Haeju
Kaesong
SOUTH KOREA

MAP REF I,33

1. Youth and exuberance is on display during the Arirang Mass Games at May Day Stadium, Pyongyang
2. Neatly authoritative, a Pyongyang policewoman tells traffic where to go
3. Heroes of North Korea are represented in the Mansudae Grand Monument
4. The mighty and imposing Tower of the Juche Idea symbolises the ideology developed by Kim Il-sung

2.

1.

Compared to its secretive neighbour to the north, South Korea is a beacon of progress, second only to Japan in its enthusiasm for scientific breakthroughs, gadgets and gizmos. Korean expats have spread the cuisine of their homeland across the globe, but surprisingly few travellers have explored this ultramodern but deeply traditional corner of Asia. For every high-tech metropolis, South Korea boasts a medieval fortress, or a verdant national park where locals come to escape the hubbub. Even after two millennia, the teachings of Confucius still resonate in Korea, but younger Koreans are famous for their national pride, which rises to a crescendo in support of the national soccer and taekwondo teams.

BEST TIME TO VISIT
September to November, for spectacular autumn colours

TOP THINGS TO SEE
- Markets, museums and medieval city gates in the bustling capital, Seoul
- Acres of tombs, temples and ruins in historic Gyeongju
- The royal mausoleums of the Baekje dynasty at Gongju and Buyeo
- Traditional Korean life on the islands of Dadohae Haesang National Park
- Mountains, forests, hot springs, temples and plenty of serenity at Seoraksan National Park

TOP THINGS TO DO
- See strange denizens of the deep on sale in Busan's fish market
- Feast on *galbi* (barbecued ribs) in Seoul's Mapo-gu district
- Trek through bear country in mountainous Jirisan National Park
- Stand as close as you safely can to the world's most volatile border on a tour of Panmunjom and the Demilitarized Zone (DMZ)
- Try to work out what all the buttons do on one of Korea's futuristic automatic toilets

GETTING UNDER THE SKIN
Read Park Kyung-ni's *Toji* (The Land), a 16-volume historical odyssey that has been made into a movie, TV series and opera

Listen to *pansori* – musical story-telling, often described as the Korean equivalent of the blues

Watch Kwak Jae-yong's romantic-comedy smash *Yeopgijeogin geunyeo* (My Sassy Girl); or Park Chan-wook's violent, extraordinary *OldBoy*

Eat *kimchi* (fiery pickled cabbage with chilli); and *galbi* (variety of grilled dishes)

Drink *soju* (local vodka); or *bori cha* (warming tea made from roasted barley)

IN A WORD
Jeong (Emotional attachment bordering on love)

TRADEMARKS
Korean barbecues; taekwondo; ginseng; *kimchi;* hot springs; free-trade zones; Mexican standoffs with North Korea across the DMZ

RANDOM FACT
Koreans are famous for their technological know-how – more than half of Koreans pay all their bills using their mobile phones

MAP REF **J,33**

1. Nuns wrap up against the winter cold at the all-female Seoknamsa Temple in Ulsan
2. Commuters wait for a train at Seoul Racecourse subway station
3. A cymbal crash of canary yellow punctuates a Seoul street parade
4. Scaly, ornate uniforms are on display at the changing of the guard at Namdaemun (Great South Gate), Seoul

1.

CAPITAL Prishtina | **POPULATION** 1,804,838 | **AREA** 10,887 sq km | **OFFICIAL LANGUAGES** Albanian (Gheg) & Serbian

Kosovo is contested territory. Populated predominately by Albanians, it is considered holy ground by minority Serbs. It formed the core of the Serbian medieval empire but was the scene of their defeat by the Turks, then it fell into obscurity. The Kosovar Albanians declared independence in 2008, a move hotly disputed by some and still not universally recognised. Now familiar to peacekeepers and NGOs, the terracotta-roofed old quarters of Prizren and Peja, remote Orthodox monasteries and poppy-splashed hillside meadows see few visitors. While tensions remain, the signature tune of Kosovo is a cacophony of nationalist voices and peace-keeping vehicles on wet roads. The hope is that one day among calls to prayer from Albanian mosques and solemnly chanted Serbian liturgy, harmony will emerge.

BEST TIME TO VISIT
May to September

TOP THINGS TO SEE
- Old Prizren, with its cobbled laneways, arched Ottoman bridge, Sinan Pasha Mosque and *hamam* (Turkish bath)
- The serenity that Decani Monastery offers from the chaos of the rest of the country
- Otherworldly stalagmites in Gadime Cave
- Slivers of sunlight carving through the atmospheric gloom in Gracanica monastery

TOP THINGS TO DO
- Talk up a storm with the philosophical crowd in the bars of Prishtina
- Enjoy the view of Prizren from Kaljaja Fortress
- Pull on your walking shoes in the wild mountain scenery of the Balkans Peace Park straddling the borders of Kosovo, Albania and Montenegro
- Hope that political differences are resolved so that the ski lifts at pristine Brezovica might start working again

GETTING UNDER THE SKIN
Read *Kosovo: What Everyone Needs to Know* by Tim Judah, a brief and admirably impartial overview of the very complex issue of Kosovo

Listen to traditional folk music featuring skirling flutes and goat-skin drums

Watch Isa Qosja's *The Kukum*, a lyrical tale of three escapees from an asylum and a poignant observation on the meaning of freedom

Eat a variety of Balkan staples including Turkish kebaps, Serbian *ćevapčići* (grilled kebap) or fabulously creamy yoghurt or goat's cheese

Drink tea by the glassful at a traditional teahouse; or locally brewed Peja beer

IN A WORD
Tungjajeta (Hello)

TRADEMARKS
Peacekeeping forces; Orthodox churches; Albanian mosques; war damage and new construction; NGO 4WDs; declaration of independence; ethnic tension; gutted monasteries

RANDOM FACT
Prishtina has streets named after two American presidents: Bill Clinton and George W Bush

MAP REF **I,22**

1. The festive burning of the *badnjak* (oak sapling) is a Serbian Christmas Eve tradition, here taking place in front of the Sveti Dimitrije church in Mitrovica

2.

3.

1.

A tiny oil-rich city state surrounded by three Middle Eastern giants, Kuwait occupies one of history's most contested regions. Iraq's 1990 invasion of Kuwait may be what most people know about the country, but civilisation here dates back millennia to the fabled Dilmun Empire. Fast forward to the present and Kuwait is one of the most intriguing corners of the Gulf. Fascinating old-style markets and dhow harbours sit alongside eye-catching feats of contemporary architecture and some of the best museums in the Middle East. Home to traditional Bedouin tribesmen and thoroughly modern oil-rich sheikhs, a bastion of Gulf tradition and an emerging battleground for women's rights and liberalising trends, Kuwait is the Gulf's past, present and future in one small space.

BEST TIME TO VISIT
February to April

TOP THINGS TO SEE
- The stunning modern architecture of the Kuwait Towers
- An extraordinary collection of Islamic art at Tareq Rajab Museum
- Giant spider crabs and crocodiles at the Middle East's largest aquarium, Scientific Center
- Failaka Island, holding some of the richest archaeological sites in the Gulf, from Dilmun to Ancient Greece
- The last outpost of Old Kuwait, Fahaheel, with a fish souq, dhow harbour and strong Bedouin traditions

TOP THINGS TO DO
- Learn about the Kuwaiti past in Kuwait City's fabulous National Museum
- Bargain for kitsch and search for treasure in Kuwait City's sprawling souq
- Tuck into a date pudding at Beit 7, one of Kuwait City's best restaurants
- Dine on Persian Gulf fish in Al-Boom Restaurant, an ancient dhow
- Dive beneath the warm waters of the Gulf, or go desert biking along the beach

GETTING UNDER THE SKIN
Read *Women in Kuwait* by Haya al-Mughni, which gives insight into the often hidden world of Kuwaiti women in this deeply traditional country

Listen to Abdullah al-Rowaishid, who blends tradition and Arabic pop

Watch *Fires of Kuwait* by David Douglas, which follows the teams cleaning up the burning oil wells after the Iraq war

Eat Gulf fish baked or stewed with coriander, turmeric, red pepper and cardamom

Drink coffee served Arabic-style

IN A WORD
Gowwa (Hello)

TRADEMARKS
Iraq's 1990 invasion of Kuwait and its 1991 liberation; staunch US ally; Kuwait Towers; blend of strong tradition and creeping liberalisation

RANDOM FACT
Kuwait takes Ramadan seriously – even chewing gum during the Islamic month of fasting is illegal

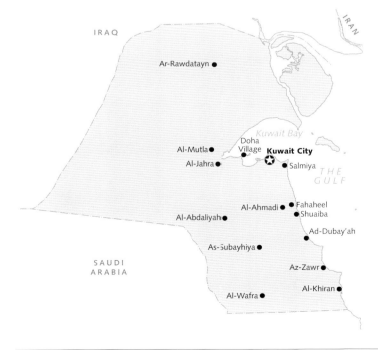

MAP REF I,24

1. A group of men gather at a cafe in Kuwait City
2. A traditional headdress transforms a Kuwaiti girl into a literal Goldilocks
3. Portraits of the sheikh arrive at Al Watan TV
4. A different drum: musicians perform in front of the strikingly modern Kuwait Towers

1.

2.

3.

A half-forgotten land of mountain valleys, glittering lakes and felt yurts, Kyrgyzstan is a dream for DIY adventurers, responsible tourists and closet nomads (visit immediately if you are all three). Left high and dry by the collapse of the USSR, tiny Kyrgyzstan turned to tourism, creating a cutting-edge network of community-based ecotourism ventures and homestays. A dozen adventures await the intrepid, from horse treks and yurt stays to eagle hunting and felt-making, safe in the knowledge that your tourist dollars are going straight to Kyrgyz families who need it most. Throw in some Silk Road bazaars, two spectacular mountain passes to China and an instinctive local hospitality and most travellers agree that Kyrgyzstan is Central Asia's don't-miss destination.

BEST TIME TO VISIT
June to September

TOP THINGS TO SEE
- Issyk-Köl, a huge inland sea fringed with beaches and framed by snowy peaks
- The pristine Alpine valleys of the Tian Shan range near Karakol village
- Tash Rabat, Central Asia's most evocative Silk Road caravanserai
- Kyrgyzstan's second city of Osh; an ancient Silk Road bazaar town on the edge of the Fergana Valley
- The blood-red sunset washing over Khan Tengri (7010m)

TOP THINGS TO DO
- Join your fellow nomads on a four-day horse trek to remote Song-Köl lake
- Cross the Irkeshtam or Torugart passes, Asia's most exciting border crossings
- Overnight in a yurt or community-tourism homestay to gain an insight into life after the USSR
- Learn how to make a *shyrdak* (felt carpet), easily the country's best souvenir
- Scare yourself heli-skiing in the Tian Shan mountains, just an hour from the capital Bishkek

GETTING UNDER THE SKIN
Read the Kyrgyz novel *Jamilla* by Chingiz Aitmatov, Central Asia's best known novelist

Listen to *Music of Central Asia Vol 1: Mountain Music of Kyrgyzstan*, (Smithsonian Folkways), a playlist of Kyrgyz music from traditional ensemble Tengir-Too.

Watch Aktan Abdykalykov's *Besh Kempir* (Five Old Women)

Eat *beshbarmak* ('five fingers'), a traditional dish of flat noodles and mutton, cooked in broth and eaten by hand

Drink *kumys* (fermented mare's milk), sold along country roads in spring and summer

IN A WORD
Ishter kanday (How are you?)

TRADEMARKS
Horses; eagle hunters; Tian Shan mountains; yurts; political demonstrations; bride-kidnapping; community-based tourism; Soviet-era apartment blocks

RANDOM FACT
The Kyrgyz oral epic, *Manas,* is the world's longest poem, 20 times longer than the *Odyssey,* and has been dubbed the 'Illiad of the steppe'

MAP REF I,27

1. Yurt sweet yurt: a man returns to his home in Naryn
2. Burana Tower, at the mouth of the Shamsy Valley, is one of Kyrgyzstan's architectural highlights
3. Horseback wrestling is a traditional nomadic sport in Kyrgyzstan
4. Women prepare *plov* (a rice and meat dish) in generous proportions

2.

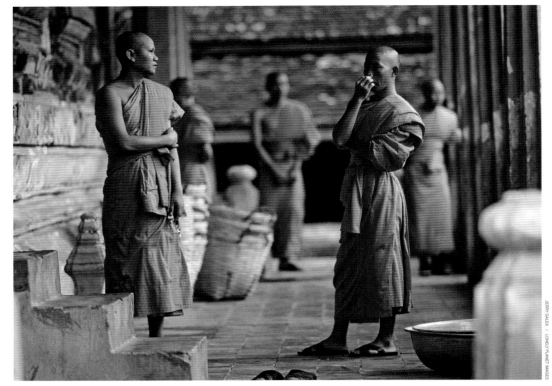

3.

1.

SARA-JANE CLELAND | LONELY PLANET IMAGES

4.

JERRY GALEA | LONELY PLANET IMAGES

Landlocked between Thailand, Myanmar, Vietnam, China and Cambodia, Laos is a sleepy Buddhist backwater whose friendly inhabitants and laid-back way of life are its biggest tourist attractions. Here, the currents of Asia swirl like the murky waters of the Mekong River – markets are piled high with durians, statues of Buddha look out over the paddy fields, and monks in saffron robes carry umbrellas to drive back the tropical sun and monsoon rain. Outside of the pocket-sized capital, Vientiane, travellers trek to tribal villages and drift along rivers in rubber rings, or spend lazy days sipping Lao Beer in the sleepy colonial city of Luang Prabang.

BEST TIME TO VISIT
November to February, to avoid the worst of the humidity

TOP THINGS TO SEE
- The angular, golden spires of the Pha That Luang stupa in Vientiane
- One monk's vision of heaven and hell in the sculpture garden at Xieng Khuan
- Irrawaddy dolphins splashing around the 4000 river islands at Si Phan Don
- Royal relics and ancient monasteries in World Heritage–listed Luang Prabang
- Dramatic limestone caverns at Vieng Xai and Vang Vieng

TOP THINGS TO DO
- Drop into a Lao *wat* (Buddhist temple-monastery) for a chat with the novices
- Drift along the Nam Song River on an old inner tube at Vang Vieng
- Trek to tribal villages in the Nam Ha National Protected Area
- Take a slow boat along the Mekong from Luang Prabang to Nong Khiaw
- Eat a Lao lunch of barbecued pork and sticky rice overlooking the Mekong River

GETTING UNDER THE SKIN
Read Brett Dakin's *Another Quiet American* or Dervla Murphy's *One Foot in Laos* for a personal take on the Lao PDR (People's Democratic Republic)

Listen to the undulating melodies of the *khэne* (the traditional reed pipe of the Lao tribes)

Watch *Good Morning, Luang Prabang*, the first ever privately funded Lao movie

Eat *laap* (spicy, marinated meat); or *tam maak hung* (green papaya salad)

Drink *lao-lao* (rice liquor); or Lao Beer, the nation's favourite brew

IN A WORD
Su kwan (The calling of the soul)

TRADEMARKS
Angular stupas; monks with umbrellas; monsoon rains and rice paddy fields; dragon boat races along the Mekong; rubber rings; unexploded ordnance (UXO)

RANDOM FACT
Laos has the unenviable status of being the most bombed nation in the world – there are estimated to be 270 million unexploded bombs in the country

MAP REF **L,31**

1. Women put their backs into their work in the rice fields of Sekong
2. A Buddha image is paraded through the streets of Luang Prabang
3. Young monks practise the art of waiting, Wat Si Saket temple, Vientiane
4. Inspired by Paris' Arc de Triomphe, Vientiane's Patuxai (Victory) Monument is unmistakably Lao

1.

2.

3.

If you've an appetite for Europe's lesser-known lights, a taste of Latvian life should stimulate the senses. Tucked between Estonia to the north and Lithuania to the south, Latvia is the meat of the Baltic sandwich, the savoury middle, loaded with colourful fillings. Thick greens take the form of Gauja Valley pine forests peppered with castle ruins. Onion-domed orthodox cathedrals cross the land from salty Liepāja to gritty Daugavpils. Cheesy Russian pop blares along the beach in Jūrmala. And spicy Rīga adds an extra zing as the country's cosmopolitan nexus, and unofficial capital of the entire Baltic region. Finish with a serve of Rīga's rich eye candy: Europe's largest and loveliest collection of art nouveau, and cobbled lanes hidden behind gingerbread trim.

BEST TIME TO VISIT
May to September

TOP THINGS TO SEE
° The view from the Skyline Bar, atop central Rīga's tallest building
° Enchantingly desolate and hauntingly beautiful Cape Kolka
° Rūndale Palace, Latvia's miniature version of Versailles (but without the crowds)
° Livonian castles and top-secret Soviet bunkers in the Gauja National Park

TOP THINGS TO DO
° Uncover emerald lakes and wispy blueberry fields in the Latgale Lakelands
° Bobsled down a 16-bend track at 80km/h in high-adrenaline Sigulda
° Hobnob with Russian jetsetters in the heart of Jūrmala's swanky spa scene
° Snack your way around the zeppelin hangars of Rīga's bounteous Central Market

GETTING UNDER THE SKIN
Read *The Merry Baker of Riga* by Boris Zemtzov, an amusing tale of an American entrepreneur setting up shop as a baker in Rīga in the early 1990s

Listen to Prāta Vētra (aka Brainstorm) for popular pop/rock; synth-heavy rock from the reborn Otra Puse, a band originally formed in the 1990s

Watch Jānis Streičs' *The Child of Man*, about a boy growing up and falling in love in Soviet-occupied Latvia; and *The Mystery of the Old Parish Church*, tackling the prickly issue of locals collaborating with Nazi and Soviet occupiers during WWII

Eat the almighty pig and ubiquitous potato; sausages; smoked fish; and freshly picked berries in summer, mushrooms in autumn

Drink Latvia's famous Black Balzām, a jet-black, 45 proof concoction that Goethe called 'the elixir of life'

IN A WORD
Labdien (Hello)

TRADEMARKS
Amber; art nouveau; Black Balzām; ballet dancer Mikhail Baryshnikov; artist Mark Rothko; song and dance festivals

RANDOM FACT
Held every five years, Latvia's Song and Dance Festival unites close to 40,000 participants in a jaw-dropping (and sweet-sounding) display of patriotism

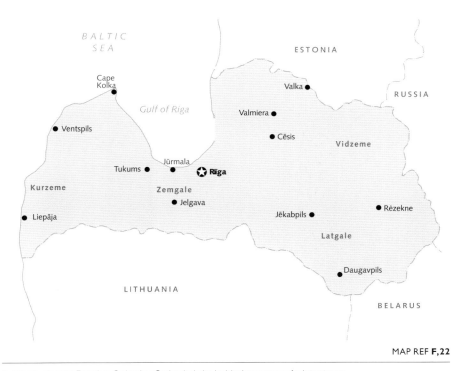

BALTIC SEA — ESTONIA — RUSSIA — Cape Kolka — Valka — *Gulf of Riga* — Valmiera — Ventspils — Cēsis — *Vidzeme* — Jūrmala — Tukums — ⚙ Rīga — *Kurzeme* — *Zemgale* — Jelgava — Jēkabpils — Rēzekne — Liepāja — *Latgale* — Daugavpils — LITHUANIA — BELARUS

MAP REF **F,22**

1. Rīga's elegant Russian Orthodox Cathedral sits behind a screen of winter trees
2. A Rīga tram plies the streets in old-world style
3. A blanket of snow lends a fairy-tale look to the Rīga cityscape
4. A local pushes past a faded beauty in Kuldīga

2.

BETHUNE CARMICHAEL | LONELY PLANET IMAGES

3.

TIM BARKER | LONELY PLANET IMAGES

1.

Lebanon is one of the most vibrant and most complicated societies on earth, grafted onto one of the Middle East's most beautiful regions. Its mosaic of peoples has coexisted here for centuries, often at war, more often at peace. Lebanon is Hezbollah and the Roman ruins of Baalbek in close proximity. It is 1500-year-old cedar trees and one of the oldest cities on earth not far from hedonistic nightclubs. It is some of the Mediterranean's best food. It all collides in Beirut, the sophisticated one-time 'Paris of the Middle East' and a true Middle Eastern melting pot, never more so than along Beirut's corniche at sunset when miniskirt-clad rollerbladers jostle for space with turban-clad mullahs and their families.

BEST TIME TO VISIT
Year-round – summer for beaches, winter for skiing and spring or autumn for hiking

TOP THINGS TO SEE
- Baalbek, possibly the best preserved, temple-studded Roman ruins in the Middle East
- One of the Middle East's most cosmopolitan cities, Beirut
- Byblos, a gorgeous fishing port and one of the oldest continuously inhabited settlements on earth
- Qadisha Valley, the Unesco World Heritage–listed site with rock-hewn monasteries and the remains of Khalil Gibran
- Stunning Mamluk architecture and a fascinating souq in Tripoli

TOP THINGS TO DO
- Wander through Aanjar, a wonderfully intact, 1300-year-old Umayyad city
- Trek 6km through the extraordinary stalactites and stalagmites of Jeita Grotto
- Ski at the Cedars, an upcountry resort and home to the last of the ancient cedar trees that adorn Lebanon's flag
- Hike through the Chouf Mountains, arguably Lebanon's most spectacular scenery
- Wander through the ruins of Tyre, crossroads of Roman and Phoenician history

GETTING UNDER THE SKIN
Read Robert Fisk's *Pity the Nation*, the best account of Lebanon's civil war; or Amin Maalouf's novel *The Rock of Tanios*

Listen to Fairuz, an enduring icon of Middle Eastern music

Watch *West Beirut*, a classic tale of civil war by Ziad Duweyri; or *Caramel* by Nadine Labaki, the story of five Lebanese women

Eat *mezze* (small dishes served as starters); *kibbeh* (spiced minced lamb in a fried bulgur-wheat shell)

Drink Lebanese wines; arak mixed with water and ice; Almaza (the local beer)

IN A WORD
Ahlan wa sahlan (Welcome)

TRADEMARKS
Destination for the Middle East's jetset; Roman ruins; sectarian melting pot

RANDOM FACT
Although little remains, the southern Lebanese coast around Tyre and Sidon is where the ancient Phoenician Empire was born

MAP REF **J,23**

1. Men gather to keep cafe culture alive and well in Beirut
2. Humble Tripoli balconies are cast in a glorious golden hue
3. A woman shows her strength near the Riviera Beach Club, Beirut
4. A food vendor seeks out customers on Beirut's Corniche, bedecked in bread

1.

2.

3.

In tiny Lesotho – the 'Kingdom in the Sky' – the thin urban veneer of Maseru, the capital, quickly gives way to traditional Basotho culture and customs. Herdboys tend their sheep on steep hillsides, horsemen wrapped in *kobo* (Basotho blankets) ride their sure-footed ponies over high mountain passes and village festivals are a focal point of local life. South Africa is just a mountain pass or two away, but Lesotho's towering peaks and isolated valleys, and the pride of the Basotho in their identity, have served to insulate Lesotho's culture from that of its larger neighbour. For anyone seeking adventure, wilderness, a laid-back pace and the chance to get acquainted with people living traditional lifestyles, Lesotho is a magical destination.

BEST TIME TO VISIT
May to October, to avoid the rains and m st

TOP THINGS TO SEE
- The rolling grasslands and wildflowers n Sehlabathebe National Park
- Vistas from the top of Thaba-Bosiu (Mountain at Night) – the old stronghold of King Moshoeshoe the Great and the birthplace of the Basotho nation
- Tapestry makers at work in Teyateyaneng – 'Place of Quick Sands' and craft centre of Lesotho
- Lovely mountain panoramas around the Moteng Pass and Oxbow
- San rock paintings around Malealea and the aptly named Gates of Paradise Pass

TOP THINGS TO DO
- Ride Basotho ponies through Lesotho's rugged interior
- Make your way up Sani Pass and take in the views from Sani Top
- Shop for Basotho blankets, hats, mats and other crafts in Maseru or Teyateyaneng
- Hike in wild and beautiful Ts'ehlanyane National Park or Bokong Nature Reserve
- Hunt for fossilised dinosaur footprints around Quthing

GETTING UNDER THE SKIN
Read *Basali! Stories by and about Women in Lesotho* edited by K Limakatso Kendall, or *Singing Away the Hunger* by Mpho 'M'atsepo Nthunya for insights into the lives of women in Lesotho

Listen to the *lekolulo*, a flute-like instrumer t played by herd boys

Watch the artists at the Morija Arts & Cultural Festival

Eat *papa* (maize meal) and *moroho* (greens)

Drink *joala* (traditional sorghum beer) – a white flag flying in a village means that it's available

IN A WORD
Khotso (Peace)

TRADEMARKS
Basotho ponies; snow-dusted mountains; Basotho hats and blankets; highest lowest point of any country in the world (1400m); the world's only country entirely above 1000m

RANDOM FACT
The Basotho are traditionally buried in a sitting position, facing the rising sun and ready to leap up when called

SOUTH AFRICA

Oxbow
Jonathane
Peka
Pitseng
Mothae
Teyateyaneng
Sefikeng
Seshote
Motsitseng
Maseru
Mokhotlong
Mazenod
Marakabei
Motsekuoa
Malealea
Semonkong
Matebeng
Sekake
Mpiti
Mekaling
SOUTH AFRICA
Ralebona

MAP REF **R,23**

1. From undulating hills, the Maletsunyane Falls spill spectacularly into the gorge below
2. A Basotho shepherd shows off his charge
3. Colour-coordinated right down to the cat: a friendly welcome is given in Matsieng village
4. A steady gaze from a Sotho man

1.

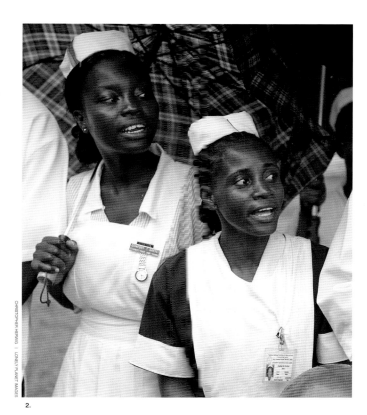

Long regarded as a byword for child soldiers and one of Africa's most brutal civil wars, Liberia is emerging from the ashes. This is a country slowly getting back on its feet, but one thing hasn't changed: Liberia is blessed with extraordinary natural beauty, its coastline lined with splendid beaches and its interior awash in barely penetrable rainforest. Founded by freed slaves from America in the 19th century and inhabited for far longer by traditional groups famous for their artistic traditions and secret societies, Liberia's complicated cultural mix hasn't always worked. And travelling in Liberia is rarely easy, thanks to its devastated infrastructure. But with peace starting to take root, it is slowly becoming one of West Africa's most fascinating countries.

BEST TIME TO VISIT
November to April (the dry season)

TOP THINGS TO SEE
- The newly optimistic village-turned-city, Monrovia, with the ruins of war and the frenetic activity of peace
- The much-damaged, but somehow-surviving Sapo National Park, with forest elephants, pygmy hippos and chimps
- Buchanan, the vibrant yet tranquil port city and home to the Fanti people
- Harper, with its charming small-town feel and a fascinating history close to Côte d'Ivoire
- Firestone Plantation, where you can learn about rubber-tapping, one of Liberia's few industries

TOP THINGS TO DO
- Join local families on the beaches southeast of the capital
- Enjoy the novelty of surfing the perfect breaks of Robertsport
- Picnic at the pretty semicrater lake of Bomi, near Tubmanburg
- Enjoy the scenery around Yekepa and climb Goodhouse Hill, Liberia's highest point
- Dive into the clamour of Monrovia's Waterside Market

GETTING UNDER THE SKIN
Read Graham Greene's *Journey Without Maps*, his 1930s trek through Liberia and Sierra Leone; for something more recent, try *The Mask of Anarchy*

Listen to *We Want Peace* by Gebah and Maudeline (The Swa-Ray Band)

Watch *Johnny Mad Dog*, a 2008 Franco-Belgo-Liberian co-production filmed in Liberia and starring former child combatants

Eat goat soup and traditional rice bread made with mashed bananas

Drink ginger beer; *poyo* (palm wine); and strong coffee

IN A WORD
Peace, man

TRADEMARKS
Diamond smugglers; rubber plantations; one of the wettest and most humid places on earth

RANDOM FACT
In 2005, former World Bank economist Ellen Johnson-Sirleaf defeated international soccer star George Weah to become Africa's first woman president

MAP REF **N,19**

1. Dressed in the manner of his forebears, this young man proudly carries on the tradition
2. Medical students enjoy watching the ceremony on Liberia's Independence Day
3. Young Liberian women are daubed in ritual white and dressed to celebrate their coming of age
4. A street vendor offers an enticing jumble of bean cakes to passers-by

1.

2.

3.

For decades hidden behind the eccentricities of its leader and international pariah status, Libya has made a stunning return to the fold: Libya is once again open for business and for tourism, although visas remain a bureaucratic nightmare. The country that has emerged has a stunning coastline studded with ruined Roman and Greek cities, poignant WWII sites, lively cities and long stretches of deserted coastline, while the interior boasts some of the most beautiful stretches of the Sahara Desert. Best of all, and unlike Egypt, Tunisia or Morocco, Libya has yet to sell its soul to the god of mass tourism. In short, this is North Africa as it used to be.

BEST TIME TO VISIT
October to March, for cooler temperatures

TOP THINGS TO SEE
° The pretty Roman city of Leptis Magna strung out along the Mediterranean
° Cyrene, the sophistication of Ancient Greece and Rome grafted onto African soil
° Ghadames, the Sahara's most captivating oasis and caravan town
° Cosmopolitan capital city, Tripoli, with a wonderfully preserved Ottoman-era medina and world-class museum
° Jebel Acacus, the haunting desert massif in the Sahara's heart with 12,000-year-old rock art

TOP THINGS TO DO
° Swim in the Mediterranean alongside the ruined Roman city of Sabratha
° Float in the salty waters of the Sahara's Ubari Lakes, surrounded by towering sand dunes
° Descend into the volcanic, black-sand crater of Waw al-Namus in one of the Sahara's remotest corners
° Tread softly through the forest of crosses in the WWII cemeteries of Tobruk
° Discover the sand dunes of your dreams in the vast sand sea of Idehan Murzuq

GETTING UNDER THE SKIN
Read *In the Country of Men* by Hisham Matar, a searing novel about modern Libya

Listen to *malouf*, a traditional musical form from Andalucía and the accompaniment to most celebrations

Watch *Lion of the Desert* by Libyan filmmaker Moustapha Akkad, about the legendary Omar al-Mokhtar's guerrilla war against Italian colonial forces

Eat at Tripoli's fish market, where you choose the freshest fish and seafood that is cooked for you at a neighbouring restaurant

Drink three glasses of strong, sweet tea with the Tuareg around a campfire in the Sahara

IN A WORD
Bari kelorfik (Thank you – a blessing)

TRADEMARKS
Colonel Gaddafi; Unesco World Heritage–listed ancient cities and rock art; vast seas of sand; lakes in the heart of the desert

RANDOM FACT
The Sahara covers 95% of Libyan territory and it was here, in 1922, that the highest temperature (57.8°C) on earth was recorded

FRANS LEMMENS | LONELY PLANET IMAGES

FRANS LEMMENS | LONELY PLANET IMAGES

MAP REF **K,21**

1. Shifting sands: waves of dunes undulate across the Unesco World Heritage–listed Jebel Acacus
2. A narrow path twists past a web of tiny rooms, built as a grain storehouse, in the old town of Nalut
3. Knowing eyes: this face among the Roman ruins at Leptis Magna has seen thousands of years of history pass before it
4. A guard reads the Quran, surrounded by the ornate carpets and frescoes of the Gurgi Mosque

4.

With a history and monarchy as storybook as its melodious mountain scenery speckled with tiled-roof stone castles and wintery snow scenes, rich old Liechtenstein puts a whole new perspective on the European tour guide's 'doing a country'. Indeed, this tiny wealthy nation landlocked between Alpine greats Austria and Switzerland can be 'done' in a day...or three at most. And what a sweet, toy-like experience it is. Its capital city, crowned with the king's castle and his vineyards, is of miniature proportion; mountains envelop two-thirds of the country, and a 25km stroll takes you from Liechtenstein's northern to southern tip. Arriving from Switzerland, pinch yourself: the Swiss franc is the currency that talks and German is the language on the streets.

BEST TIME TO VISIT
December to March for winter sports; May to late September for summer hikes

TOP THINGS TO SEE
○ Schloss Vaduz, the castle on a hill where the king lives – beautiful vistas
○ Postage stamps issued in the principality since 1912 at the Post Museum in Vaduz
○ The snowy slopes of Malbun where British royal Prince Charles learnt to ski
○ Austria, Switzerland and most of little Liechtenstein from the lofty crests of Malbun's circular Fürstin-Gina hiking trail

TOP THINGS TO DO
○ Toast His Majesty on 15 August – the only day when he opens the grounds of his castle in Vaduz for all and sundry to visit (and watch a magnificent firework display)
○ Lunch amid royal vines at Torkel, the ivy-clad royal restaurant in the capital
○ Enjoy a concert in style at Balzers's fairytale 13th-century castle, Burg Gutenberg
○ Hike the Fürstensteig, a rite of passage for every Liechtensteiner
○ Skate along the Väluna Valley on cross-country skis

GETTING UNDER THE SKIN
Read David Beattie's *Liechtenstein: A Modern History* for the complete story on how this tiny country almost got wiped off the world map

Listen to Vaduz-born classical composer Joseph Gabriel Rheinberger (1831–1901)

Watch movies beneath the stars during July's atmospheric Vaduz film festival

Eat traditional local dishes like savoury *Käsknöpfle* (tiny cheese-flavoured flour dumplings) and sweet *ribel* (a semolina dish served with sugar and fruit compote or jam)

Drink local, rarely exported, wine

IN A WORD
Guten Tag (Hello, good day)

TRADEMARKS
Quality living; downhill skiing; fairy-tale castles; story-book panoramas; Prince Hans-Adam II and Crown Prince Alois; constitutional monarchy; tax haven; exporter of false teeth and sausage skins

RANDOM FACT
Liechtenstein is the only county in the world named after the people who purchased it

MAP REF **H,21**

1. During winter the purest white snowdrifts blanket the mountains of Liechtenstein

1.

2.

3.

Mother Nature has sprinkled a decent dose of fairy dust over enigmatic Lithuania, but you'll find that humans have left their stamp too, in undeniably weird and wonderful ways. White sandy beaches edge the Curonian Spit, an enchanting pig-tail of land dangling off the country's western rump, and deep magical forests guard twinkling lakes. The capital, Vilnius, is a beguiling artists' enclave, with mysterious courtyards, worn cobbled streets and crumbling corners overshadowed by baroque beauty beyond belief. The country's oddities – among them a hill covered in crosses and a sculpture park littered with Lenins – add a flavour found nowhere else. Add a colourful history, and raw pagan roots fused with Catholic fervour, and you've got a country full of surprises.

BEST TIME TO VISIT
May to September

TOP THINGS TO SEE
- Vilnius, the baroque bombshell of the Baltics
- Thousands of crosses – some tiny, others gigantic – at the Hill of Crosses
- The slither of shifting sands that constitutes the remarkable Curonian Spit
- The red-brick gothic castle of Trakai, in a fairy-tale lakeside locale
- A former secret Soviet underground missile base that once housed nuclear missiles with enough power to destroy most of Europe

TOP THINGS TO DO
- Take a hot-air balloon flight across the rooftops and church spires of Vilnius
- Go fishing, boating, bathing and berry-collecting in the country's beloved Lakeland
- Brave the winter and go ice fishing on the Curonian Spit
- Ponder the past at Grūtas Park, dubbed Stalin World

GETTING UNDER THE SKIN
Read *The Last Girl* by Stephan Collishaw bringing Vilnius to life in a brilliant historical novel covering WWII to the 1990s

Listen to avant-garde jazz from the Ganelin Trio; rock from Andrius Mamontovas, a household name in Lithuania for more than two decades; Skamp, for hip hop and R&B

Watch *Dievų miškas* (Forest of the Gods), about a man imprisoned by both the Nazis and the Soviets

Eat the formidable national dish of *cepelinai* (zeppelins), airship-shaped parcels of potato dough stuffed with cheese, meat and mushrooms, topped with a creamy sauce

Drink *midus* (mead; honey boiled with water, berries and spices, then fermented with hops); *stakliskes* (a honey liqueur)

IN A WORD
Labas (Hello)

TRADEMARKS
Baroque architecture; Catholicism; *cepelinai*; folk festivals; Stalin World

RANDOM FACT
Basketball is akin to religion in Lithuania – the worshipped national team has finished in the top four at the Olympic Games since 1992

LATVIA

Palanga
Plungė
Šiauliai
Klaipėda
Nida
Panevėžys
Tauragė
Ignalina
Ukmergė
Molėtai
Jurbarkas
Ěvenčionys
RUSSIA
(Kaliningrad
Region)
Kaunas
Marijampolė
Trakai
✪ Vilnius
Alytus
BELARUS
POLAND
Druskininkai

Baltic
Sea

Curonian
Lagoon

MAP REF **G,22**

1. A footbridge arcs over the frozen lake towards the famous 14th-century island castle in Trakai
2. Rhapsody in blue: the lovely colour of this orthodox church in Druskininkai echoes the endless blue of the skies above
3. The Hill of Crosses was built, cross by cross, as a symbol of defiance against invaders
4. The traditional dress donned by these Lithuanian girls lends an old-world charm

1.

Luxembourg is one of those wonderful little European countries that can easily be undressed from head to toe in a week – many a traveller's dream. Its capital city – a fortress spectacularly built on a promontory with an eagle-eye view of the deep valleys it so slavishly protected for centuries – easily competes for title of 'Europe's most dramatically picturesque'. Indeed, there is no fast-paced urban frenzy in small affluent Luxembourg City or, for that matter, elsewhere in this essentially rural country knitted from thick forest, fairy-tale feudal castle and enchanting vineyard. Proud and independent define those who live here, and the royal family, headed by Grand Duke Henri and his Cuban-born queen, are as down-to-earth as you can get. How refreshingly quaint!

BEST TIME TO VISIT
May to August, the sunniest months

TOP THINGS TO SEE
- Modern art in a building designed by IM Pei of Paris Louvre fame at Luxembourg City's Musée d'Art Moderne Grand-Duc Jean
- The panorama along the capital's stone walkway Chemin de la Corniche
- Primeval rock formations in the Müllerthal region
- Echternach, a town steeped in Christian history and ensnared by forest
- Château de Bourscheid, a castle straight out of a fairy tale

TOP THINGS TO DO
- Delve into the honeycomb innards of Luxembourg City's fortress casements dating back to 1744
- Stroll the capital's Old Town – lunch alfresco on tree-lined Place d'Armes
- Mosey from one winery to another along the Route du Vin in the Moselle Valley
- Play 'king of the castle' in Vianden
- Visit the Unesco World Heritage–listed exhibition by Luxembourg photographer Edward Steichen (1879–1973) inside a castle in Clervaux

GETTING UNDER THE SKIN
Read *How to Remain What You Are,* a humorous look at Luxembourg ways by writer and psychologist George Müller
Listen to the Luxembourg Philharmonic Orchestra
Watch *Lèif Lëtzebuerger* (Charlotte: A Royal at War) to catch Luxembourg's WWII history through the eyes of exiled grand duchess Charlotte
Eat the national dish, *judd mat gaardebounen* (smoked pork in a creamy sauce with broad beans and potato chunks)
Drink a bubbly or fruity white Moselle wine bearing the quality label *'Marque Nationale du Vin Luxembourgeois'*

IN A WORD
Moien (Hello! in Letzeburgesch)

TRADEMARKS
Banking; fairy-tale castles; good-value alcohol, tobacco, perfume; beautiful china

RANDOM FACT
In 1919, with monarchies collapsing around them, the Grand Duchy put its royal family up for referendum. The result was 'yes' and never again has their existence been questioned

MAP REF **H,20**

1. Fairytale kingdom: magical terraces and improbably perched houses lend the area around the Bockfelsen cliffs an ethereal, dreamlike quality

1.

2.

3.

The last outpost of the Portuguese empire, Macau only became part of China in 1999, two years after the British withdrawal from Hong Kong. Even today, the city state at the mouth of the Pearl River has a tangible Mediterranean feel, with baroque basilicas, cobblestone lanes, colonial mansions and grand civic squares. Nevertheless, Chinese culture shines through in the form of caged songbirds, clicking chopsticks, Buddhist statues, incense-filled joss-houses and signs illuminated with neon *hanzi* characters. For tourists from the mainland, the main attraction is the chance to gamble in Macau's glittering casinos; international visitors come for the Portuguese relics, the shopping and the beaches of Coloane, the former island at the tip of the Macau peninsula.

BEST TIME TO VISIT
October to December, to avoid the muggy summer weather

TOP THINGS TO SEE
° The floating facade of the vanished Church of St Paul
° Winding lanes and grand colonial mansions on Ilha de Coloane
° Incense smoke drifting around the A-Ma Temple
° Swirls of black and yellow sand at Hac Sa Beach
° Giant statues of Matsu, Goddess of the Sea, and Kun Iam, Goddess of Mercy

TOP THINGS TO DO
° Admire the views from the top of the Macau Tower – or, if you feel brave, bungee-jump off the top
° Feast on Portuguese delicacies like *ca'do verde* (potato and greens in soup) and *bacalhau* (salt cod) in Taipa village
° Enjoy the roar of engines at the Macau Grand Prix
° Try to spot Hong Kong's Lantau Island from the top of Guia Fort
° Win or lose a few hundred pataca (the Macau currency) at the Venetian-Macao casino

GETTING UNDER THE SKIN
Read Austin Coates' *City of Broken Promises*, a fictionalised account of the life of Martha Merop, Macau's most famous *taipan* (trader)

Listen to the captivating melodies of Cantonese opera, performed at religious and cultural festivals throughout the year

Watch Cai Yuan-yuan's *The Bewitching Braid*, the first ever Macanese feature film

Eat *galinha à Portuguesa* ('Portuguese chicken' cooked in a coconut sauce)

Drink Portuguese *vinho verde* wine; or locally brewed Macau Beer.

IN A WORD
Dó bōk (To gamble)

TRADEMARKS
Casinos; Chinese gamblers; Portuguese churches; boisterous carnivals; fusion cuisine; milk pudding; great shopping

RANDOM FACT
With more than half a million people crammed into 28.2 sq km, Macau is the most densely populated place on earth

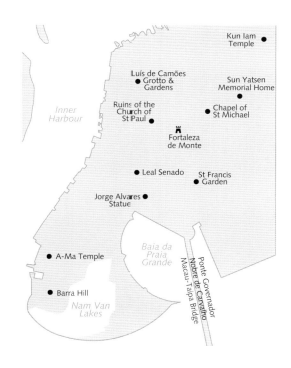

Kun Iam Temple
Luís de Camões Grotto & Gardens
Sun Yatsen Memorial Home
Inner Harbour
Ruins of the Church of St Paul
Chapel of St Michael
Fortaleza de Monte
Leal Senado
St Francis Garden
Jorge Alvares Statue
Baía da Praia Grande
A-Ma Temple
Ponte Governador Nobre de Carvalho Macau-Taipa Bridge
Barra Hill
Nam Van Lakes

MAP REF **L,32**

1. Space age: the spangled dome of Grand Lisboa Casino pulses light into the darkness
2. An artisan expertly crafts pillowy mounds of fresh noodles
3. Worshippers gather outside A-Ma Temple
4. A family sits down to tables beautifully laden with the night's feast

1.

The French call fruit salad *macédoine*, and this harmonious melange of distinctive flavours provides a neat analogy for modern Macedonia. With a staunchly Slavic Orthodox majority and a plethora of graceful monasteries and Byzantine-style churches, Macedonia also accommodates an Albanian minority and smaller communities of Turks, Jews, Vlachs and Roma. Harmony prevails and the small, land-locked republic boasts a diversity that belies its size. Chilly winters see fir-capped mountains wreathed in snow, while spring brings forth meadows full of flame-red poppies, and through summer friends gather outdoors to nibble sunflower seeds and chat through the sultry nights. Dusty Skopje is the national hub, but in the countryside, among slate-roofed villages, road-side cafes, lake panoramas and watermelon stalls, you find the soul of Macedonia.

BEST TIME TO VISIT
April to September

TOP THINGS TO SEE
- Graceful domes and views of Lake Ohrid at diminutive 13th-century Church of Sveti Jovan at Kaneo
- The 'Republic of Vevčani', a hamlet inhabited by notably independent villagers who have created their own flag, passports and currency
- Undulating hillsides and placid lakes in the Tikveš wine region
- Vivid frescoes alongside Roman remains and tombs at Treskavec Monastery
- The sublime Albanian floral motifs of the Painted Mosque at Tetovo, and the nearby Arbati Baba Tekke dervish lodge

TOP THINGS TO DO
- Haggle for traditional crafts, carpets and dolls in Skopje's Čaršija quarter
- Kneel down to hear Sveti Naum's heartbeat at his tomb in his monastery
- Charter a water-taxi row boat for a languid tour of Ohrid town's waterfront
- Hike into Mt Pelister National Park, passing through the Vlach village of Malovište

GETTING UNDER THE SKIN
Read *Black Lamb and Grey Falcon*, Rebecca West's Balkan travel masterpiece; or *Hidden Macedonia*, a travelogue by Christopher Deliso

Listen to Tanec, an ensemble of folkloric musicians and dancers

Watch *Before the Rain,* a cycle of three linked stories directed by Milco Mancevski

Eat *skara* (grilled meat), the national favourite, accompanied by *nafora* (crusty bread sprinkled with white cheese and baked) and *ajvar* (red-pepper relish)

Drink *rakija* (grape brandy) or hearty red wines from the Kavardaci region

IN A WORD
Haydemo (Let's go)

TRADEMARKS
Lake Ohrid; untouched countryside; Skopje bazaar; orthodox monasteries; Roman ruins; the endangered Ohrid trout; naming controversy

RANDOM FACT
In 2008, 200,000 Macedonians (10% of the entire population) planted two million trees in the first Macedonian Tree Day, which has since become a regular event

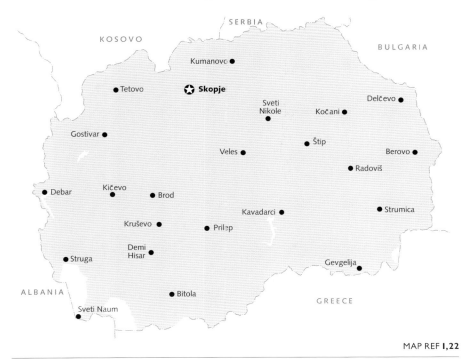

MAP REF **1,22**

1. A young girl gazes from a window, surrounded by the ornate painted patterns of the Alaca Mosque
2. In Skopje, a shoemaker concentrates on the task at hand
3. An exercise in devotion: a new church is constructed in Ohrid
4. There's room for two in this little horse-drawn cart

1.

2.

3.

ANDERS BLOMQVIST | LONELY PLANET IMAGES

ANDERS BLOMQVIST | LONELY PLANET IMAGES

MADAGASCAR

CAPITAL Antananarivo | **POPULATION** 20,653,556 | **AREA** 587,041 sq km | **OFFICIAL LANGUAGES** Malagasy, French & English

Who says science isn't fun? The great Madagascar experiment began some 165 million years ago when it was ripped from Africa and sent floating off into the newly formed Indian Ocean. Isolated, the island's plants and animals evolved, creating thousands of dumbfounding species that Madagascar could call its very own. The remaining forests still teem with this outlandish life, and encounters with it can't help but make you giggle with delight. The Malagasy, who are relatively recent arrivals, are equally captivating. Although fiercely patriotic, they believe family is central to life, and their startling exhumation ceremonies prove the dead are just as important to them as the living. Pure fantasy? No. Unforgettable? Yes.

BEST TIME TO VISIT
April to October (the dry season)

TOP THINGS TO SEE
○ *Tsingy,* surreal limestone pinnacles that would make Antoni Gaudí proud
○ Remote Madagascar from a pirogue floating down the Tsiribihina River
○ Avenue du Baobab, a road lined by giants
○ Famadihana, or 'turning of the bones', a sacred ceremony of exhumation
○ Malagasy life in fast forward, the colourful streets of Antananarivo are full of it

TOP THINGS TO DO
○ Try not to get caught up in it all while walking through the remarkable 'spiny forest' in Parc National d'Andohahela
○ Trek deep into the lush cloud forests of Parc National de Ranomafana to swap looks with lemurs
○ Step into an envy-evoking postcard at Andilana's beach on Nosy Be
○ Experience the geological, biological and spiritual wonders of Parc National de l'Isalo
○ Find your own personal treasure when diving the reef off Nosy Ve, a former haunt of Malagasy pirates

GETTING UNDER THE SKIN
Read *A History of Madagascar* by Mervyn Brown, an eminently readable, authoritative description of the island's history

Listen to *hira gasy*, live storytelling spectacles in Madagascar's central highlands

Watch Raymond Rajaonarivelo's *Quand les Étoiles Rencontrent la Mer* (When the Stars Meet the Sea), the story of a boy born during a solar eclipse; Rajaonarivelo's *Tabataba*, a film about the bloody rebellion against the French in 1947

Eat *vary hen'omby* (rice served with stewed or boiled zebu)

Drink *rano vola* (rice water), a brown, smoky-tasting concoction – it's an acquired taste!

IN A WORD
Manao ahoana ianao (How do you do?)

TRADEMARKS
Lemurs; *tsingy;* chameleons; Avenue du Baobab; zebu-drawn carts; aggressive forestry

RANDOM FACT
Rice is so significant in Malagasy culture that words used to explain the growth of it are the same as those used to describe a woman becoming pregnant and giving birth

Comoros
Mayotte
Antsiranana (Diego Suarez)
Sambava
Mahajanga (Majunga)
Mozambique Channel
Toamasina (Tamatave)
Antananarivo ✪
Morondava
INDIAN OCEAN
Morombe
Fianarantsoa
Toliara (Tuléar)
Vangaindrano
Manambondro
Androka
Taolagnaro (Fort Dauphin)

MAP REF **Q,24**

1. The Avenue du Baobab is lined with these spectacular and strange trees
2. As with so much of Madagascar's extraordinary wildlife, sifakas aren't found anywhere else in the world
3. Women from a religious community wend their way through the Soatanana village, expertly carrying cargo on their heads
4. Time for tea: train passengers purchase snacks at a stop in Fianarantsoa

4.

2.

3.

1.

Malawi is dominated by its lake – alternately known as Lake Malawi, Lake Nyasa or 'Lake of Stars' – and by its reputation for friendly people and easy travel. But, step away from the stereotypes and you'll find much more. The country has beautiful and diverse landscapes, ranging from dramatic peaks to rolling grasslands, from hills and waterfalls to a tropical shoreline. Its national parks are home to zebras, impalas, crocodiles, hippos and birds galore. Traditional culture thrives in villages and on the islands in Lake Malawi. Stay for a week or three, relax on the lake, hike in the hills, explore the Nyika Plateau, and – best of all – get to know Malawians. Before long, you'll be hooked.

BEST TIME TO VISIT
April/May to September

TOP THINGS TO SEE
- A wealth of birds in the swamplands of Elephant Marsh, an ornithologist's paradise
- Hundreds of colourful cichlids in the clear waters of Lake Malawi
- The beaches, the cathedral, the baobabs and the mango trees on lovely Likoma Island
- Elephants, impalas and buffaloes at Vwaza Marsh Wildlife Reserve
- A performance of *gule wamkulu* or other traditional dances

TOP THINGS TO DO
- Hike or ride a horse past zebras and antelopes in magnificent Nyika National Park
- Scale majestic Mt Mulanje
- Meander down Lake Malawi on the *Ilala* ferry, Malawi's grande dame of river vessels
- Paddle a dugout canoe along the Lake Malawi shoreline, listening to the calls of fish eagles circling above
- Spot hippos and crocs in the Shire River in Liwonde National Park

GETTING UNDER THE SKIN
Read *The Rainmaker,* a poetic drama by Steve Chimombo; or Legson Kayira's *The Looming Shadow*, an exploration of conflicts between traditional and modern beliefs

Listen to Lucius Banda's 'Malawian-style' reggae

Watch *Up in Smoke*, a documentary exploring the effects of the tobacco industry in Malawi

Eat *nsima* (maize meal) and *chambo* (a fish from Lake Malawi)

Drink *chibuku* (shake-shake beer), a commercially produced local brew

IN A WORD
Zikomo (Thank you)

TRADEMARKS
Lake Malawi; carved wooden chief's chair; laid-back beach resorts; friendly locals; tobacco; *Ilala* ferry; wildlife

RANDOM FACT
Malawi is home to over 600 species of bird. There are more fish species (500-plus) in Lake Malawi than in any other inland body of water in the world

MAP REF **P,23**

1. Dugout canoes provide an essential means of transport and livelihood for those living along the shores of Lake Malawi
2. A friendly smile from a young Malawian epitomises her people's hospitality
3. A small, eager crowd forms around a street vendor preparing tasty morsels for sale
4. Elephant transport: a bird hitches a big, bumpy ride across the Shire River in Liwonde National Park

1.

2.

3.

CAPITAL Kuala Lumpur | POPULATION 25,715,819 | AREA 329,847 sq km | OFFICIAL LANGUAGE Bahasa Malaysia

Malaysia offers two countries for the price of one – Peninsular Malaysia, with its sprawling cities, forested highlands and fringing islands, and East Malaysia, the northern half of the island of Borneo, whose dense rainforests provide a haven for orangutans and indigenous tribes. 'Unity in diversity' is the national motto of this famous melting pot, a heady blend of Malay, Indian and Chinese culture, with a garnish of animist traditions, courtesy of the Orang Asli – literally 'original people' – of Sabah and Sarawak. A steamy colonial air hangs over the mainland cities of Georgetown (Penang), Melaka and Kuala Lumpur, while Malaysian Borneo is a playground for divers, trekkers and modern-day explorers.

BEST TIME TO VISIT
May to September, for the best chance of clear skies

TOP THINGS TO SEE
- Kuala Lumpur from the walkway between the Petronas Towers
- Tea plantations sprawling across the Cameron Highlands
- The dawn view from the summit of Mt Kinabalu, Southeast Asia's highest mountain
- Colonial grandeur and dragon-tiled temples in Georgetown (Penang)
- Surreal acts of self-mortification during the festival of Thaipusam

TOP THINGS TO DO
- Stay in an Iban longhouse on Borneo's mighty Batang Rejang river
- Dive with sharks and turtles on the awesome reefs of Sipadan
- Enjoy the full tropical island experience at Pulau Perhentian or Pulau Langkawi
- Get up close and personal with the 'old man of the forest' at Sepilok Orangutan Rehabilitation Centre
- Munch on *nasi lemak* (coconut rice steamed in banana leaves) in a traditional Melaka coffeeshop

GETTING UNDER THE SKIN
Read Tash Aw's *The Harmony Silk Factory* or Rani Manicka's *The Rice Mother* for two different takes on Malaysian multiculturalism

Listen to *dondang sayang* (Chinese-influenced love ballads); or the wholesome Malay pop of Siti Nurhaliza and Mawi

Watch Yasmin Ahmad's award-winning *Sepet*, which challenges taboos about cross-cultural relationships in Malaysia

Eat *roti canai (*fried, flat bread with a rich curry dipping sauce) at one of Malaysia's 24-hour *mamak* (Tamil Muslim) canteens

Drink *teh tarik* ('pulled' tea with condensed milk); or *tuak* (rice wine from Borneo)

IN A WORD
Malaysia boleh! (Malaysia can do it!)

TRADEMARKS
The Petronas Towers; orangutans; dense jungles; logging; Michelle Yeoh; tribal longhouses; colonial relics; hawker food; the Malaysian F1 Grand Prix

RANDOM FACT
Malaysia is home to the largest flower in the world, the foul-smelling *Rafflesia*, which can grow to more than a metre in diameter

MAP REF **N,31**

1. This horse and its little rider, a Sabah 'cowboy', have a good grasp on pomp and ceremony
2. A sadhu (holy man) at the Sri Mariamman Temple in Penang maintains the Hindu religion and heritage in Malaysia
3. Follow the leader: proboscis monkeys find a path through the mangrove roots in Bako National Park
4. At night the Petronas Towers form a shining landmark that can be seen throughout Kuala Lumpur

2.

3.

1.

MALDIVES

Floating just above the surface of the Indian Ocean, the islands of the Maldives are a glamorous playground for sun-seekers and explorers of the undersea world. Pinpricks in a sea of blue, these tiny coral atolls are home to some of the most exclusive resorts on earth, each set on its own private paradise island. The postcard perfection of the islands is matched only by the staggering richness of the coral reefs that lie between the atolls, attracting divers from across the globe. Away from the surf and sand, the Maldives is notable for its intriguing Islamic culture, shaped by centuries of seafaring and trade. However, the islands face a growing challenge from rising sea levels caused by climate change.

BEST TIME TO VISIT
December to April for fine weather, manta rays and whale sharks; or May to December for schooling hammerheads

TOP THINGS TO SEE
- Sunrise over the surf from a palm-draped coral sand beach
- The mesmerising underwater world within metres of your beach towel
- The mosques and bustling market of Male', the pocket-sized Maldivian capital
- Laid-back villages and the ruins of the British WWII air base on Gan island
- Whale sharks, manta rays and hammerheads performing a natural ballet beneath the surface of the Indian Ocean

TOP THINGS TO DO
- Sunbathe on some of the world's most perfect beaches
- Dive or snorkel on spectacular *thilas* and *giris* (isolated reefs) and *kandus* (deepwater channels)
- See the Maldives from above on a scenic seaplane flight between the atolls
- Take a cruise to an outlying island on a *dhoni* (traditional Maldivian boat)
- Drop into a local cafe in Male' for a snack-sized feast of *hedika* (short eats)

GETTING UNDER THE SKIN
Read Imogen Edward-Jones' *Beach Babylon*, allegedly based on true events at a luxury Maldives resort
Listen to *bodu beru* (big drum), the traditional folk music of the islands
Eat *garudia* (smoked-fish soup); or *hedika* – delicious, spicy fish-based snacks
Drink *raa* (a sweet and tasty toddy tapped from the coconut palm)

IN A WORD
Mabuti naman (I'm fine)

TRADEMARKS
Coral atolls; white sand; swaying palms; coconuts; honeymoons; Conde Nast friendly resorts; world-class diving; the ever-present threat of climate change

RANDOM FACT
The highest point in the Maldives is just 2.4m above sea level – if sea levels continue to rise, plans are afoot to move the entire population to a new homeland overseas

MAP REF **N,27**

1. The pristine waters around the islands provide a playground for the children of the Maldives
2. Muslim girls make their way to school in the Northern Islands
3. Water bungalows fan out into the water, their orientation designed to give a sense of luxurious isolation
4. Sunglasses help defend against the glare from the sun, the sparkling seas and even the super-white school uniforms

1.

2.

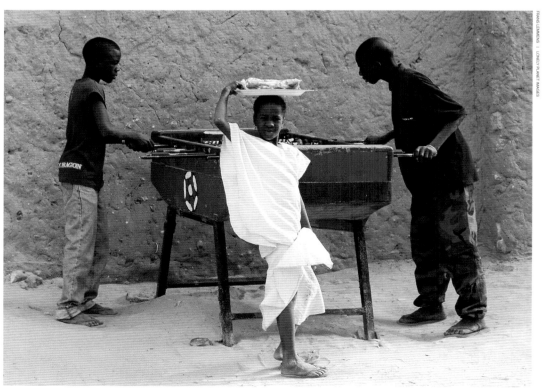

3.

If you could only visit one country in West Africa, Mali would be a prime candidate. Few countries in the region can boast such an array of sights, from fabled Timbuktu and the mysterious Dogon Country to riverside mosques that seem to spring from a child's imagination. Adding considerable depth to these attractions is Mali's illustrious history, a story of ancient gold-rich empires along the Sahara's southern fringe that has yielded to a stable West African democracy famed for the largely peaceful coexistence of its multifarious ethnic groups. And accompanying you on your journey through the country will be Mali's world-famous musical soundtrack, a beguiling playlist of soulful desert blues, ancient *griot* tunes and frenetic dance rhythms.

BEST TIME TO VISIT
October to February (before the heat, after the rains)

TOP THINGS TO SEE
- Djenné's breathtaking Grand Mosque and colourful Monday market
- The legendary (yet humble) city of Timbuktu crouching amid the Saharan sands
- Bamako's live music venues where Mali's master musicians play
- The sleepy riverside town of Ségou with its wonderful music festival and *bogolan* (mud cloth) workshops
- The deliciously remote city of Gao, with sunset views from a towering riverside dune

TOP THINGS TO DO
- Trek down off the Bandiagara Escarpment and into the timeless villages of the Dogon Country
- Ride a camel out into the Sahara and spend a night in a Tuareg camp close to Timbuktu
- Travel on a slow boat up the Niger River from Mopti to Timbuktu
- Track down the Sahel's last elephants in northeastern Mali
- Dance under stars in the Festival in the Desert, the world's most remote music festival

GETTING UNDER THE SKIN
Read *Ségu* by Maryse Condé, a sweeping generational tale that captures the essence of Malian history and its ethnic groups

Listen to Tinariwen, Toumani Diabaté, Amadou and Mariam, the late Ali Farka Touré, Salif Keita, Oumou Sangaré…the list is endless

Watch *Yeleen* by Souleymane Cissé, which won the Special Jury Prize at Cannes in 1987

Eat *capitaine* (Nile Perch)

Drink *bissap* or *djablani* juice (brewed from hibiscus petals); Castel (Malian beer)

IN A WORD
Bonjour, ça va? (Hello, how are you?)

TRADEMARKS
Mud architecture; the Mali and Songhaï empires of the Middle Ages; the ancient manuscripts of Timbuktu; Bambara woodcarvings and *bogolan* cloth

RANDOM FACT
King Kankan Musa of the Mali Empire distributed so much gold en route to Mecca in the 14th century that it was a generation before the world gold price recovered

MAP REF L,19

1. Everyone lends a hand in the difficult task of pounding the grain
2. The ingenious mud-brick construction of the Grand Mosque of Djenné gives it a seamlessly sculpted appearance that is breathtakingly impressive
3. Table football is hungry work: a midgame snack awaits
4. These intriguing carvings prop up a *toguna*, a place for men to discuss the workings of the community

1.

2.

3.

4.

A trio of sun-bleached islands on the southernmost edge of Europe, Malta is an eccentric and compelling blend of 9th-century Arabia, 1950s colonial Britain and Sicilian-styled gastronomy. Most travellers know the diminutive nation, independent since 1964, for its summertime beaches and sizzling nightlife. But scratch beneath that blue-sky, gold-sand holiday-brochure gloss and unearth an evocative canvas of ancient temples, passion-fuelled *festas* celebrating patron saints and baroque architecture. This is a unique country menaced by medieval pirates, saved by 16th-century crusading knights, nurtured as a 19th-century British naval base. Sure, dance until dawn in the party towns of St Julian's, Sliema and Paceville. But take time to slow down the pace and ponder ancient stone monuments built before the Egyptians even thought of the pyramids.

BEST TIME TO VISIT
February to June

TOP THINGS TO SEE
- The fortified capital of Valletta built by the Knights of St John
- The view from the elegant 'silent city' citadel of Mdina
- Hypogeum, a mysterious subterranean necropolis
- Malta's megalithic temples: Ġgantija, Ħaġar Qim and Mnajdra
- Marsaxlokk, a picture-postcard fishing village with fresh seafood to die for

TOP THINGS TO DO
- Get lost in Roman, Maltese and British history at Vittoriosa's dazzling Maritime Museum – or in the town's cinematic web of dusty back alleys
- Watch the curtain rise at Valletta's sumptuous Manoel Theatre, one of Europe's oldest dating to 1731 – don't miss a pre-theatre drink in its courtyard bar
- Splash, swim and frolic like a fish in the turquoise waters of the Blue Lagoon
- Learn to scuba-dive off the island of Gozo
- Party like a Maltese during a *festa* – an infectious mix of music, food and fireworks

GETTING UNDER THE SKIN
Read British historian Ernle Bradford's *The Great Siege*, a gripping account of the epic 1565 battle between Ottoman Turks and the Knights of St John

Listen to edgy riffs strung on rock guitars by alternative rock-pop artist Ira Losco

Watch Ridley Scott's *Gladiator,* and the blockbuster *Troy* with Brad Pitt – two of dozens of movies shot in Malta

Eat a ricotta-stuffed *pastizza* (puff-pastry parcel); *aljotta* (garlic-spiked fish and tomato broth with rice); and *fenek* (rabbit) with spaghetti or baked in a pie

Drink a thirst-quenching rum and Kinnie (bitter orange and herb-flavoured soft drink); or a fridge-cold bottle of local Cisk lager or Hopleaf ale

IN A WORD
Kif inti (How are you?)

TRADEMARKS
Crusading knights; falcons; the Maltese Cross; beaches; British tourists

RANDOM FACT
Malta is the only country in Europe where divorce is illegal

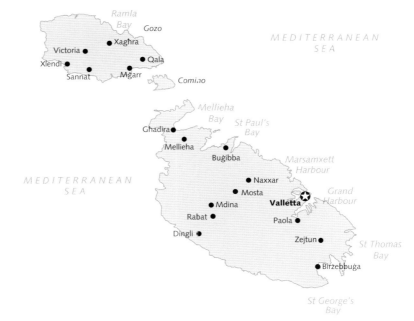

MAP REF J,21

1. A narrow street in Valletta funnels traffic, and indeed one's gaze, towards the sea
2. Brightly hued boats bob jauntily in Marsaxlokk Harbour
3. These men are dressed as the Knights of St John, who in 1530 took over Malta as one of their fiefdoms
4. The renowned beauty of the Blue Grotto draws visitors from all over the world

2.

3.

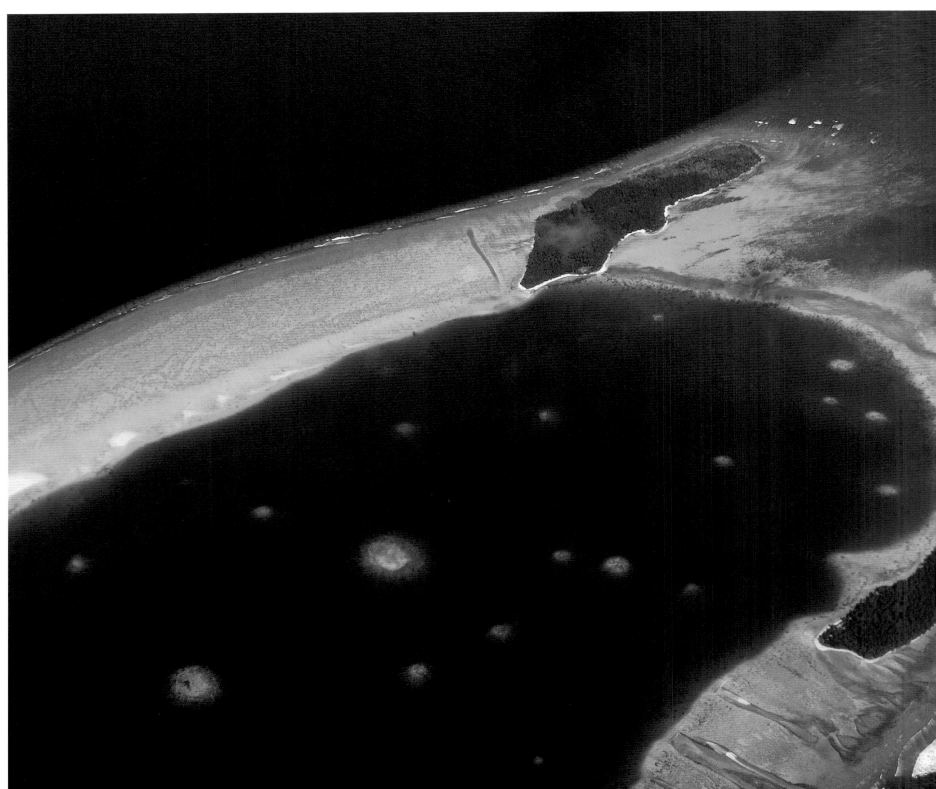

1.

It's a neon-blue water world out in the Marshall Islands. This expanse of slender, flat coral atolls is so surrounded by tropical sea that anywhere at any time you can see, hear, smell and feel salt air and water. The people have embraced their remote, ocean-locked environment to become some of the world's finest fishermen, navigators and canoe builders. Throughout history, the British, Spanish, Germans, Japanese and Americans have all claimed these strategically located atolls. Today US military presence is still huge and the lingering effects of bomb testing still sting. The charm however lies in the country's outer islands, which still retain the pristine feel of a Pacific paradise.

BEST TIME TO VISIT
The dry season from December to August in the south; the northern Marshalls are dry year-round and during September to November rains can be a blessing

TOP THINGS TO SEE
- A red-hot sunset from the Delap-Uliga-Darrit (DUD) lagoon
- Navigational stick charts, model canoes and shell tools at the Alele Museum
- The twisted wreckages of Japanese WWII Zeros, Betty Bombers and more in the jungle foliage on Maloelap Atoll
- Beautiful, intricately woven mats, fans, baskets and 'kili bags' (once a favourite of Jackie Onassis) on sale

TOP THINGS TO DO
- Dive the WWII wrecks on Bikini Atoll
- Sail the waters of the Majuro lagoon in a Waan Aelon in Majol, a traditional Marshall Islands–style canoe
- Picnic on the pristine beaches at Laura village
- Deep-sea fish off Longar Point on Arno Atoll
- Gaze at the pyrotechnics of US missile-testing on Kwajalein, the world's largest coral atoll

GETTING UNDER THE SKIN
Read *Al In Aelon Majol*, a locally published 2005 anthology of Marshall Islands–inspired writing

Listen to Cha-Nin-Way, a modern danceable syth-group singing in Marshallese

Watch 2008's *Morning Comes So Soon* – filmed in the islands, it's a story of a Marshallese boy and a Chinese girl who fall in love

Eat a snack of boiled, sweet pandanus fruit (just watch out for the hairy insides!)

Drink an ice-cold coconut

IN A WORD
Yokwe yuk (Love to you)

TRADEMARKS
Canoes; stick charts; sports fishing; diving; nuclear testing; US military; bikinis

RANDOM FACT
Bikini Atoll was the site for the first peacetime explosion of an atomic bomb. Subsequently the two-piece swimming costume (thought to be as awe-inspiring as the blasts) was named after the explosion site

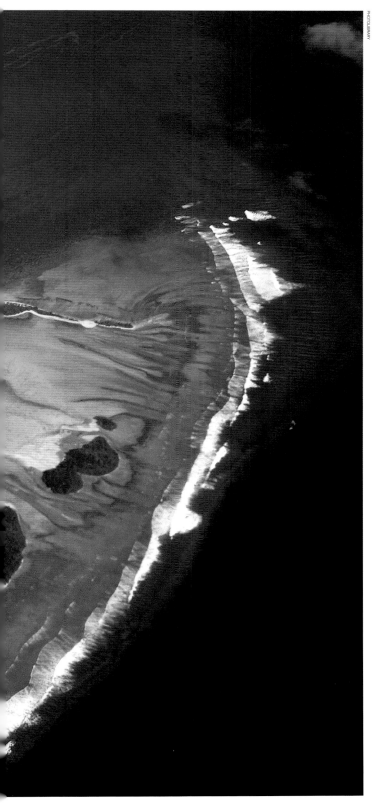

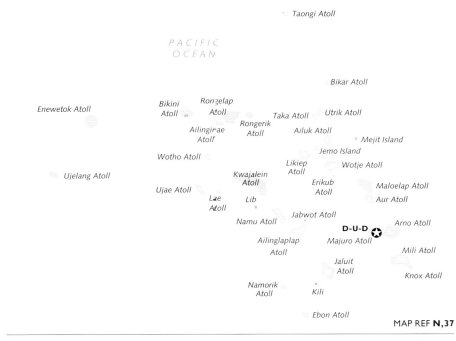

MAP REF **N,37**

---

1. Seen from above, Majuro Atoll appears as just a few brights spots in the vast blue of the Pacific Ocean
2. Being immersed in water is almost as natural as breathing for Marshallese children
3. The bountiful sealife of the Marshall Islands makes for irresistable snorkelling
4. An enormous coconut crab (which has also earned the unfortunate moniker, 'robber crab') takes refuge in a palm tree

Who can resist a place with the moniker 'Isle of Flowers'? Indeed Martinique is awash in hibiscus, frangipani and bougainvillea. And their colour accents an island with a sunny charm that makes it one of the most appealing Caribbean holiday spots. There's a strong French accent to life here, that combines with languid Caribbean customs to create an intoxicating Creole culture. Just as flowers speckle the verdant tropical forests, the piquant local sensibilities spice the food, which is among the best in the region. And everything is enlivened by hulking Mt Pelée, an often steaming and occasionally spouting volcano. The lava flows of the north and the jungles of the centre make good counterpoints to the lavish resorts of the south.

BEST TIME TO VISIT
December to May when rains are moderate and hurricanes are few

TOP THINGS TO SEE
- Ste-Luce, a charmer of a fishing village where a profusion of underwater life now lures divers
- The ruins of St-Pierre, the former capital destroyed by the eruption of Mt Pelée in 1902
- Pesqu'île de Caravelle, a romantic mix of natural tropical beauty and tiny timeless villages
- Fort-de-France has a crumbling Creole charm and spectacular water views
- The lonely black sand beaches dotting the north coast

TOP THINGS TO DO
- Pop a champagne bottle in Pointe du Bout, the très chic yacht harbour and fashion centre
- Create a very few and very tiny tan lines on the golden sands of Les Salines
- Try to speak some French, even if it is just a *'Bonjour'*
- Surf the uncrowded breaks at Anse l'Etang, which is fronted by a palm-ringed beach
- Traverse the rainforest-clad interior on the mountainous Route de la Trace

GETTING UNDER THE SKIN
Read *The Collected Poetry of Aimé Césaire*, the force behind the Black Pride phenomenon known as négritude; *Texaco* by Patrick Chamoiseau and *Malemort* by Edouard Glissant are also excellent reads

Listen to landmark *zouk* band Kassav' whose 30 albums include *Shades of Black*

Watch *Sugar Cane Alley*, by Euzhan Palcy, documenting the love and sacrifice of a poor black family living on a sugar plantation in Martinique in the 1930s

Eat *accras* (fish fritters); or perfectly proper French pastries

Drink Fleur de Canne St James rum, redolent with the flowery essence of cane

IN A WORD
Bonjour (Hello)

TRADEMARKS
Creole cuisine; lush mountains; volcanoes; sugar plantations; *zouk* music; fragrant flowers

RANDOM FACT
Paul Gauguin spent five months on Martinique in 1887, the bright flowers and other colours of the island are clearly visible in his later works

MAP REF **M,13**

1. Under a moody sky, the cliffs of Martinique loom dramatically over the Grande-Rivière

2.

3.

1.

4.

Consumed by the Sahara, Mauritania is a bridge between North Africa and sub-Saharan regions. As the safest trans-Saharan route for overlanders, Mauritania has long been an essential waystation en route from Europe to West Africa. But those that do more than pass through rarely regret it, with stunning natural landforms, lovely oases that bring life to isolated pockets of the country and a Unesco World Heritage–listed bird sanctuary along the Atlantic Coast. Perhaps more than anything else, however, what strikes you about Mauritania is that it is unlike any other country in Africa, a deeply traditional Islamic Republic and an in-between place that is part-Arab, part-African, but with an identity all its own forged in the sands of the Sahara.

BEST TIME TO VISIT
November to March, when it's hot but not unbearable

TOP THINGS TO SEE
- Ben Amira, at 633m-high, it's the world's second-largest rock monolith
- Terjît, one of the most verdant oases in the Sahara
- The dramatic old town of Ouadâne, built of brown stone
- Matmata's Saharan rock pools inhabited by Africa's unlikeliest crocodiles
- The nomad-built capital city of Nouakchott facing the desert

TOP THINGS TO DO
- Scramble aboard the world's longest train, the iron-ore-carrying colossus from Nouâdhibou to Choum
- Become a birder in Parc National du Banc d'Arguin
- Take a camel ride into the dunes from charming Chinguetti
- Go beyond the last town to Guelb er Richat, a crater-like depression of vast concentric circular ridges
- Venture deep into the desert to Oualâta, a Saharan ghost-town-in-the-making

GETTING UNDER THE SKIN
Read Peter Hudson's *Travels in Mauritania*, which follows the author's early 1990s exploration of the country on foot, donkey and camel

Listen to Malouma, who has modernised the Moorish traditional music

Watch *Heremakono* (Waiting for Happiness) by Mauritanian director, Abderrahmane Sissako, set in Nouâdhibou

Eat at a *méchui* (traditional nomad's feast), where an entire lamb is roasted over a fire and stuffed with cooked rice

Drink strong sweet tea; or the nomad's staple *zrig* (curdled goat or camel milk)

IN A WORD
Salaam aleikum (Hello, or Peace be with you)

TRADEMARKS
The Sahara's beauty and the threat of desertification; Islamic Republic with diplomatic relations with Israel; priceless manuscripts in the desert

RANDOM FACT
Mauritania has one of the world's lowest population densities, with just three people per square kilometre

MAP REF **L,18**

1. The snowy domes of this traditional inn in the Adrar stand stark against the desert horizon
2. Life in a traditional Mauritania dwelling, as glimpsed through the doorway
3. In a Chinguetti library gentle hands hold a delicate, historic manuscript
4. A local girl's smile is as bright as her dress is colourful

1.

2.

3.

Adrift in the Indian Ocean, this island paradise has collected many hangers-on since its fiery volcanic beginnings. One of the latest arrivals to wash up on its tropical shores was the human species. Today, Mauritius' social, gastronomic and architectural melange of Asian, African and European elements provides visitors with plenty to experience when not floating in azure seas, lounging on white-sand beaches or trekking through virgin rainforests. Minor tensions do exist between the Hindu majority, Muslims and Creoles, but respect and tolerance are intrinsic to Mauritian society. The cultural melting pot has been too hot for some to handle, however, with the island's most famous endemic species going the way of the dodo.

BEST TIME TO VISIT
May to November, for pleasant temperatures and the driest skies

TOP THINGS TO SEE
- Lily pad power at Sir Seewoosagur Ramgoolam Botanical Gardens in Pamplemousses
- Rempart Serpent, La Passe St François and Colorado, three of Mauritius' best dive sites
- Virgin tropical rainforest in La Vanille Réserve des Mascareignes
- Yourself on Trou d'Argent, an altogether staggering beach on the remote island of Rodrigues
- Maha Shivaratri, a captivating Hindu festival bringing 500,000 pilgrims to the holy lake of Grand Bassin

TOP THINGS TO DO
- Surround yourself with swaying casuarina trees and trek past tumbling waterfalls in Black River Gorges National Park
- Join local Mauritians on Belle Mare beach for a traditional Sunday picnic
- Saunter past Port Louis' revamped colonial architecture before diving into its fragrant market
- Soar over Rivière des Galets, past waterfalls and through lush forest on a 2km-long set of high-flying zip lines at St Felix
- Learn the Mauritian art of fusing Creole, Indian, French and Chinese cuisine on a cooking course in Rodrigues

GETTING UNDER THE SKIN
Read Bernardin de St-Pierre's 18th-century classic *Paul et Virginie*, a romantic, moralistic tragedy inspired by real life events

Listen to 'Anita' by the late Ti-Frère, a Mauritian singer who led the séga renaissance

Eat *rougaille* (a sauce of tomatoes, garlic and chilli with Creole-flavoured meat or fish)

Drink *alouda* (an almond-based concoction best topped with ice cream)

IN A WORD
Tapeta! (Cheers! in Mauritian Creole)

TRADEMARKS
Land of the lost dodo; sugar-cane plantations; fusion cuisine; honeymooners

RANDOM FACT
A significant proportion of the country's electricity is produced from sugar cane, with condensing extraction steam turbines running in sugar mills

MAP REF **Q,26**

1. Sandwiched between dramatic geography and sublime seas is the sweep of Morne Brabant Beach
2. A Sikh woman kneels in prayer at a Tamil temple in Port Louis
3. The dreadlocked tresses of these local children create an impression of carefree island life
4. A tailor works in the open doorway of his shop, perhaps hoping to catch the breeze

2.

3.

1.

DANIEL BONG | LONELY PLANET IMAGES

4.

GUYLAIN DOYLE | LONELY PLANET IMAGES

Mexico is like its food: varied, colourful, spicy, over-commercialised, fresh and often underappreciated. Much of Mexico's popular perceptions are shaped by its uneasy relations with its neighbour to the north. Border towns ripped by violence over vast sums from American drug sales and ceaseless migrations to a supposed better life are but two of the modern realities. But plunge deep into this vast nation that varies from arid to verdant and you'll find an intoxicating cultural mix of Europe, indigenous America and lost civilisations. Colours, and life, have a vibrancy here as seen in the heaving markets, the people-filled public squares and an often flamboyant love of life. Forget what you think you know and like a good salsa, start fresh.

BEST TIME TO VISIT
October to May, to avoid extreme temperatures

TOP THINGS TO SEE
° A city even bigger in many ways than its already enormous size: vast, heaving Mexico City
° Mayan temples rising above impenetrable deep green jungle at Palenque
° The stately old-world charms of colonial Oaxaca
° The vast sinuous abyss of the Copper Canyon
° Classy beach resort charms at Playa del Carmen, away from the squalor of Cancún yet close to evocative ruins and splendid diving

TOP THINGS TO DO
° Surf the waves washing the endless white beaches of mellow Puerto Escondido
° Go on the ultimate road trip down Baja's endless coast and forbidding interior
° Savour the simple pleasures of exquisite fresh fare sold for mere pesos at a market
° Surmount the steaming peak of Pico de Orizaba
° Feel the breeze of a billion butterfly wings at the winter refuge of Reserva Mariposa Monarca

GETTING UNDER THE SKIN
Read *The Air is Clear* by the great Carlos Fuentes; *Frida Kahlo and Diego Rivera* by Isabel Alcantara and Sandra Egnolff, the story of two pop culture icons

Listen to Los Tigres del Norte and Cafe Tacuba – pioneers of *rock en español*

Watch the landmark 1970s guerrilla struggles in the countryside in *The Violin*; a taste of near-hallucinatory romance in *Like Water for Chocolate*

Eat from a huge range of regional styles like chocolate *mole*, sweet *tamales* with milky *atole*, *nopales* (cactus leaves) and much more

Drink *jugos naturales,* especially the bloodlike vampiro fruit juice (beet and carrot); all three alcohols from the maguey plant: tequila, mezcal and pulque

IN A WORD
Hola (Hello)

TRADEMARKS
Mariachis; trying to get to the US; *telenovelas*; *mañana*; lawless border towns; margaritas

RANDOM FACT
Old civilisations like the Olmecs and Aztecs had achievements and cultures beyond what's thought possible today

MAP REF **K,9**

1. Performers prepare in the *corrida* (bull fight) ring for the impending contest
2. This folk-art skeleton, bedecked in all its colourful finery, looks positively cheerful
3. The bright dwellings of the city of Zacatecas spread across the hill like a strangely hued rainbow
4. Traditional Mexican style has been emulated all over the world

1.

2.

3.

And now for somewhere completely different. The Federated States of Micronesia (FSM) is made up of four unique and otherwise unrelated island states: Kosrae, Pohnpei, Chuuk and Yap. Each region has cultures, and traditions as colourful, distinct and diverse as the fish and coral formations that paint the fringing reefs. Kosrea is a Pacific paradise and arguably FSM's most beautiful island; Pohnpei is home to mysterious ancient ruins and a plethora of lush landforms; Chuuk is renowned for its wreck diving and Yap is a fiercely traditional state retaining a true island spirit. If you can't find something in the diversity of FSM to expand your view of the world, check your pulse.

BEST TIME TO VISIT
Temperatures hover around 27°C (81°F) year round, but it's a little less humid December to June

TOP THINGS TO SEE
- Yap's enormous stone money banks
- The ramshackle, pulsing hub of Kolonia, FSM's biggest towm
- Hard working artisans and local dance performances at Yap's Ethnic Art Village
- The 'Venice of Micronesia', Pohnpei's ancient stone city Nan Madol

TOP THINGS TO DO
- Dive Chuuk's veritable museum of WWII wrecks and spot Yap's graceful manta rays
- Imagine ancient life in hidden-feeling Lelu Ruins on Kosrae
- Hike the lush volcanic swells on Pohrpei and Kosrae
- Kayak through Kosrae's magical mangroves
- Stain your mouth red chewing *buw* (betel nut) with the locals

GETTING UNDER THE SKIN
Read *His Majesty O'Keefe* by Lawrence Klingman, the true story of David O'Keefe who landed on Yap in the late 1800s and became a very successful entrepreneur

Listen to the compilation *Spirit of Micronesia*, recordings of traditional songs from around the region

Watch *Globe Trekker's* Megan McCormick island hop through Pohnpei, Yap and Chuuk

Eat with locals to try adventurous island specialties such as Chuukese preserved breadfruit and Pohnpeian dog

Drink *sakau* (the local potently narcotic kava drink made from the roots of pepper shrubs)

IN A WORD
Fager (Yapese), *Kompoakepai* (Pohnpeian), *Pwipwi* (Chuukese), *Kawuk* (Kosraean) – the word 'friend' from the respective islands

TRADEMARKS
Giant stone money; traditional magic; betel nut; wreck diving; ancient stone cities; preserved cultures; seafood

RANDOM FACT
It's rumoured that the notorious international swindler Bully Hayes buried loot from the brigantine *Leonora* somewhere on Kosrae in 1874; many treasure hunts have ensued but nothing has been found

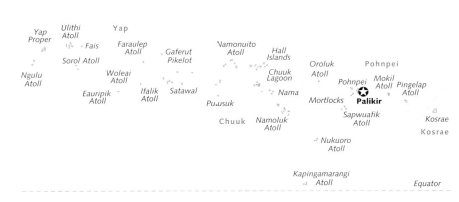

PACIFIC OCEAN

Yap Proper / Ulithi Atoll / Yap / Fais / Faraulep Atoll / Gaferut / Pikelot / Namonuito Atoll / Hall Islands / Oroluk Atoll / Pohnpei / Sorol Atoll / Ngulu Atoll / Woleai Atoll / Chuuk Lagoon / Pohnpei / Mokil Atoll / Pingelap Atoll / Eauripik Atoll / Ifalik Atoll / Satawal / Nama / Mortlocks / **Palikir** / Puluusuk / Chuuk / Namoluk Atoll / Sapwuafik Atoll / Kosrae / Kosrae / Nukuoro Atoll / Kapingamarangi Atoll / Equator

PACIFIC OCEAN

MAP REF **M,35**

1. Grass skirts swish as traditional Yapese dancers move to the rhythms of the bamboo stick dance
2. The detritus on the ground reveals how hard this man is working to carve out the canoe
3. This really is a place where the forest meets the sea
4. On Ifalik Atoll, these boys crouch by a canoe, ready to set out to sea

Long-forgotten and little-known, Moldova struggles to throw off its post-communist trappings and reputation as one of the poorest nations in Europe. Its gently undulating landscape fosters a vibrant wine industry with a wealth of lush vineyards and cavernous cellars, but is riven by the disputed breakaway region of Transdniestr and semi-autonomous Gagauzia. Its out-of-the-way aspect makes travel in Moldova a challenge and an adventure, but the unhurried and timeless way of life, where there is always time to chat in the shade of summer's fruit trees, are part of its appeal. Then, of course, there are the wineries and the understated welcome of the locals, who are given to forgetting workaday worries in exuberant night-time revelry in the capital, Chişinău.

BEST TIME TO VISIT
May to September, though there's no peak season, as such

TOP THINGS TO SEE
- Sprawling, lush Cathedral Park, framed by Chişinău's own Arc de Triomphe, flower market and Orthodox Cathedral
- The Cave Monastery at Orheiul Vechi Monastery Complex
- The Kvint factory, distillery for Transdniestr's finest brandy since 1897
- The Pushkin Museum, in Chişinău, where the great writer was exiled and wrote some of his classic novels
- Comrat, capital of the Gagauz autonomous region, and home to the world's only Gagauz university

TOP THINGS TO DO
- Investigate the gloom to explore literally hundreds of kilometres of wine cellars beneath the earth at Cricova or Mileştii Mici
- Kick back over a bottle of wine with the locals in Chişinău's buzzing clubs and bars
- Travel back in time to Tiraspol, capital of breakaway Transdniestr, a last surviving bastion of communism

GETTING UNDER THE SKIN
Read *The Moldovans: Romania, Russia and the Politics of Culture* by Charles King, a scholarly look at this small nation divided by Romanian and Russian spheres of interest

Listen to the unique 'bang and boom' sound of Zdob si Zdub

Watch The films of Moldovan-born Emil Loteanu, including *Lautarii* and *Red Meadows*

Eat *pelmeni* (Russian-style ravioli); or *shorba* (a Turkic-style spicy mutton soup)

Drink Local wine varietals including Feteasca and Black Rara

IN A WORD
Buna (Hello)

TRADEMARKS
Wineries and vineyards in rolling countryside; horse-drawn carts and labourers swinging scythes in meadows; communist throwbacks; separatist tendencies; Romany townships; local handicrafts

RANDOM FACT
Several Moldovan underwater hockey teams have attempted to claim refugee status while at international sporting competitions

UKRAINE

Edinița
Soroca
Bălți
Fălești
Orhei
Strășeni
Căpriana
Crivoca
Cojuşna
Chişinău
Bendery
Tiraspol

ROMANIA

Comrat

Vulcaneşti

BLACK SEA

MAP REF **H,23**

1. A cave monastery at Orheiul Vechi is gently illuminated by the intimate glow of votive candles

2.

3.

1.

Prince Albert II is king of this dynastic fairy tale, roughly wedged between France and Italy on Europe's most mythical, celebrity-studded coastline – the Côte d'Azur or French Riviera. Glitzy, glam and bubbling over with self-assurance, this teensy-tiny seaside state sizzles with resident millionaires, millionaire yachts and day trippers by the millions who traipse up to 'the Rock' to see the palace, sip champagne at Café de Paris and have a flutter at the casino. Yes. Monégasque life is the high life, all-embracing the second you step off the train into Monaco's swanky subterranean marble-clad station. Above ground, Hong Kong–style skyscrapers jostle for sunlight as billion-dollar plans to expand Dubai-style out to sea hover on this unusual country's glittering-blue horizon.

BEST TIME TO VISIT
April to June, September, October

TOP THINGS TO SEE
- The changing of the guard at the Palais du Prince
- Sharks above your head at the Musée Océangraphique
- The graves of Grace Kelly and her Monégasque prince charming, Rainier III, in the cathedral
- Billionaire yachts moored at the port
- World-class racing drivers tearing around during the Formula 1 Grand Prix in May

TOP THINGS TO DO
- Risk a lot (or a little) amid belle époque opulence at Monte Carlo Casino
- Spoil yourself rotten with a gold-dust bath at the Thermes Marin de Monte Carlo
- Lunch at Louis XIV, Monaco's most prestigious dining address
- Hike between century-old cactus in the Jardin Éxotique
- Motor into France between sea and cliff along the hair-raising Grande Corniche

GETTING UNDER THE SKIN
Read Graham Greene's *Loser Takes All* – a couple honeymoons in 1950s Monte Carlo

Listen to 1930s music-hall singer Charles Colbert (1852–1953) sing *The Man Who Broke the Bank at Monte Carlo*

Watch a beetle speed through the Formula 1 Grand Prix tunnel in the Walt Disney classic *Herbie Goes to Monte Carlo*

Eat Monégasque specialities *barbajuan* (spinach and cheese pasty) and *stockfish* (dried cod flavoured with aniseed)

Drink champagne aperitifs at celebrity-cool Kare(ment) on the waterfront

IN A WORD
Bon Giurnu (Hello!) in Monégasque

TRADEMARKS
Millionaire lifestyle; banking; tax-free haven; Formula One Grand Prix; Grace Kelly; Monte Carlo Casino; the Grimaldi dynasty

RANDOM FACT
Monaco grew by 20% in the late 1960s when land was reclaimed from the sea to build Fontvieille; on-off plans this millennium to build an artificial island could see the world's second smallest country grow by another 5%

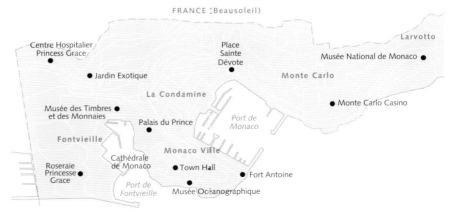

MAP REF **H,20**

1. It's not for nothing that Monte Carlo is known as the millionaires' playground
2. A lesson in grace: young dance students rehearse with their costumes at the ready
3. There's a hair's breadth between the track and the spectators at the Monaco Formula 1 Grand Prix
4. It's not magic making these fairy lights twinkle: electricians inspect the chandelier in the throne room of the Palais du Prince

1.

RICHARD I'ANSON | LONELY PLANET IMAGES

CLAIRE LUCAS | LONELY PLANET IMAGES

2.

3.

Blessed with huge horizons from the Gobi Desert to the Altai Mountains, Mongolia is the place for anyone who values a bit of personal space. Almost devoid of fences, roads or even towns, the best thing to do here is to hire a horse (or its modern equivalent the 4WD) and set off on an epic trip across the grasslands. And just when you think you have reached the middle of nowhere, a herder will appear on horseback looking like a lost foot soldier from the time of Genghis Khan, to greet you like a long-lost friend and invite you to back to his *ger* (yurt). Put aside your creature comforts and Mongolia rewards with a timeless sense of space and freedom that's simply intoxicating.

BEST TIME TO VISIT
June to September

TOP THINGS TO SEE
- The Naadam festival, a kind of 'nomad Olympics', featuring horse races, archery competitions and wrestling in silly underpants
- Khövsgöl Nuur, a spectacular sub-Siberian lake whose water is so pure you can drink it
- Altai Tavan Bogd National Park, home to snowcapped peaks, sparkling blue lakes and Kazakh eagle hunters
- The ruined ancient Mongol capital of Karakorum and nearby Tibetan-style monastery of Erdene Zuu Khiid

TOP THINGS TO DO
- Buy a horse and gallop across the open grasslands in your best Genghis Khan impersonation
- Get a crash course in Russian jeep repair while stuck in the middle of absolutely nowhere
- Dig for dinosaurs or trek with Bactrian camels in the southern Gobi
- Overnight in a local *ger*, stumble outside after a night of vodka and mare's milk and gaze up at the incredible ceiling of stars

GETTING UNDER THE SKIN
Read *Mongolia: Travels in the Untamed Land* by Jasper Becker, for insights into the present; and *The Mongols* by David Morgan, for a rundown of the nomadic past

Listen to the otherworldly sound of *khöömii* (Mongolian or Tuvan throat singing)

Watch Sergei Bodrov's *Mongol*, the first in a planned trilogy depicting the life of Genghis Khan

Eat *boodog* (barbecued roast marmot, cooked from the inside with hot stones and crisped to perfection with a blow torch)

Drink *airag* (fermented mare's milk); or *suutei tsai* (salty milk tea)

IN A WORD
Sain baina uu (Hello)

TRADEMARKS
Grasslands; endless steppe; horses; Gobi desert; Altai Mountains; eagle hunters; Genghis Khan; big blue skies; wrestlers; sub-Arctic winters; throat-singing; barbecue

RANDOM FACT
Mongolia has the lowest population density of any country on earth

RUSSIA

Ulaangom •   Amarbayasgalant   Khiid • • Sükhbaatar
Ölgii •   Mörön •   • Darkhan
Khovd •   • Bulgan   Choibalsan
    • Uliastai   Ulaanbaatar ✪   • Öndörkhaan
Altai •   • Kharkhorin   Baruun Urt
Bayankhongor   • Arvaikheer
    • Mandalgovi
     • Sainshand
   • Dalandzadagad

CHINA

MAP REF **H,31**

1. The almighty wingspan of an alighting golden eagle dwarfs its human perch
2. A pilgrim turns a prayer wheel at the many-coloured Ochidara Temple, Gandantegchinlen Khiid (Gandan Monastery)
3. Beast of burden: a hard-working motorcycle transports a family of four
4. In Ulaanbaatar a sharply dressed performer is an impressive sight

2.

3.

1.

RICHARD NABSON | LONELY PLANET IMAGES

4.

SIME | GRANDADAM LAURENT

Montenegro may have remained unknown to the West for centuries, but it was certainly well known to Adriatic pirates, Venetian plunderers, Ottoman pashas and Yugoslav technocrats. The unforgiving landscape and dogged people resisted all and maintained their own course, emerging as an independent nation in 2006. It is a country that prides itself on 'humanity and bravery' – to which we might add hospitality – and that comfortably accommodates Orthodox monasteries, Albanian mosques and communal promenading every evening. While the Montenegrins have their no-nonsense charm, it is the land itself that is the star. Lavender-tinged scree-covered mountains plummet to an emerald shore bustling with pomegranate trees along the Adriatic, and the northern mountains are so ruggedly untamed they are surely the refuge of mythical beasts.

BEST TIME TO VISIT
April to September

TOP THINGS TO SEE
- Almighty panoramas over Kotor and the opal-green sea, from Mt Sv Ivan
- The idiosyncratic mix of historic capital meets cosy village in Cetinje
- The gleaming white walls of Ostrog Monastery, the spiritual heart of Montenegro
- Stupendous scenery in Durmitor National Park, home to eagles, bears, wolves and – quite possibly – wood nymphs and satyrs as well

TOP THINGS TO DO
- Hang on for the white-knuckle ride around the hairpin-bending ascent from Kotor to Cetinje
- Feel the rush of white water – and adrenalin – as you raft down the Tara River
- Soak up the sun, and then cool off in the limpid waters of the Adriatic at the beaches around Budva
- Peer through your binoculars at Lake Skadar, one of Europe's most important wetlands

GETTING UNDER THE SKIN
Read *Realm of the Black Mountain* by Elizabeth Roberts, a lively history

Listen to epic poetry sung to the accompaniment of the *gusle* (a single-string fiddle)

Watch Marija Perovic's *Packing the Monkeys, Again* and *Look at Me*

Eat grilled squid on the coast; or, in the mountains, *ispod saca* (lamb baked in a metal pot under hot embers)

Drink *loza* (grape brandy); or Nikšićko, the fabulous local beer

IN A WORD
Dobro došli (Welcome)

TRADEMARKS
Dreamy Adriatic coastline; Orthodox monasteries; pomegranates in season; resistance and resilience; wild mountain spaces; the translucent Adriatic; stone architecture

RANDOM FACT
During the Romantic age, Western European observers suddenly developed a distinctly rose-tinted view of the Montenegrins, describing them as a 'race of heroes' and 'born warriors'

MAP REF **I,22**

1. Our Lady of the Rock church sits serenely on a man-made island in the Bay of Kotor
2. Through lush forest, sheep head for greener pastures
3. Beachgoers soak up the sun on Sveti Stefan beach
4. The seaside town of Budva offers spectacular vistas

1.

2.

3.

A casual visitor to Morocco might wonder if they hadn't been whisked there by magic carpet. Cities like Marrakesh, Tangier and Fez instantly spark a word association game of *Arabian Nights* style images of souqs and kasbahs, spices and date palms. It's a cultural collision of Africa and Islam, plus a dose of Andalucia from across the Straits of Gibraltar, offering Roman ruins and ancient medinas to hip city nightlife and all things between. Its handicrafts are famous, but away from the hustle it's possible to find solitude along wild coastlines, high mountain passes and an endless sea of sand dunes.

BEST TIME TO VISIT
October to April

TOP THINGS TO SEE
º Marrakesh's Djemaa el-Fna square, a joyful riot of music, food, storytellers and snake charmers
º The ancient medina in Fez, the most intact medieval Arab city in the world
º Sunset over the Sahara Desert, where an ocean of sand dunes washes up at Erg Chigaga
º The quiet mountain town of Chefchaouen, where every house is painted cornflower blue
º The palm oases and rocky red cliffs of the central Dadès Gorge

TOP THINGS TO DO
º Trek deep into the Atlas Mountains with mules, sleeping at local Berber homestays
º Haggle for souvenirs in the souqs until you're knee-deep in carpets
º Lounge in a trendy *riad* (townhouse-cum-boutique hotel)
º Soak your cares away in a *hammam* (bath house) – go traditional or for the trendy spa experience
º Indulge your sweet tooth with a pot of scalding mint tea and a plate of pastries

GETTING UNDER THE SKIN
Read *The Caliph's House* by Tahir Shah, an account of restoring a *djinn*-haunted house in Casablanca

Listen to the hypnotically bluesy grooves of *gnawa* (the Sufi- and slave-inspired music of Marrakesh and Essaouira)

Watch *Hideous Kinky*, an odyssey of 1960s hippie dreams, with Kate Winslet and Morocco itself competing for top billing

Eat *seksu* (couscous) – steamed for hours and heaped with meat or vegetables, the highpoint of any feast

Drink local wine – red or white, Morocco has some surprisingly good wineries

IN A WORD
Lebas? (How are you?)

TRADEMARKS
Mint tea; Berbers; Marrakesh riads; couscous; quality rugs; Bogart and Bergman in *Casablanca*

RANDOM FACT
Casablanca's Hassan II Mosque accommodates 25,000 worshippers at prayer, and its minaret is 210m high – the tallest in the world

MAP REF J,19

1. There's plenty of room to move in Casablanca's enormous Hassan II Mosque
2. Chilling out inside the Ensemble Artisanal, Marrakesh
3. Marrakesh's Djemaa el-Fna square is rich with sights, smells and sounds
4. Piercing eyes gaze out of a weathered face

2.

3.

1.

4.

Mozambique's star is on the rise. After almost two decades of peace, the economy is growing. Glitzy high-rises and lively street cafes compete for attention with remote island archipelagos and a steadily increasing population of wild animals. A new bridge over the Zambezi River links north and south for the first time. Yet, despite the development, centuries-old rhythms still dominate and the country moves to its own beat – a unique fusion of African, Arabic, Indian and Portuguese influences. Slip away from the Western mindset and immerse yourself for a while: a dhow ride through silent mangrove channels, an Indian Ocean sunrise or the pulsating rhythms of *mapiko* dancing should do the trick. Once you're seduced, it's hard to break away.

BEST TIME TO VISIT

May to November, during the cooler, drier season

TOP THINGS TO SEE

- The Quirimbas Archipelago – just as stunning whether seen from above in a flyover or from the prow of a dhow
- Dugongs, corals and colourful fish in the waters of the Bazaruto Archipelago
- The lions and elephants that are now back at home in Gorongosa National Park
- Cahora Bassa Dam and the mighty Zambezi River
- Works by Malangatana and other artists at Maputo's National Museum of Art

TOP THINGS TO DO

- Sail on a dhow past deserted white sandbanks and beautiful beaches in remote island archipelagos
- Wind your way through the heart of rural Africa on the Nampula–Cuamba train
- Explore Lake Niassa, with its clear waters, secluded coves and star-filled skies
- Hike over precipitous log bridges and through rushing mountain streams in the cool Chimanimani Mountains
- Dance until dawn at Maputo's lively nightclubs

GETTING UNDER THE SKIN

Read *The Last Flight of the Flamingo* or any other work by Mia Couto for lyrical insights that take you into Mozambique's soul

Listen to the upbeat rhythms of *marrabenta*, Mozambique's national music

Watch an explosive, rhythmic, colour-filled performance of the Mozambican National Company of Song and Dance

Eat *matapa* (cassava leaves with peanut sauce)

Drink a 2M (Dois M) beer – cold, if you can find it

IN A WORD

Paciência (Patience)

TRADEMARKS

Marrabenta music; Makonde woodcarvings; giant prawns; *mapiko* dancing; dhows; Mozambique Island; idyllic beaches

RANDOM FACT

Before an engagement can be approved, the matrilineal Lomwe-Makua peoples around Gurúè require the man to prove he can work

MAP REF **Q,23**

---

1. A village rests next to the jewel-like Indian Ocean on Vamizi Island
2. Women pick cotton beneath cottony clouds
3. The sun-saturated streets of Mozambique Island fill as the day draws to a close
4. A man takes a precious, quiet moment of contemplation in a mosque

1.

2.

3.

Many travellers boycott the nation formerly known as Burma because of its oppressive military government, but those who visit have nothing but praise for the kindness and hospitality of the Burmese people and the cultural richness of this backwater of Asia. Golden stupas dot the landscape like giant candlesticks and the pace of life is dictated by the inexorable flow of the mighty Ayeyarwady River. Isolation has preserved a centuries-old way of life and the superficial trappings of the 21st century – mobile phones, advertising, email – are largely absent. However, travellers are always under the watchful eye of the junta, which strives to keep locals unaware of the outside world and the outside world unaware of human rights abuses inside the country.

BEST TIME TO VISIT
November to February (the cool season)

TOP THINGS TO SEE
- The breathtaking plain of temples at Bagan
- Mighty Shwedagon Paya, perhaps the grandest Buddhist monument in the world
- Wonky bridges and hilltop stupas in the villages around Mandalay
- Motorised canoes swirling through the morning mist on Inle Lake
- The timeless pace of village life in sleepy Hsipaw

TOP THINGS TO DO
- Cruise along the Ayeyarwady on a charmingly decrepit passenger boat
- Trek to fascinating tribal villages around Kalaw or Kengtung
- Run through the surf on idyllic Ngapali Beach
- Climb Mt Popa to commune with the *nats* (animist spirits)
- Shop for Buddhist trinkets at Yangon's Bogyoke Aung San Market

GETTING UNDER THE SKIN
Read Pascal Khoo Thwe's moving memoir *From the Land of Green Ghosts;* or George Orwell's classic *Burmese Days*

Listen to the *Maha Gita* (the traditional classical music of the Burmese court); or the rousing rock of Lay Phyu and Iron Cross

Watch the bravely satirical comedy performances of the Moustache Brothers in Mandalay

Eat at a traditional Burmese canteen – a typical meal includes *htamin* (rice), *hin* (curries), *peh-hin-ye* (lentil soup) and *balachaung* (fiery shrimp and chilli paste)

Drink Dagon Beer, Myanmar Beer or Spirulina Beer, which claims to have antiageing properties

IN A WORD
Mingalaba (We are blessed)

TRADEMARKS
Golden stupas; teak bridges; monks in maroon robes; jade mines; the Ayeyarwady River; *cheroots* (cigars); opium and the Golden Triangle; Aung San Suu Kyi; brutal military crackdowns

RANDOM FACT
Officially, the Burmese kyat is worth around one seventh of one US dollar, but on the black market, one dollar will buy you more than 1000 kyat

MAP REF **L,30**

1. The temples of Bagan spread out across the plain beside the Ayeyarwady
2. Two generations of a hilltribe family look out from their Pin Tauk village home
3. Women work the bright fields of spring onions
4. Floral tributes: prayers are offered at Shwedagon Paya, Yangon

279

2.

3.

1.

JOHNNY HAGLUND | LONELY PLANET IMAGES

4.

JOHNNY HAGLUND | LONELY PLANET IMAGES

It's life and death. And never has the battle been so beautifully fought. One look at the Namibian landscape and you will understand. Nowhere in the world is such visual splendour matched with such unmerciful harshness – if anything is to survive here, in the sea of dunes, within the rocky canyons, or along the Skeleton Coast, it has to be equally extraordinary. Thankfully, nature has provided just such a cast. Its members include desert-adapted elephant, rhino and lion, fog-basking beetles, great white sharks, rare mountain zebra, cartwheeling spiders and some of the most intriguing people you'll meet on the planet.

BEST TIME TO VISIT
May to September (the dry season)

TOP THINGS TO SEE
- Classic safari wildlife emerging from the heat haze on Etosha Pan
- The hungry sands of the Skeleton Coast consuming the massive rusty relics that ran aground on this mist-shrouded shore
- The earth opening up before you as you approach the edge of the gaping Fish River Canyon
- Spitzkoppe, the 'Matterhorn of Africa', rising boldly from the Damaraland plains
- The wild horses of the Namib

TOP THINGS TO DO
- Cruise the Caprivi Strip and embrace the wet and wild life on the banks of the Chobe River
- Skydive over the extraordinary meeting place of two great seas, the Namib Desert and the Atlantic Ocean
- Hike along the serpentine spine of a dune at Sossusvlei at sunrise
- Track endangered black rhino through the parched landscape of the Kaokoveld
- Slide down the garnet-laced dunes near Terrace Bay to hear (and feel!) them roar

GETTING UNDER THE SKIN
Read *Born of the Sun*, which follows the coming of age and political awakening of author Joseph Diescho

Listen to the vibrant voices of the Mascato Coastal Youth Choir

Watch *Namibia: The Struggle for Liberation*, a story about the nation's first president and his fight for independence

Eat *oshiwambo* (a memorable mixture of spinach and beef)

Drink prickly-pear-cactus schnapps

IN A WORD
Goegaandit?/Matisa?/Kora? (How are you? in Afrikaans/Damara/Herero)

TRADEMARKS
Mountainous parabolic dunes; shipwrecks; Sperrgebiet, or 'Forbidden Zone' (aka Diamond Area 1); the Skeleton Coast; sandboarding

RANDOM FACT
Believed to have been slowed by skipping along the atmosphere, much like a stone on water, Hoba touched down softly (in meteoric terms) in what is now northeastern Namibia – weighing over 60 tons, it's the world's largest intact meteorite

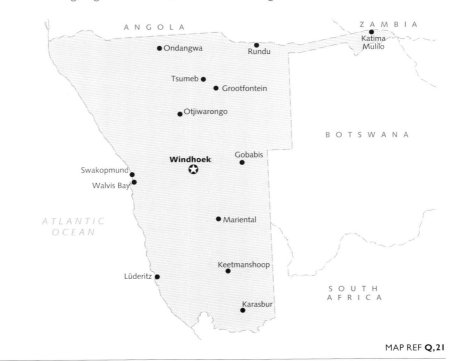

MAP REF **Q,21**

1. A man is dwarfed by nature at the Sossusvlei sand dunes
2. Ochre-covered braids are traditional adornment for the Himba tribe
3. Four Burchell's zebras have a strobe effect at a waterhole in Etosha National Park
4. And not a drop to drink: one ocean meets another on the Atlantic Coast

Nauru's beauty can be glimpsed along its coast: seabirds swoop over green cliffs, aqua reigns along wild-ocean vistas and sunsets are nothing short of spectacular. Head to the island's interior however, and you'll find deforestation from phosphate mining and an eerie landscape of limestone pinnacles. The exposed rock reflects the sun's rays and chases away the clouds so there's lots of sunshine but frequent drought. Meanwhile, the wealth accrued from mining, followed by the poverty once the stores were depleted, have brought the country to near collapse. Freight deliveries are rare and employment scarcer. Perhaps tourism, once thought unneeded, could help Nauru get back on its feet. Transport and hospitality services are thin on the ground but smiles are plentiful.

BEST TIME TO VISIT
Though hot and humid year-round, the rainiest months are November to February, so it's best to visit from March to October

TOP THINGS TO SEE
o A fiery South Seas sunset over coconut trees and salt brush
o WWII relics scattered around the island including a Japanese jail built into and around phosphate pinnacles
o A light-hearted game of Australian Rules football at dusk
o Ekawada, string figures stretched across the hands like 'cat's cradle' to tell traditional stories
o The ruins of the once-splendid presidential palace burned down by a local mob in 2001

TOP THINGS TO DO
o Swim and snorkel off the boat ramp at Anibare
o Hunt black noddy birds, a Nauruan delicacy, with the locals
o Catch marlin, yellow-fin tuna, barracuda and more with the island's fishermen
o Walk the pinnacled remnants of the now defunct phosphate mines
o Run and drink with the expat Hash House Harriers

GETTING UNDER THE SKIN
Read *Freeing Ali – the Human Face of the Pacific Solution* by Michael Gordon for an insight into the detention of asylum seekers on Nauru

Listen to the strange cry of the noddy bird

Watch *Nauru: An Island Adrift,* a documentary about Nauru's rise and fall

Eat a fresh seafood barbecue

Drink *demangi*, the island's take on fermented toddy made from coconut palm sap

IN A WORD
Kewen (Gone, dead)

TRADEMARKS
Phosphate; camps of Australia-bound asylum seekers; weightlifting; noddy birds; limestone pinnacles; 1875 civil war; Nauruan high-rollers in the 1970s and '80s

RANDOM FACT
During the phosphate boom in the 1980s, Nauru was the second-richest country in the world in terms of per capita income; 30 years later the estimated average income is US$2500 per year

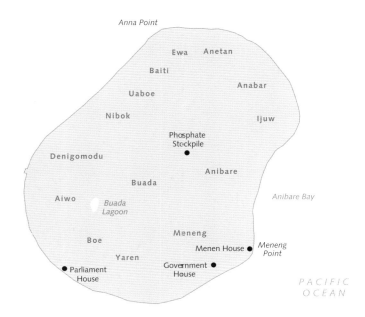

MAP REF **O,37**

1. Take time out, Nauruan style

2.

3.

1.

4.

A land of mountains, monasteries and mystery, the former kingdom of Nepal has been calling out to adventurers ever since it first opened its borders to the outside world in the 1950s. With the end of the Maoist rebellion, this little piece of Shangri-La is once again open for business, and thrill-seekers are flocking back to the foothills of the Himalaya to indulge in some of the best trekking, mountaineering and rafting in the world. Beyond these natural highs, travellers are drawn to Nepal by the sound of chiming temple bells, the chanting of Buddhist monks, the enduring traveller scene in Kathmandu and the timeless drama of day-to-day life in the remote villages of the Himalaya.

BEST TIME TO VISIT
September to November and March to May, to avoid summer rains and icy winters

TOP THINGS TO SEE
- The winding, temple-strewn backstreets of Kathmandu
- Stupendous stupas at Bodhnath and Swayambhunath
- The magnificent royal squares in Patan and Bhaktapur
- Views of the snowpeaks from Nagarkot, Dhulikhel and Sarangkot
- Chariot parades and other fantastic festivals in the Kathmandu Valley

TOP THINGS TO DO
- Test muscle against mountain on the trek to Everest Base Camp
- Take a row boat across the placid waters of Phewa Tal in Pokhara
- Haggle for singing bowls and Tibetan rugs in the bazaars of Thamel in Kathmandu
- Raft or kayak on the wild white waters of the Bhote Kosi or Sun Kosi
- Track rhinos and tigers from the back of a jumbo at Chitwan National Park

GETTING UNDER THE SKIN
Read *Arresting God in Kathmandu* by Samrat Upadhyay; or WE Bowman's mountaineering spoof *The Ascent of Rum Doodle*

Listen to the evocative Nepali folk music of Sur Sudha

Watch Eric Valli's classic *Himalaya*, with all characters played by Dolpo villagers

Eat *dal bhat* (lentils, vegetables and rice) – it's what you'll be eating twice a day, every day if you go trekking

Drink salted butter tea; *chang* (milky beer made from rice or barley); or hot *tongba* (millet beer).

IN A WORD
Ke garne? (What to do?)

TRADEMARKS
High altitude thrills; hippies; the Himalaya towering temples; Buddhist lamas; Maoists; mountaineers with icicles in their beards; prayer flags; mandalas; yaks and yetis; buffalo steaks

RANDOM FACT
Sagarmatha (Mt Everest) is growing by 6mm every year as a result of plate tectonics

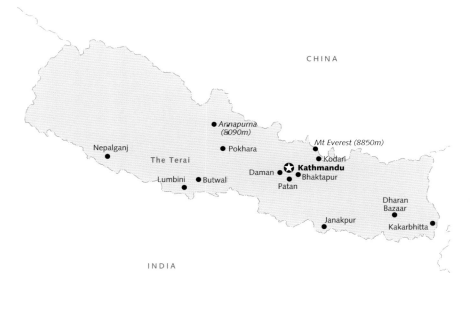

MAP REF **K,28**

1. Himalayan peaks rise above the impossibly blue Gokyo Lake
2. A sadhu is a Hindu ascetic who has left home, job and family on a spiritual search
3. Messages that spin into the ether – mantras in Pali script adorn these prayer wheels
4. The form of Nyatapola Temple in Bhaktapur echoes Nepal's soaring peaks

1.

2.

3.

NETHERLANDS

CAPITAL Amsterdam (Government seat is the Hague) | **POPULATION** 16,715,999 | **AREA** 41,526 sq km | **OFFICIAL LANGUAGE** Dutch

The Dutch are among the least prolific pot smokers in Europe, yet their nation is a magnet for pot-smokers worldwide. They are also unlikely to visit prostitutes but Amsterdam's red-light district is a major tourist draw. Making money off others has always been a Dutch talent and it's paid off for centuries. Beautiful old cities such as Amsterdam, Haarlem, Leiden, Delft, Utrecht and many more attest to the wealth that fuelled their growth. The ever-tolerant Dutch have always excelled at making the most with what they have. They've created a modern, comfortable country out of swamps and shallows and made it the world's best place to ride a bike; constant winds off the North Sea power pumps that keep it all dry.

BEST TIME TO VISIT
April for tulips, May to October for cafe-friendly weather

TOP THINGS TO SEE
- Amsterdam is one of Europe's best-preserved great cities, with canals, 17th-century vistas and an incongruous mix of neighbourhoods
- Rotterdam is as modern as Amsterdam is old, an open-air gallery of cutting edge architecture
- Cheery Maastricht is hilly and has a Belgian-German accent
- Millions of tulips pose as pixels every spring at Keukenhof
- Hoge Veluwe National Park with its world-class art museum set among vast royal gardens and forest

TOP THINGS TO DO
- Bicycle to your heart's content in the world's best country for riding
- Retrace the life of Vermeer in tidy old Delft
- Painlessly school yourself in Dutch Art 101 at the picture-perfect Mauritshuis in the Hague
- Set sail on land in one of the creaking old windmills at Zaanse Schans
- Hike the dunes of the last natural place left in this densely packed nation: Unesco-recognised Schiermonnikoog National Park

GETTING UNDER THE SKIN
Read the classic, timeless *Diary of Anne Frank*, which never loses its impact

Listen to Tiësto, the undisputed trancemeister and famous face of the killer Dutch club scene

Watch Paul Voerhaven's *Turks Fruit*, made before he found vast fame in Hollywood

Eat crispy *frites* (chips) doused with mayonnaise or any of dozens of other sauces

Drink rich ales like Palm, rather than the bland best-selling lagers

IN A WORD
Dag (Hello/goodbye)

TRADEMARKS
Bikes; dykes; windmills; clogs; tulips; red-light district; pot smoking; Van Gogh; canals; Rembrandt; tall people

RANDOM FACT
Of the area claimed as the Netherlands, 20% is underwater (canals, lakes, marshes etc) while another 20% is below sea level and protected by 2400km of dykes

MAP REF **G,20**

1. In the depths of winter, frozen canals become icy highways
2. Not a hill in sight: excellent bike-riding awaits in the Netherlands
3. Amsterdam's canals showcase magnificent gables
4. Farmland in Flevoland creates a precise patchwork when viewed from above

Très French yet warmly Melanesian, New Caledonia is a place for gourmet meals beneath palm trees and flip-flops worn with designer clothing. A massive, World Heritage–listed lagoon encircles the main island of Grande Terre imbibing the coasts with light in every shade of blue. From cosmopolitan Noumea down through the south's red earth to Île des Pins' araucaria pines and the depths of the indigo lagoons, New Caledonia feels much bigger than most island nations. And it's no wonder: Grande Terre is the third-largest island in the Pacific with the largest enclosed lagoon in the world.

BEST TIME TO VISIT
September to December when it's not too hot or cold and there's the least chance of rain

TOP THINGS TO SEE
- Noumea's magnificent Tjibaou Cultural Centre, Aquarium des Lagons and the colonial Musée de la Ville de Noumea – all on one handy pass
- Fishermen unloading their catch, and the weekend string band at Noumea's Le Marché
- Panoramic views over sea-turtle territory and the unusual rock formations at La Roche Percée
- A *grande case* (chief's hut), and political and community centres of the Kanak districts

TOP THINGS TO DO
- Glide across Baie d'Upi on Île des Pins in a traditional sailing outrigger canoe
- Dive and dine on fresh lobster on the Loyalty Islands
- Kayak through a drowned forest, abseil down waterfalls and hike the landscapes of the Far South
- Experience Kanak life at a homestay in Hienghène
- Enjoy fine wine and French cuisine at Noumea's chic restaurants

GETTING UNDER THE SKIN
Read *The Kanak Apple Season* by Déwé Gorodey, a collection of short stories exploring Kanak political and cultural issues

Listen to mellow beautiful melodies crooned by Gulaan

Watch *Le Bal du Gouverneur*, a romance set in 1950s New Caledonia

Eat *bougna* (a delicious meal of taro, sweet potatoes, bananas and pieces of chicken, crab or lobster cooked in banana leaves in an earthen oven)

Drink *nalamal* (the local kava sold only from private houses)

IN A WORD
Ti-Va-Ouere (Brothers of the Earth)

TRADEMARKS
Kanak communities; French tourists; grass huts on the beach; colonial strife; Grande Terre's immense lagoon; clan societies; tin mines; Catholicism; colourful yet conservative missionary style dresses

RANDOM FACT
The rare Kagu bird (Cagou in French), endemic to New Caledonia, is nearly flightless and has a call that sounds like a dog bark

MAP REF **Q,37**

1. The buildings of the Tjibaou Cultural Centre stretch skyward out of the greenery in Noumea

1.

2.

3.

There's a reason the sun shines on New Zealand before anywhere else – every day here feels like a new world has begun. Mother Nature decided to take her best features and condense them all in this South Pacific gem, from snowcapped Alps, winding fjords and expanses of pristine beach to lush rainforests and active volcanoes. Trek, ski, raft or paraglide – all through decadent scenery – then take sleepy inland roads to find superb local wineries and a thriving Maori culture. Complete the package with cosmopolitan cities and a distinctly Kiwi lust for life, and it's easy to understand why nearly all who visit fall in love with this country.

BEST TIME TO VISIT

November to April for fun in the sun, June to August for fun in the snow

TOP THINGS TO SEE

- Volcanic mud bubbles, spurting geysers and neon geothermal pools at Rotorua
- Fifty-one metre-high Tane Mahuta, the world's largest kauri tree that's between 1200 and 2000 years old
- Rare kiwi birds in the wild on Stewart Island
- A view of Mt Cook, New Zealand's highest peak from impossibly blue Lake Tekapo
- The icy grandeur of the Franz and Fox Glaciers from the ground or the air

TOP THINGS TO DO

- Kayak or trek the golden-sand beaches and turquoise inlets of Abel Tasman National Park
- Sip world-famous sauvignon blanc at gorgeous wineries and gourmet restaurants throughout the Marlborough wine region
- Jump off a bridge or out of a plane in Queenstown
- Experience New Zealand's best nightlife and caffeine-scene in Wellington
- Dive the subtropical underwater cliffs in the crystal-clear waters off the Poor Knights Islands

GETTING UNDER THE SKIN

Read *The Bone People* by Keri Hulme, a haunting story of New Zealand identity and child abuse

Listen to anything on the double CD *Great New Zealand Songbook,* a compilation of the greatest Kiwi tunes from the last two centuries

Watch *Whale Rider,* a mystical glimpse into modern Maori life

Eat grass-fed lamb off the grill followed by pavlova, an addictive meringue cake topped with fruit and cream

Drink 'boutique beer' from any of the country's growing selection of microbreweries

IN A WORD

Sweet as, bro

TRADEMARKS

Sheep; Maori; the All Blacks rugby team; nuclear-free; bungee jumping; *The Lord of the Rings;* Kiwi birds and fruit; *Flight of the Conchords*

RANDOM FACT

No matter where you are in New Zealand you are never more than 120km from the sea

MAP REF **T,38**

1. The Southern Alps erupt from the smooth Canterbury Plains near Methven
2. A rare clear day on Milford Sound
3. The Moeraki Boulders are scattered on the beach like a giant kid's discarded marbles
4. Loud and proud: Maori women perform a *kapa haka*

2.

3.

1.

4.

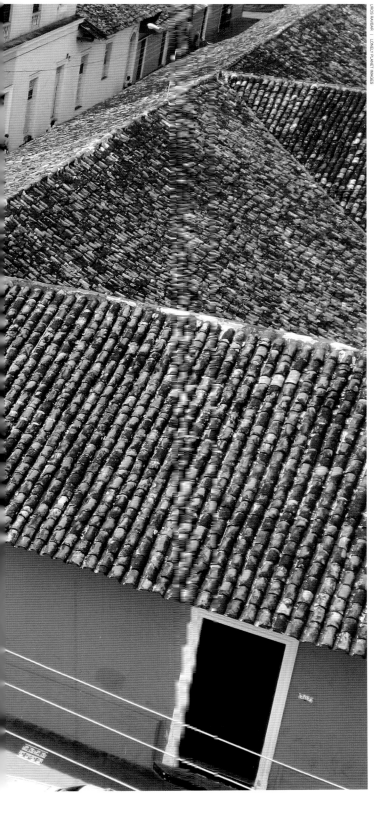

Poet Rubén Darío called it 'Our America, trembling with hurricanes, trembling with love'. Recent history rollercoastered residents through dictatorships, revolution, civil war and economic collapse, but Nicas, as they're known, are persistent and proud. Fast forward and today's Nicaragua is considered among the safest countries in Central America. The politics are still far from settled or straightforward. Yet travellers are starting to come in large numbers. With its seductive colonial settings, a passion for poetry and big beach breaks, Nicaragua has become a regional hot spot. Dollars stretch far here, and a warm tropical welcome eases the transition. Just don't offend your hosts by calling it 'the next Costa Rica'.

BEST TIME TO VISIT
June to March, to avoid the dusty end of the dry season

TOP THINGS TO SEE
o Moonrise over the cathedral in colonial Granada
o One island, two volcanoes on the biggest lake in Central America: Isla de Ometepe
o Jungle-covered Spanish fortresses along the Río San Juan
o Bright handicrafts piled high at Masaya's Mercado Viejo
o Giant papier-mâché people strolling León's Carnaval Mitos y Leyendas

TOP THINGS TO DO
o Lay low in the rugged and restful surf haven of San Juan del Sur
o Climb up Cerro Negro then sandboard down its soft steeps
o Dive with hammerheads and eagle rays off Little Corn Island
o Paddle the corridors of Central America's largest mangrove stand in Reserva Natural Estero Padre Ramos
o Play castaway on the white sand of the Pearl Keys

GETTING UNDER THE SKIN
Read *Stories and Poems* by Rubén Darío, the founder of Spanish modernism; Salman Rushdie's *The Jaguar Smile: A Nicaraguan Journey*; and Gioconda Belli's *The Country Under My Skin: A Memoir of Love and War*

Listen to electro-pop goddess Clara Grun; the Bossa-pop of Belén; the Manu Chau–influenced Perrozompopo; and legendary marimba-folk artists Los Mejía Godoy

Watch *Nicaragua Was Our Home* – a documentary about Miskito Indian repression; the Oscar-nominated *Alsino and the Condor,* about a boy in war-torn Nicaragua

Eat *nacatamales (*a mixture of cornmeal, potato, pork, tomato, onion and sweet chillies packed into a banana leaf and steamed to perfection)

Drink Flor de Caña rum; *pinol,* toasted corn powder sweetened with sugar or taken with *cacao* (chocolate)

IN A WORD
¡Va pue'! (All right!)

TRADEMARKS
Contras and Sandinistas; dusty farms and chicken buses; earthquakes and hurricanes; US intervention; baseball

RANDOM FACT
Nicaragua is the least densely populated country in Central America but that's child's play: 72% of the population is under 30 years old

HONDURAS

Puerto Cabezas

Ocotal

Guasaule
Somotillo
Matagalpa

Caribbean Sea

Corinto
León
Boaco

Managua ✪
Juigalpa
Bluefields

Masaya
Granada
Lago de Nicaragua

Monkey Point

PACIFIC OCEAN

Rivas
Isla de Ometepe

San Carlos
San Juan del Norte

COSTA RICA

MAP REF **M,10**

1. A schoolbus makes its way through the lolly-hued streets of Granada
2. Young dancers wait to perform at a festival in León
3. Bareback, barefoot and bare-chested: the only way to ride in La Prusia
4. A woman comes out swinging during a softball match in Tasbapauni

1.

2.

3.

ANTON GIBLIN | LONELY PLANET IMAGES

According to the UN, Niger is the world's worst place to live – life here can be unrelentingly tough. But Niger's diverse peoples – Tuareg, Fulani, Hausa, Djerma and Songhaï to name just five – bear these difficult times with remarkable dignity, and getting to know these peoples of the Sahel is a journey into the real Africa. Niger is also dominated by two of Africa's most iconic natural features – the Niger River in the southwest and the Sahara in the north. Together they form a focal point for so many of Niger's attractions and whether you're drifting down the river in a wooden dugout canoe or plodding through the Sahara astride a camel, life here moves to a different rhythm.

BEST TIME TO VISIT
October to February, dry and relatively cool

TOP THINGS TO SEE
- Agadez, one of the most romantic caravan towns of the Sahara, with an iconic mud mosque
- The languid riverside capital of Niamey, which has a terrific museum and traditional pirogue trips
- Zinder's ancient Hausa sultanate with a palace, weekly market and fine old quarter
- The Niger River town of Ayorou, which has a wonderful Sunday market, pirogue trips and hippos
- Kouré, home to the Sahel's last, highly endangered giraffe herd

TOP THINGS TO DO
- Ride a camel into the Aïr Mountains, the barren and beautiful desert massif and Tuareg homeland
- Sip a sunset beer at Niamey's Grand Hotel overlooking the Niger River
- Mount a deep desert expedition into the endless dunes of the Ténéré Desert
- Venture into Niger's south to see elephants and lions at the Parc Regional du W
- Celebrate the world-famous La Cure Salée festival with the nomads near In-Gall

GETTING UNDER THE SKIN
Read *Riding the Demon: On the Road in West Africa* by Peter Chilson, which sees Niger through its bush taxis

Listen to Mamar Kassey *(Alatouni)*, or to Etran Finatawa *(Desert Crossroads)*, a Tuareg and Wodaabe band famous for their desert blues

Watch *The Sheltering Sky*, directed by Bernardo Bertolucci and filmed partly in Agadez

Eat dates, yoghurt, rice, mutton, rice with sauce and couscous

Drink Bière Niger, a local lager

IN A WORD
Bonjour (Hello)

TRADEMARKS
Tuareg nomads and salt caravans; dinosaur bones and ancient rock art in the desert; a difficult life; uranium mines

RANDOM FACT
The Sahara Desert covers around 80% of Nigerien territory and less than 3% is suitable for agriculture

CAPITAL Niamey | **POPULATION** 15,306,252 | **AREA** 1,267,000 sq km | **OFFICIAL LANGUAGE** French

FRANS LEMMENS | LONELY PLANET IMAGES

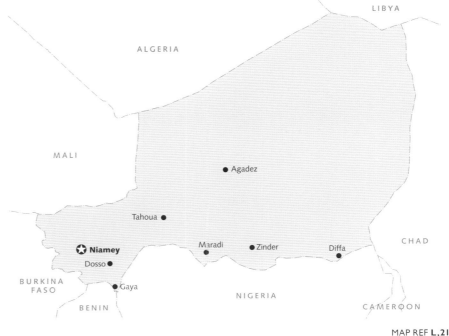

MAP REF **L,21**

1. The magnificent clothing of the Wodaabé tribe adds drama and colour to the Cure Salée (Salt Festival) in Agadez
2. A startling blue headscarf hides a shy smile
3. Tuareg nomads in the Sahara sail across an ocean of undulating dunes
4. Life springs out of the desert at Timia, near an oasis in the Aïr Mountains

4.

1.

2.

3.

4.

Africa writ large, Nigeria can be an overwhelming experience. Indeed, such is its fame that few travellers dare to venture into Africa's most populous country. But this is also West Africa's most exciting country, a place where the sensory overload of Lagos yields to the wilds of the Gashaka Gumpti National Park, where tranquil sacred forests of animist provenance coexist with the deeply religious Muslim north and its ancient trading towns with distinguished and colourful histories. Yes, this coexistence is often fraught with tension, blighted by corruption and sometimes erupts into violence. But for the most part, ordinary Nigerians, when faced with an uncertain future, throw themselves wholeheartedly into the present. Join them and you'll really 'get' Nigeria.

BEST TIME TO VISIT
November to February

TOP THINGS TO SEE
- West Africa's oldest surviving city, Kano, with beguiling Muslim and Hausa architecture and traditions
- Intimidating and exciting in equal measure, Lagos, the capital in all but name
- Benin City, the rich legacy of ancient Benin with brass casting, museum and the Oba's Palace
- The small but ancient walled city of Zaria in Nigeria's north
- Calabar, one of Nigeria's most agreeable cities set high above Cross River

TOP THINGS TO DO
- Spot elephants, lions and hippos in the terrific Gashaka Gumpti National Park
- Wander through the World Heritage–listed Sacred Forest in Yoruba Oshogbo
- Walk through the rainforest canopy at the Afi Mountain Drill Ranch, home to rehabilitated drills
- Stroll through a medieval epic amid the well-preserved architecture of Katsina
- Make a musical pilgrimage to the New Afrika Shrine, the enduring epicentre of Afrobeat in Lagos

GETTING UNDER THE SKIN
Read anything by Chinua Achebe, Ben Okri, Chimamanda Ngozi Adichie or Nobel Prize winner Wole Soyinka

Listen to Afrobeat, that unmistakeably Nigerian musical style mastered by the late Fela Kuti and his son and heir-apparent Femi Kuti

Watch any film from 'Nollywood', the world's third-largest film industry

Eat 'chop' (food), such as pepper soup and *suya* (spiced kebabs)

Drink Star beer or Guinness

IN A WORD
Dash (Bribe or tip)

TRADEMARKS
The cultural powerhouse of Anglophone Africa for music, literature and artistic traditions; squandered oil wealth

RANDOM FACT
By some estimates, one out of every five Africans is a Nigerian

MAP REF **M,21**

1. Rush-hour traffic on a Lagos street leaves little room to manoeuvre
2. Check mates: a game of outdoor checkers passes the time in Lagos
3. Crowned in gold, the Nigerian National Mosque is an impressive landmark in Abuja
4. A swirl of pattern frames friendly face

2.

3.

1.

Norway is the supermodel of Scandinavia, a peak- and fjord-blessed country that gives its neighbours a serious case of mountain envy. There's a reason why artists, photographers and outdoor enthusiasts rave over this country: at almost every corner, stunning wilderness lurks to overwhelm the senses. Much of Norway lies above the Arctic Circle, home to the midnight sun's ceaseless light, the polar night's gloomy darkness, or the ghost-like, swirling northern lights. Set amid these natural phenomena is some of the world's most scenic hiking and skiing. There's a rugged frontier feel to much of the country, but this is still Scandinavia – design-driven bars and hotels are never too far away.

BEST TIME TO VISIT
May to September for sunshine, or December to February for skiing and the northern lights

TOP THINGS TO SEE
○ Oslo's Vigeland Park, with its walkway lined with photogenic statues of screaming babies and entwined lovers
○ Lofoten Islands – mountain-islands littered with fishing villages so postcard-perfect they look fake
○ The jawdropping beauty of the Geirangerfjord, by boat or on foot
○ Bryggen, the old medieval quarter of Bergen, with its long timber buildings housing museums, restaurants and shops

TOP THINGS TO DO
○ Take a trip on a Hurtigruten coastal steamer, heading north from Bergen
○ Steam up the windows on the spectacular, seven-hour Oslo–Bergen train route
○ Spot polar bears in the Arctic archipelago of Svalbard, the ultimate polar-adventure destination
○ Hike among the high peaks and glaciers of the sublime Jotunheimen National Park

GETTING UNDER THE SKIN
Read *Gods and Myths of Northern Europe* by HR Ellis Davidson; *A Doll's House* by Henrik Ibsen; *Sophie's World* by Jostein Gaarder

Listen to the synthtastic '80s sounds of A-ha; the dark and controversial tones of black metal; the cool electro stylings of Röyksopp

Watch *Max Manus* (Man of War), Norway's biggest budget blockbuster, recounting the true story of a resistance fighter during WWII

Eat *laks* (smoked salmon); warm *moltebær syltetøy* (cloudberry jam) with ice cream

Drink coffee; *aquavit* (or *akevitt*; a potent liquor distilled from potato)

IN A WORD
Skal vi gå på ski? (Shall we go skiing?)

TRADEMARKS
Fjords; glaciers; playwright Henrik Ibsen; midnight sun; artist Edvard Munch; high taxes, high prices; oil tycoons; polar explorers; skiing; stave churches; trolls; Vikings

RANDOM FACT
'Ski' is a Norwegian word, and thanks to aeons-old rock carvings depicting hunters travelling on skis, Norwegians make a credible claim to having invented the sport

MAP REF **E,21**

1. Sunrise at noon: winter takes hold of Moskenesøy
2. The remarkable Preikestolen (Pulpit Rock) plummets 604m to Lysefjord below
3. The coastal town of Ålesund showcases Art Noveau style with traditional local motifs
4. The Briksdalsbreen glacier takes things slowly

1.

2.

3.

The sultanate of Oman could be the Arabian Peninsula's most rewarding destination. More accessible than Saudi Arabia, safer than Yemen and more traditional than the Gulf emirates, Oman nonetheless has plenty to rival these countries' attractions and more. A stirring history that combines the great sweep of Bedouin tradition with some extraordinary forts and other traditional architecture. And Mutrah Souq in Muscat is a fantasy of an Arabian bazaar come-to-life, with glittering gold and clouds of incense. But it's Oman's diverse natural beauty that is the main drawcard. Here you'll find wildly beautiful beaches, the jagged ramparts of mountain ranges and the perfectly sculpted sands of the fabled Empty Quarter.

BEST TIME TO VISIT
November to mid-March, to avoid the monsoon

TOP THINGS TO SEE
- Muscat, the lovely port city with a beautiful bay, atmospheric souq and Portuguese forts
- Yitti's gloriously unspoiled beach with craggy mountains
- Masirah's palm-strewn oases, postcard-perfect beaches and flamingos
- Nizwa, the beguiling inland town with a 17th-century fort and expansive souq
- Mughsail's jaw-dropping bay with sheer cliffs and frankincense trees close to Yemen

TOP THINGS TO DO
- Walk in wonder though Wadi Shab, the verdant gorge that feels like paradise
- Explore the copper-coloured dunes of the Wahiba Sands by camel or 4WD
- Drive over the Hajar Mountains from Al-Hamra to Wadi Bani Awf, Oman's most spectacular road
- Ponder the mysteries of Ubar, Arabia's fabled 'Atlantis of the Sands'
- Get off the beaten track on the Musandam Peninsula, a dramatic Omani outpost guarding the gates of the Gulf

GETTING UNDER THE SKIN
Read *Sultan in Oman* by renowned travel writer Jan Morris; or *Atlantis of the Sands* by Ranulph Fiennes
Listen to *Symphonic Impressions of Oman* performed by the London Symphony Orchestra, which captures the mood, scenery and traditions of Oman
Watch *7 Days Sultanate of Oman* – Oman's cinematic history is nonexistent but at least you can take a tour around the country
Eat *harees* – steamed wheat, boiled meat, lime chilli, onions and garnished with *ma owaal* (dried shark); *shuwa* (marinated meat cooked in an earth oven)
Drink camel's milk

IN A WORD
Tasharrafna (Nice to meet you)

TRADEMARKS
A former hermit sultanate that has become one of the most open Arabian Peninsula states; frankincense; ancient forts; Bedouin and the sands of the Empty Quarter

RANDOM FACT
The coastal oasis of Sohar will forever be remembered from the *Arabian Nights* as the starting point for Sinbad's epic journeys

MAP REF **L,26**

1. Jockeys spur their camels on during pre-Eid celebrations in Bidya
2. Al-Riyam Park houses a giant replica of an incense burner that looms over Muscat Harbour
3. Move to the beat of the drum: dancers celebrate in Asylah
4. The intricate patternwork on the *khanjar* (curved dagger) belies its dangerous potential

2.

3.

1.

Always off the beaten track, Pakistan is one of the last great frontiers for travellers seeking white-knuckled adventure. However, with growing political turmoil and religious fundamentalism, this is not a destination for the faint-hearted. Although Pakistan has spectacular attractions in the form of ruined cities, mesmerising mosques, fascinating tribal culture, crumbling Raj-era relics and stunning Himalayan scenery, many parts of the country are off-limits because of the risk of violence. Nevertheless, with some strategic planning, it is perfectly possible to travel through Pakistan and experience a captivating Islamic culture that has changed only superficially since the time of the Mughals.

BEST TIME TO VISIT
November to April in the south, May to October in the north

TOP THINGS TO SEE
- The Mughal brilliance of Lahore Fort and the Badshahi Masjid
- A courtyard with room for 300,000 of the faithful at the Faisal Masjid in Islamabad
- The ruins of a vanished civilisation at Moenjodaro
- Sufi shrines and spectacular Mughal monuments in historic Multan
- Pantomime sabre-rattling at the Wagah–Attari border crossing between Pakistan and India

TOP THINGS TO DO
- Eat mutton biryani – the perfect quick lunch – in the bazaars of Hyderabad
- Sway along with the singers of qawwali (Sufi devotional music) at the Data Darbar in Lahore
- Rattle along the bone-shaking Karakoram Highway to Kashgar in China
- Marvel at the outrageous ornamentation of Pakistan's lavishly decorated trucks and buses
- Get carried away by the heated atmosphere of a cricket match at Karachi's National Stadium

GETTING UNDER THE SKIN
Read Kamila Shamsie's *Burnt Shadows* or Mohsin Hamid's *The Reluctant Fundamentalist*, to see the world from a Pakistani perspective

Listen to the ballads of Nusrat Fateh Ali Khan, the most famous performer of qawwali

Watch Shoaib Mansoor's *Khuda Kay Liye* (In the Name of God), a thought-provoking exploration of some of the key issues facing Pakistan today

Eat chicken *karahi*, the national curry of Pakistan and the forerunner to the British balti

Drink fresh fruit juice; *chai* (tea); or *badam* milk, flavoured with almonds

IN A WORD
Insha'Allah (If God wills it)

TRADEMARKS
Mangos, mosques and mountains; the Karakoram Highway; Raj-era relics; climbing K2; nuclear stand-offs; military coups

RANDOM FACT
The Sufi mystics of southern Pakistan follow an esoteric interpretation of Islam with a focus on music, dancing and smoking marijuana

MAP REF **K,27**

1. The Karakoram Highway leads towards the toothy snarl of the Passu peaks
2. Worshippers enter through the dusky red facade of the Badshahi Mosque, Lahore
3. Hunzakut women dry the fruits of their labour, apricots, in the sun
4. Prayers are offered inside the Badshahi Mosque

Above and below water, Palau showcases the best of Micronesia. The diving here is world renowned for its flourishing reefs, blue holes, WWII wrecks, caves, tunnels, sumo-sized clams and more than 60 vertical drop-offs. Without gills (or a breathing apparatus) you can witness exotic birds, crocodiles slipping into the mangroves and orchids flourishing in shady corners. The archipelago is incredibly diverse from coral atolls and tranquil specks with haunting WWII pasts, to Babeldoab, Micronesia's second largest island. With signs everywhere of feel-good acronyms like: WAVE (Welcome All Visitors Enthusiastically!), it's just as easy to fall in love with the people here as it is with their particularly blessed geography.

BEST TIME TO VISIT
February and March are the driest months although it's warm year-round and can rain anytime

TOP THINGS TO SEE
- The mushroom-shaped limestone islets of the Rock Islands from a kayak
- Carved wooden 'storyboards', Palau's unique art form portraying myths and legends
- The history and art of Palau on display at the Belau National Museum
- Ngardmau Waterfall, the highest falls in Micronesia
- Eerie Japanese WWII ruins on Peleliu

TOP THINGS TO DO
- Dive by trees of black coral, mammoth gorgonian fans, sharks and sea turtles around Peleliu
- Snorkel the alien-like, stingless-jellyfish world of Jellyfish Lake
- Take it really, really easy on the charming island of Angaur
- Travel between Koror and Peleliu by local ship

GETTING UNDER THE SKIN
Read *Words of the Lagoon: Fishing and Marine Lore in the Palau District of Micronesia*, marine biologist RE Johannes' account of the knowledge of Palau's fishermen

Listen to *Natural...*, the first album by the popular Palauan band, InXes

Watch *Palau – The Enchanted Islands*, a scuba adventure by filmmaker Avi Klapfer

Eat Palau specialties like taro-leaf soup

Drink a cold Red Rooster, Palau's only microbrewed beer

IN A WORD
Omelengmes (The concept of politeness and respect)

TRADEMARKS
Giant clams; storyboard art; Jellyfish Lake; wall diving; WWII battle scars; welcoming people; social responsibility

RANDOM FACT
Although peaceful now, Palau still has a scattering of live WWII ammunition in the bush; there's a US$15,000 fine for the removal of war relics if you get caught without getting blown up

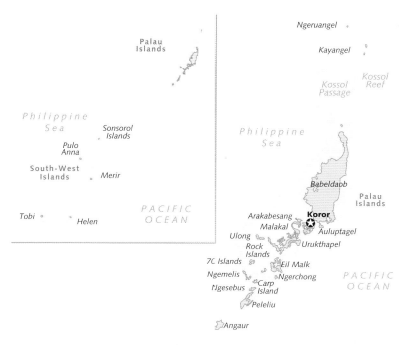

MAP REF **N,34**

1. A little rain won't stop welcoming smiles in Palau

1.

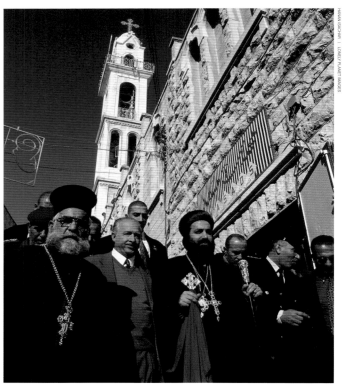

2.

3.

The world's best-known country-in-waiting, Palestine is one of the most troubled corners of the planet. Split between the West Bank and Gaza Strip and punctuated by islands of Israeli settlements, Palestine is fragmented and overcrowded. Travelling here is difficult – Israeli checkpoints are common, and security restrictions are a routine part of life – although it's nothing compared to the daily trials of Palestinians living under occupation. And yet for all its geographical and political limitations, Palestine has a proud history – Christ was born here, sacred signposts abound, and the Crusades also left their mark – and, in spite of everything, an enduring dream of peace and independence. And the chance to meet real, live and unfailingly hospitable Palestinians is Palestine's greatest gift.

BEST TIME TO VISIT
Year-round, but check the political climate rather than the temperature

TOP THINGS TO SEE
° The thriving arts scene of Ramallah, the de facto capital of the West Bank
° Jericho, one of the world's oldest continuously inhabited cities and sacred to three faiths
° Bethlehem, fabled birthplace of Christ
° Hebron, a profoundly important site for Muslims, Jews and Christians, with an architecturally stunning souq stalked by conflict and melancholy
° Nablus' enchanting old quarter and skyline pierced by more than 30 minarets

TOP THINGS TO DO
° Sample Palestine's best beers on a visit to Taybeh Brewery
° Hike through the canyon of Wadi Qelt to the 5th-century St George's Monastery
° Stroll to Shepherds' Fields, where shepherds who visited Jesus tended their flocks
° Take a Turkish bath in Nablus at Al-Shifa, which dates back to 1624
° Learn Hebrew of Arabic in Jerusalem

GETTING UNDER THE SKIN
Read anything by the late Edward Said, scholar, political activist and conscience of the Palestinian nation

Listen to Oriental Music Ensemble's *Emm el Khilkhal*, a landmark album reviving traditional Palestinian instruments and musical traditions

Watch *Paradise Now*, directed by Hany Abu-Assad, a harrowing, controversial and Oscar-nominated look at the last 24 hours of two suicide bombers

Eat *shwarma* (grilled meat sliced from a spit and served in pita bread)

Drink Taybeh Beer; *shay bi-naana* (mint tea); or pomegranate juice

IN A WORD
Al-hamdu lillah 'al as-salama (Thank God for your safe arrival)

TRADEMARKS
Birthplace of Christ; Yasser Arafat, Mahmoud Abbas, Hamas and Edward Said; a desire for Jerusalem to be the capital of an independent Palestinian state

RANDOM FACT
By one estimate, Palestinians have the highest ratio of PhDs per head of population than any other 'country' in the world

MAP REF **J,23**

1. A Palestinian shepherd pauses for thought
2. A solemn Syrian Orthodox Christmas procession passes through Bethlehem
3. Jerusalem is a city steeped in history – and conflict
4. The curved roof of Maqam Hasan al-Rai nearly blends into its Judean Desert surrounds

2.

3.

1.

4.

The waistline of the Americas, Panama is also the crucial connection. Its 80km belt of locks brings the Atlantic to the Pacific, wedding east to west in global commerce. The canal has defined Panama in the last century. But what lies just beyond could define the next. Pristine beaches, lush rainforest and big city nightlife give a taste of the country's outstanding assets. Paradoxes are plenty – the US legacy means that English is widely spoken, yet one hour outside the city, indigenous Embera paddle dugout canoes. The Panama Canal expansion will mean even more business than usual. But for now, you can pick an empty islet and play *Survivor* for the day.

BEST TIME TO VISIT
Mid-December to mid-April (the dry season)

TOP THINGS TO SEE
- Monster freighters and Capuchin monkeys sharing the Panama Canal
- The hip, regal and ruinous intersect in the 17th-century Panama City neighbourhood of Casco Viejo
- Perfect beaches and poisonous dart frogs in the Bocas del Toro Archipelago
- The great roadless wilderness of rainforest and waterways known as the Darién Gap
- Sunrise over the Pacific and sunset over the Caribbean

TOP THINGS TO DO
- Snorkel with sea turtles, sharks and schools of jack in Parque Nacional Coiba
- Trek through Parque Nacional Volcán Barú in search of the elusive quetzal
- Water-sopping and rum-soaked, revel on the crowded streets at Carnavales de Azuero
- Barter with shrewd Kunas, an autonomous indigenous group, in English, Spanish and Kuna on the sun-soaked islands of San Blas
- Sip award-winning local java in the cool mountain town of Boquete

GETTING UNDER THE SKIN
Read *The Path Between the Seas* by David McCollough, on the elephantine undertaking of the Panama Canal; *The Darkest Jungle* by Todd Balf, which chronicles the US Army's disastrous 1854 Darién expedition

Listen to the salsa of Rubén Blades; the jazz of Danilo Pérez; the Panamanian folk of Samy and Sandra Sandoval; *plena* (known internationally as reggaeton)

Watch the Academy Award–winning documentary *The Panama Deception,* by Barbara Trent, which investigates the US invasion of Panama

Eat *sancocho* (chicken, *ñame* and cilantro soup); or *carimañolas* (meat-filled *yucca* puffs)

Drink *chicheme* (sweet corn, cinnamon and vanilla in milk); or *seco* (sugar-cane liquor served with milk and ice)

IN A WORD
¡Chuleta! (Wow!)

TRADEMARKS
The umbilical cord between Central and South America; the world's most famous shortcut; Manuel Noriega; Panama hats; baseball

RANDOM FACT
The Panama Canal makes almost US $4million daily

MAP REF **M, 11**

1. The burnished desert sands of Sarigua National Park bake red under the sun
2. A bright smile from the gorgeous Archipiélago de San Blas
3. Centuries-old Casco Viejo is a good vantage point from which to take in the skyscrapers of Panama City
4. The white-throated Capuchin monkey is polygamous, communal and highly intelligent

1.

2.

3.

One of Earth's megadiverse regions, PNG has a common history with Australia going back tens of millions of years. Yet while Australia is predominantly dry and flat, PNG is wet and mountainous. As a result, Australian kangaroos bound across plains while in PNG tree kangaroos climb the rainforest canopy. As night falls, *Kundu* and *garamut* drums beat out rhythms in the sweet sticky heat, frogs and geckos bark only to be silenced by a sudden deluge of tropical rain. Beyond the modern wilds of Port Moresby are tribes living like they have for thousands of years surrounded by great mountain ranges, mighty rivers and sparkling tropical beaches.

BEST TIME TO VISIT
June to September is cooler, drier and takes in the majority of the provincial celebrations and Highlands *sing sings* (festival or dance)

TOP THINGS TO SEE
- A visual overload of en-masse body decoration at the carnival-like Highland Shows
- Dancing, singing, whistle blowing and sometimes magic involved in a crowded game of Trobriand cricket
- A traditional *sing sing* celebrating the ascension of a chief, adult initiation rites and more
- Tree kangaroos, turtles and birdlife at the Rainforest Habitat in Lae
- The rumbling, billowing string of volcanoes in New Britain

TOP THINGS TO DO
- Travel up the quintessentially primitive Sepik River into a treasure trove of Pacific art
- 'Muck dive' at Milne Bay to see tiny critters and pelagics including manta rays
- Pay respect to WWII soldiers by surviving the difficult, leech-infested Kokoda Track
- Chew betel nut

GETTING UNDER THE SKIN
Read biologist Tim Flannery's *Throwim Way Leg,* an account of his trips to the remote interior in search of tree kangaroos

Listen to Telek's *Serious Tam* CD, showcasing the singer's extraordinary voice

Watch Robin Anderson and Bob Connelly's triptych *First Contact, Joe Leahy's Neighbours and Black Harvest*, an outstanding exposition of Highlanders' first encounters with the outside world and their emergence into modern times

Eat *sasak* (sago), the staple in the swampy Sepik; and *kaukau* (sweet potatoes) in the Highlands; fresh fish and lobsters whet the palate on the coasts

Drink PNG Highland-grown Arabica coffee

IN A WORD
Em nau! (Fantastic! Right on!)

TRADEMARKS
Penis-gourds; betel nut; *sing sings*; bilum bags; tribal art; beautiful beaches; Kokoda Track; Asaro mud men; yam worship; *The Phantom*

RANDOM FACT
Over 820 languages are spoken in PNG with adults speaking an average of three languages

MAP REF O,35

1. The face paint used by the Karamui dance group hints at the bones beneath the skin
2. A tattooed dancer pauses for a solemn moment beneath his crown of feathers
3. Houses seem poised to stalk on their stilts out into the sea near Port Moresby
4. The dramatic topography of the Bismarck Range reveals undulating mountain ranges and lush valleys scored into the landscape

2.

3.

1.

PHOTOLIBRARY

4.

CHRISTOPHER PILLITZ / THE IMAGE BANK / GETTY IMAGES

Dwarfed by Brazil and Argentina, small, landlocked Paraguay is sometimes described as South America's 'forgotten country'. Like its better-known neighbours, football madness and a burgeoning beef industry are national hallmarks, while Jesuit ruins mark their shared Catholic heritage. Paraguayans, however, have followed a far different course through history. Most citizens are bilingual, proudly touting their Guaraní heritage, and scratch out a living at small-scale microenterprises or subsistence farming. The country is a remarkable study in contrasts, with horse-drawn carts sidling up to luxury automobiles, while huge Mennonite farms and rustic *campesino* (peasant farmer) settlements share space on the hard-scrabble Chaco. Paraguayans are famously laid back, quick to share a *terrere* (iced herbal tea) with a visitor over long siestas that sometimes stretch into dusk.

BEST TIME TO VISIT
May to September (winter)

TOP THINGS TO SEE
- The engineering behemoth of Itaipu, one of the world's largest hydroelectric dams and supplier of 90% of Paraguay's energy
- The haunting Jesuit Missions of Trinidad and Jesus, 18th-century colonial remnants and a Unesco World Heritage site
- Parque Nacional Cerro Corá, with its forest and savannah, caves and petroglyphs
- The colourful Carnaval of Encarnación, smaller but no less wild than Rio's big fest

TOP THINGS TO DO
- Spot jaguars, tapir and bird life in Parque Nacional Defensores del Chaco
- Go horseback riding, camp or simply admire the beauty of Laguna Blanca
- Spot monkeys, macaws and other wildlife on a slow boat ride up the Río Paraguay
- Visit the intriguing Mennonite colonies in the Chaco

GETTING UNDER THE SKIN
Read *I the Supreme* by Augusto Roa Bastos, a fascinatingly complex novel delving into the mind of a dictator

Listen to the song 'Pajaro Campana', which uses the bizarre call of the bellbird (Paraguay's national bird) as the main rhythm

Watch Roland Joffe's epic film *The Mission* for depictions of Guaraní and Jesuit settlements in colonial days

Eat succulent cuts of *tapa de cuadril* (similar to rump steak); and *empanadas* (pasties stuffed with chicken, cheese and ham, or beef)

Drink *terere* (iced herbal tea); and *mosto* (sugar-cane juice)

IN A WORD
Mba'eichapa? (How are you?)

TRADEMARKS
Football (soccer); jaguars; corruption and contraband; impassable jungle roads

RANDOM FACT
The War of the Triple Alliance (1864–70) destroyed Paraguay with a loss of over 50% of its population and 25% of its territory in the conflict against Argentina, Brazil and Uruguay

BOLIVIA

BRAZIL

The Chaco

Fortín Toledo

Filadelfia • Loma Plata

Eastern Paraguay

Asunción ✪   Nueva Australia
Itaguá • Piribebuy

ARGENTINA

Villa Florida • Santa Mariá
San Ignacio Guazú •

MAP REF R,13

1. As another day ends, the muted colours and welcoming glow of a roadside bar beckon passers-by
2. These oxen make slow progress down the road, drawing along their cart and its passengers
3. Rites of passage: adolescent girls are initiated into womanhood by the female elders of the Nivaclé tribe in Barrio Obrero
4. Trinidad, a once-grand Jesuit mission, is slowly crumbling into history

1.

2.

3.

Birthplace of the great Inca civilisation, Peru remains deeply connected to its storied ancestral heritage. Nearly half the population is purely indigenous, inhabiting some of the most fantastical settings on earth. Quechua-speaking highlanders mingle in colourful markets in the shadow of towering Andean peaks, while Uros peoples eke out a living on the surreal floating islands in Lake Titicaca. A world away, remote tribes (some uncontacted) maintain ancient traditions deep in the Amazon. Peruvian cities provide a vivid contrast, a blend of frenetic and cosmopolitan neighbourhoods, scenic Spanish-colonial centres and folk-music clubs. Innovative ideas – like sustainable tourism projects run by indigenous groups – are helping to ensure Peru's treasures will be around for generations to come.

BEST TIME TO VISIT
June to August (the dry season)

TOP THINGS TO SEE
° Machu Picchu, the great Inca ruins hidden deep in mist-covered cloud forest
° Cuzco, a beautiful Andean town with Inca-made walls, cobblestone streets and gilded colonial churches
° The enchanting islands on Lake Titicaca, one of the world's highest navigable lakes
° Arequipa, a charming colonial city near smouldering volcanoes and the world's deepest canyons
° Parque Nacional Manu, home to cloud- and rainforest and astounding biodiversity

TOP THINGS TO DO
° Listen to live *trova* (folk music) at an atmospheric nightspot in Lima
° Hike the Santa Cruz trail through the towering peaks of the Cordillera Blanca
° Charter a flight over the Nazca Lines, the mystical drawings in the earth left by a past civilisation over 1000 years ago
° Visit the ruins of Chan Chan, once the largest pre-Colombian city in the Americas

GETTING UNDER THE SKIN
Read Mario Vargas Llosa's famed *Conversations in the Cathedral* about power and politics in 1950s Peru, but with universal repercussions

Listen to the sublime Afro-Peruvian rhythms of Susana Baca

Watch Claudia Llosa's award-winning fable *MadeinUSA* about the clash between old and new in a somewhat surreal Andean town

Eat *ceviche (*fresh seafood marinated in lemon juice and chilli peppers)

Drink Inka Kola, bubble-gum flavoured soda; *pisco* (a white grape brandy)

IN A WORD
Buenos días (Good day)

TRADEMARKS
Pan pipes; Andean peaks; llamas; Incan ruins; colourful textiles; indigenous villages; 16th-century Spanish architecture and artefacts

RANDOM FACT
Peru's pre-Colombian civilisations left such a mine of archaeological riches that treasures are still being unearthed, like the recently discovered 'lost city of the cloud people', a cliff-top citadel with rock paintings and 1000-year-old stone houses

MAP REF **P,12**

1. You can leave your hat on: spectators enjoy a dance competition at the Virgen de la Merced festival in Incahuasi
2. The ominously named Funerary Rock towers over Machu Picchu
3. The best way to travel: hand-woven blankets provide a snug cocoon for this passenger
4. A band beats out the rhythm of the streets during the Señor de Torreschally festival parade in Lima

2.

3.

1.

TOM COCHREN | LONELY PLANET IMAGES

4.

DALLAS STRIBLEY | LONELY PLANET IMAGES

Scattered like jewels across the Pacific Ocean, the 7107 islands of the Philippines lie well off the radar of most travellers, despite the lure of riotous fiestas, stunning beaches and some of the best diving in the world. Many are put off visiting this former Spanish and American colony by the reputation of its hectic capital, Manila, and by the sex tourists who flock to the largest Catholic country in Asia. However, it is the islands rather than the cities that define the Philippine experience – each has its own unique character, most are covered in dense jungles and volcanoes, and almost all have glorious beaches and fringing coral reefs. Drifting from island to island by outrigger ferry only adds to the sense of being an explorer on a new frontier.

BEST TIME TO VISIT
September to May, to avoid the typhoon season

TOP THINGS TO SEE
- The almost too perfect sands of Boracay Island
- Rice terraces on an epic scale at Banaue
- *Butanding* (whale sharks) on their annual migration past Luzon Island
- Peaceful island backwaters like Siquijor, Camiguin and Bohol
- The spooky hanging coffins of Sagada

TOP THINGS TO DO
- Ride in a jeepney – the wildly decorated stretched jeeps that serve as buses across the Philippines
- Dive into an eerie graveyard of WWII shipwrecks at Coron on Busuanga
- Survive a night out in Manila – Asia's most notorious metropolis
- Travel by outrigger ferry between the islands of the Visayas
- Ride a dirt bike across rugged Palawan

GETTING UNDER THE SKIN
Read *In Our Image* by Stanley Karnow, a harrowing exposé of the American colonial period in the Philippines; or F Sionil José's Spanish-era epic *Dusk*

Listen to the sentimental croonings of karaoke favourite Jose Mari Chan; or the agreeable Pinoy-rock of Eraserheads

Watch Ishmael Bernal's emotional classic *Himala*; or Chito Rono's crowd-pleasing blockbuster *Sukob*, starring Kris Aquino, daughter of former president Corazon Aquino

Eat *adobo* (pork or chicken stewed in vinegar and soy sauce) – the national dish of the Philippines

Drink Tanduay rum, typically served *Cuba Libre*-style with Coke and a twist of lime

IN A WORD
Mabuti naman (I'm fine)

TRADEMARKS
Jeepneys; San Miguel beer; cock-fighting; Catholicism; coral reefs; coco-palm plantations; revolutions; Manila's seedy underbelly; more beaches than you can count; Imelda Marcos' shoes

RANDOM FACT
Every Easter dozens of devout Filipino Catholics offer themselves up to be crucified with real nails at San Fernando de Pampagna

MAP REF **M,33**

1. Enchanting rays of light settle on a stilt village in Coron
2. Skilful ball masters shoot some hoops in Puerto Princesa
3. Mixing Spanish and local styles, the Miagao Church in Iloilo City depicts St Christopher holding a baby Jesus under the Philippine 'palm tree of life'
4. A proud moment for costumed boys waving their straw hats at the annual Sinulog Fiesta in Cebu City

1.

2.

As the smallest territory in the world and one of the most remote destinations on earth, Pitcairn Island feels both claustrophobic and wildly exhilarating. The island's 4.5 sq km surface is almost entirely sloped and has landscapes that vary from desolate rock cliffs to lush tropical hillsides. Yet it's the 50 or so residents, descended from the Bounty mutineers, who make the place famous. If you can find a way to get here, spend time hiking and meeting the locals – you'll quickly understand why these Anglo-Polynesians are proud to call Pitcairn home and preserve their unique heritage. The archipelago also consists of two atolls plus Henderson Island – a raised coral island with a virtually untouched environment and endemic birdlife.

BEST TIME TO VISIT
April to October is the dry season

TOP THINGS TO SEE
- All the *Bounty* leftovers from the rusty canon and anchor to the faded old bible on display at the island's museum
- Flightless and fearless Henderson rails trundling on the mosquito-free shores of Henderson Island
- Mysterious Polynesian petroglyphs at Down Rope, the island's only beach
- The island's resident Galapagos turtle, Mrs T over on Tedside
- Sawdust-covered local artists making *Bounty* models and wood sculptures

TOP THINGS TO DO
- Take a dip in the neon-blue waters of cathedral-like St Paul's Pool
- Hike down the steep cliffs to Down Rope to go fishing
- Whiz around on the back of a quad bike up and down red-dirt slopes
- Follow Fletcher Christian's footsteps by gazing over Adamstown from high up in Christian's Cave
- Eat, drink and get to know the locals at Christian's Cafe

GETTING UNDER THE SKIN
Read *Fragile Paradise* by Glynn Christian (Fletcher's great-great-great-great-grandson), an investigation of the mutiny and the mutineers' fate on Pitcairn

Listen to locals speaking Pitkern, a strange mix of old English sailor slang and Tahitian

Watch *The Bounty* (1984) starring Anthony Hopkins and Mel Gibson, the best re-enactment of the mutineer's tale

Eat local Pitcairn honey, said to be the world's purest

Drink a tipple with the locals at Christian's Cafe on Friday nights

IN A WORD
Whutta-waye? (How are you?)

TRADEMARKS
Mutiny on the *Bounty*; Fletcher Christian; pirates; precipitous slopes; Seventh Day Adventists; honey; isolation; breadfruit

RANDOM FACT
The islanders are Seventh Day Adventists, but few attend church and almost everyone drinks alcohol

MAP REF **R,6**

1. A cruise ship anchors off the stunning coastline of Bounty Bay at Adamstown
2. A cricket match takes place against a distractingly beautiful backdrop
3. Big brother is watching: young boys sporting HMS *Bounty* gaze at the camera

2.

3.

1.

Stretching from the Baltic Sea to the Carpathian mountains, Poland's fortunes, and territory, have waxed and waned over centuries. Having shrugged off the Soviet mantle, Poland is embracing modernity with the energy and passion characteristic of its staunch Catholic faith and ages-tested doggedness in the face of adversity. With its upbeat capital, Warsaw, and the timeless elegance of Kraków, industrial heartland cities and Unesco Biosphere Reserves, Poland is nothing if not diverse. Locals tend to be family-oriented church-goers, and fiercely proud of John Paul II, the first Polish pope. Visitors can expect a warm welcome comprised of a raised glass of vodka, always drunk neat, accompanied by a hearty handshake. A second glass usually follows the first; then a third, and so on...

BEST TIME TO VISIT
May to September

TOP THINGS TO SEE
- The architectural treasures of the Old Town and Wawel Hill in the former capital of Krakow
- The Warsaw Rising Museum, testament to the bravery and determination of local Poles
- Malbork Castle, the largest Gothic castle in Europe and once headquarters of the Teutonic Knights
- Sandy beaches and dunes, and amber on sale in Gdańsk, on the Baltic coast
- The countless lakes and canals of the Great Masurian Lake system

TOP THINGS TO DO
- Pay your respects at the infamous Nazi death camps of Auschwitz and Birkenau
- Spot a European bison emerging out of the undergrowth at Białowieża National Park
- Join the pilgrims trekking to see the Black Madonna at the Jasna Góra monastery
- Hike into the Tatra Mountains, the highest range within the Carpathians, or catch the cable car to Mt Kasprowy Wierch

GETTING UNDER THE SKIN
Read *Heart of Europe* and *God's Playground* by revered historian Norman Davies

Listen to the works of Frederic Chopin; or Henryk Gorecki's *Symphony No 3*

Watch the films of Krzysztof Kieslowski, either *the Decalogue*, 10 short films set in a Warsaw tower block, or *Three Colours: White,* a black comedy

Eat *pierogi* (dumplings stuffed with minced meat); or *borscht*, either hot or cold, depending on the season

Drink vodka, which the Poles claim to have invented and which is always downed in a single swig

IN A WORD
Dzien dobry (Good day)

TRADEMARKS
Pope John Paul II; *pierogi*; Baltic Sea amber; Solidarity; vodka shots; astrologer Nicolaus Copernicus; author Joseph Conrad

RANDOM FACT
Nobel Prize–winning physicist Marie Curie completed her studies in Paris because, as a woman, she was denied a place at Kraków University

MAP REF **G,22**

1. The Czocha Castle in Leśna is dusted with fresh powdered snow
2. Take a stroll among the fallen leaves of autumn in Las Wolski (Wolski Forest)
3. Soldiers parade in historic uniforms during the 3rd of May Constitution Day celebrations in Warsaw
4. The resplendent beauty of St Mary's Church in Kraków's Old Town dates back to the 14th century

1.

2.

3.

There is good reason why locals call Lisbon 'Lisa'. A slow-paced, siesta-fuelled place that lazes in the Iberian sun between palm-treed plazas, brightly coloured houses and ivory-white domes, this city is one very beautiful lady – and a natural beauty at that. Born to be wandered, her tangle of cobblestone lanes trimmed with stylish boutiques and an eclectic mix of edgy bars and dining hideouts is a heart-stealer. Move away from the capital, and medieval castles, white-washed villages, old-fashioned wine estates and rambling cork groves unfold. Up north, granite peaks, lush river valleys and virgin forest beckon. Add to the cocktail its exuberant people wildly passionate about family, food and the soul-searching sound of bittersweet fado, and seduction is head-over-heels complete.

BEST TIME TO VISIT
March to June and September, July and August to bake on the Algarve's busy beaches

TOP THINGS TO SEE
- Capital views from Lisbon's Castelo de São Jorge
- The tourist icon of Portugal: Torre de Belém in Lisbon's Belém quarter
- World-class modern art, Moorish architecture and fairy-tale palaces in Sintra
- Coimbra, the Cambridge of Portugal, with a medieval heart and live fado in packed student bars
- Walled 14th-century Évora, a Unesco World Heritage Site

TOP THINGS TO DO
- Uncover bijou boutiques down dusty alleys and an eclectic mix of bars, restaurants and clubs in ubercool Lisbon
- Poke around Alfama, Lisbon's ever charming Moorish old-timer
- Dramatic cliffs, gold-sand beaches and scalloped bays on the Algarve
- Tour a port-wine lodge and taste Portugal's legendary tipple in Porto
- Hike rugged peaks in the Parque Nacional da Peneda-Gerês

GETTING UNDER THE SKIN
Read the funny, 18th-century love story *Memorial do Convento* by Nobel Prize–winner José Saramago

Listen to Mariza, whose album *Terra* fuses traditional fado with world sounds

Watch Manoel de Oliveira's *The Convent,* in which John Malkovich and Catherine Deneuve travel to Portugal to find out if Shakespeare was Spanish-Jewish

Eat *caldeirada* (seafood stew); *cataplana* (seafood and rice stew in a copper pot)

Drink Sogrape's Barca Velha *vinho* (wine) with your meal, followed by vintage port from the Douro Valley

IN A WORD
Bom dia (Hello!)

TRADEMARKS
Fado; football; Ronaldo; salted cod; the Algarve; cork; wine

RANDOM FACT
The sleeves-up people of Porto recite an old saying about the country's biggest cities – 'Porto works, Coimbra studies, Braga prays and Lisbon plays'

MAP REF 1,19

1. Barrels of wine make their way down the Rio Douro in *barcos* (barges), past the soft-pink city skyline
2. Constructed from rare lioz limestone, the four-storey Torre de Belém defends the Rio Tejo
3. *Tranvía eléctricos* (trams) whizz by each other on a busy Lisbon street
4. Mere mortals attempt to rub shoulders with royalty at Lisbon's Discoveries Monument

2.

3.

1.

Old Spain lives on in Old San Juan, the centuries-old walled seaside town within the vast urban sprawl that is modern San Juan. There's no ossified museum peace – the cobblestone streets are alive with Puerto Ricans day and night. Shopping, cafes, clubs, corner bars and more attract streams of locals for whom *passeo* (strolling) is *the* cultural institution. Elsewhere on this large island heaving with life, the influences are myriad, but none less so than from America, the protecting, exploiting and culturally colonising force in Puerto Rico. Locals are forever torn between independence, dependence or outright statehood and opinions are passionately expressed. Adding to the mix are African traditions dating to slave times and even older native Caribbean beliefs.

BEST TIME TO VISIT
November is lovely but crowds are few; December to April is the most popular time

TOP THINGS TO SEE
○ Old San Juan, the 500-year-old centre of the nation and an engrossing, vibrant window into the past
○ Fuerte San Felipe del Morro is an enclessly fascinating and enormous Spanish fort dating from 1539
○ Ponce, a colonial gem known for its criollo architecture and a centre for traditional dance
○ The myriad fauna in the dry forests of Bosque Estatal de Guánica
○ The 'cathedral of rum' at the Bacardi factory

TOP THINGS TO DO
○ Listen to the silence in the nature reserves of Vieques, an island once used for target practice
○ Follow the bouncing frogs in El Yunque, the island's surviving tropical rainforest
○ Burrow like a turtle into the warm, and turtle-friendly, sands of Culebra
○ Party along the playful beachside stretch of Condado
○ Surf on and dive below the waters of laidback Rincón, with its '60s hippie vibe

GETTING UNDER THE SKIN
Read Rosario Ferre's revisionist stories in *Sweet Diamond Dust*

Listen to the infamous sounds of Tito Puente and Willie Colon

Watch the acclaimed *West Side Story* that represents stateside Puerto Ricans of the day; also Rachel Ortiz's heartfelt documentary *Mi Puerto Rico*

Eat plantain dishes like *mofongos* and *tostones; tembleque* (coconut pudding), *comido criollo* (an everchanging stew)

Drink piña coladas; *Cuba libres; mojitos* or any other rum drink

IN A WORD
Qué pasa? (What's happening?)

TRADEMARKS
Living *la vida loca*; the 51st state; Bacard rum cocktails; baseball players

RANDOM FACT
If you want to hear raised voices, ask about the pros and cons of independence and statehood; the US may authorise a plebiscite to decide the island's future

MAP REF **L,13**

1. A couple of locals are framed by the Puerto Rican flag in Old San Juan
2. Terrifying horns feature on an ornate papier mâché mask worn in Ponce
3. The elegant neoclassical facade of the Casa Armstrong-Poventud graces Ponce's Plaza Las Delicias
4. An accordion player pumps out the tunes at Fuerte San Cristóbal in San Juan

1.

2.

3.

Perhaps tired of living in one of the least known countries on earth, Qatar's rulers seem determined to put the country firmly on the international map as a regional financial capital and rival to Dubai for oil-rich glitz and Gulf glamour. Qatar has also made headlines as a liberal Arab state, at once the base for Al-Jazeera and the only Gulf country to maintain relations with Israel. Yes, there are sand dunes, desert excursions and ancient rock carvings, and Qatar may be traditional in the sense of being ruled over by an old-style Gulf dynasty. But its charms are almost entirely contemporary and Qatar's essence is found in Doha, with its futuristic architecture and rush to embrace the modern.

BEST TIME TO VISIT
November to March, to avoid the fierce heat and humidity

TOP THINGS TO SEE
○ Al-Corniche: Qatar in a nutshell along 7km of waterfront with innovative architecture and old-style dhows
○ Palm Tree Island: Doha's answer to Dubai's feats of modern engineering in the Gulf waters
○ Sheraton Doha Resort, an Arabian institution and the place for panoramic views of Doha's skyline
○ Al-Wakrah: with fine mosques, glorious beaches and shallow waters where flamingos wade
○ Rock carvings dating back thousands of years at Jebel Jassassiyeh

TOP THINGS TO DO
○ Sleep overnight in Khor al-Adaid, a lovely stretch of water surrounded by sand dunes
○ Pass the evening eating wonderfully well in the restaurants of Al-Bandar in Doha
○ Engage in some retail therapy at City Center Doha
○ Go birdwatching in the mangroves and gardens of Al-Khor
○ Explore the country's northern tip with lovely beaches and evocative abandoned villages

GETTING UNDER THE SKIN
Read *Arabian Time Machine: Self-Portrait of an Oil State*, a collection of interviews with Qataris and window on local society

Listen to Ali Abdul Sattar, Qatar's only musical export of note

Watch *Qatar: A Quest for Excellence*, exploring Qatari culture and music

Eat *labneh* (a type of yoghurt cheese made from goat's milk)

Drink strong black coffee; fruit juices; alcohol in top-end hotel bars and restaurants

IN A WORD
Salaam (Hello)

TRADEMARKS
Al-Jazeera; old wind-towers alongside sleek modern architecture; fierce summer heat; Arabian oryx

RANDOM FACT
Foreign maps of Arabia drawn before the 19th century didn't show Qatar

MAP REF **K,25**

1. Wanna buy a falcon? Then head to this well-stocked shop in Doha
2. A one-hump race: camels training on the track at Al-Shahaniyah
3. Women catch up on the latest news in Qatar
4. A lustrous pearl rests in an oyster shell that looks ready to devour the Doha skyline

2.

3.

1.

Transylvania is hands-down Romania's most well-known region, and Count Dracula its best-known resident. But Romania has a great deal more to it than hoary old vampire legends. With a mighty section of the Carpathian mountains, a white-sand stretch of Black Sea coast, bucolic vistas wherever you turn your gaze, Orthodox churches and a clutch of medieval walled cities, Romania is more picturesque than Bram Stoker would have you believe. This easternmost outpost of the long-gone Roman Empire retains a Latin attitude to time and authority. The Romanians are spontaneously convivial, always willing to stop for a lengthy chat under blossoming pear trees, to move with the rhythms of the seasons and to make the most of the sun while it shines.

BEST TIME TO VISIT
May to June and September to October

TOP THINGS TO SEE
- The medieval delights of Braşov, centre of bucolic Transylvania, home to Gothic churches and Europe's narrowest street
- Maramureş, the last redoubt of medieval rural life in Europe
- The world's second biggest building, Ceausescu's imposing Palace of Parliament in Bucharest
- Dazzling icons and frescoes full of Biblical scenes, allegories and cautionary tales in the Bucovina Monasteries

TOP THINGS TO DO
- Check over your shoulder as you tour so-called Dracula's Castle in Bran
- Enjoy the views from the medieval citadel of Sighişoara, perched on a hillock and ringed with 14th-century towers
- Push a rowboat out into the Danube delta to tour an expansive wetland teeming with birdlife
- Soak up the sun on the golden sand of the most popular Black Sea resort, Mamaia

GETTING UNDER THE SKIN
Read *Along the Enchanted Way* by William Blacker, an account of life in rural Romania and a doomed love affair with a Roma person

Listen to the inspirational, upbeat, improvised Romany mayhem of Taraf de Haidouks

Watch *12:08 East of Bucharest*, a deadpan look at the decline of the communist regime; *Gadjo Dilo* by Tony Gatlif, a tale of a Frenchman pursuing a Romany musician

Eat *mamaliga* (a cornmeal staple); or *ciorba da burta* (tripe soup that allegedly cures hangovers)

Drink local wines, including Murfatlar, Odobesti and Tarnave

IN A WORD
Buna (Hello)

TRADEMARKS
Count Dracula and all that Transylvanian business; rolling countryside; the tyranny of Ceausescu; local wine; sturgeon from the Danube delta

RANDOM FACT
In 1884, Timişoara became the first European city to have electric street lighting

MAP REF H,22

1. Priests in ceremonial vestments conduct a baptism at the Cathedral of Sts Peter and Paul in Constanţa
2. Overlooking the Danube is the gargantuan 40m-high monument to King Decebalus, Europe's tallest rock sculpture
3. A suspicious flock in Transylvania spot a wolf in sheep's clothing lurking among them
4. The dome on Biserica Studentilor in Bucharest is exquisite in its detail

1.

2.

3.

Stretching across 11 time zones from the Baltic to the Bering Sea, Russia is a country of epic proportions. Although home to the world's largest forest (the taiga) and its deepest lake (Lake Baikal), Russia is better known for its man-made wonders: stunning tsarist palaces, monolithic Stalinist skyscrapers, glittering onion-domed cathedrals and lavish theatres where world-class ballets, symphonies and operas pack the seasonal calendar. Famous for a gloomy exterior, Russians are extraordinarily generous with those who've earned their trust. An invitation to a Russian home usually means memorable feasting and storytelling over a seemingly endless flow of vodka; long train trips and weekend stays at the dacha (summer country house) provide another setting to swap stories about Russia's enduring legacy.

BEST TIME TO VISIT
May to October

TOP THINGS TO SEE
º The Kremlin in Moscow, home to striking cathedrals and tsarist treasures
º St Petersburg's awe-inspiring Hermitage Museum, an 18th-century palace holding one of the world's finest art collections
º The grand imperial estate of Tsarskoe Selo, outside of St Petersburg, with its lavish palace halls and pretty, landscaped gardens
º Kamchatka, the remote 'land of fire and ice' with its snow-covered volcanoes, reindeer herds, lush forests and other-worldly landscapes

TOP THINGS TO DO
º Wander through the fortress of Novgorod, followed by a Volkhov River boat ride
º Take a 9289km journey on the Trans-Siberian Railway from Moscow to Vladivostok
º Feel the beat of birch on your back as you sweat it out in a *banya* (bathhouse)
º Take in the views of crystal-clear Lake Baikal from the cliffs on Olkhon Island

GETTING UNDER THE SKIN
Read *War and Peace* by Leo Tolstoy, the great and highly readable epic given new life by Pevear and Volokhonsky's celebrated translation

Listen to the Romantic piano concerti of Rachmaninov; the sweet lyricism of Tchaikovsky; and the dissonant modernism of Stravinsky

Watch *Russian Ark*, a mesmerising journey through St Petersburg's Winter Palace

Eat *pelmeni* (meat dumplings); or borsch with *smetana* (sour cream)

Drink vodka; Baltika beer; and piping hot tea poured from a samovar

IN A WORD
Zdrastvuyte (Hello)

TRADEMARKS
Vodka; free-spending oligarchs; *matryoshka* dolls; fur hats; caviar; stocky babushkas; *dachas;* cabbage and potatoes; Soviet high-rises

RANDOM FACT
One of Russia's most urgent problems is its grave population decline; in response, the Kremlin has created incentives, including cash awards, for families to have more children

MAP REF **F,28**

1. Cavernous communist art adorns Moscow's Kievskaya metro station
2. All aboard! The Trans-Siberian arrives in Irkutsk
3. Dashing through the snow...Buryat horses head off for a brisk gallop in Ulan-Ude
4. The swirling domes and red-brick towers are unmistakably those of Russia's most recognisable landmark – St Basil's Cathedral in Moscow's Red Square

2.

3.

1.

4.

Although more associated with death, this petite African nation exudes vitality. *Le Pays des Milles Collines* (The Land of a Thousand Hills) is draped with life: mountain gorillas play in pockets of virgin rainforest; patchwork fields cling to steep slopes; and Rwandans radiate the unfathomable strength and endurance of the human spirit. The beauty of it all shatters preconceptions, just as the stories of the past can break hearts. Travels here are incredibly rewarding, taking visitors to new highs as well as leading them on an introspective trip into the depths of the human condition. Meanwhile Rwandans, on a remarkable journey of their own, have regained their feet and continue to stride forward to a peaceful future.

BEST TIME TO VISIT
Mid-May to mid-March, to avoid the long rains

TOP THINGS TO SEE
- The National Museum in Butare, with one of Africa's best ethnographical exhibits
- Papyrus gonolek and other rare bird species in the rich Nyabarongo wetlands
- Elephant, buffalo and giraffe on Parc National de l'Akagera's open savannah
- King Yuhi V Musinga's restored royal palace in Nyanza

TOP THINGS TO DO
- Share a gleeful hour with endangered mountain gorillas on the rainforest-clad slopes of Parc National des Volcans
- Travel the length of Lake Kivu, sampling unspoilt beaches every step of the way
- Contemplate humanity's darkest side at the Kigali Memorial Centre, a haunting tribute to those lost in the genocide
- Track chimps, L'Hoest's monkeys and colobus troops beneath Afromontane forest's canopy in Parc National Nyungwe

GETTING UNDER THE SKIN
Read *We Wish to Inform You that Tomorrow We Will Be Killed with Our Families* by Philip Gourevitch, which delves into the horrors of the 1994 genocide and sheds light on how the international community failed Rwanda

Listen to Jean-Paul Samputu, an international award-winning recording artist famous for his neo-traditional Rwandan music

Watch *Gorillas in the Mist*, based on Dian Fossey's compelling autobiography about her life's work with gorillas

Eat grilled *tilapia* (Nile perch); or goat brochettes with *ugali* (maize porridge)

Drink *icyayi* (sweet, milky tea)

IN A WORD
Muraho (Hello, in Kinyarwanda)

TRADEMARKS
Mountain gorillas; the apocalyptic 1994 genocide; forgiveness; volcanoes; *Le Pays des Milles Collines*; patchwork fields of green

RANDOM FACT
Once defined by their respective tribes, the Rwandans are being asked to shed this aspect of their identity; with no more Hutus, no more Tutsis, only Rwandans, it's hoped the country will take another step away from the genocidal past

MAP REF O,23

1. Where the wild things are – mountain gorillas keep their hands warm in the Parc National des Volcans
2. Get swept away by Intore dancers performing the 'Dance of Heroes'
3. Villagers drink home-made beer in a bar at a weekly market in Gotovo
4. A couple of goats get a good cuddle near Butare

1.

2.

3.

Driving around the northern reaches of St Kitts, you pass mile after mile of sugar cane gone wild. The once all-encompassing lifeblood of the nation is no more and the huge plantations have been abandoned. Meanwhile beaches across the island rattle with the percussion of construction as a new economy based on tourism takes hold. Even the train once used for hauling cane now hauls tourists. But if change is coming fast to this classic eastern Caribbean island, it is managing to retain its essential qualities: a laid-back culture given to loud, boisterous celebration and an utter contempt for stress. Nevis is much the same albeit in a package that's almost impossibly alluring. Circumnavigating the island on a two-hour drive is one of life's meandering pleasures.

BEST TIME TO VISIT
Year-round, although the hurricane season (June to October) has more storms

TOP THINGS TO SEE
- Basseterre, the capital of St Kitts is equally thriving and shambolic
- Brimstone Hill Fortress, a rambling 18th-century fort and a Unesco site
- Historic Charlestown, the small main town on Nevis has a mellow vibe that makes you want to settle back on a park bench
- Plantation houses with sweeping sea views on St Kitts
- Frigate Bay, with a string of fun beach shacks serving lobster for dinner and drinks till dawn

TOP THINGS TO DO
- Ride one of the many ferries linking the two islands
- Drive right round Nevis, enjoying rainforests and beaches in equal measure
- Take a guided hike on the lush mountainsides of Nevis
- Windsurf on the Oualie Bay, a world-class site
- Dive in Sandy Point Bay far below the ramparts on Brimstone Hill

GETTING UNDER THE SKIN
Read *Out of the Crowded Vagueness* by Brian Dyde, and *A History of St Kitts* by Vincent K Hubbard, two histories that fully cover the islands' past dramas

Listen to Christmas music; there's a strong local tradition to set old chestnuts to Calypso and other Caribbean beats

Watch out for some film talent as St Kitts is spending big money to establish film production facilities

Eat pepperpot, a stew made with any imaginable combination of meats and vegies

Drink CSR (Cane Spirit Rothschild), a potent potion made from sugar cane and most often mixed with Ting, a grapefruit soda

IN A WORD
Menono (I don't know)

TRADEMARKS
Snorkelling; laid-back attitude; old sugar plantation estates; fine beaches; cricket

RANDOM FACT
The federation of the two islands forms the smallest nation in the Western Hemisphere

MAP REF **L,13**

1. Puppy love is on display at Pinney's Beach, Nevis' most famous beach
2. Worth its weight in gold? This vendor will happily sell you 18 carrots at the Basseterre market
3. The Unesco World Heritage–listed Brimstone Hill Fortress contains this citadel, which holds 24 cannons and offers superb coastal views
4. So much sugar cane, so little time – harvesters at work in the fields

The colour wheel is simple on St Lucia: rich green for the tropical land, pure white for the ring of beaches and brilliant blue for the surrounding sea. And if you look closely, you can fill out the rainbow. Yellows, oranges and reds emerge once you spot the flowers in the lush forest and take in the jaunty little villages with their brightly painted homes. (Yellow also gets help from the many banana plantations dotting the hilly countryside.) Take time for all the pleasures of surf and sand while tasting the garish cultural stew of loud reggae, piquant food and rum-fuelled escapades. Away from the coasts, there are hikes amid the towering limestone pitons that are alive with the echoes of waterfalls.

BEST TIME TO VISIT

Enjoy perfect weather with plenty of other visitors from December to May; at other times, you get rain, humidity and solitude

TOP THINGS TO SEE

- Pigeon Island, a former hangout for pirates with evocative names like Wooden Leg de Bois
- Diamond Botanical Gardens, a mannered and artful presentation of local flora beauty
- Soufrière, an authentic fishing town that's welcoming yet unaffected by tourists
- The buzzing markets of Castries, the capital, are windows into island life
- Gros Islet, a genial mix of loafers, Rastas and beach bums

TOP THINGS TO DO

- Dive in Anse Chastanet, a marine park that's also ideal for snorkelling
- Chat up the St Lucia parrot in the Edmond and Quilesse Forest Reserves
- Crew one of the many transiting yachts on the glass-smooth waters of Marigot Bay
- Avoid becoming lunch for the boa constrictors of the Frigate Islands Nature Reserve
- Catch the breeze with kite-surfing on the south coast

GETTING UNDER THE SKIN

Read Derek Walcott's *Collected Poems, 1948–1984*, an anthology by St Lucia's Nobel prize winner

Listen to the local version of the banjo called the *bwa poye*

Watch various films that used St Lucia for palm-tree scenes including *Dr Doolittle* (1967), *Superman 2* and *White Squall*

Eat West Indian fare made with grilled fish, plus fresh bread, a legacy of the French

Drink Piton, a locally brewed lager

IN A WORD

Bon jou (Good day, in Kwéyòl, which the French Creole islanders sometimes use)

TRADEMARKS

Pirate hideouts; impenetrable jungles; bananas aplenty

RANDOM FACT

Although the British invaded in 1778 and the French ceded the island for good in 1814, old traditions linger: most people speak a French-accented patois, are Catholic and live in towns with French names

MAP REF **M,13**

1. Dare to summit the primeval twin peaks of the Pitons, volcanic plugs on the southwestern coast at Soufrière

1.

Caribbean fantasies converge on this collection of 32 islands at the south end of the Leeward Islands. Party like a rock star in the fabled $150,000-a-week estates on Mustique; hang out with reggae-addled locals and itinerant fishers on St Vincent; or live your own pirate fantasy amid Tobago Cays. In fact SVG (as it's known) might be the ideal place to finally live out that fantasy of owning a yacht, as you can avoid the commitment by simply renting one and lazing your way about the islands, letting the winds and your moods guide you from one perfect spot to the next. Or indulge your inner sailor and hop a ride aboard somebody else's yacht – the ultimate in carefree wanderlust.

BEST TIME TO VISIT
Most people arrive December to May but the summer wet months like July can be nice and uncrowded

TOP THINGS TO SEE
- Tobago Cays, a five-spot of tiny islands that could be a model of Caribbean perfection
- Kingstown, the very buzzing capital with its maze of old stone alleyways
- Windward Highway, a seemingly scripted mix of wave tossed shores, placid beach coves and pastel-hued villages
- Fort Charlotte, an 1806 edifice with commanding views of a dozen islands clear to the horizon
- Port Elizabeth on the sweep of Admiralty Bay

TOP THINGS TO DO
- Pass through plantations on a trek up La Soufrière volcano
- Lose all inhibitions on Mustique, a private pleasure island favoured by wealthy luminaries
- Hope for treasure amid the myriad variations of coral reefs and shipwrecks
- Claim your sandy patch on Saltwhistle Bay, a beach so fine it needs a sixth star
- Playing Captain Jack on the *Sacra Nouche*, a boat used in *Pirates of the Caribbean*

GETTING UNDER THE SKIN
Read about life in St Vincent's oh-so-picturesque capital in *City Of Arches: Memories Of An Island Capital* by Vivian Child

Listen to reggae; steel bands; and local boy made good, Kevin Lyttle

Watch the *Pirates of the Caribbean* movies, which used SVG as a principal location

Eat *bul jol* (roasted breadfruit and saltfish with tomatoes and onions)

Drink the locally distilled Captain Bligh Rum

IN A WORD
Check it? (Do you follow what I'm saying?)

TRADEMARKS
Rock stars and royalty; yachts; volcanoes; pirate movies

RANDOM FACT
The British dreamed of making the islands a plantation paradise for growers after the French were expelled in 1783, but volcanic eruptions, hurricanes, the abolition of slavery and more thwarted the scheme

MAP REF **M,13**

1. Racing boats gather in the aquamarine waters of Carriacou for a regatta
2. A bubbly spirit delivers a crate of cola in Kingstown
3. Dive into another world among the reefs of Tobago Cays
4. Escape to a beautiful island hideaway on Mustique

1.

2.

3.

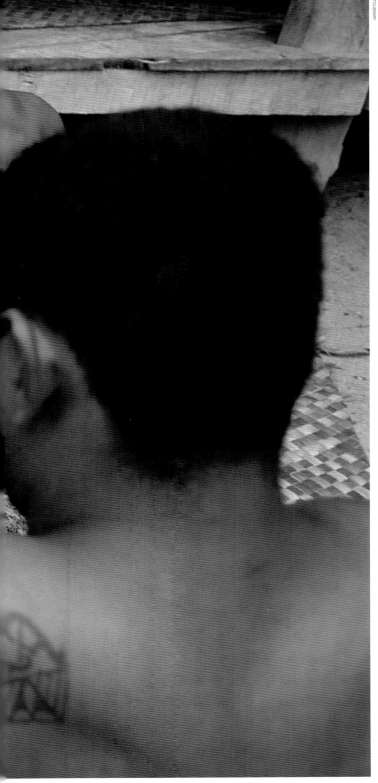

Slow down, way down, to Samoa time. Hardly anything disturbs the balmy peace except for the occasional barking dog or passing pickup truck. All the attributes of an island paradise are here – cascades, jungles and endless blue lagoons – but all the tourist hoopla isn't. While resort experiences are at a minimum, authentic cultural experiences abound. Music is everywhere: exuberant drumming resounds through the *fiafia* dance nights, choral music emanates from churches on Sundays while Samoan hip hop is played day and night on boom boxes. Made up from two entities, independent Samoa and the US territory of American Samoa, the Samoan Islands share a history of being one of the strongest cultural forces in the Pacific.

BEST TIME TO VISIT
Between May and October, the dry season when many major Samoan festivals are held

TOP THINGS TO SEE
- The Robert Louis Stevenson Museum in the author's former home, lovely Villa Vailima
- The eerie desolation of the Lava Field
- An edge of the world sunset at Cape Mulinu'u
- A game of *kirikiti,* Samoan-style cricket where dancing is as important as catching the ball
- Gorgeous traditional tattoos against bronze skin

TOP THINGS TO DO
- Gaze at the sky while floating in the To Sua Ocean Trench
- Drift through the spectacular coral colonies of the Palolo Deep Marine Reserve
- Bathe in the jungle pool at Afu Aau Falls before standing atop Pulemelei Mound
- Soak up the island vibe while strolling around the island of Manono
- Stride along Tutuila's mountainous spine to the top of Mt Alava

GETTING UNDER THE SKIN
Read local author Sia Figiel's first novel, *Where We Once Belonged* about dispossession in modern Samoa

Listen to locally grown Samoan hip hop – Mr Tee or New Zealand–based Samoan groups King Kapisi and Scribe

Watch the 2007 New Zealand comedy *Sione's Wedding (Samoan Wedding)* about 30-year-old New Zealand–based Samoans who have to 'grow up'

Eat local favourites such as *oka* (raw fish in lime juice and coconut milk) and *palusami* (taro leaves cooked with coconut cream)

Drink an ice cold Valima, one of the best known beers in the Pacific

IN A WORD
Fa'a Samoa (The Samoan way)

TRADEMARKS
Tattoos; Robert Louis Stevenson; Polynesian-style hip hop; *fiafia* dances; 2009 tsunami

RANDOM FACT
Samoa has one of the world's highest suicide rates; Although it's hard to believe, it's thought to be due to the strictness of religion and society

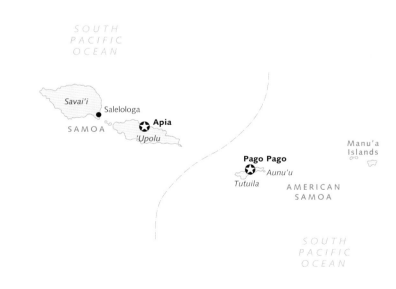

SOUTH
PACIFIC
OCEAN

Savai'i
Salelologa
Apia
SAMOA
'Upolu

Manu'a
Islands

Pago Pago
Aunu'u
Tutuila
AMERICAN
SAMOA

SOUTH
PACIFIC
OCEAN

MAP REF **P,I**

1. Tiatia Tafili Faitele, a tatooist on Savai' i, carefully applies his art
2. Not afraid to blow his own horn, a police-band player shows off his instrument in Apia
3. Verdant rainforest envelopes the water cascading over the 53m-high Sopo'aga Falls at 'Upolu
4. As far as the eye can see, rowers practise for the *fautasi* (long boat) race, an important part of Samoan culture

It's all very toy-town, and the packed streets and kitsch souvenir shops are not everyone's cup of tea. But the novelty value of this enclave cannot be overestimated. Wedged in on all sides by Italy, a dozen kilometres from the Adriatic Coast in the Apennine Mountains, San Marino has been an independent republic since AD 301 when a Croatian stone-cutter built a church atop a windswept bluff here. San Marino's constitution, the world's oldest, dates to 1600 and its stunningly picturesque location on top of Mount Titano certainly justifies the myriad postcard and souvenir boutiques in which visitors spend a large part of the day browsing. Views of the deep blue from the clifftop fortress are jewel-like.

BEST TIME TO VISIT
May, June and September; July and August get crowded

TOP THINGS TO SEE
- Palazzo Pubblico with its richly decorated facade
- The relics of Saint Marinus inside the neoclassical Basilica del Santo
- A sweeping coastal panorama atop Castello della Cesta, the highest and mightiest of San Marino's three fortresses
- A 13th-century prison, 8m deep, in the darkest depths of the Montale tower
- Skinning devices, knee breakers and other ghastly torture devices at the Museo della Tortura

TOP THINGS TO DO
- Revel in pure unadulterated kitsch in San Marino's overdose of souvenir shops
- Take snaps of the republican soldiers, track down local euro coinage (or buy a souvenir set) and send a postcard home using a San Marino stamp
- Get your passport stamped at the tourist office – there are no border controls between San Marino and Italy
- Nip into Italy and dance until dawn on the Rimini Riviera

GETTING UNDER THE SKIN
Read *A Freak of Freedom*, an evocative portrait of San Marino penned in 1879 by English explorer James Theodore Bent

Listen to tracks by Sammarinese boy band Miodio

Watch Darryl Zanuck's *The Prince of Foxes* – the American director 'rented out' the entire republic to film the 16th-century period drama

Eat quintessential Italian pasta dishes against a stunning Adriatic Coast backdrop

Drink a full-bodied Brugneto red, dry white Biancale or sweet dessert Oro dei Goti from San Marino's steeply terraced vineyards

IN A WORD
Ciao (Hello/Bye)

TRADEMARKS
Stamp and coin collecting; fortresses; Mount Titano; rampant postcard production

RANDOM FACT
To mark Italian victory in the 2006 FIFA World Cup, San Marino issued a commemorative stamp starring 92-year-old Granny Isetta, who could remember all four Italian football championship titles since 1934

MAP REF **H,21**

1. Castello della Guaita offers a commanding view of San Marino

1.

2.

3.

Life is beautiful, and this nation is full of it: rainforests blanket rolling hills and backdrop spellbinding beaches; tropical birds circle stark volcanic rock formations; and aquatic life aplenty patrols immaculate shores. Paradise it is, but this has not always been the case for the people who've called it home. Uninhabited when discovered by Portuguese seafarers in 1470, the fertile islands were soon inhabited by African slaves and *degredados* (undesirables sent from Portugal), all of whom were forced to work new sugar plantations. While travellers can't help but notice the colonial vestiges – the Portuguese language, Roman Catholicism and magnificent architecture – it is the peaceful, easygoing São Toméan vibe that will stick with them forever.

BEST TIME TO VISIT
June to September (the dry season)

TOP THINGS TO SEE
- Turtle hatchlings poking their noses out of the sand and hurrying down the beach to the great blue sea
- Cão Grande, a massive volcanic tower rising from the jungle floor
- The poignant display in the Museu Nacional dedicated to the Batepá Massacre of 1953
- Distinctive forests, orchids and birds as you hike up Pico São Tomé
- Pristine reefs, crystal-clear waters and more aquatic species than bubbles leaving your diving regulator

TOP THINGS TO DO
- Slide into a São Tomé cafe and savour each and every sip of your *bica* (tiny cup of coffee)
- Pinch yourself when you first glimpse Príncipe's Banana Beach
- Peruse the aged architectural remains of Roça Agostinho Neto, the most elaborate colonial plantation estate
- Converse with São Toméans, young and old – you'll leave a richer person
- Feast at the rejuvenated plantation Roça de São João

GETTING UNDER THE SKIN
Read Miguel Sousa Tavares' novel *Equador*, an enchanting story about the governor of the islands' life turning upside down following his arrival from Portugal

Listen to *Vôa Papagaio, Vôo!*, the seminal work of Gilberto Gil Umbelina

Watch *Extra Bitter: The Legacy of the Chocolate Islands*, Derek Vertongen's exploration of slavery in São Tomé

Eat *calulu* (smoked fish with a sauce of *oca* leaves, palm oil, local chillies and fresh herbs)

Drink palm wine

IN A WORD
Lévé lévé (Easy, easy) – it's a mellow hello, and the motto of São Tomé

TRADEMARKS
Cocoa; *roças* (plantation estates); sublime beaches; warm Atlantic water; *motoqueiros* (motorcycle taxis); *bicas*

RANDOM FACT
It was on the island of Príncipe where Albert Einstein's theory of relativity was proven

MAP REF **N,20**

1. Mists descend over the mountains behind an old rural house in Santa Trinidade, Príncipe
2. Gorgeous braids and beads are almost as pretty as this girl's smile
3. A baptismal procession makes its way through the streets of São Tomé
4. Bountiful baskets of fish from the morning's catch, São Tomé

2.

3.

1.

Reclusive yet an influential player on the world stage, Saudi Arabia can seem like the sum total of its contradictions. Tourist visas are almost impossible, even as countless expats and millions of Muslim pilgrims flood into the country – the birthplace and self-appointed custodian of Islam – from all corners of the earth every year. The result is a country pulled in two directions at once – into the future and into the past – which collide in a sometimes disconcerting present. In short, Saudi Arabia is *the* place to take the pulse of modern Islam. The prizes for those who do make it here include an ancient Nabataean city to rival Petra, world-class diving and avant-garde architecture alongside cities built of coral.

BEST TIME TO VISIT
November to February

TOP THINGS TO SEE
- Madain Salah, the rock-hewn Nabataean city in an otherworldly desert landscape
- Saudi Arabia's most beguiling city, Jeddah, with souqs and a wood-and-coral old quarter
- Najran, echoes of Yemen with its forts and multistorey mud homes
- An ancient fortress and audacious modern architecture in Riyadh
- Hejaz Railway's old stations and tracks made famous in Lawrence of Arabia

TOP THINGS TO DO
- Dive or snorkel the Red Sea with scarcely another diver in sight
- Take the cable car down the cliff to the hanging village of Habalah
- Venture into one of the world's most famous deserts, the Rub al-Khalil, or Empty Quarter
- Journey back to the 19th-century origins of Wahhabi Islam and al-Saud ruling dynasty in Dir'aiyah
- Cheer on the camels lumbering across the sand just north of Riyadh

GETTING UNDER THE SKIN
Read *Arabian Sands* by Wilfred Thesiger, a travel literature classic through the Empty Quarter with the Bedouin

Listen to the call to prayer; or to Abdou Majeed Abdullah, the closest Saudi Arabia comes to a rock star

Watch National Geographic's *Inside Mecca*, the only way for a non-Muslim to see inside this Muslims-only city

Eat *khouzi* (lamb stuffed with a chicken that is stuffed with rice, nuts and sultanas)

Drink cardamom-flavoured coffee

IN A WORD
Allahu akbar (God is Great)

TRADEMARKS
Oil-rich sheikhs and Bedouin nomads; Mecca and Medina, Islam's holiest cities; vast shopping malls; *mutawwa* (religious police charged with upholding Islamic orthodoxy)

RANDOM FACT
During Bedouin feasts, excessive conversation among the normally garrulous Bedouin is considered a sign of poor manners

MAP REF **K,24**

1. North of Tabuk, the rocks of the Hisma Desert soar skyward
2. A sea of worshippers engulfs the Kaaba in Mecca's Masjid al-Haram
3. Men gather in in Umm Ruqaybah for a decadent dinner of mutton and rice
4. Mounted guards raise their ceremonial swords on parade

1.

2.

3.

JONATHAN SMITH | LONELY PLANET IMAGES

What a luxuriant oil painting Scotland is: a beguiling mix of sophisticated city and brooding landscape, no place quite eats into the traveller's soul like this. True, the weather – buckets of rain and wind-whipped cloud – is hardly Mediterranean. But tramp beneath castle-crowned crags and cinematic skies mirrored in myriad lonely lochs, and it doesn't matter. This *is* Europe's last outpost of rugged arresting beauty, serenaded by an island-laced coastline with waltzing seals, dolphins and whales. Cosmopolitan student town and capital Edinburgh appeases culture fiends with wonderful museums, festivals and arts; while traditional rival Glasgow cuts the grain with innovative architecture, dining and nightlife. Pour yourself a nip of fine Scottish malt whisky, sit back and savour...

BEST TIME TO VISIT
May to September; August for the Edinburgh festival season

TOP THINGS TO SEE
- The fine view of Firth of Forth atop Edinburgh Castle
- Ben Nevis, a true taste of the magnificent Scottish Highlands
- A Neolithic stone village built in 3100 BC in Skara Brae, Orkney Islands
- The deserted beaches and walking trails of the inspirationally remote Outer Hebrides
- Mt Stewart, one of the most spectacular stately homes in the UK
- Hogmanay in Edinburgh

TOP THINGS TO DO
- Get a hole in one on the world's oldest golf course in St Andrews
- Hike spectacular cliff tops on the northern islands of Orkney
- Catch salmon, visit castles and enjoy lazy forest walks in Royal Deeside – the British Royal family has their country retreat, Balmoral, here
- Admire Victorian architecture and shop in Glasgow, Scotland's most bustling city
- Catch a festival: Shetland's Up Helly Aa in January, and August's Edinburgh Festival and Fringe are favourites

GETTING UNDER THE SKIN
Read about Iain Banks' search for the perfect single malt whisky in *Raw Spirits*

Listen to the Corries for real McCoy Scottish folk

Watch *Trainspotting* by Danny Boyle – a Scottish youth tries to wean himself away from Edinburgh's druggie underworld

Eat haggis with *neeps 'n' tatties* (turnips and potatoes)

Drink a dram of single malt whisky; to get the better of a hangover, knock back Barr's Irn-Bru, a bubble-gum-scented, radioactive-orange-coloured soft drink

IN A WORD
Slàinte mhath (Cheers!)

TRADEMARKS
Haggis; malt whisky; smoked salmon; caber-tossing; kilts and sporrans; bagpipes; novelists Robert Louis Stevenson and Robert Burns; Loch Ness monster

RANDOM FACT
Bevvied, blootered, hammered, fleein', fou, steamin', stotious, plastered and just plain pished...all these words mean 'drunk' in Scotland

NEIL SETCHFIELD | LONELY PLANET IMAGES

ATLANTIC OCEAN
Lewis
Outer Hebrides
Stornoway
Ullapool
Skye
Kyle of Lochalsh
Inner Hebrides
Mull
Oban
Islay
Arran
NORTHERN IRELAND
Stranraer

Orkney Islands
Thurso
Wick
North Sea
Elgin
Inverness
Aberdeen
Arbroath
Perth
Dundee
St Andrews
Kirkaldy
⭐ Edinburgh
Glasgow
Ayr
Melrose
Dumfries
ENGLAND
North Channel

MAP REF **F,19**

1. Watch the sun set over Edinburgh Castle and the old town from Arthur's Seat
2. Highland cows put on a fringe festival of a different kind
3. As dusk falls on Eilean Donan Castle on the Isle of Skye, reflections in the loch resemble a monster rearing its head
4. Tartan takes over as a bagpiping band storms through George Square in Glasgow

4.

2.

1.

CHRISTIAN ASLUND | LONELY PLANET IMAGES

4.

CHRISTIAN ASLUND | LONELY PLANET IMAGES

Devout yet dedicated to having a good time, Senegal is one of West Africa's most rewarding countries. The terrain here tells a diverse story, from coastal beaches and mangrove forests to savannah woodland and the dusty Sahel of the interior. It all provides the backdrop for attractions as varied as birdwatching (Senegal sits on the migratory path between Africa and Europe for millions of birds), poignant monuments to slavery, the sophistication and elegance of French and African cultural fusion, and one of Africa's most powerful yet tolerant religious traditions, the Mouride Sufi brotherhood. Accompanying you along the way will be music from some of the continent's most celebrated international stars, who'll soon get you dancing in Dakar.

BEST TIME TO VISIT
November to February – the dry season and relatively cool

TOP THINGS TO SEE
○ Francophone West Africa's most lively and compelling capital, Dakar
○ The car-free and tranquil island, Île de Gorée, with its monuments to Africans cast into slavery
○ Touba, home to the Mouride Sufi brotherhood and the extraordinary Grand Mosque
○ The fascinating and beautiful colonial-African architecture and culture in St-Louis
○ Cap Skiring, among West Africa's most beautiful beaches

TOP THINGS TO DO
○ Dance to live music at Dakar's Just 4 U, where you might hear Youssou N'Dour or Orchestra Baobab
○ Listen to Gregorian chants in Wolof at the Keur Moussa Monastery
○ Watch millions of migratory birds in the Parc National des Oiseaux du Djoudj
○ Take a pirogue through the bird-rich Parc National de la Langue de Barberie
○ Traverse the wilderness and look for threatened wildlife in the Unesco-listed Parc National du Niokolo-Koba

GETTING UNDER THE SKIN
Read *God's Bits of Wood* by Sembène Ousmane, a classic tale of colonial West Africa; or Mariama Bâ's *So Long a Letter*, a window on the world of Senegalese women

Listen to Youssou N'Dour; or Orchestra Baobab

Watch *Moolaade*, directed by Ousmane Sembène, a beautifully told tale about female circumcision

Eat *tiéboudieune* (rice cooked in tomato sauce with chunks of fish, vegetables and spices); *yassa poulet* (grilled chicken marinated in a thick onion and lemon sauce)

Drink hibiscus *bissap* (hibiscus juice); *gingembre* (ginger beer); *bouyi* (baobab juice)

IN A WORD
Asalaa-maalekum (Greetings, peace – in Wolof)

TRADEMARKS
The Wolof and Mandinka peoples; migratory birds in their millions; internationally renowned music scene; *marabouts* (holy men)

RANDOM FACT
Touba is the site for one of Africa's largest pilgrimages – 48 days after the Islamic New Year, two million people descend on the town for the Grand Magal pilgrimage

MAP REF **M,18**

1. Sorry to butt in…goats go to market in Kidira
2. A decorative arched gateway leads to Dakar's Marché Kermel (Kermel Market)
3. Mmmm, something smells good – a woman tends to a bubbling pot in Dakar
4. A never-ending line of pirogues awaits passengers in Dakar's harbour

1.

2.

3.

During the 1990s Serbia went from being the powerhouse of Yugoslavia to the bully boy of the Balkans. Today, the Serbs' innate sense of industry, creativity and initiative sees their homeland EU-bound and assuming a pivotal role in the region again. The bad press of the '90s still casts a shadow, but Serbia has a long history of multiculturalism and intellectual thought, rich folklore and thriving art and music scenes. The Serbs are single-minded, and earnest in their Orthodox faith, yet quietly hospitable, given to coffee-house philosophising and spontaneous picnics, where a rug can be thrown down anywhere – beside a road or lake, or under an apple tree – a fire lit and the day passed in eating and making merry.

BEST TIME TO VISIT
Between May and September

TOP THINGS TO SEE
- Kalemegdan Citadel in Belgrade, over the confluence of the Danube and Sava
- The bucolic rolling hills of Fruška Gora, a realm of vineyards, orchards and Orthodox monasteries
- Art nouveau architectural treasures, including a synagogue, in Hungarian-influenced Subotica
- The chalky hews and Cyrillic script of the vibrant frescoes of Manasija Monastery
- Drvengrad, a 'traditional' Serbian mountain village created by film director Emir Kusturica

TOP THINGS TO DO
- Cruise the 'hidden' basement bars of Belgrade for pulsating nightlife and eclectic decor
- Mosh at the Exit festival in Petrovaradin Fortress on the Danube
- Hit the piste at Kopoanik, Serbia's premiere ski resort, or enjoy summertime alpine meadows and walking trails in Zlatibor
- Lap up the multicultural ambience of Novi Pazar, with its Orthodox monasteries and Ottoman-era *hamam* (Turkish bath) and caravanserai

GETTING UNDER THE SKIN
Read *The Serbs: History, Myth and the Destruction of Yugoslavia* by Tim Judah, a nonpartisan observation of the Serbs and their history

Listen to the Guča Trumpet Festival, a three-day Balkan frenzy of blaring brass bands

Watch the films of Emir Kusturica, including *Black Cat, White Cat*, a shambolic, comic, colourful Romany tale; or *Life is a Miracle*, detailing the traumas of the Balkan wars

Eat meaty fare like *ćevapčići* (grilled kebab) or *pljeskavica* (spiced beef patties)

Drink *šljivovica* (a fiery plum brandy taken neat); any of the great locally brewed beers

IN A WORD
Živəli (Cheers!)

TRADEMARKS
Brass bands; piano accordions; meat dishes on the grill; intense patriotism; Eurovision winner Marija Serifovic; Orthodox monasteries

RANDOM FACT
The Serbs use both Cyrillic and Latin alphabets, switching between them without a second thought

CAPITAL Belgrade | **POPULATION** 7,379,339 | **AREA** 77,474 sq km | **OFFICIAL LANGUAGE** Serbian

MAP REF **H,22**

1. The formidable Kalamegdan Citadel is synonymous with the history of Belgrade itself
2. Floodlit in the Belgrade night sky is Sveti Marko (St Mark's) Orthodox Church
3. In the run-up to elections, candidates give away free bags of beans in Belgrade
4. Splashes of colour enliven Belgrade's formerly bleak backstreets

353

3.

2.

1.

4.

A hundred million dollars worth of pirate treasure may lurk nearby, but you won't care. When you're in this tropical Indian Ocean paradise, surrounded by white-sand beaches, intoxicating waters and swaying palms laden with exotic fruit, you'll already feel like the richest person on the planet. And who wants to get dirty digging on holiday? Hewn seductively from granite or grown from corals, the Seychelles' 115 islands were uninhabited until the 18th century – many still are. The burgeoning society is primarily African in origin, though it's infused with touches of French, Indian, Chinese and Arab influence. The only thing known to test the Seychellois' renowned Pacific nature is their long-standing government.

BEST TIME TO VISIT
March to May and September to November

TOP THINGS TO SEE
- Thunderous clouds of feathers flocking in the skies over Bird Island
- Anse Source d'Argent, a heavenly stretch of white sand and crystal-clear water punctuated by naturally sculpted granite monoliths
- The rare and ever so suggestive coco de mer palms growing in primordial Vallée de Mai on Praslin Island
- The remote raised corals of Aldabra Atoll, the spellbinding home to 150,000 giant tortoises
- A perfectly prepared plate of succulent seafood being placed in front of you

TOP THINGS TO DO
- Forget *Jaws* and share the depths with sea creatures big and small at the aptly named Shark Bank
- Satisfy any *Robinson Crusoe* fairy-tale urges on the shores of the Outer Islands
- Set your pace to slow and sink into the laid-back vibe on the beautiful granite island of La Digue
- Unleash your inner Indiana Jones hiking in the jungle-clad hills of Morne Seychellois National Park
- Nothing (as long as you're planted on one of the planet's most astounding beaches)

GETTING UNDER THE SKIN
Read *Seychelles Since 1770: History of a Slave and Post-Slavery Society* by Deryck Scarr

Listen to Jean-Marc Volcy, who's fused modern Creole pop with traditional folk music

Watch *Le Monde de Silence*, Jacques Cousteau's ground-breaking documentary, much of which was filmed at Seychelles' Assumption Island

Eat *trouloulou* and *teck teck*, two local varieties of shellfish

Drink *calou* (a palm wine that will put a bounce in your step)

IN A WORD
Bonzour (Good morning, in Kreol Seselwa)

TRADEMARKS
Aldabra giant tortoises; coco de mer palms; fairy-tale beaches; coral atolls

RANDOM FACT
Weighing up to 20kg, the seed in the famously erotic fruit of the Seychelles' female coco de mer palm is the plant kingdom's largest

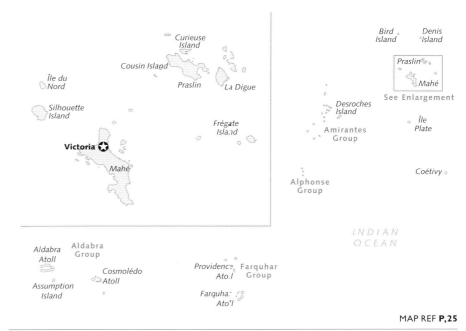

MAP REF **P,25**

1. Kick up the sand on Anse Source d'Argent beach on La Digue
2. Crowning glory – a Seychellois man sports an impressive do in Praslin
3. Many hands make light work: children help fishermen land their catch in Mahé
4. Not surprisingly, an archaic botanical name for the remarkable Coco de Mer coconut, *Lodoicea callipyge,* means 'beautiful rump'

1.

2.

3.

Sierra Leone is a country on the upswing. In the dark days of the 1990s, when the country flickered briefly onto the world's news screens, Sierra Leone was ravaged by brutal conflict. It was an extreme case of Africa's resource curse, with lucrative natural resources (in this case diamonds) the preserve of warlords who took their greed out on ordinary people. Sierra Leone may no longer make headlines, but that is in itself good news as the resilient, friendly people of Sierra Leone set about rebuilding their lives and their country. The results have been impressive enough to entice travellers back and there's much to discover: idyllic beaches, rainforest-clad mountains and terrific wildlife-watching opportunities with scarcely another tourist in sight.

BEST TIME TO VISIT
November to April

TOP THINGS TO SEE
- Busy and brimful of optimism, Freetown, is the symbol of newly peaceful Sierra Leone
- Bunce Island, an important landmark in the tragic history of slavery
- Outamba-Kilimi National Park, a beautiful, peaceful refuge for elephant, leopard and hippo
- Turtle Islands, a small slice of rarely visited paradise off the Sierra Leonean coast
- Sulima, a timeless place to kick back and rest from life on the African road

TOP THINGS TO DO
- Dance the night away at Paddy's, one of Africa's most famous bars
- Laze on beautiful beaches within striking distance of Freetown
- Search for pygmy hippos and primate species in the Tiwai Island Wildlife Sanctuary
- Hike through lowland rainforest and spot 333 bird species in the Gola Forest Reserve
- Climb to the summit of Mt Bintumani, watching for wildlife along the way

GETTING UNDER THE SKIN
Read *The Devil that Danced on the Water* (memoir) and *Ancestor Stones* (novel) by Aminatta Forna for their fascinating insights into modern Sierra Leone

Listen to palm wine music (or *maringa* as it's known locally), whose finest exponent was the late SE Rogie

Watch *Blood Diamond*, directed by Edward Zwick, a brutal yet uplifting civil-war tale with Leonardo DiCaprio; or the disturbing documentary *Cry Freetown* by Sorius Samura

Eat rice served with *plasas* (a sauce of pounded potato or cassava leaves, palm oil and fish or beef)

Drink Star, the top-selling beer; light and fruity *poyo* (palm wine)

IN A WORD
Owdibody (How are you? – literally 'How's the body?')

TRADEMARKS
Civil war; blood diamonds; war amputees; an impressive return to peace

RANDOM FACT
Sierra Leone has one of the highest population growth rates in the world (over 4%)

MAP REF **M,18**

1. The landmark green and white minarets of the central mosque dominate the townscape in Makeni
2. A Freetown woman demonstrates her skilful balancing act
3. Mende women process palm oil
4. These men bang to the beat of a different drum during a celebration in Freetown

2.

3.

1.

Travellers often knock Singapore for its corporate mindset, draconian laws and relentless urban sprawl, but some of that is probably sour grapes about the cost of travel here compared to the rest of Southeast Asia. Fans of the city rave about the shopping, the fabulous food and the intoxicating blend of Indian, Chinese and Malay culture. So Singapore may not be as edgy as Bangkok or Phnom Penh, but there's plenty to see, from quirky ethnic neighbourhoods and world-class museums to historic temples where the air is thick with incense, and things are fabulously well-organised – perfect for families breaking the journey between Europe and Australasia.

BEST TIME TO VISIT
February to October, the dry season

TOP THINGS TO SEE
- The rainbow-coloured glory of the Sri Mariamman Temple
- Market mayhem, temples and crowds on Waterloo St
- Treasures from across Asia at the Asian Civilisations Museum
- A menagerie of exotic beasties at the Singapore Zoological Gardens and Night Safari
- Gloriously garish tourist attractions on Sentosa Island

TOP THINGS TO DO
- Light a joss stick at the historic Thian Hock Keng temple
- Soak up the sounds and smells of the subcontinent in Little India
- Pick up a plastic beckoning cat at a religious emporium in Chinatown
- Feast your way around the Malay Straits in one of Singapore's legendary hawker courts
- Sip a Singapore sling at Raffles, the famous hotel where the cocktail was invented in 1915

GETTING UNDER THE SKIN
Read *Foreign Bodies*, Hwee Hwee Tan's gripping tale of young people on the wrong side of the Singapore justice system

Listen to Singaporean and international DJs spinning disks on the ground-shaking sound system at Zouk

Watch Woo Yen Yen and Colin Goh's *Singapore Dreaming* or Tay Teck Lock's *Money No Enough* for insights into the Singapore psyche

Eat hawker food – top treats include Hainanese chicken rice and *roti prata* (fried flat bread with curry dipping sauce)

Drink Tiger beer, the national brew; or *teh tarik* (strong, sweet tea with condensed milk)

IN A WORD
Kiasu (Fear of losing) – one of the defining traits of the competitive inhabitants of Singapore

TRADEMARKS
Asian tiger economics; Raffles; rogue traders; Changi Airport; Tiger beer; the dynasty of Lee Kuan Yew; 'No Durians' signs; fines for littering and spitting

RANDOM FACTS
Singapore is the world's largest exporter of exotic aquarium fish

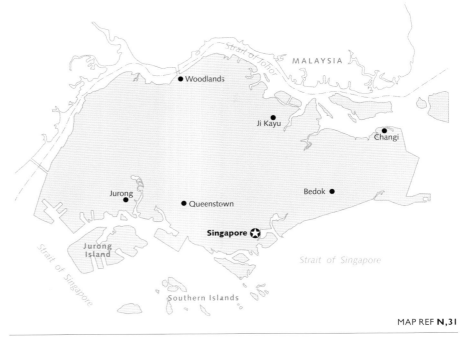

MAP REF **N,31**

1. Indian girls get ready to dance
2. A flurry of fish push their way through the annual Chinese New Year parade
3. The soft pastel hues of a heritage building in Little India perfectly complement the pink and blue sari of a passing woman
4. Get tactile with interactive displays at the Chinatown Heritage Centre

1.

2.

3.

Slovakia long played second fiddle to the Czech Republic but with the demise of Czechoslovakia in the Velvet Revolution of 1989, the Slovaks moved on with a characteristic lack of rancour and went about their business unperturbed. Here, folk traditions still hold sway, family life is paramount, and no one is particularly bothered with glitz and glamour. Slovakia offers a wealth of outdoor attractions, with well-marked paths criss-crossing forested hills, the High Tatras mountains and Malá Fatra National Park. Unpretentious Gothic cities, stately castles and picturesque villages with wooden churches made without nails, punctuate the landscape. The locals appreciate the unspoiled nature of their surrounds so wherever you go you're sure to be greeted by a Slovak striding out bearing a backpack.

BEST TIME TO VISIT
May to September

TOP THINGS TO SEE
o The sprawling, rocky mass of Spiš Castle, a ruin rambling over four hectares
o Neat pastel facades on the Gothic-Renaissance burghers' houses in Bardejov
o Precipitous peaks and pine-topped ridges in the Malá Fatra National Park
o Prickly spires and battlements on Bojnice Castle, the most vistied chateau in Slovakia

TOP THINGS TO DO
o Wander the streets beneath Bratislava Castle dropping in at the narrow Museum of Clocks and Museum of Jewish Culture
o Plunge into a thermal pool, breathe 'seaside' breezes in a salt cave, or be wrapped naked in hot mud at a Piešťany thermal treatment
o Dip your toes over the edge of a *plte* (wooden raft) down Dunajec Gorge
o Clamber up the ladder and chain ascents to the precipice in Slovenský Raj
o Crunch through the snow on the walking trails of the High Tatras

GETTING UNDER THE SKIN
Read the straightforward tales of feisty Slovakian women in *That Alluring Land: Slovak Tales* by Bozena Slancikova-Timrava

Listen to wailing *gajdy* (bagpipes) and *konkovka* (shepherd's flutes) that are central to much Slovakian folk music

Watch internationally acclaimed *Krajinka*, directed by Martin Sulik, 10 vignettes of Slovakian rural life, landscape and ways throughout the 20th century

Eat schnitzel, *bryndzove halusky* (potato dumplings with sheep's cheese and bacon)

Drink local beers such as dark, sweet Martiner or full-bodied Zlatý Bažant; or very quaffable local wines

IN A WORD
Ahoj (Hello)

TRADEMARKS
Wooden churches; communist-era 'socialist-realist' tower blocks; hearty food; folk arts and traditions

RANDOM FACT
Venus of Moravany, a headless female fertility symbol carved from mammoth bone found near Piešťany in 1938, is almost 23,000 years old

MAP REF **H,22**

1. The majestic Vysoké Tatry range looms over the village of Štôla
2. The view from St Michael's Tower, Bratislava, takes in the historical old town nestled beneath Bratislava Castle
3. Performers dance in folk dress at the annual Gemer folk festival, Rejdová
4. Take a ride up to Slovakia's biggest ski resort, Jasná, in Low Tatras National Park

2.

3.

1.

4.

Contrasts abound in tiny Slovenia. It's a modern, forward-looking nation where tales of fairies and mountain spirits retain currency. It is thoroughly Slavic yet displays obvious Italianate and Germanic influences. It boasts a clutch of Alpine peaks where snow may last into summer, but where Mediterranean breezes may suddenly raise temperatures. With almost half of its total area covered in forest, it is one of the greenest countries on earth, something that its residents – generally multilingual and suntanned, and always welcoming – appreciate and take advantage of. Perhaps out of necessity due to its Thumbelina proportions, Slovenia is neat and precise. Villages are orderly, churches picturesque and castles imposing, yet the pagan spirit of the people lives on in their raucously colourful festivals.

BEST TIME TO VISIT
May to September

TOP THINGS TO SEE
- The view over Ljubljana's old town and the bridges of the Ljubljanica River from the ramparts of Castle Hill
- Shimmying dancers in shaggy sheepskin and masks at the Kurentovanje festival
- The translucent lake, valleys and alpine hamlets of Bohinj
- The snow-white horses of Lipica, bred for the Spanish Riding School in Vienna
- The mesmerising opal-azure waters of the Soča River

TOP THINGS TO DO
- Ring the 'lucky' bell in postcard-perfect Church of the Assumption on Bled Island, then return to shore in a piloted gondola
- Hike between mountain huts on well-marked trails in the Julian Alps
- Lap up Ljubljana's afternoon sun in any of the cafes on the banks of Ljubljanica
- Enjoy the Venetian ambience and the sparklingly azure Adriatic Sea at Piran

GETTING UNDER THE SKIN
Read *Forbidden Bread* by Erica Johnson Debeljak, a memoir of an American woman coming to terms with life in Slovenia

Listen to traditional folk 'big band' music, featuring panpipes and zithers alongside usual folk instrumentation; or for hard rock with a Slovenian bent listen to Siddharta

Watch Damjan Kozole's *Rezerni Deli* (Spare Parts), a provocative and award-winning tale of the trafficking of illegal immigrants through Slovenia

Eat *zlikrofi* (dumplings filled with cheese, bacon and chives) followed by *struklji* (sweet, cottage-cheese dumplings) or *palacinke* (pancakes)

Drink wine such as peppery red Teran; or *zganje* (fruit brandy distilled from many fruits)

IN A WORD
Dober dan (Hello)

TRADEMARKS
Alpine sports; Lipizzaner horses; three-headed Mt Triglav; fairy-tale castles; forested mountains

RANDOM FACT
The national icon of Slovenia is the *kozolec* (hayrack), which was invented to lift hay off the ground in damp Alpine areas and allow it to dry swiftly

MAP REF **H,21**

1. Jamnik Church sits amid the picture-perfect surrounds of the Jelovica mountains, Kranj
2. Women make final adjustments to an elaborate headdress at a wedding in Ljubljana
3. Pedestrians and cyclists alike navigate the quaint cobbled streets of Ljubljana
4. The Church of the Assumption stands gracefully on an island in the glacial Lake Bled, with the Julian Alps in the background

Want to get off the beaten path? That's easy: there is no beaten path in the Solomon Islands. It's just you, the ocean, dense rainforests and traditional villages and it feels like the world's end. With a history of headhunting, cannibalism and (more recently) civil unrest, the islands are much safer than their preceding reputation and are now an ecoadventurer's heaven. The volcanic, jungle-cloaked islands jut up dramatically from the tropical Pacific and are surrounded by croc-infested mangroves, huge lagoons, beaches and lonely islets. Islanders are laid back, friendly and still practice ancient arts and till their village gardens the way they have for thousands of years.

BEST TIME TO VISIT
From late-May to early-December there's less chance of rain and the breezes are cooling

TOP THINGS TO SEE
° Spooky WWII relics around Honiara
° The artificial stone and coral islands of Malaita's lagoon
° The sensory overload, variety and bustle of the Honiara market
° Leaf-mound nests of megapodes, birds that use volcanic heat to incubate their eggs
° Eerie skull caves, the final resting places of vanquished warriors and chiefs

TOP THINGS TO DO
° Dive the fantastic 'Iron Bottom Sound' WWII wrecks of Guadalcanal
° Assist rangers tag sea turtles on ecofriendly Tetepare Island
° Take a dip in the natural pools beneath Mataniko or Tenaru Falls
° Kayak or dive through the dramatic double-barrier enclosed Marovo lagoon
° Surf hollow, crowd-free waves at Ghizo

GETTING UNDER THE SKIN
Read *Solomon Time*, Englishman Will Randall's funny and insightful account of trying to start a chicken-farming business on Rendova

Listen to Tipa's 2005 album *Maiae*, breezy island sounds fused with modern music and multipart harmonies

Watch Terrence Malick's *The Thin Red Line*, a grim war film based on James Jones' 1963 novel about the WWII battle for Guadalcanal

Eat, or more palatably chew, a gob of betel nut

Drink Solbrew pale lager, the local brew

IN A WORD
No wariwari ('No worries')

TRADEMARKS
Spear-fishing; animist beliefs; blond-haired Melanesians; shark calling; skull caves; underwater volcanoes; sunken WWII warships; deep-sea fishing; snorkelling and scuba diving

RANDOM FACT
There are 67 indigenous languages in the Solomons so, even though English is the official language, Pijin is what's used in day-to-day communication

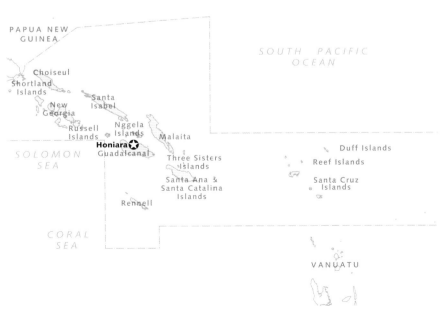

MAP REF **P,36**

1. Taking panpiping to a new level on Malaita Island, the 'Are'are people are renowned for their traditional music

2.

3.

1.

4.

Three countries for the price of one. Sound like a bargain? In Somalia's case, you may think not. But for travellers wanting to break new ground, one of this patchwork state's nations provides the ultimate adventure. Somaliland, with archaeological treasures, world-class beaches and the welcoming Isaq clan of Somalis, is this promised land. Wedged between Ethiopia and the southern shore of the Gulf of Aden, Somaliland has been a self-proclaimed republic since 1991 and has had success maintaining both peace and order. The nation of Puntland, perched on the Horn of Africa's tip, has had less instability than war-torn Somalia, which sits to its south, but both are still considered serious no-go areas.

BEST TIME TO VISIT
December to March, when it is coolest

TOP THINGS TO SEE
- The inconceivable treasures of Las Geel, a series of caves containing hundreds of the world's best preserved Neolithic rock art
- Peace on the streets of Mogadishu (patience required)
- The blissful white sands of Baathela Beach on the outskirts of Berbera
- An unheralded wealth of aquatic life along the island reefs north of Zeila

TOP THINGS TO DO
- Get to grips with the fact that you may be the only tourist in the country
- Stroll the streets of Hargeisa, greet the intrigued locals and peruse the multitude of market shops, all with your mandatory armed escort in tow
- Snake your way up the scenic switchbacks from Berbera to Sheekh, the site of a 13th-century necropolis
- Wade into the atmospheric livestock market in Burcao and enjoy letting it all sink in (smells excepted)

GETTING UNDER THE SKIN
Read *Understanding Somalia and Somaliland: Culture, History and Society* by Ioan Lewis

Listen to *The Journey* by Maryam Mursal, the first woman to sing Somali Jazz (Peter Gabriel sings back-up in this effort)

Watch *Black Hawk Down*, Ridley Scott's dramatic take on the disastrous 3 October 1993 US military combat mission in Mogadishu

Eat *anjeero* (local flatbread) topped with sheep liver and onions

Drink *shaah* (Somali black tea) with *heel* (cardamom) and *qarfe* (cinnamon)

IN A WORD
Ma nabad baa? (greeting; literally meaning 'Is it peace?')

TRADEMARKS
Pirates; civil war; Islamic militias; warlords; narcotic *qat* leaves; Las Geel; some of the planet's longest beaches

RANDOM FACT
The daily cost to hire a gang of armed guards in Mogadishu is over $500; the cost of an armed guard in Somaliland is less than $20 (their meals are extra)

MAP REF **M,25**

1. Seemingly posing for the camera, camels await a new home at a livestock market in Hargeisa
2. Boys practise their football goal celebraton moves in Bosasso
3. Kickin' back and playing some tunes, these men take it easy on the streets of Berbera
4. A woman sifts through desert soil for edible seeds

1.

2.

3.

South Africa overshadows almost every other country on the continent with its economy, its influence and the turbulence of its history. Yet, it's only in the microcosm of daily life where the country's real spirit emerges. Share a drink with locals in a tin-roofed shebeen (illegal drinking establishment); glance into a township school; sip a glass of wine on a blue-sky day on a Winelands Cape Dutch estate; sit at dawn at a watering hole in any of South Africa's national parks; spend a morning at Johannesburg's Apartheid Museum. Wherever you go, South Africa's human drama – with its pain, its injustice and its hope – mixes with an unsurpassed natural beauty. The result is sobering and challenging, fascinating and inspiring – and alluring enough to keep most visitors returning time and time again.

CAPITALS Pretoria (administrative), Bloemfontein (judicial), Cape Town (legislative) | **OFFICIAL LANGUAGES** Zulu, Xhosa, Afrikaans, Sepedi, English, Tswana, Sesotho, Tsonga, Swati, Venda & Ndebele | **POPULATION** 49,052,489 | **AREA** 1,219,090 sq km |

BEST TIME TO VISIT
Year-round, with spring (September to November) and autumn (April to May) ideal almost everywhere

TOP THINGS TO SEE
- Cape Town, Robben Island and Table Bay from the top of Table Mountain
- Namaqualand's vast, colourful carpets of spring flowers
- The convergence of two oceans at the Cape of Good Hope
- Stark and solitary landscapes of shifting sands in Kgalagadi Transfrontier Park
- Stunning panoramas from almost anywhere amid the peaks and valleys of the Drakensberg

TOP THINGS TO DO
- Bush walk at dawn past elephants and zebras in Kruger National Park
- Spend time in Soweto, Johannesburg's sprawling, turbulent, hope-filled soul
- View dolphins, crashing waves and waterfalls while trekking along the Wild Coast
- Discover Cape Town, with its lively vibes and cosmopolitan rhythms
- Explore the beauty and birdlife of lovely iSimangaliso Wetland Park

GETTING UNDER THE SKIN
Read *Long Walk to Freedom* – Nelson Mandela's inspirational autobiography

Listen to *Nkosi Sikelel' iAfrika* (God Bless Africa) – part of the South African national anthem of unity

Watch *Amandla! A Revolution in Four-Part Harmony*, which uses music, song and the voices of political activists and other prominent South Africans to document the anti-apartheid struggle

Eat *biltong* (dried and cured meat); *mealies* (maize); and *boerwors* (sausages)

Drink wines from the Cape Winelands; or *rooibos* herbal tea

IN A WORD
Howzit?

TRADEMARKS
Table Mountain; Springboks rugby team; Nelson Mandela; Kruger National Park; wildlife; whales; surf; *braai* (barbecue)

RANDOM FACT
Almost half of South Africa's wealth is concentrated among just 10% of the population

MAP REF **S,22**

1. Unsuspecting prime rump is enough to make any predator's eyes light up, as Burchell's Zebras quench their thirst in Kruger National Park
2. Sheltered from the wind, the beaches at Clifton are regarded as Cape Town's top sunbathing spots
3. Fancy a cuppa? San people (Kalahari Bushmen) prepare a brew
4. A young lion plans his next move while lapping water from a pool in Sabi Sands Game Reserve

1.

2.

3.

4.

Spain is Europe's most exotic country, a heady mix of often curious traditions and a relentless energy that propels Spaniards into the future. You see it in Spain's architecture: the Islamic confections of Al-Andalus and soaring Gothic cathedrals rub shoulders with avant-garde creations by Gaudí and Santiago Calatrava. Or you taste it in the food: you're just as likely to find three generations of the same family in the kitchen as you are three Michelin stars honouring the innovations of new Spanish cuisine. There are jagged sierras, wild coastlines, soul-stirring flamenco and world-class art galleries that span the centuries. But for all this talk of past and future, Spaniards live very much in the present where life is one long fiesta.

BEST TIME TO VISIT
May, June, September and October

TOP THINGS TO SEE
- The Alhambra, the exquisite highpoint of Andalucía's Islamic architecture
- Córdoba's Mezquita, perfection rendered in stone
- Gaudí's Barcelona, the astonishing architectural legacy that came to define a city
- Madrid's golden mile of art, three of the world's best art galleries
- Santiago de Compostela's cathedral, Spain's most sacred corner and a flight of architectural extravagance

TOP THINGS TO DO
- Go on a tapas crawl sampling San Sebastián's world famous *pintxos* (Basque tapas)
- Hike the Pyrenees in Catalonia or Aragón
- Drive along the dramatic Galician coastlines of Rías Altas or the Costa da Morte
- Laze on a secluded and postcard-perfect beach on Mallorca or Menorca
- Escape the modern world in inland Spain's stone-and-timber pueblos (villages)

GETTING UNDER THE SKIN
Read *Don Quijote de la Mancha* by Miguel de Cervantes; or *Roads to Santiago* by Cees Nooteboom, a fascinating journey through modern Spain

Listen to El Camarón de la Isla, Paco de Lucía, Enrique Morente and Chambao for the essence and evolution of flamenco

Watch any film by Pedro Almódovar, especially *Todo Sobre Mi Madre* (All About My Mother) or *Volver* (Return)

Eat wafer-thin slices of *jamón ibérico de bellota;* and paella (especially in its birthplace, Valencia)

Drink *vino tinto* (red wine) from La Rioja wine region, *vino blanco* (white wine) from Galicia, or *fino* (sherry) from Jerez de la Frontera

IN A WORD
¿Qué pasa? (What's happening?)

TRADEMARKS
Flamenco; paella; bullfighting; football; fiestas; Picasso, Dalí and Goya; fiestas; summer invasions of vacationing northern Europeans on the Costa del Sol; Camino de Santiago pilgrimage route

RANDOM FACT
Spaniards spend more on food per capita than anyone else in Europe

MAP REF I,19

---

1. Antoni Gaudí's most ambitious and famous piece, the staggering La Sagrada Família, continues to be a work in progress, Barcelona
2. Dancers keep tradition very much alive through celebations during the Feria de Abril fiesta, Seville
3. Slow it down a bit to browse the shopfronts in sophisticated Madrid
4. Tapas is a culinary artform that is many a visitor's highlight of the Basque region

1.

2.

3.

It seems somehow incongruous that a tropical Buddhist island should be associated with so much political turmoil, but the end of the civil war marks a new chapter for this land of sand and cinnamon at the southern tip of India. Travellers can once again focus on the languorous beaches, the steamy tropical air, the tea plantations and the historic cities scattered around the interior. Sri Lanka is a place where you can start the day sipping from a fresh coconut with your toes in the Indian Ocean, and end it scouring the jungle for leopards or gazing at monumental statues of the Buddha. Think of it as India-on-sea, with a sprinkling of Southeast Asian Buddhism and Arabian spice.

BEST TIME TO VISIT
December to March, to avoid the southwest monsoon

TOP THINGS TO SEE
- Museums, monuments and colonial trim in the frenetic capital, Colombo
- Ruined palaces and super-sized Buddhas in the old royal capital of Polonnaruwa
- A window onto the Dutch colonial past in historic Galle
- Elaborate gardens and exquisite frescoes in the ancient fortress at Sigiriya
- A very different side of Sri Lanka in the Tamil city of Jaffna

TOP THINGS TO DO
- Kick back on the sparkling sands of Sri Lanka's southern beaches
- Watch the rising sun cast its rays over the island from Adam's Peak
- Search for leopards and elephants in the foliage of Yala National Park
- Surf the wild breaks at Arugam Bay
- Make the pilgrimage to the Temple of the Tooth in World Heritage–listed Kandy

GETTING UNDER THE SKIN
Read Shyam Selvadurai's unconventional love story *Funny Boy;* or Romesh Gunesekera's coming-of-age drama *Reef*

Listen to www.lankabroadcast.com for streaming broadcasts of local pop and *baila* (Sri Lankan dance music)

Watch the antiwar films of Asoka Handagama – his *Aksharaya* (A Letter of Fire) was banned in Sri Lanka, but copies are circulating online

Eat 'hoppers' (or more properly *appa*), delicious pancakes made from fermented rice and coconut milk

Drink *toddy (*a local wine made from fermented palm sap); or *arrack,* the same thing, distilled and bottled

IN A WORD
Ayubowan (May you live long)

TRADEMARKS
Bendy palm trees; sun-kissed beaches; Ceylon tea; colonial hand-me-downs; jumbos in the jungle; fresh coconuts; short eats; batik; cricket-obsessed locals; Tamil Tigers

RANDOM FACTS
Sri Lanka gave the world cinnamon – the island has been trading the spice since at least 2000 BC

MAP REF **N,28**

1. Hugging the coast, the chaotic Kollupitiya station in Colombo is not necessarily the safest in the world, but is certainly memorable
2. Kandyan dancers put in a rattling performing during a *perahera* (procession) in Colombo
3. A mahout has his work cut out during bathtime at the Pinnewala Elephant Orphanage in Kegalle
4. Not a bad office: a woman picks tea leaves in the beautiful surrounds of Nuwara Eliya

2.

3.

1.

4.

There is no country on earth that travellers are as apprehensive to visit as they are pained to leave. Sudan stretches over swathes of the Sahara, the swamps of the Sudd and the singed shoreline of the Red Sea, and is dotted with impressive relics of civilisations dating back to pre-Pharaonic Egypt. Yet for visitors its greatest treasures are the Sudanese – diverse as they are mysterious, generous as they are welcoming. The world often wrongly paints the entirety of Sudan – Africa's largest nation – in the same perilous shade even though its conflicts have been restricted to the south and west. The peaceful northeast, a region exuding the country's true nature, offers travellers both incredible solitude and hospitality.

BEST TIME TO VISIT
October to March (the dry season)

TOP THINGS TO SEE
- The colossal 3500-year-old remains of the kingdom of Kerma's capital
- Whirling dervishes stirring up more than dust at Omdurman's Hamed el-Nil Mosque
- A shiver of hammerhead sharks circling above you in the Red Sea – their silhouettes are eerily unmistakable
- The holy mountain of Jebel Barkal and the vestiges of the Temple of Amun, the centre of the kingdom of the Kush

TOP THINGS TO DO
- Let your eyes wander in the fascinating *souqs* (markets) of Kassala before letting your legs take over in the extraordinarily shaped Taka massif
- Witness colourful fluid dynamics in action as the two Niles, Blue and White, meet and meld in Khartoum
- Wade through the ancient sands enveloping the astounding pyramids at the royal cemetery of Begrawiya, the resting place of the Meroitic Pharaohs
- Board a barge and voyage south up the White Nile from Kosti

GETTING UNDER THE SKIN
Read *Emma's War* by Deborah Scroggins, not only a compelling, real-life tale of a British aid-worker marrying a Sudanese warlord, but also a great introduction to the nation and its civil war

Listen to *Stars of the Night*, Abdel Gadir Salim's LP laced with songs of his homeland

Watch *The Devil Came on Horseback*, a powerful documentary exposing the war crimes in Darfur

Eat *fuul* (stewed brown beans) for a traditional breakfast – complete with cheese, egg, salad and flatbread

Drink sweet black *shai* (tea); or coffee infused with cinnamon and cardamom

IN A WORD
Salaam aleikum (Peace upon you)

TRADEMARKS
Hospitality of the highest order; the meeting of the Niles; ancient pyramids; Nubia; civil war; ethnic cleansing in Darfur

RANDOM FACT
Sudan is dotted with more ancient pyramids than Egypt

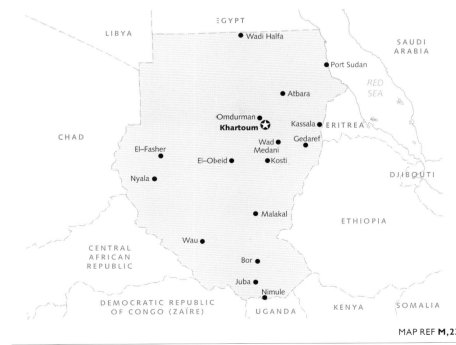

MAP REF **M,23**

1. The Khatmiyah mosque basks in the setting sun amid classic African desert scenery in Kassala
2. Designed to represent a sail, the five-star Boji Al-Fateh Hotel will take the wind out of you in Khartoum
3. Man and beast rest up in the desert outside Omdurman
4. Found mainly on older people, the declining trend of tribal scarification markings is a cultural practice in Sudan that represents identity and social status

One of South America's smallest countries, Suriname packs in a surprising jumble of cultures. The heavily forested nation is home to a mix of people descended from West African slaves; Javanese, Chinese and Indian labourers; as well as native Amerindian groups; and Dutch, Lebanese and Jewish settlers. Paramaribo, where half the population resides, is a blend of synagogues and mosques, Indian roti shops and Chinese dumpling houses spread among Dutch colonial buildings. Outside the capital, dirt tracks and meandering rivers lead to Suriname's natural wonders, which include African-like savannahs, vast swaths of protected rainforest and remote beaches that are a major breeding site for endangered sea turtles.

BEST TIME TO VISIT
February to April, and August to early December

TOP THINGS TO SEE
- Paramaribo, Surinam's vivacious capital and Unesco World Heritage site with its fantastic blend of cultures (and cuisines)
- The Central Surinam Nature Reserve, a staggering 1.6 million-hectare reserve of diverse ecosystems and incredible wildlife
- The Amerindian village of Palumeu, offering a locally run ecotourism experience on the remote banks of the Boven Tapanahoni River
- Sunrise atop the Voltzberg, a 240m granite dome offering stunning views

TOP THINGS TO DO
- Stand watch over the sands of Galibi Nature Reserve as giant leatherback turtles emerge from the sea to lay their eggs on the beach (April to August)
- Spy howler monkeys in the jungle canopy of the Brownsberg Nature Reserve
- Summit Mt Kasikasima after days of canoeing and trekking through deep jungle
- Take a memorable boat journey along the Suriname River stopping at Amerindian and Maroon villages along the way

GETTING UNDER THE SKIN
Read *Tales of a Shaman's Apprentice* by Mark Plotkin, about one Harvard ethnobotanist's surprising discoveries living among Amerindians in Suriname and Brazil

Listen to incredibly talented flautist Ronald Snijders, who blends indigenous sounds with jazz, beatbox and classical melodies

Watch Pim de la Parra's *Wan Pipel*, which provides a fascinating glimpse into Surinamese society through a cross-cultural relationship

Eat salt fish; *bami goreng* (fried noodles); or *petjil* (a type of green bean)

Drink ice-cold Parbo beer; Borgoe and Black Cat are the best local rums

IN A WORD
Fa waka? (How are you?)

TRADEMARKS
Pristine rainforest; bauxite

RANDOM FACT
Although Dutch is the official language the lingua franca is Sranan Tongo, an English-based creole with African, Portuguese and Dutch roots that emerged from the plantations, where it was spoken between slaves and slave owners

MAP REF **N,14**

1. Get into the thick of the action during celebrations marking the end of Ramadan in Paramaribo

2.

3.

1.

JOCHEM D WIJNANDS | THE IMAGE BANK, GETTY IMAGES

4.

ARNAUD VAN ZANDBERGEN | LONELY PLANET IMAGES

In Swaziland – Africa's last remaining monarchy – traditional culture is strong. You're just as likely to see a man garbed with an *amahiya* (traditional robe) and spear as with jeans and a brief case, and traditional crafts and customs abound. Mbabane – the capital – has a western gloss at first glance, but get away from the malls and central area, and you'll be treated to the laid-back hospitality, pride and vibe for which tiny Swaziland is renowned. Whether it's hiking in the hills, watching wildlife in a small but stellar collection of parks and reserves, trying to catch a glimpse of the king or shopping for crafts, this quirky country offers a wealth of surprises to anyone who lingers long enough to discover its secrets.

BEST TIME TO VISIT
March to November

TOP THINGS TO SEE
- Rare black rhinos in lovely Mkhaya Game Reserve
- The annual *umhlanga* (reed) dance in Swaziland's royal heartland
- Preparations for the sacred Incwala ceremony around the royal kraal at Lobamba
- Rolling hill panoramas around Piggs Peak in northern Swaziland
- Brilliant orange flame trees and lavender jacarandas dotting the woodlands of the Ezulwini Valley, with its abundance of comfortable lodges and fine craft shops

TOP THINGS TO DO
- Hike or birdwatch in wild Malolotja Nature Reserve
- Shop for Swazi candles, wood carvings and other traditional crafts around Malkerns and in the Ezulwini Valley
- Shoot the rapids on the Usutu River
- Explore the forests and rugged scenery in and around Ngwempisi Gorge
- Walk amid the wildlife in tranquil Mlilwane Wildlife Sanctuary or the large Hlane Royal National Park

GETTING UNDER THE SKIN
Read *The Kingdom of Swaziland* by D Hugh Gillis – a look at the influences shaping modern-day Swaziland

Listen to the songs and traditional rhythms of Bholoja's 'Swazi Soul' music

Watch the mix of performers at the annual Bush Fire Festival, with theatre, music, poetry and more

Eat *sishwala* (maize porridge) and other traditional dishes

Drink *tjwala* (home-brewed beer), often served by the bucket

IN A WORD
Yebo ('Yes', but also an all-purpose greeting)

TRADEMARKS
Black rhinos; sugar cane; Swazi crafts; HIV/AIDS; King Mswati III; *amahiya* and spear

RANDOM FACT
During preparations for the Incwala ceremony, young Swazi men harvest branches of the *lusekwane* bush and bring these to the royal kraal at Lobamba. A wilted branch is interpreted as a sign that the young man bearing it has had illicit sex.

Piggs Peak
Mhlume
★ Mbabane
Lobamba
Manzini
Siteki
Mankayane
Big Bend
Hlathikulu
Nhlangano
Lavumisa

MOZAMBIQUE

SOUTH AFRICA

MAP REF **R,23**

1. Remember to use your right hand only to dig into your food in Swaziland
2. A *sangoma* (traditional spiritual doctor) in Man'enga village
3. Looks can be deceiving: this 3-tonne hippopotamus at Mlilwane Wildlife Sanctuary may appear docile, yet it is regarded as one of the world's most aggressive animals
4. Unmarried women attend the Umhlanga, or Reed Dance, for eight days of dancing

1.

2.

3.

For a small, far-flung country, Sweden has a big international reputation. Preconceptions of this land abound – midnight sun, snowbound winters, ABBA, blonde bombshells, meatballs, herrings, Vikings and Volvos. Whatever your pre-existing notions, a visit to Sweden will both confirm and confound them. The plundering Vikings won't be greeting you at the shore; today you're more likely to be slayed by cutting-edge music, fashion and food, or visions of pretty-as-a-picture countryside, forested fantasylands and island idylls. So yes, look for the stereotypes and you won't be disappointed. Taste the meatballs, admire the blondes and dig the Viking relics, but don't stop there – history hasn't.

BEST TIME TO VISIT
May to August if you're after sunshine, December to March if you want to ski

TOP THINGS TO SEE
- The glittering beauty of Stockholm from Söder Heights
- A manageable portion of the 24,000 islands of the Stockholm archipelago, ideally on a boat cruise
- The midnight sun above the Arctic Circle, preferably from Abisko National Park
- Glass blown to perfection in the glassworks of Glasriket (the Glass Kingdom)
- Rocky islands and idyllic fishing villages of the picturesque Bohuslän coast

TOP THINGS TO DO
- Celebrate Midsummer in the story-book villages surrounding lovely Lake Siljan
- Do a bicycle loop (with camping gear) around the island of Gotland
- Bed down for a night in the supercool Ice Hotel at Jukkasjärvi
- Explore the attractions in Stockholm's Djurgården, including Skansen open-air museum and the Vasa Museum
- Hang out with verified Vikings at the Foteviken Viking Reserve

GETTING UNDER THE SKIN
Read crime-busting novels courtesy of Stieg Larsson's blockbuster *Millennium Trilogy,* or Henning Mankell's Kurt Wallander series; or the sweet tales of *Pippi Longstocking*

Listen to ABBA or Roxette, if that's your thing; or give the Hives or Millencolin a spin Something mellower? Try José González

Watch any of the 62 films directed by the great Ingmar Bergman; the acclaimed *My Life as a Dog*; the romantic vampire film *Let the Right One In*

Eat *lax* (salmon) in its various guises; game such as elk and reindeer; and the requisite *köttbullar* (Swedish meatballs), served with mashed potatoes and lingonberry sauce

Drink *kaffe* (coffee); Absolut vodka; or the beloved *aquavit* and *öl* (beer)

IN A WORD
Jättebra! (Fantastic!)

TRADEMARKS
ABBA; Ingmar Bergman; blondes; Ericsson; Greta Garbo; Ikea; meatballs; the Muppet Chef; Saabs and Volvos; sexually liberated socialists; tennis players; Vikings

RANDOM FACT
The best-known Swedish inventor is Alfred Nobel, who discovered dynamite and also, ironically, founded the Nobel Institute (giver of peace prizes)

MAP REF **E,21**

1. Nature's spectacular lightshow, the aurora borealis, flashes over a quaint church
2. Get into character and visit the Foteviken Viking market in Höllviken
3. A Scottish highland cow is protective of her shaggy calf, Kullaberg Nature Reserve
4. Turning heads since 2005, the Turning Torso dominates the skyline of Malmö

1.

2.

3.

SWITZERLAND

CAPITAL Bern | **POPULATION** 7,604,467 | **AREA** 41,277 sq km | **OFFICIAL LANGUAGES** German, French, Italian & Romansch

Few places beg self-indulgence quite as much as Switzerland, one of these enviably smart, tidy, well turned-out girls with a great sense of organisation, impeccable manners, four languages and charisma by the bucket-load. Not that you'll find cause to complain as you roam Switzerland's picture-postcard castles and villages, pause for a schnapps or hot chocolate in a chalet strewn with geranium boxes, ride a little red mountain train between pine wood and glacial peak or glide silently on skis around the pyramid-shaped Matterhorn. Switzerland is a country that really has it all: linguistic dexterity, cultural diversity, mountain vistas, heavenly chocolate and natural landscapes so extraordinarily magnificent even the gods get goosebumps. Go on, spoil yourself.

BEST TIME TO VISIT
Year-round

TOP THINGS TO SEE
- The Matterhorn
- Lucerne with its medieval painted bridges, lakeside vistas and alfresco cafe life
- Europe's largest glacier, the Aletsch, sticking out its iced serpentine tongue for 23km
- Lauterbrunnen's fairy-tale Staubbach Falls, so beautiful that the poets Goethe and Lord Byron immortalised them in verse
- The medieval chateau-village of Gruyères and its working cheese dairy

TOP THINGS TO DO
- Shop for urban fashion and dance until dawn in Europe's hippest city, Zürich
- Wallow, quite literally, in modern architecture at the spa of Therme Vals
- Ski, snowboard, snow-trek or snow-shoe in Zermatt
- Hike through pastures filled with cows and the melodious chink of bells: the Engadine, Monte Rosa or in the shadow of giant trio Eiger, Mönch and Jungfrau
- Jive to live jazz lakeside at the legendary Montreux Jazz Festival in July

GETTING UNDER THE SKIN
Read *At Home,* a collection of short stories by Zürich cabaret artist Franz Hohler

Listen to folk band Sonalp, a fusion of Swiss yodelling, cow bells and world sounds

Watch the James Bond 1960s classic *On Her Majesty's Secret Service* for action-packed shots of Bern, Grindelwald and snowy Saas Fee

Eat *rösti* (crispy, fried shredded potatoes) and *würste* (sausages) in German-speaking Switzerland and a cheesy fondue or raclette when there's snow

Drink prestigious Calamin or Dézaley *grand cru* from the Unesco-protected vineyards of Lavaux facing Lake Geneva

IN A WORD
Grüezi ('Hello' in Swiss German)

TRADEMARKS
Matterhorn; *Heidi; Swiss Family Robinson;* yodelling; clockwork efficiency; chocolate; cows; private banks; luxury watches; Swiss Army knives; Sigg water bottles

RANDOM FACT
Röstigraben (literally '*rösti* trench') is the cultural divide between German- and French-speaking Switzerland

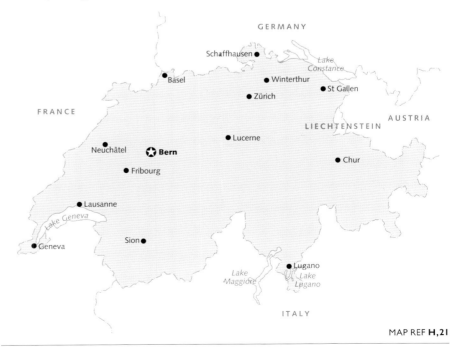

MAP REF **H,21**

1. The serene-looking rocky mountains of Klausenpass provide the backdrop for a popular cycle route
2. One of the highest peaks in the Swiss Alps, the legendary Matterhorn (4478m) overlooks the quaint town of Zermatt
3. A frozen lake makes for a unique track surface for horse racing in St Moritz
4. Zip through the picturesque Old Town of Bern on a tram

2.

3.

1.

It may be known to the world as a rogue state, but travellers to Syria know better. This is a place where the long-standing tradition of warm Arab hospitality has survived the tumult of a region beset by conflict. Although Syrians themselves are what travellers remember most fondly from their visit, this country, which has always stood at history's crossroads, has so much more to offer. Roman ruins, Crusader castles, some of the oldest cities on earth and some of the Mediterranean's best food are all Syrian specialties. And despite what you may have read, Syria is an extremely safe country to visit and one of the Arab world's most accessible entry points for beginners and experienced travellers alike.

BEST TIME TO VISIT
March to May (spring)

TOP THINGS TO SEE
- The extraordinarily beautiful old city of Damascus, with abundant signposts to the Middle East's great civilisations
- The ancient Roman city of Palmyra, like an evocation of a fairy tale in the desert
- Crac des Chevaliers, the stunning hilltop Crusader castle with a labyrinth of rooms and panoramic views
- Bosra's wonderfully intact 15,000-seat Roman theatre and citadel
- Apamea, the little-known Roman city with an extraordinary colonnaded street

TOP THINGS TO DO
- Get lost beneath the vaulted ceilings of Aleppo's souq, one of the world's most evocative bazaars
- Listen to the Arab world's last storyteller, then head for the peerless Umayyad Mosque in Damascus after sunset
- Stay in a hotel occupying one of the old courtyard homes in Old Damascus
- Listen to mass in Aramaic, the language of Christ, in Maalula
- Wander through peaceful Qala'at Samaan, where St Simeon Stylites once sat

GETTING UNDER THE SKIN
Read *The Dark Side of Love* by Rafik Schami, a beautifully written love letter to his troubled nation

Listen to Lena Chamamian's *Shamat*, which has seen her dubbed Syria's new diva

Watch *Out of Coverage*, directed by Abdel atif Abdelhamid, a nuanced study of Syrian society that somehow satisfied Syrian censors

Eat at a converted courtyard restaurant in Old Damascus or Aleppo; an ice cream at Bakdash, a world-famous Damascene institution

Drink *shay na'ana* (mint tea), the essential complement to Syrian hospitality

IN A WORD
Ahlan wa sahlan (Welcome)

TRADEMARKS
Larger-than-life posters of the Assad dynasty that has ruled Syria since 1970; two of the oldest continuously inhabited cities on earth (Damascus and Aleppo)

RANDOM FACT
One out of every three Syrians is under 15 years old

MAP REF J,24

1. Umayyad Mosque in Damascus features the legendary shrine of John the Baptist
2. Ruined colonnades stand as a reminder of the former glories of the Temple of Nebo in ancient Palmyra
3. Home sweet home: a boy arrives at his conical mud-brick beehive house in central Syria
4. A drink vendor with an impressive set-up serves up cold drinks in Damascus

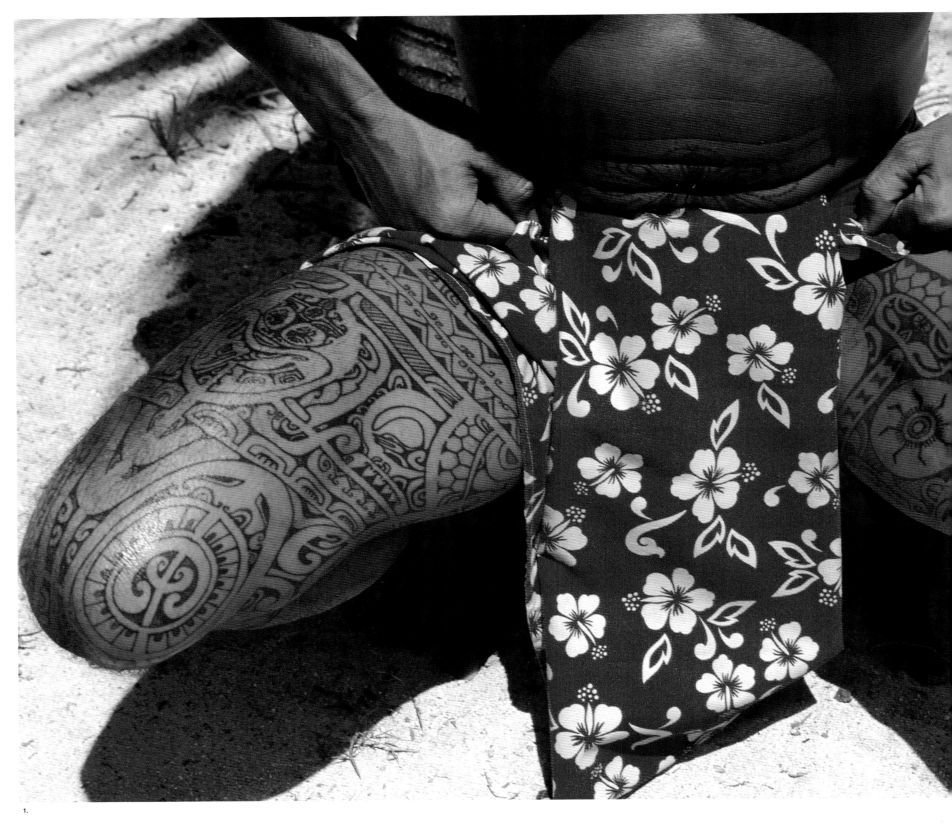

1.

2.

3.

CAPITAL Pape'ete | POPULATION 245,405 | AREA 3500 sq km | OFFICIAL LANGUAGE French

Seductively tranquil and lushly gorgeous, French Polynesia offers much more adventure than its jet-set reputation suggests. From the vast lagoons of the Tuamotu atolls, to the culturally intense Marquesas Archipelago, the country's 117 islands are spread over a marine area the size of Europe and hold an impressive amount of diversity. Divers will find clear-water Nirvana, hikers steamy-jungle bliss and foodies a delicious French cuisine with Polynesian flavours. Whether you're beach lounging or surfing, the scent of *tiare* (gardenia) flowers is ubiquitous in the air and a warm tropical softness caresses the skin. Splurge at luxury resorts or stay in more affordable rustic rooms or boutique-style bed and breakfasts – the French Polynesian dream isn't just for movie stars.

BEST TIME TO VISIT

The cooler, drier months between May and October – especially July for the Heiva i Tahiti festival

TOP THINGS TO SEE

- Ra'iatea's Taputapuatea *marae* (ancient temple), thought to be one of the most important in the Pacific
- The county's best dancers shaking their hips at the Heiva i Tahiti festival
- Shell necklaces, woven hats and flowers à go-go at Pape'ete's market
- The outrageous view over Mo'orea's two bays from the Belvedere view point
- The best surfers in the world gliding through cavernous tubes at Teahupo'o

TOP THINGS TO DO

- Learn to love sharks while diving the passes of immense Rangiroa atoll
- Hike to rugged vistas, valleys and waterfalls on Nuku Hiva
- Live like a rock star at one of Bora Bora's opulent resorts
- Snorkel with humpback whales in the clear subtropical waters of Rurutu
- Party with sailors, surfers and transvestites in Pape'ete's raucous bars and clubs

GETTING UNDER THE SKIN

Read *Frangipani* by Célestine Vaite for insight into modern Polynesian life

Listen to *Bobby & Angelo*, a dreamy, utterly Polynesian collaboration of two of Tahiti's most popular artists

Watch the 2009 comedy *Couples Retreat* filmed on stunning Bora Bora

Eat raw fish in its many forms: coconut-milk *poisson cru*, Mediterranean-flavoured carpaccio and Asian-inspired sashimi

Drink a Hinano, the country's signature beer with a label image of a Tahitian woman wearing a *pareo* (sarong-type garment)

IN A WORD

Haere maru (Take it slow)

TRADEMARKS

Tiare flowers; Tahitian pearls; Paul Gauguin; Mutiny on the *Bounty*; bungalows over the water; surfing the monster wave of Teahupo'o

RANDOM FACT

Over 300,000 *tiare* flowers are harvested per day for making flower leis and fragranced coconut oil, as well as to simply tuck behind the ear

PETER HENDRIE | LONELY PLANET IMAGES

PHOTOLIBRARY

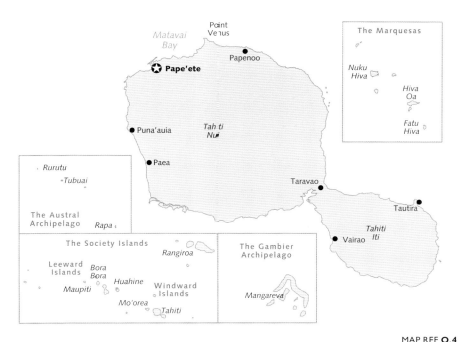

MAP REF **Q,4**

1. Impressive tribal tattoos cover a man's legs in Tahiti
2. Get some barrel action at the legendary Teahupo'o break
3. A horse strikes a noble pose while looking out upon a memorable Tahitian view
4. Flower power: a young girl wears a lei and garland of flowers

4.

2.

3.

1.

4.

CAPITAL Taipei | POPULATION 22,974,347 | AREA 35,980 sq km | OFFICIAL LANGUAGE Mandarin

One of the four Asian tigers, the island of Taiwan is divided from the Chinese mainland by the Formosa Strait, and by a yawning political divide. Officially known as the Republic of China, Taiwan has been ruled by the nationalist government founded by Chiang Kai-shek since 1945, but the island is simultaneously claimed by the People's Republic of China (PRC). Politics aside, this is a land where skyscrapers rub shoulders with misty mountains and mysteries. Away from the futuristic capital, Taipei, Taiwan is a tapestry of forested peaks, giant Buddhas, hot springs, basalt islands and tribal villages. No wonder the island was christened Ilha Formosa (the Beautiful Island) by the Portuguese.

BEST TIME TO VISIT
September to November, for ravishing autumn colours

TOP THINGS TO SEE
- The view over Taipei from the 509m-high Taipei 101 tower
- A staggering array of Chinese artefacts in Taipei's National Palace Museum
- Historic temples and gourmet dining in Tainan, the ancient capital
- Stunning roadside scenery while cycling the South Cross-Island Hwy or Hwy 11
- Basalt outcrops and delightfully sculptural stone fish traps on the Penghu islands

TOP THINGS TO DO
- Trek through marble canyons beside a jade-green river in Taroko Gorge
- Learn to drink tea the Chinese way in the tea gardens of Pinglin
- Hike to hidden waterfalls and hot springs in the jungles around Wulai
- Encounter Yami tribal people on lovely Lanyu island
- Test your commitment to adventurous eating at one of Taipei's legendary stinky tofu stands

GETTING UNDER THE SKIN
Read Hsiao Li-hung's classic love story *A Thousand Moons on a Thousand Rivers*

Listen to the slickly packaged Mandarin pop of Jay Chou, F4, Farenheit and S.H.E

Watch Taiwanese 'idol dramas' to see the next generation of Mandarin pop stars being launched onto the scene

Eat *chou doufu* ('stinky tofu'), marinated in a brine made from decomposing vegetables and shrimps)

Drink Taiwan beer, brewed with Taiwanese *ponlai* (Japonica) rice – if nothing else, it will take away the taste of the stinky tofu…

IN A WORD
Chiah pa boeh? (Have you eaten yet?)

TRADEMARKS
Territorial disputes with the PRC; the Taipei 101 tower; Chiang Kai-shek; labels saying 'Made in Taiwan'

RANDOM FACTS
Taiwan has its own aboriginal people, the Yuanzhumin, related to the tribes of Indonesia, who today make up less than 2% of the population

MAP REF **K,32**

1. Catch an elegant performance at the Chinese opera in Taipei
2. On full alert: witness the changing of the guards at the Martyrs' Shrine in Taipei
3. There's plenty to take in at the Dragon and Tiger Pagodas on Lotus Lake in Kaohsiung
4. Competition for advertising space is fierce in bustling Taipei

1.

2.

3.

Tajikistan is very much the odd man out in Central Asia. A Persian speaker in a Turkic world, cut adrift in a mountain cul-de-sac at the furthest corner of the former USSR and the only republic to have so far suffered from civil war – hence tourists are still relative novelties here. Aside from bustling Silk Road towns and colourful bazaars, Tajikistan's main pull is the Pamir Mountains, an awesomely beautiful high-altitude plateau of intensely blue lakes, Kyrgyz yurts and rolling valleys that has impressed everyone from Marco Polo to Francis Younghusband. If your favourite places include Tibet, Bolivia or northern Pakistan, chances are you'll be blown away by little-known Tajikistan.

BEST TIME TO VISIT
June to September (mountains), March to April, September to November (lowlands)

TOP THINGS TO SEE
- Pamir Hwy, one of the world's great road trips, linking Khorog and Osh
- The Wakhan Corridor, a gloriously scenic valley of Silk Road forts, Buddhist stupas and 7000m peaks
- Marguzor Lakes, a string of seven turquoise lakes and homestays near Penjikent
- Istaravshan, with a great bazaar, mosques and madrasas hidden in its side streets

TOP THINGS TO DO
- Fasten your seatbelt on the scenically outrageous flight from Khorog to Dushanbe
- Trek the Fan or Pamir Mountains, up there with the world's best mountain scenery
- Stay overnight in a remote homestay or yurtstay, to experience the region's humbling hospitality
- Stroll the neoclassical facades of Rudaki, Dushanbe's main drag, which owes more to St Petersburg than inner Asia
- Watch *buzkashi* (polo with a headless goat) at Hissar Fort during the March Navrus festival

GETTING UNDER THE SKIN
Read *Land Beyond the River: The Untold Story of Central Asia* by Monica Whitlock, for a rundown of recent history

Listen to a folk singer belting out a Rudaki poem to the tune of a six-stringed *rubab* (Persian lute) in the western Pamir

Watch Bakhtyar Khudojnazarov's *Luna Papa*; or Jamshed Usmonov's *Angel on the Right*

Eat a home-made bowl of *kurtob* (a deliciously cool and creamy mix of flat bread, yoghurt, onion, chives and coriander)

Drink a Dushambinksy *piva* (beer) at the fountains of Dushanbe's Ayni opera house

IN A WORD
Roh-i safed (Have a good trip)

TRADEMARKS
Drug traffickers; civil war; mountains; yurts; bazaars; humbling hospitality; Marco Polo sheep; skullcaps; Persian poetry; 'roof of the world'

RANDOM FACT
Ancient Sogdian, the language of the Silk Road, is still spoken in the more remote parts of Tajikistan's Yagnob Valley

MAP REF I,27

1. A game for *real* men, *buzkashi* is a sport played on horseback that uses an animal carcass, such as a calf, as the 'ball' – it is one of the festivities during Navrus celebrations in Hissar
2. A Tajik family have their portrait taken in the wheat fields of the Wakhan Valley, Vichkut
3. Kyrgyz men keeping warm with their traditional *kalpaks* (felt hats) in Murghab
4. The statue of Ismail Samani, the 10th-century Samanid ruler, stands defiantly in Dushanbe

2.

3.

1.

Some countries make noise. Tanzania makes music. Its largest soundstage – the vast Serengeti plains – hosts earth's most spectacular natural show, the great migration. Not only do grasses sway to the millions of wildebeest hoof beats, but so do the lucky visitors who drop in each year. Melodies of different sorts, whether the chants of leaping Maasai warriors, the lilting songs of Kilimanjaro guides or the rhythmic lapping of turquoise waters on Zanzibar's shores, are as intrinsic to travellers' experiences as Tanzania's epic visuals – dramatic Rift Valley landscapes, colourfully clad locals and spellbinding wildlife. Although the nation is home to one of Africa's most diverse populations, tribal rivalries are almost nonexistent. As you'd expect from a great maestro, harmony reigns.

BEST TIME TO VISIT
June to October or December to January

TOP THINGS TO SEE
- A stream of countless wildebeest risking life and limb as they cross the Serengeti's croc-infested Grumeti River
- Dawn breaking over the African savannah from your spot atop Kilimanjaro
- Turquoise waters cresting Zanzibar's reefs and flowing over the white sands
- Thousand-strong buffalo herds on Katuma River's wild floodplain in Katavi National Park
- The interior of Kilwa Kisiwani's Great Mosque lit by a sun low on the horizon

TOP THINGS TO DO
- Paint a rippled picture on a glassy canvas while sailing in a traditional dhow
- Drop into the wildlife-laden depths of Ngorongoro Crater
- Calm your racing heart on a tropical beach in Mahale Mountains National Park
- Weave slowly past brass-studded, intricately carved Swahili doors while taking in the intoxicating air of Stone Town in Zanzibar
- Kayak past hippo, elephant and smaller species in Selous Game Reserve

GETTING UNDER THE SKIN
Read *Empires of the Monsoon: A History of the Indian Ocean* by Richard Hall, for an understanding of the country's past

Listen to Bongo Flava, a form of Swahili hip hop incorporating Afrobeat and arabesque melodies

Watch *Kilimanjaro – To the Roof of Africa*, a stunning IMAX documentary by David Breashears

Eat *ugali* (maize and/or cassava flour); or *mishikaki* (marinated meat kebabs)

Drink *mbege* (banana beer); or *uraka* (a brew made from cashews)

IN A WORD
Hakuna matata (No worries)

TRADEMARKS
Serengeti; the great migration; Kilimanjaro; Zanzibar; Maasai people

RANDOM FACT
The Anglo-Zanzibar conflict on 27 August 1896 stands as the world's shortest war – it lasted a grand total of 38 minutes

MAP REF O,24

1. A herd of wildebeest amble through the Ngorongoro Conservation Area
2. A young Maasai warrior sports traditional attire, including unique ear piercings, outside Arusha
3. The Islamic-majority island of Zanzibar features some fascinating colonial architecture in the old Stone Town
4. Flocks of pink-hued greater flamingos can be spotted in the lakes of many of Tanzania's national parks

1.

2.

3.

When it comes to traveller appeal, Thailand has everything – perfect beaches, dense jungles, ruined cities, exotic islands, golden monasteries, captivating coral reefs, laid-back locals, fast and furious cities, cascading rice terraces, tranquil Buddhist backwoods, steamy tropical weather, blistering cuisine, five-star extravagance and indulgence on a shoestring. Despite the occasional revolution, people just keep coming back to Thailand, lured by a wealth of travel experiences and an anything-goes attitude that finds its best expression in the hedonistic beach parties of the southern islands, and its worst expression in the girlie bars of Bangkok and Pattaya.

BEST TIME TO VISIT
November to April to escape the rains

TOP THINGS TO SEE
- Culture, chaos and Buddhist splendour in Bangkok, Thailand's energetic capital
- The atmospheric ruins of the old Thai capitals at Sukhothai and Ayuthaya
- Pristine rainforests teeming with wildlife at Khao Yai National Park
- Humbling relics from the Thailand–Burma Railway at Kanchanaburi
- Unspoiled islands of the kind that inspired Alex Garland's *The Beach* at Ko Tarutao National Marine Park

TOP THINGS TO DO
- Dance barefoot on the sands at a full-moon bash on Ko Pha-Ngan
- Conjure up a Thai feast on a cooking course in Chiang Mai
- Test your head for heights by climbing the awesome karst outcrops at Krabi
- Trek to atmospheric tribal villages around Chiang Rai and Mae Hong Son
- Dive with magnificent megafauna at Richelieu Rock, Hin Daeng and Hin Muang

GETTING UNDER THE SKIN
Read *Monsoon Country* by Nobel Prize–nominated Thai author Pira Sudham

Listen to the jazz compositions of His Majesty King Bhumibol Adulyadej, including the classic *Sai Fon* (Falling Rain)

Watch Chatrichalerm Yukol's historical romp *Legend of Suriyothai*; or the unconventional, arthouse films of Apichatpong Weerasethakul

Eat *tom yam kung* (hot and sour prawn and lemongrass soup); or the outrageously moreish satay sticks served by vendors on Thanon Khao San

Drink Singha Beer; or Sang Som whisky, successor to the infamous and now banned Sang Thip

IN A WORD
Sanuk (Fun – the cornerstone of the Thai psyche)

TRADEMARKS
Golden stupas; floating markets; colour-coded curries; monks with bowls; high-spirited *kathoey* (lady boys); Thai silk; hill tribes; elephant rides; backpacker beach parties; Khao San Road

RANDOM FACTS
No Thai would think of building a new house without erecting an accompanying *san phra phum* (spirit house) for the animist spirits dwelling on the site to live in

MAP REF **L,30**

1. Setting the sky alight, Buddhist monks release lanterns during the festival of Loi Krathong in Chiang Mai
2. A girl wears the signature neck rings of the Kayan people
3. Moor yourself in paradise on Ko Phi-Phi Don
4. Watch on as locals go about their shopping at the floating market in Damnoen Saduak

395

2.

3.

1.

4.

Tibet is without doubt one of the most beautiful, tragic and uplifting corners of Asia. An ambiguous relationship with China came back to haunt Tibet when China invaded in 1950, reclaiming the plateau for the 'motherland'. Today an immigrant-fuelled economic boom has transformed towns across the plateau into miniature Chinese cities. But scratch under the surface and you'll find the Tibetan spirit still strong. Join pilgrims for a tour of a centuries-old monastery, a circuit of a holy mountain or simply a bowl of yak butter tea and you'll find an irrepressible, intensely likeable people whose Buddhist faith remains the cornerstone of their cultural survival.

BEST TIME TO VISIT
Mid-May to September

TOP THINGS TO SEE
- Potala Palace, the empty former home of the exiled Dalai Lama, bustling now with Chinese tourists
- Mt Everest, the literal high point of Tibet, for better views of the mountain than the Nepal side
- Nam-tso, a breathtaking high-altitude lake home to hardy nomads and rich birdlife
- Gyantse Kumbum, a unique stupa filled with magnificent murals
- Tashilhunpo Monastery, home of the Panchen Lama and Tibet's second city Shigatse

TOP THINGS TO DO
- Watch maroon-cloaked monks at Sera Monastery debate Buddhist dialectics with a slap and a shout
- Hire a 4WD for the classic overland route along the Friendship Hwy from Lhasa to Kathmandu
- Take the world's highest train ride across the Tibetan plateau to Lhasa
- Trek over 5200m passes from Ganden to Samye, two of Tibet's finest monasteries
- Cleanse a lifetime of sins on Mt Kailash, the world's holiest peak

GETTING UNDER THE SKIN
Read *The Story of Tibet: Conversations with the Dalai Lama* by Thomas Laird for a mix of history and insight from Tibet's spiritual leader

Listen to CDs *Chö* or *Selwa* by Choying Drolma, the sublimely spiritual Tibetan nun

Watch Martin Scorsese's *Kundun* for a splendid look into the life of the Dalai Lama

Eat *momos* (dumplings); a sizzling yak steak; or *tsampa* (ground roasted barley)

Drink salty *bo cha* (yak butter tea) at a remote monastery or sip sweet milky *cha ngamo* tea in a bustling Tibetan teahouse

IN A WORD
Tashi Delek! (Hello, literally 'Good fortune')

TRADEMARKS
'Roof of the world'; the Land of Snows; yaks; sky burial; Han people immigration; religious crackdowns; ethnic riots; the Dalai Lama; monks; pilgrims; butter lamps; juniper incense; destroyed monasteries

RANDOM FACT
Yak tails from Tibet used to be exported to the US to make Father Christmas beards

MAP REF J,29

1. A sea of maroon as Tibetan Buddhist monks study at Galden Jampaling Monastery in Chamdo
2. You'll find ample character in the faces of pilgrims at the atmospheric Barkhor, Lhasa
3. Brave the high altitude for some unforgettable Tibetan scenery at Kambala Pass
4. Friendly Tibetans with spinning prayer wheels are a warming sight throughout Lhasa

1.

2.

3.

Togo could have been designed to cram as much of Africa as is geographically possible into one small space. For a start, its palm-fringed beaches are a world away from the verdant hills and savannah of the north. Its human geography, too, boasts a diversity way out of proportion to the country's size: a staggering 40 ethnic groups live within its borders. Thanks to intermittent unrest and four decades of rule by the same family, Togo's once-thriving tourism industry has taken a battering, but in its stead have come little guesthouses and small-scale ecotourism projects. And the appeal of the attractions that once drew tourists here in droves – wildlife, stunning natural beauty and intriguing cultura traditions – remains undiminished.

BEST TIME TO VISIT
Mid-July to mid-September

TOP THINGS TO SEE
- The Unesco World Heritage–listed area, Koutammakou, famous for its fortified Tamberma compounds
- Lomé's extraordinary Musée International du Golfe de Guinée, busy markets and fine beaches nearby
- Badou, located in the heart of picturesque mountains and a base for good hiking
- The once-threatened Parc National de Fazao-Malfakassa, with elephants and great birdwatching
- The crossroads town of Dapaong, which has a stunning cave settlement nearby

TOP THINGS TO DO
- Hike through the cocoa and coffee plantations around Kpalimé
- Journey by pirogue to Togoville, then immerse yourself in voodoo traditions
- Dance the night away in Lomé
- Haggle for a porcupine skin or warthog tooth in Lomé's Marché des Féticheurs
- Catch a glimpse of Muslim Togo in pretty countryside in the peaceful town of Bafilo

GETTING UNDER THE SKIN
Read *The Village of Waiting*, the first book by George Packer (who now writes for the *New Yorker*) about his time as a Peace Corps Volunteer in a Togolese village

Listen to drums, *lithophones* (stone percussion instruments), then more drums

Watch Togolese director Anne-Laure Folly's *Femmes aux Yeux Ouverts* (Women with Open Eyes)

Eat *pâte* (a dough-like substance made of corn, manioc or yam) accompanied by sauces like *arachide* (peanut and sesame) or *gombo* (okra)

Drink *Tchoukoutou* (fermented millet), the preferred tipple in the north

IN A WORD
Be ja un sema (How are you? in Kabyé)

TRADEMARKS
Castle-like clay houses of the Tamberma; the ruling Eyadéma dynasty; the Sparrow Hawks (Togo's national football team) and Emmanuel Adebayor

RANDOM FACT
Togo is one of only two countries in Africa where more than 40% of its land is suitable for agriculture

MAP REF **M,20**

1. Assuming a meditative pose, a teenage boy rests up in a typical mud-hut village
2. Mother and baby in the Tamberma Valley, one of the least accessible regions in Togo
3. Sharply dressed pastors file into church to begin a service
4. Feel the power of voodoo as a priest leads a ceremony in a sacred forest in Lomé

2.

3.

1.

Say goodbye to tourist hype – the Kingdom of Tonga is pure Polynesia. You won't find resorts selling packaged fun and you won't have to try to gain authentic experiences because they're everywhere. From the monarchy, to church services, feasts and traditional dancing, Tonga pulsates with cultural identity. The backdrop to the thriving way of life is sublime: perfect beaches, rainforests, soaring cliffs and underwater caves; migrating humpbacks are frequently spotted from June to November. Go with the flow and let the Tongan way of life carry you into the calm of island time.

BEST TIME TO VISIT
May to October when it's cooler and drier

TOP THINGS TO SEE
- The imposing Ha'amonga Trilithon, the 'Stonehenge of the South Pacific', constructed to track the seasons
- Tongan arts and crafts, and pyramids of tropical fruit at the Talamahu Market
- Sultry traditional dancing inside Hina Cave while dining on a Tongan feast
- The hundreds of Mapu'a 'a Vaca Blowholes spurting at once along a 5km stretch of coastline
- A Sunday church service to hear lovely, hypnotic singing

TOP THINGS TO DO
- Swim with, or watch humpback whales that come to breed in Tongan waters
- Kayak through the turquoise waterways, islands and deserted beaches of Vava'u
- Explore the collapsed, doughnut-shaped volcanic isle of Niuafo'ou
- Hike through 'Eua's limestone caves and tropical forests to dramatic cliff edges
- Dive the cathedral-like underwater caves of the Arch, Foa Caves, Hot Spring Cave or Ha'ano Castle

GETTING UNDER THE SKIN
Read *Tonga Islands: William Mariner's Account* by Dr John Martin, is a masterpiece of Pacific literature that offers a first-hand experience of the ancient Tongan culture

Listen to *Malie! Beautiful: Dance Music of Tonga*

Watch *My Lost Kainga*, the story of a Tongan woman raised in Australia who returns to Tonga and discovers her own culture

Eat a feast prepared in an *umu* (underground oven): taro and sweet potatoes, roasted suckling pig, chicken, corned beef, fish and shellfish

Drink kava, the murky forget-your-cares-and-stare-at-the-sunset tipple that's a part of the Tongan experience

IN A WORD
Ha'u 'o kai (Come and eat!)

TRADEMARKS
Polynesian monarchy; migrating humpback whales; *tapa* (bark cloth) adorning the walls of every building; packed churches on Sunday

RANDOM FACT
Tonga has the only monarchy in the South Pacific and is the only island nation in this region to have never been officially colonised

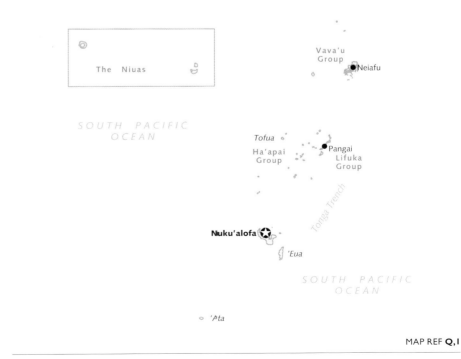

The Niuas

SOUTH PACIFIC OCEAN

Vava'u Group

Neiafu

Tofua

Ha'apai Group

Pangai
Lifuka Group

Tonga Trench

Nuku'alofa

'Eua

SOUTH PACIFIC OCEAN

'Ata

MAP REF **Q,1**

1. A woman applies the finishing touches to a *tapa*
2. St Joseph's Cathedral acts as a beacon for arriving boats in Neiafu, Vava'u Island
3. A proud local shows off a prized catch at the Nuku'alofa wharf, Tongatapu Island
4. Checking the quality of sweet potatoes at the central market, Nuku'alofa, Tongatapu Island

1.

2.

Like a perfect *callaloo* (a thick green soup), Trinidad and Tobago are a rich hotpot of flavours, cultures and influences. You can hear it in the music, which combines everything for Caribbean (calypso, reggae, soca, steel pan, parang and much more) and see it in the locals, a melange of African, island, Spanish, Asian and native peoples. Half of the capital, Port of Spain, is falling apart while the rest buzzes with an energy that can over-power; often you can't separate the two. Elsewhere oil and gas production are the economic engine, which means tourism can be an afterthought; good if you hate well-trodden paths or worry about scaring the myriad birds in the many preserves. Trinidad and Tobago are always authentic.

BEST TIME TO VISIT
It is slightly wetter May to September; the real joy is at Carnival in February

TOP THINGS TO SEE
º Trinidad's remote east coast with its Atlantic storms and deserted, wave-tossed beaches
º Queen's Park Savannah, where all of Trinidad comes to sip fresh coconut juice and people-watch
º Brasso Seco, the rainforest village that's in the green heart of Trinidad
º Buccoo, a Tobago town where you can go completely local while hanging out at the beach
º The Asa Wright Nature Centre, where a full list of bird species tops 430

TOP THINGS TO DO
º Lose yourself at Port of Spain's world-class Carnival, an annual party for the ages
º Surf Mt Irvine Bay on Tobago and wheedle out tips to secret spots from locals
º Snorkel the shallow coral gardens on Tobago
º Cycle past waterfalls while watching for wildlife along the coastal Northern Range
º Jam to Trinidad's raucous, vibrant and everchanging music, the liveliest scene in the Caribbean

GETTING UNDER THE SKIN
Read *A House for Mr Biswas* by VS Naipaul – a vivid portrait of life as an East Indian in Trinidad

Listen to long-time 'Calypso King of the World', the Mighty Sparrow

Watch *SistaGod*, about a girl who thinks she's the Messiah

Eat *callaloo* (a thick green soup made with varying combos of okra, onions, spices, peppers and other seasonings)

Drink sorrel (made from a type of hibiscus, mixed with cinnamon and other spices)

IN A WORD
You limin' tonight? (Are you hanging out tonight?)

TRADEMARKS
Carnival; cricket matches; boisterous music; birdwatching

RANDOM FACT
Carnival on Trinidad rivals New Orleans for the most raucous in the hemisphere – parties start a month in advance and reach a climax of vast outdoor revelry that's followed by days of exhaustion

MAP REF **M,13**

1. Laying down the rules: playing cards can be serious business in Tobago
2. Women shake their tail feathers during Carnival, Port of Spain, Trinidad
3. Kids play it cool, hanging out on the hood of an old pick-up truck in Tobago

2.

3.

1.

Wedged between two reclusive North African giants, Tunisia prides itself on being open to the world. From ancient times when the Carthaginians controlled much of the Mediterranean's seagoing trade, Tunisia has always turned its face towards Europe, and it's from there that countless sun-starved Europeans flock to Tunisia in summer. But Tunisia is about far more than beach-sized tourist resorts, although it does have these in abundance. Tunisia has the Sahara and troglodyte architecture of Hollywood imagination, Roman cities of antiquity, clamorous medinas and walled towns, and one of Islam's holiest cities. As if all that weren't enough, Tunisia's past interaction with the outside world makes it an easily accessible entry point into North Africa and all its charms.

BEST TIME TO VISIT
November to April

TOP THINGS TO SEE
- El Jem, the world's third-largest colosseum, one of Africa's most impressive Roman sites
- Jerba's whitewashed buildings, a rare synagogue in the Arab world, fortress architecture and beaches
- The charming old town of Mahdia untouched by Tunisia's coastal tourism explosion
- Sweeping views from Roman city Dougga's capitol, theatre and other fine monuments
- Sidi Bou Saïd, the clifftop village that is among the Mediterranean's prettiest

TOP THINGS TO DO
- Trek into the dunes of the Grand Erg Oriental for a deep-desert experience
- Imagine yourself in a *Star Wars* movie amid the architecture of the Ksour region
- Lose yourself in the labyrinth of Tunis medina
- Haggle for carpets amid the glorious architecture and mosques of Kairouan
- Wander through Tozeur, a lovely oasis town in the heart of some stunning country

GETTING UNDER THE SKIN
Read Mustapha Tlili's novel *Lion Mountain*; or *Pillar of Salt* by exiled Tunisian Jewish writer Albert Memmi

Listen to Dhaffer Youssef's *Electric Sufi,* a ground-breaking fusion of contemporary jazz and traditional instruments

Watch *The English Patient*, *Life of Brian* and various movies in the *Star Wars* series all were filmed in part in Tunisia

Eat *harissa* (a fiery red-chilli paste); *brik* (deep-fried pastry filled with egg and other delights); seafood; couscous

Drink Celtia (a local lager); Turkish coffee with orange blossom or rose water

IN A WORD
Shukran (Thank you)

TRADEMARKS
Ancient Carthage (close to modern Tunis); Island of the Lotus Eaters (Jerba); tourist resorts along the Mediterranean Coast; *Star Wars* film sets

RANDOM FACT
Tunisia's Cape Blanc (Ras al-Abyad) is the northernmost tip of Africa

MAP REF J,21

1. A four-storey *ksar* (fortified granary) offers a striking contrast against the vivid blue Tunisian sky
2. A Berber man sits below an imposing hilltop fortress in Tataouine
3. Moorish arches and fine mosaic work surround the central courtyard of the Zaouia Sidi Abid el-Ghariani in Kairouan, which houses the tomb of the Hafsid sultan Moulay Hassan
4. A solitary horseman passes a mosque in a desolate landscape near Chenini

1.

2.

3.

CAPITAL Ankara | POPULATION 76,805,524 | AREA 783,562 sq km | OFFICIAL LANGUAGES Turkish & Kurdish

The history of Turkey is akin to a Turkish meal: long and full of different flavours. The result is a country of great diversity that is entirely satisfying to visitors. Sun and sea may be the drawcards, but the landscape rewards with rivers perfect for rafting, quiet villages where fig trees droop over stone walls and a rugged mountain interior peaking at biblical Mt Ararat. That tasty history has left a legacy of clifftop castles, palaces and caravanserais where you can almost still hear the camels bellowing. And tradition coexists with modernity, as watermelon vendors peddle in traffic jams, mobile phones ring in vaulted bazaars scented with saffron and traditional Turkish nomadic hospitality beckons to you to come and join the feast.

BEST TIME TO VISIT
April to June, and September to October

TOP THINGS TO SEE
- The soaring interior domes of İstanbul's Aya Sofya and the Blue Mosque
- Glassy blue waters of Ölüdeniz lagoon and nearby, untouched Butterfly Valley
- A glimpse of Turkey as it once was in the elegant Ottoman-era *konaks* (mansions) of Safranbolu
- Ephesus, the best-preserved Roman city in the eastern Mediterranean
- The trenches, cemeteries and the tranquillity of the beach at Anzac Cove

TOP THINGS TO DO
- Wander among the 'fairy chimneys' and rocky outcrops of Cappadocia, or float over them in a hot-air balloon at dawn
- Get pummelled, soaped and rinsed on the marble in a *hamam* (Turkish bath)
- Watch the sunset amid the monumental stone heads on Nemrut Dağı
- Haggle for carpets, cushions, copperware or ceramics in the Grand Bazaar
- Abandon yourself to the winds and tides on a Blue Voyage from Fethiye

GETTING UNDER THE SKIN
Read *Istanbul: Memories of a City* by Nobel Prize–winner Orhan Pamuk; and Barbara Nadel's İstanbul whodunits featuring detective Çetin Ikmen

Listen to the pop of Tarkan; or Anatolian-folk infused albums from Sezen Aksu

Watch *Uzak (Distant),* an observation of Turkey's modern dilemmas by Nuri Bilge Ceylan; and *Crossing the Bridge: the Story of Music in Istanbul* by Fatih Akin

Eat the ubiquitous kebap; or *hunkar begendi* (pureed aubergine with lamb and bechamel) which is sublime

Drink *çay* (tea) in tulip-shaped glasses; *rakı* (grape brandy flavoured with aniseed); or *ayran* (a refreshing yoghurt drink)

IN A WORD
Hoş geldiniz (Welcome!)

TRADEMARKS
Domes and minarets; kebaps; carpet salesmen; Turkish delight; beaches; blue-glass eye amulets; prayer beads; İstanbul ferries; *hamam*

RANDOM FACT
Van cats, native to southeastern Turkey, have different coloured eyes (one blue, one green) and love swimming

MAP REF I,23

1. The illuminated Ortaköy Camii mosque looks towards the Bosphorus Bridge, İstanbul
2. Turquoise waters beckon sunlovers at Kaputaş Cove, Antalya
3. Get hot and steamy at Çemberlitaş Hamamı, İstanbul
4. Succulent fresh fish are grilled to perfection near the Galata Bridge, İstanbul

2.

3.

1.

4.

Let's not beat around the bush, Turkmenistan is weird; not quite North Korea–weird but pretty damn close. Isolated from the rest of the world since independence from the USSR in 1990, Turkmenistan's first two decades were dominated by eccentric late President 'Turkmenbashi' (Father of the Turkmen), who set about recreating the country in his image, using as funds one of the world's largest reserves of natural gas. The result is a fascinating fiefdom of oddball sights and quirky historical remains. Gasp at the huge Turkmenbashi Mosque, stare in awe at the Ministry of Fairness, wonder at the revolving statue of the late president and be one of the few people to have glimpsed the strangest corner of Central Asia.

BEST TIME TO VISIT
April to May, and September to November

TOP THINGS TO SEE
○ The capital Ashgabat for its wacky monuments to megalomania, the Turkmen equivalent of Disneyland; and the world's largest carpet
○ The ancient Seljuq capital of Merv, once the world's largest city until levelled by Genghis Khan
○ Konye-Urgench, the 13th-century ruined capital of the Khorezmshahs
○ The views of the capital from the top of the Arch of Neutrality or the Turkmenbashi Cableway

TOP THINGS TO DO
○ Search for the footprints of Turkmenosaurus Rex at Kugitang Nature Reserve
○ Ride an Akhal-Teke horse across the foothills of the Kopet Dagh mountains
○ Shop for Bukhara carpets at Tolkuchka Bazaar, Central Asia's greatest bazaar
○ Take a 4WD trip through the desert to the burning Darvaza Gas Craters, as close to the Gates of Hell as we hope you ever get

GETTING UNDER THE SKIN
Read *Unknown Sands: Journey's Around the World's Most Isolated Country* by John Kropf, which chronicles travels through Turkmenbashi-era Turkmenistan

Listen to *City of Love* by Ashkabad, a lilting five-piece Turkmen ensemble

Watch Waldemar Januszczak's *Travels with My Camera: The Happy Dictator*, filmed undercover in Ashgabat by a film crew pretending to be on a drunken stag weekend (in Turkmenistan!)

Eat black Caspian caviar for a song on the Turkmen Caspian coast

Drink a cooling cup of *chal* (sour fermented camel's milk) as the sun rises over the Karakum desert

IN A WORD
Siz nahili? (How are you?)

TRADEMARKS
Personality cult; Turkmenbashi statues; horses; desert; natural gas; hospitality; Bukhara carpets; shaggy hats; bizarre holidays; carpets

RANDOM FACT
Natural gas is free in Turkmenistan but matches aren't, with the result that many people keep their gas stoves burning 24 hours a day

MAP REF **1,26**

1. The lunar landscape of Yangykala Canyon is an ancient sea bed where fossils can still be found
2. These two children are at home in the haunting beauty of the Karakum Desert
3. The stately golden statue of ex-President Niyazov, aka Turkmenbashi, surveys Ashgabat
4. A *telpek* (traditional Turkmen hat) protects the wearer from summer heat and winter chill

1.

2.

3.

The oddly named Turks & Caicos are a group of about 40 islands dotting their own patch of warm water just north of the Caribbean Sea and south of the Bahamas. Although Miami is a mere 90 minutes by plane, these little gems are blissfully untrammelled by wintering masses. Providenciales, the main island, is renowned for its silky smooth white sand in a part of the world famous for its granular delights. Even the conch, that ubiquitous mollusc, seems both fresher and sweeter here. Time vanishes as you putter about between the islands, with their old pastel villages and languid, reef-protected shores. Locals (called 'belongers') are thoroughly attuned to this pace, saving much of their energy for well-attended church services come Sunday.

BEST TIME TO VISIT
December to July; August to November can be hot and humid

TOP THINGS TO SEE
- Grace Bay, the setting for the best resorts and the most vivid sunsets
- Grand Turk, the government hub, is a sleepy mix of dilapidated buildings, salt ponds and narrow lanes
- Mudjin Harbor, a hidden beach on Middle Caicos reached by stairs amid the cliffs
- Chalk Sound, a vibrant blue, almost neon in its intensity
- Caicos Conch Farm, which tells you everything you could hope to know about great pink molluscs

TOP THINGS TO DO
- Dive anywhere – the underwater treats are top form amid stiff competition
- Spot humpback whales off Salt Cay
- Delight in conch-everything at seafood shacks in Blue Hills on Providenciales
- Spot flamingos and iguanas on West Caicos
- Catch the balmy breezes while windsurfing off Grand Turk

GETTING UNDER THE SKIN
Read J Dennis Harris' *A Summer on the Borders of the Caribbean Sea*, a classic 19th-century travelogue

Listen to ripsaw music, a local style combining conga drums, concertina and actual saws; top talents include Lovey Forbes and Tell and the Rakooneers

Watch your own wedding video, the resorts are popular for nuptials

Eat golden brown, moist and chewy conch fritters or have conch curried, sautéed, in ceviche, perched on a salad

Drink any of several kinds of Turks Head beer

IN A WORD
Alright, alright (Hello)

TRADEMARKS
Shady expats living off 'investments' or involved in 'exports'; lavish resorts; birdwatching; diving

RANDOM FACT
Technically, the Turks and Caicos (like the Bahamas) lie outside the Caribbean Sea; they are washed on the north and east by the Atlantic and on the south and west by the Gulf Stream

MAP REF L,12

1. Making a splash – a skilful display of aquabatics takes places in the crystal-clear waters of Cockburn Town, Grand Turk
2. Is it a bird? Is it a fish? A boy shows off his iridescent parrot fish with its super-sharp beak
3. He sells sea shells by the sea shore; the shells he sells are by the barrowful, I'm sure
4. A man ferries his cargo across the azure waters between Grand Turk and Haiti

Tuvalu is one of the smallest, remotest and low-lying nations on earth; the highest point is only 4.6m (15ft) above sea level. Approaching the island by plane after endless ocean, a dazzling smear of turquoise and green appears, ringed with coral and studded with coconut palms. On the ground, experience the slow pace of the unspoiled South Pacific: stroll around town, chat with the locals at the airport if the plane is arriving or float in the translucent lagoon. The most energetic activity is to motorbike up and down the country's only tarmac road on Funafuti with the local boy racers. Unfortunately, Tuvalu is most renowned today for being extremely threatened by rising sea levels, an effect of global warming.

BEST TIME TO VISIT
May to October, the dry season, when cooling trade winds provide natural air conditioning

TOP THINGS TO SEE
- A *fatele*, a Tuvalu song and dance show with building percussion rhythms and crescendo singing
- *Te ano*, a sport unique to Tuvalu, where two balls get hit around by co-ed teams
- Faleatau (house of God), a rustic pre-Christian archaeological site of raised standing stone platforms on Nukulaelae Atoll

TOP THINGS TO DO
- Realise your desert-island fantasies on the sparkling islets of the Funafuti Conservation Area
- Take a sunset or early morning dip in the waters surrounding Funafala Islet
- Hire a bicycle and explore the length of Fongafale
- Maroon yourself on the outer islands where the supply ship might pick you up again in a few weeks – or maybe not

GETTING UNDER THE SKIN
Read *Where the Hell is Tuvalu?*, a comic tale by Philip Ells who spent two years in Tuvalu as 'the people's lawyer'; *Time & Tide: The Islands of Tuvalu,* a collection of photography by Peter Bennetts and Tony Wheeler

Listen to Radio Tuvalu, the country's radio station

Watch *Pacific Women in Transition*, featuring a Tuvaluan woman adapting to the changes of modern life on the island

Eat a streetside snack of chicken curry or fish roti

Drink coconut water straight from the nut

IN A WORD
Fifilemu (To be very peaceful, quiet)

TRADEMARKS
Fine-sand beaches on clear seas; dot tv millionaires; isolation; rising sea levels; outrageous *fatele* dances

RANDOM FACT
The 'top-level domain' internet suffix for Tuvalu is dot tv. In 2002 the country sold a 15-year lease of the rights to their suffix to VeriSign for US$45 million

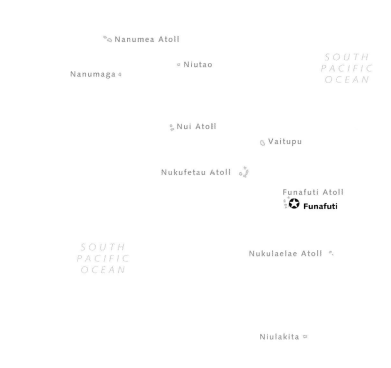

MAP REF **P,39**

1. Schoolchildren on Nukufetau Atoll celebrate the anniversary of their primary school

1.

2.

3.

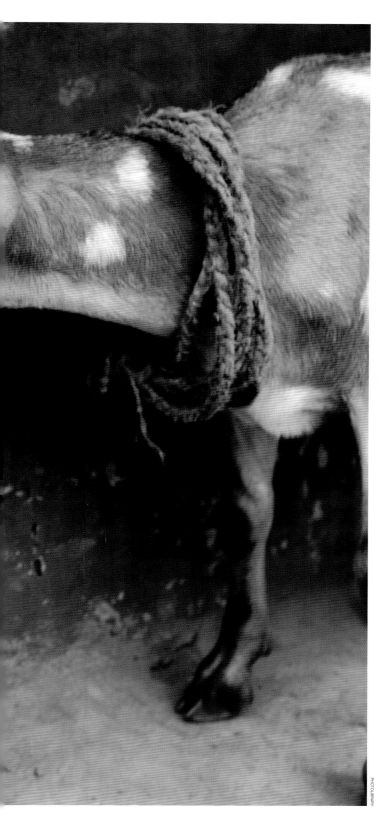

Emphatically fecund, this petite nation punches well above its weight in terms of nature. Its lush forests reverberate with life, their dense canopies shielding the playground of hundreds of bird and mammal species, including half the planet's mountain gorillas. Its savannahs, nestled in some of Africa's most stunning settings, nurture classic safari wildlife, and the Rwenzoris, Africa's highest mountain range, are clad in endemic plant species and topped with equatorial glaciers. Yet although Ugandans have received many body blows, particularly during Idi Amin's rule, remarkably, they've retained their warmth of spirit. Open, eloquent and always polite, Ugandans continue to debate their future. Will nationalism ever take hold? Or will politics and life continue to be split along tribal lines?

BEST TIME TO VISIT
January to February, or June to September

TOP THINGS TO SEE
- Cheetahs giving chase in the incredible mountain-fringed savannah of Kidepo Valley National Park
- Candlelit vegetable stalls punctuating the darkness on Kampala's backstreets
- A narrow gorge trying to strangle the powerful Nile at Murchison Falls – the result is rather extraordinary
- Lush terraced hills flowing down to the serenity of Lake Bunyonyi

TOP THINGS TO DO
- Do the unthinkable – penetrate Bwindi's impenetrable forest and come face to face with mountain gorillas
- Endure the cold and wet to reach mystical highs in the glaciated 'Mountains of the Moon' (Rwenzoris)
- Listen to the chorus of chimp calls while following in their actual footsteps in Kibale Forest National Park
- Stir the Nile with your paddle before it shakes you (and your raft) to the core

GETTING UNDER THE SKIN
Read *Waiting* by Goretti Kyomuhendo, one of Uganda's pioneering female writers – it tells of the rituals of rural life as well as the omnipresent fear during the fall of Idi Amin

Listen to the rumba sounds of Afrigo Band, one of Uganda's longest-running groups

Watch *The Last King of Scotland*, Kevin Macdonald's adaptation of Giles Foden's eponymous novel about the emotional whirlwind surrounding Idi Amin's physician

Eat *matoke* (cooked plantains) and groundnut sauce

Drink Bell Beer, infamous for its 'Great night, good morning!' ad-jingle – hangover-free it's not, but it's tame in comparison to *waragi* (millet-based alcohol)

IN A WORD
Habari? (What news?)

TRADEMARKS
Gorillas; Lake Victoria; Idi Amin; 'Mountains of the Moon'

RANDOM FACT
Winston Churchill was one of Uganda's earliest tourists – his 1907 visit had a lasting impact, with his 'Pearl of Africa' description becoming one of the nation's monikers

MAP REF N,23

1. A mother goat watches over her kid snuggled up in the arms of another kid in Gulu
2. Come no closer – a gorilla bears its powerful fangs
3. Sacred Heart sisters in crisp white habits step out into the deep red dust of the Gulu region
4. Blanketed by mist, Mt Baker rises over Irene Lakes

2.

3.

1.

Once the dynamo of the Soviet economy, Ukraine has come a long way since throwing off the shackles of its bigger neighbour to the east. While the push and pull between Europe and Russia still defines a significant part of Ukrainian identity, many citizens are equally torn between old traditions and pulsing modernisation. Ukraine is, after all, the birthplace of Eastern Slavic civilisation, with a capital at least 1500 years old, and home to seminomadic Hutsuls who still inhabit the rugged Carpathian Mountains. At the other end of the scale is the rush of cosmopolitanism – including the Eurovision song contest, rapidly changing urban neighbourhoods and spruced-up resort towns fronting the Black Sea.

BEST TIME TO VISIT
May to October

TOP THINGS TO SEE
- The caverns with mummified remains of monks at Kyiv's Caves Monastery
- Khan's Palace, the 16th-century home to Crimean rulers in Bakhchysaray
- The town of Kamyanets-Podilsky in a majestic setting above the Smotrych River
- Carpathian National Park, Ukraine's largest wilderness preserve and home to lynx, bison, brown bears and wolves

TOP THINGS TO DO
- Unwind in the laid-back resort town of Yalta, set with pebble beaches, pretty gardens and neo-Byzantine architecture
- Stroll the seaside promenade in Odesa, taking in elegant 19th-century buildings and the cinematic icon of the Potemkin Steps
- Lose yourself in the atmospheric back lanes of pretty Lviv, a Unesco World Heritage site, with buildings dating back to the 14th century
- Delve into Kyiv: marvel at 1000-year-old St Sophia Cathedral, shop along cobblestone Andriyivsky Uzviz and catch a show at the National Opera Theatre

GETTING UNDER THE SKIN
Read *Death and the Penguin* by Andrey Kurkov, an absurdist and socially incisive novel about a man and a penguin living in modern-day Kyiv

Listen to the fast-paced dance melodies of traditional folk ensemble Suzirya

Watch Oksana Bayrak's *Avrora*, the evocative story of a 12-year-old orphan and aspiring dancer who witnesses the Chornobyl disaster

Eat tasty *varenyky* (boiled dumplings served with cheese or meat); *holubtsi* (cabbage rolls stuffed with rice and meat or buckwheat); and *salo* (salted or smoked pork fat)

Drink vodka; and *kvas* (a sweet beer made from fermented bread)

IN A WORD
Vitayu (Hello)

TRADEMARKS
Cossacks; *pysanky* (hand-painted eggs); costumed folk singers; ice fishing; Chornobyl; Soviet architecture; borsch; Orthodox churches; *shapkas* (fur hats)

RANDOM FACT
Some biblical literalists believe the nuclear meltdown at Chornobyl was predicted in the *Book of Revelations*

MAP REF **H,23**

1. A blur of tuille surrounds the principal dancers of *Swan Lake* at Odesa's Opera and Ballet Theatre
2. Perched precariously on a cliff overlooking the Black Sea, Swallow's Nest castle could be plucked right out of *The Lord of the Rings*
3. Any requests? Accordian players in traditional attire get into the swing of it
4. Brightly painted *matryoshka* (sets of wooden dolls within dolls) blush at a craft market in Lviv

1.

2.

3.

Welcome to one of the greatest shows on earth, an astonishing blend of Arabian tradition and race-for-the-future innovation. Few countries have undergone such an extraordinary transformation as the seven emirates of the UAE. A century ago, this was an impoverished Bedouin backwater and Dubai and Abu Dhabi were quiet little villages huddled by the water's edge. But fabulous oil wealth, wedded to sharp business nous, have made these two of the world's most energetic and architecturally exciting cities that together represent the future of Arabia. But scratch beneath the surface and you'll discover the proud Bedouin traditions that provide the foundation for UAE society, not to mention date-filled oases, stirring sand dunes, dramatic mountains and coral rich waters.

BEST TIME TO VISIT
Late October to late February

TOP THINGS TO SEE
- Dubai, where Miami meets the Middle East with old-style souqs, wind towers, the National Museum and modern architecture that will take your breath away
- Hatta, a Dubai getaway with a wonderfully reconstructed heritage village
- UAE's cultural capital, Sharjah, with a state-of-the-art heritage precinct
- Abu Dhabi, one of the richest cities on earth with an extravagant modern skyline
- Khor Fakkan, the most beautiful port in the UAE with a long corniche and fine beaches

TOP THINGS TO DO
- Enjoy the novelty of early-morning camel racing in Dubai
- Head out into the sand dunes of Liwa Oasis, the first ripples of the Rub' al-Khali (Empty Quarter)
- Discover the other UAE in the oasis town of Al-Ain with busy souqs and a fort
- Dive and snorkel at the world-class sites off Badiyah
- Drive from Fujairah to Oman's Musandam Peninsula between the mountains and the Arabian Sea

GETTING UNDER THE SKIN
Read *Dubai: The Story of the World's Fastest City* by Jim Krane

Listen to *Ahlam*, the eponymous album by UAE's first lady of song

Watch contemporary Arab cinema at the prestigious Dubai International Film Festival

Eat *khuzi* (a stuffed whole roast lamb); *Umm Ali* (a pudding with raisins and nuts)

Drink strong *shay na'ana* (mint tea); dark muddy *qahwa* (coffee)

IN A WORD
Al-Hamdu lillah (Thanks be to God)

TRADEMARKS
Dubai, Abu Dhabi and the glitz of oil wealth; wadi-bashing (four-wheel-driving around UAE's oases); a shopper's paradise; Burj al-Arab; a cultural mix of Arab and millions of expats from the West and Asia

RANDOM FACT
Oil was discovered in 1958 in Abu Dhabi and UAE has the world's third-largest oil reserves

MAP REF **K,25**

1. Camels take a leisurely stroll past the construction cranes of Dubai's everchanging skyline
2. Another perfect Dubai sunset lingers behind Burj al-Arab, the world's first seven-star hotel
3. UAE and Dubai flags adorn the walls of a bazaar in Dubai
4. A modern art installation frames the stately domes and minarets of Jumeira Mosque, Dubai

2.

3.

1.

4.

There can be no activity more American than travelling in America. Residents of the USA think nothing of moving thousands of kilometres for a job, on a whim, because of love or simply due to boredom. An eternal optimism fuelled by the hope of better times around the next curve is coupled with the promise of discovery. The culture is everchanging and this vast nation has a corner for every taste. Extraordinary beauty is bound together by commercial squalor, cities beguile and horrify while franchised taste seems to be the national fabric even as individual creativity is celebrated. The variations are myriad, find your own adventure from New York to California, Alaska to Florida, Chicago to New Orleans.

BEST TIME TO VISIT
Year-round

TOP THINGS TO SEE
° New York City, which locals already assume you know is the centre of the universe
° California, which combines boundless beauty in the world's eighth-largest economy
° The hopped-up ethereal netherworld that is Las Vegas, city of a billion lights
° New Orleans, where American clichés go to die
° The natural fireworks of autumn leaves in New England

TOP THINGS TO DO
° Walk Chicago, where you'll discover everything quintessentially American, good and bad
° Escape the hordes on a back trail of Yellowstone National Park
° Joyfully join the smiling masses at the real Disneyland
° Get out on the roads of the great American west, where the only limit is the horizon
° Surf at SoCal (Southern California) beaches, settings for a culture embodied in music, film and fashion

GETTING UNDER THE SKIN
Read three great American road-trip books: John Steinbeck's *Travels With Charley*; William Least Heat Moon's *Blue Highways,* and Jack Kerouac's *On the Road*

Listen to Willie Nelson's *On the Road Again*; Johnny Cash's *American Recordings*, which is a melting pot of blues, rock, country and punk; *James Brown's Greatest Hits*, songs that changed music forever

Watch nominees for best picture Oscars: *Citizen Kane*; *Dr Strangelove*; *American Graffiti*; *Taxi Driver*; *The Color Purple*; *Million Dollar Baby*; *No Country for Old Men*

Eat the array of regional cuisines

Drink microbrewed beers; California reds; coffee drinks with names like short stories

IN A WORD
Yo! Howdy! Hi!

TRADEMARKS
Cheeseburgers; red, white and blue everything; oversized cars; oversized portions; oversized people; national parks; guns; Hollywood; vast, open spaces

RANDOM FACT
In January, the average low in Boston is -6°C, the average high in Miami is 24°C

MAP REF I,9

1. The mighty Colorado River cuts its way through the Grand Canyon, viewed from Toroweap Overlook
2. The dazzling lights of the Flamingo casino have been a Vegas icon since 1946
3. Jazz pros blow the house down at Preservation Hall, New Orleans
4. Ice skaters glide through the winter wonderland of New York's Central Park

1.

2.

3.

Often called the Switzerland of South America, Uruguay remains a country of relative peace and prosperity in a sometimes-troubled region. It's one of Latin America's most secular countries, with legalised same-sex civil unions, a high literacy rate, a strong independent press and low levels of corruption. Flanked by Brazil and Argentina, tiny Uruguay shares with its bigger neighbours a love of football (the first World Cup took place here in 1930), gaucho culture (horsemen, cattle ranches and big open skies) and surf-pounded beaches, several of which have gained an international reputation as the hot spot du jour.

BEST TIME TO VISIT
December to March (summer)

TOP THINGS TO SEE
° Montevideo, Uruguay's culturally rich capital with 19th-century neoclassical buildings and a photogenic Old Town
° The picturesque cobblestone streets of Colonia del Sacramento, beautifully set above the Río de la Plata
° Cabo Polonio, a fishing village that attracts a staggering amount of wildlife – sea lions, seals and penguins, with whales spotted offshore
° The stretch of beaches, surfing-fishing villages and parks along the Atlantic Coast

TOP THINGS TO DO
° Discover Uruguay's cowboy culture at the Fiesta de la Patria Gaucha (March) in Tacuarembó, featuring rodeos, parades and folk music
° Join the international party crowd at the dance clubs in Punta del Este
° Catch the ferry for a memorable jaunt to Buenos Aires
° Enjoy a soak in the thermal baths of Termas de Dayman
° Feast on steak at a *parrilla* (steakhouse) inside Montevideo's Mercado del Puerto

GETTING UNDER THE SKIN
Read *Tree of Red Stars* by Tessa Bidal, a moving coming-of-age story in a time of political upheaval

Listen to the talented singer-songwriter and Academy Award winner Jorge Drexler

Watch *Stranded,* the powerful documentary that brings together the 16 survivors of the infamous 1972 plane crash who spent 72 days in the Andes

Eat huge steaks cooked over a sizzling barbecue, followed by *chaja* (a meringue and ice cream concoction)

Drink maté, the smooth tea made from the leaves of yerba maté, sometimes served in a hollow gourd with *bomba* (metal straw)

IN A WORD
Hola (Hello)

TRADEMARKS
Football (soccer); military dictators; beach resorts; beef; tango; *gauchos* (cowboys)

RANDOM FACT
Gnocchi is traditionally eaten on the 29th day of each month – a custom referencing both Uruguay's Italian heritage and earlier days of hardship when potatoes and flour were all that remained by month's end

MAP REF S,14

1. The perfect beach is at your fingertips – *El Mano* beach sculpture, Playa Brava
2. Tacuarembó's Fiesta de la Patria Gaucha is the *gauchos'* (cowboys) traditional festival
3. The ultimate green machine – foliage overtakes an antique car in Colonia del Sacramento
4. Listen to soulful strumming as you explore Port Market, Montevideo

1.

2.

3.

Any Silk Road romantic who's daydreamed of travelling the Golden Road to Samarkand or the desert tracks to Bukhara will already have their sights firmly set on Uzbekistan. As the cultural and historic heart of Central Asia, the country's Islamic architecture of floating turquoise domes and towering minarets easily ranks among the region's greatest sights, while in the foreground old men with white beards and stripy cloaks haggle over melons in the bazaar or savour a pot of green tea beside a crackling kebab stand. Despite an authoritarian government and strong police presence, travel through this essential slice of the Silk Road is hassle-free and dripping with epic history at every turn.

BEST TIME TO VISIT
March to May, September to October

TOP THINGS TO SEE
◦ Samarkand's Registan Square, one of the world's great architectural ensembles
◦ Shah-i-Zinda, Samarkand, a necropolis that marks the highpoint of Timurid tilework
◦ The old slave-raiding walled city of Khiva, frozen in time and surrounded by desert
◦ The History Museum of the Uzbek People, Tashkent, a walk through the Central Asian past
◦ The scattering of ruined palaces built by Timur (Tamerlane) in his hometown of Shakrisabz

TOP THINGS TO DO
◦ Explore the desert citadels of Khorezm, overnighting en route in a desert yurt
◦ Haggle for carpets, embroidery and striped silks in backstreet bazaars
◦ Ride the beautiful Tashkent metro, while dodging a shake-down by the local police
◦ Get lost in the mosques, mausolea and madrasas of Bukhara's backstreets

GETTING UNDER THE SKIN
Read Peter Hopkirk's *The Great Game*, to gem up on the region's imperial shenanigans

Listen to *Yol Boisin*, by world-music diva Sevara Nazarakhan; or try something by the Tashkent taxi cab favourite Yulduz Usmanova

Watch Michael Winterbottom's *Murder in Samarkand*, starring Steve Coogan as the controversial British ambassador sidelined by his own government

Eat a round of shashlyk kebabs; *shorpa* (soup of boiled mutton with potato, carrot and turnip) or *plov* (rice, meat and carrots)

Drink *kok choy* (green tea) at a traditional teahouse, returning the tea to the pot twice to let it brew, just as the locals do

IN A WORD
Yol boisin (May your travels be free of obstacles)

TRADEMARKS
Timur; shashlyk; blue-domed mosques; minarets; political repression; desert; *plov;* cotton; the Silk Road; skullcaps; white beards; the Aral sea disaster

RANDOM FACT
Uzbekistan is only one of two countries in the world to be double land-locked (ie two countries away from the sea)

MAP REF I,26

4.

1. The sun sets over a game of football beneath the Kalon Minaret at the Mir-i-Arab Medressa in Bukhara
2. The brilliant blue glazed tilework of the unfinished Kalta Minor Minaret dominates Ichon-Qala in Khiva
3. The characterful grin of a Bukhara local
4. Long shadows are cast by a diligent streetsweeper as the sun rises in Samarkand

1.

2.

3.

An ancient living culture, accessible volcanoes, world-class diving and some of the best cuisine in the Pacific make Vanuatu an extraordinary place to visit. Home to the fiercest cannibals during the European exploration era, islanders today have changed their dietary preferences and welcome visitors with authentic warmth. Smiles are as easy to come by as *laplap* cooked in a pit oven, crusty French bread or fresh fish flavoured with herbs and coconut. Port Vila, the capital and tourist centre, is colonial-cool with views of the glorious harbour from every chic restaurant. From here set off to the outer islands to find perfect beaches and clear waters – and also black magic, fiery spouts of lava and authentic Melanesian *kastom* (custom).

BEST TIME TO VISIT
April to October (the southern winter)

TOP THINGS TO SEE
- The brilliant volcanic fireworks of Mt Yasur
- The land divers of Pentecost, who leap from man-made wooden towers
- The Dog's Head cannibal site, complete with dismemberment tables and fire pits
- *Rom* dances, magic, cultural demonstrations or even a fashion show at one of north Ambrym's festivals
- The chambers, tunnels and underground lake of Valeva Cave from a kayak

TOP THINGS TO DO
- Camp in the active caldera of Mt Marum surrounded by lava beds, jungle and cane forests
- Swim through an underwater world of luxury liners, caves and coral gardens off Luganville
- Keep your eyes peeled for dugongs while snorkelling in Lamen Bay
- Parasail over Port Vila's beautiful harbour
- Abseil down the 35m Mele Cascades for a dip in an aquamarine freshwater pool

GETTING UNDER THE SKIN
Read *The Story of Eel & Other Stories*, myths and legends from the Uripiv Islands

Listen to *Jewel in a Crown* by the Vanuatu-style reggae/country/rock band Nauten Boys of Tanna

Watch the videos made by Wan Smolbag Theatre in Port Vila, particularly the musical comedy *Pacific Star*

Eat *laplap*, a hearty meal in a banana leaf cooked in an earthen oven

Drink *aelan bia* (island beer), otherwise known as kava, a becalming nonalcoholic, slightly narcotic brew

IN A WORD
Tank yu tumas (Thank you very much)

TRADEMARKS
Volcanoes; drumming; friendly locals; penis sheaths; wild boars; carvings; spears; French-inspired cuisine; snorkelling and scuba diving; land divers

RANDOM FACT
The last recorded act of cannibalism in Vanuatu was in 1969 by the Big Nambas tribe on Malekula who are also said to be the last islanders to convert to Christianity

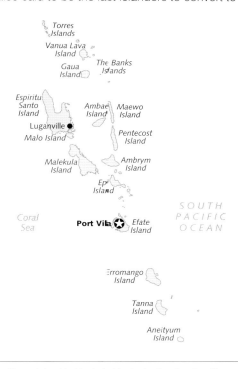

Torres Islands

Vanua Lava Island

Gaua Island — The Banks Islands

Espiritu Santo Island — Ambae Island — Maewo Island

Luganville — Pentecost Island

Malo Island

Malekula Island — Ambrym Island

Epi Island

Coral Sea — Port Vila — Efate Island

SOUTH PACIFIC OCEAN

Erromango Island

Tanna Island

Aneityum Island

MAP REF Q,37

1. A welcoming ceremony on Tanna Island is blanketed in dust, stirred up by villagers pounding their feet
2. A cautious observer watches a ritualistic ceremony on Espiritu Santo Island
3. Ambrym Island's Mt Marum releases powerful blasts of volcanic vapours from its active vents
4. Pentecost Island's death-defying land dive is the forerunner of the modern bungee jump

1.

2.

3.

4.

It is quite extraordinary really, not just its small area, but how marvellously unique this city state is. Ensconced w thin walls in the centre of Italian capital Rome and enshrined in a bevy of sacrosanct traditions and rituals, the Vatican City is one of those rare places that must be visited. This – the world's smallest nation – is the seat of the Catholic Church, ruled with absolute authority by the pope, who lives in a palace with over a thousand rooms, and is protected by a century of single Swiss men in ceremonious red, yellow and blue costume. Not only that: the art and architecture here is priceless, a perfect masterpiece.

BEST TIME TO VISIT
April and June (the low season); Wednesdays when the Pope meets his flock

TOP THINGS TO SEE
- Michelangelo's Sistine Chapel – his cei ing frescoes and *The Last Judgement* are awe-inspiring
- The pope at 11am on Wednesdays
- The Swiss Guard – all male, Swiss and single – and their marvellous, Renaissance-styled skirt pants
- Sacred art and treasures inside the Vat can Museums

TOP THINGS TO DO
- Hike 320 steps up the world's largest come, St Peter's Basilica – the panorama is dizzying and dazzling
- Zigzag around Doric columns and lap up the extraordinary air of St Peter's Square
- Kiss or rub for luck the right foot of bronze St Peter inside the basilica
- Take a 90-minute tour of the 'City of the Dead' and see St Peter's tomb beneath the basilica
- Pay your respects to John Paul II, the second-longest serving pontificate and first non-Italian for centuries – his tomb lies in the Vatican grotto complex

GETTING UNDER THE SKIN
Read *A Season for the Dead* by David Hewson for a fast-paced thriller about a serial-killer cardinal

Listen to papal speeches and news from the city on Radio Vatican – live-streaming or podcasts in English – at www.radiovaticana.org

Watch Tom Hanks flit around the Vatican City in Ron Howard's film adaptation of Dan Brown's *Da Vinci Code* sequel, *Angels & Demons*

Eat Roman pasta such as creamy carbonara (egg yolk, parmesan and bacon); and fiery *alla matriciana* (tomato, bacon and chilli)

Drink local wines such as Frascati and Torre Ercolana

IN A WORD
Amen

TRADEMARKS
The Pope; Catholicism; Sistine Chapel; Swiss Guard; pilgrims; saintly souvenirs

RANDOM FACT
The Popes' previous pad was in Avignon, southern France; they moved to the Vatican City in 1377

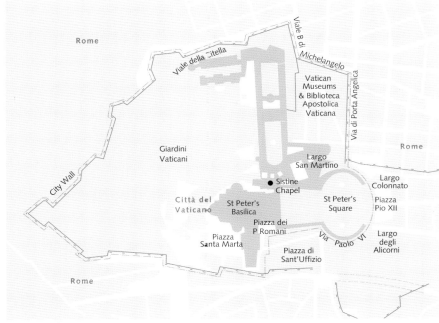

MAP REF I,21

1. The Vatican Museums' grand double-helix sta rcase was designed by Giuseppe Momo in 1932
2. Wander through the glorious high-vaulted inte ior of St Peter's Basilica
3. A heavenly light illuminates St Peter's Basilica
4. Pontifical Swiss Guards are on duty in their distinctive uniform

1.

2.

3.

Simon Bolivar, the lionised 'great liberator' who freed South America from Spanish rule, was born in Venezuela, and it's just one of many reasons why citizens take such pride in their country. The oil-rich nation has always followed its own course, and stands apart from South America, with its love of baseball (rather than football), a relatively small indigenous heritage (just 2% of the population) and a surprising number of beauty queens (more competition winners than any other nation on earth). In recent years, the country's reputation for strong-armed rulers has kept away foreign crowds, leaving the great wonders of Venezuela – its marvellous Caribbean islands, Amazonian wilderness and breathtaking waterfalls – largely to domestic visitors.

BEST TIME TO VISIT
December to April (the dry season)

TOP THINGS TO SEE
- Angel Falls, the highest waterfalls on earth, which drop over 300 stories in Parque Nacional Canaima
- Los Roques, tiny Caribbean islands with fine snorkelling and a friendly vibe
- Los Llanos, an immense wildlife-rich savannah with anteaters, capybaras, anacondas, caiman and astounding birdlife
- Cueva del Guácharo, Venezuela's magnificent cave system
- The laid-back beach town of Santa Fe, well positioned for boat trips to the coral reefs and pretty islands of Parque Nacional Mochima

TOP THINGS TO DO
- Feel the adrenaline rush in the mountain town of Mérida, where rafting, paragliding, canyoning and hiking rule the day
- Hike to the top of Roraima, a massive table mountain with a wild landscape
- Explore the waterfalls, beaches and rain forests along the meandering Río Caura
- Learn to salsa in the steamy capital of Caracas

GETTING UNDER THE SKIN
Read the masterpiece *Dona Barbara* by Romulo Gallegos for insight into the resilience of the Venezuelan character

Listen to *The Venezuelan Zinga Son* by the indie-rock favourite Los Amigos Invisibles

Watch *The Revolution Will Not Be Televised*, the documentary directed by Kim Bartley and Donnacha O'Briain, about the attempted coup to overthrow Hugo Chavez

Eat *pabellon criollo* (shredded beef, rice, black beans, cheese and fried plantain)

Drink *guarapita* (a cocktail made from sugar-cane spirit and fresh juices)

IN A WORD
Como esta? (How are you?)

TRADEMARKS
Oil; dictators; beauty queens; *tepuis* (table mountains); Simon Bolivar; Caracas nightlife; Angel Falls

RANDOM FACT
Sir Arthur Conan Doyle's book *The Lost World* is based on the plateaulike mountain of Roraima, with plant and animal species found nowhere else on earth

MAP REF **N,13**

1. Friends relax amid brightly painted fishing boats in Sucre
2. A sheer 974m drop makes Angel Falls in Parque Nacional Canaima the world's tallest waterfall
3. Perfect blocks of colour line a street in the historic centre of Ciudad Bolívar
4. A fisherman weighs up his freshest fish for sale on Isla de Margarita

2.

3.

1.

CAPITAL Hanoi | POPULATION 86,967,524 | AREA 331,210 sq km | OFFICIAL LANGUAGE Vietnamese

No longer held down by its past (or its politics), the slender nation of Vietnam makes for easy itineraries, book-ended as it is with two very different cities: poetic, tight-lipped Hanoi and zestful, go-go-go Ho Chi Minh City. You can fly into one and out from the other, seeing the dialect, temperament and diet change as you move from the south's rice paddy fields to the centre's white-sand beaches and the north's hill-tribe villages and limestone cliffs. It's still cheap, but has increasingly become a mini China, with a growing nose of business, yet push-cart vendors amid the sports cars. Despite the surge in attention, there are undiscovered pockets everywhere; to find them, you usually just need to walk a couple of blocks from the main street.

BEST TIME TO VISIT
March and April, September to November

TOP THINGS TO SEE
o Hanoi's Hoan Kiem Lake, particularly when lined with morning exercisers at 5am
o Ho Chi Minh Mausoleum in the capital, Hanoi
o Dragon-shaped mountains and blue-green water of Halong Bay
o The citadel and royal tombs along the Perfume River in Hué
o Terraced rice fields, mountains and traditional homes in Sapa

TOP THINGS TO DO
o Eat *pho* (noodle soup) from a tiny plastic stool at a sidewalk eatery
o Pick one of the many Hoi An tailors to make a shirt, suit or dress
o Boat through the Mekong Delta
o Escape tourist ghettos, where it's easier to mix with friendly locals

GETTING UNDER THE SKIN
Read *Dumb Luck* by Vu Trong Phung, a fun 1936 tale of Red-Haired Xuan, a Charlie Chaplin–type character

Listen to the motorbike engines, beeps and street vendor calls from a street cafe in Ho Chi Minh City

Watch a film having little to do with war, Tran Anh Hung's *The Vertical Ray of the Sun,* showing life in modern Hanoi

Eat as much local food as you can; the *pho*, *banh cuon* (steamed rice rolls with minced pork) and *goi cuon* (summer spring rolls) are fresher, better and cheaper than Vietnamese restaurants abroad

Drink *bia hoi* (draught beer), particularly at Hanoi's infamous '*bia hoi*' corner in the Old Quarter: a hundred stools, 101 drinkers and cheap beer

IN A WORD
Troi oi! (Oh my!)

TRADEMARKS
Conical hats; cyclos; *ao dai* (traditional dresses); scooter gridlocks

RANDOM FACT
Hanoi turned 1000 in 2010

MAP REF **M,31**

1. Drift silently through the water towards the limestone mountains of Tam Coc
2. Black H'mong girls are about to begin the autumn rice harvest in the village of Khanh Hoa, Yen Bai province
3. Basketware is piled up high on a two-wheeled shop in Ho Chi Minh City
4. Nha Trang's fish market bustles with activity

CAPITAL Roadtown (BVI), Charlotte Amalie (USVI) | **POPULATION** 24,491 (BVI), 109,825 (USVI) | **AREA** 505 sq km | **OFFICIAL LANGUAGE** English

Although considered one archipelago, the Virgin Islands are divided between two countries (the British Virgin Islands, BVI; and the United States Virgin Islands, USVI). And the curiosities don't stop there. St Thomas on the USVI is mobbed for much of the year by hordes of tourists (ships larger than some islands dock here by the dozen) yet at the other end of the island, you'll find preserved mangroves. Its siblings, St Croix and St John, are much quieter and feature beaches and wild places as beautiful as any in the Caribbean. Meanwhile the 40 islands of the BVI are more than content to remain as quiet as possible, except for requisite island rhythms. The star is Virgin Gorda, the silver-sanded playground of movie stars.

BEST TIME TO VISIT
The weather is fine all year, November and May see less crowds

TOP THINGS TO SEE
- Virgin Islands National Park on St John (USVI), with perfectly preserved beaches
- Devil's Bay (BVI), a natural play land of a perfect beach surrounded by grottos, boulders and more
- Christiansted on St Croix (USVI), which has a vast 18th-century fort and an appealing waterfront
- Buck Island Reef National Monument of St Croix (USVI), a haven for sea turtles
- The Baths on Virgin Gorda (BVI), a collection of volcanic boulders forming pools

TOP THINGS TO DO
- Deaden your pain with a trademark Painkiller cocktail at White Bay (BVI)
- Laze away your cares on the hideaway of Anegada (BVI)
- Dive sites like the sunken *RMS Rhone* (BVI) and the wall at Cane Bay (USVI)
- Make friends underwater at Leinster Bay and Waterlemon Cay (USVI)
- Kayak through the mangroves on the wild end of St Thomas (USVI)

GETTING UNDER THE SKIN
Read Robert Louis Stevenson's *Treasure Island*, a classic yarn of buried treasure and Long John Silver

Listen to Quelbe, a blend of local folk music; a top group is Stanley and the Ten Sleepless Knights

Watch *Christopher Columbus: The Discovery,* and *1492: Conquest of Paradise*, two 1992 movies featuring the Italian explorer washing ashore in the New World (in both cases St Thomas)

Eat soups, stews and pot roast (*daube* is a spicy version) with johnnycakes (fried bread)

Drink a debilitating range of fruity rum drinks

IN A WORD
Limin' (Universal West Indian slang for hanging out)

TRADEMARKS
Huge cruise ships; reggae rhythms; Cruzan and Pusser's rums; yachties; flamingos

RANDOM FACT
The USVI is an unincorporated territory of the USA; the BVI is a Crown Colony of the United Kingdom

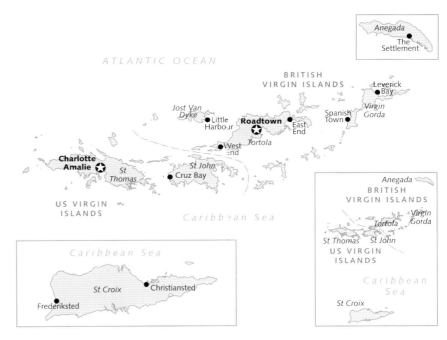

MAP REF **L,13**

1. Yachts dot the Caribbean Sea around the spectacular coral reef of Marina Cay

2.

3.

1.

4.

Wales at its best is tramping in splendid isolation across magnificent green hills and purple-heather moors, valleys ringing with the song of male voice choirs and poetry of 6th-century bards, local pubs beckoning with a pint of Best Bitter. One man and his dog (and sheep by the millions) are the only souls for miles around; King Arthur fires the imagination with his treasury of ancient Welsh lore; and you can be sure it will rain. Political devolution has long dominated national politics and no one shows a greater pride in this raw, underrated land of heady rough-cut landscapes, mighty stone castles and lyrical morning mists than those fiercely patriotic, rugby-loving, song-mad, Welsh-speaking Cymry (Welsh).

BEST TIME TO VISIT
March to June, September

TOP THINGS TO SEE
- Pontcysyllte, the world's longest navigable aqueduct on the Llangollen Canal
- Snowdon, Wales' highest and headiest peak at 1085m
- The Six Nations Rugby Championships in Cardiff
- Conwy, Caernarfon, Harlech and Beaumaris castles
- The Brecon Beacons National Park – rugged hills, moors and fantastic pubs

TOP THINGS TO DO
- Hike, mountain bike, camp, get wet, feel alive in the Snowdonia National Park
- Shop for china in Portmeirion, a whimsical vision of Italian classicism
- Be roused by male voice choirs performing at Llangollen's International Eisteddfod
- Follow the Pembrokeshire coastal path through quaint fishing villages and around secluded coves – play spot a puffin!
- Frolic across sandy beaches and limestone cliffs on the Gower Peninsula

GETTING UNDER THE SKIN
Read *Random Deaths and Custard* by Catrin Davydd, one of Wales' best contemporary creative writers

Listen to operatic arias by Welsh tenor Aled Wyn-Davies

Watch *Solomon and Gaenor,* a turn-of-the-20th-century tale of forbidden love set against South Wales' coalfields

Eat *bara brith* (tea-soaked fruit loaf); a Welsh cream tea (fruit scone with strawberry jam and whipped cream); or a lunchtime plate of Welsh rarebit (an 18th-century version of beer-soaked Cheddar cheese on toast)

Drink a pint of Cardiff-brewed Brains or ale from a local microbrewery

IN A WORD
Bore da (Hello, good morning)

TRADEMARKS
Mountains; sheep; coal mines; male voice choirs; rugby; tongue-twisting place names starting with double L; King Arthur and Merlin; leeks; the Welsh red dragon

RANDOM FACT
Genuine Welsh products: Richard Burton, Anthony Hopkins, Laura Ashley, Roald Dahl, Tommy Cooper, Peter Greenaway, Alfred Sisley

MAP REF **G,19**

1. The magnificent medieval Caernarfon Castle presides over the Afon Seiont
2. Take in the bird's-eye view over the old rooftops of Caernarfon
3. Tension on the green – the home side bowls up a storm during a close game
4. Contestants prepare for some tough fishing competition beneath the cliffs of Porth Nefyn

1.

2.

3.

Yemen may be the Arabian Peninsula's poor cousin, but therein lies its charm. With none of the oil wealth of its neighbours, the country is like a time capsule to old Arabia. Yemen's history reads like the retelling of a legend – to the Romans, Yemen was Arabia Felix (Happy Arabia), Noah launched his ark from here, the Queen of Sheba once ruled the land and there was once dazzling wealth from the frankincense trade. This journey into the past has many diverse focal points, from the Arabian Nights–like capital of San'a in the west to mud skyscrapers in the east, from the stunning mountain scenery and villages of the north to the weird and wonderful landscapes of Suqutra off the south coast.

BEST TIME TO VISIT
October to March

TOP THINGS TO SEE
- San'a, the 2500-year-old Unesco World Heritage–listed city with 14,000 ancient buildings
- Wadi Hadramawt's otherworldly mud villages, especially Shibam which has been dubbed the 'Manhattan of the Desert'
- Shaharah, the ancient mountain village with a 17th-century suspended bridge and fantastic scenery
- Thilla, the historic fortified village with stone walls and lovely architecture
- Aden, Yemen's most modern city with some fine beach resorts nearby

TOP THINGS TO DO
- Pick your way through San'a's Souq al-Milh, the Arabian Peninsula's finest market
- Hike through the Jebel Kawkaban from the fortified citadel of Kawkaban
- Step back into Yemen's ancient history at Ma'rib, home to Sabean temples
- Explore wildlife-rich Suqutra where you can go diving, caving and hiking
- Drive into the clouds in the Jabal Razih, a mountain region with remote villages

GETTING UNDER THE SKIN
Read *Yemen: Travels in Dictionary Land* by Tim Mackintosh-Smith – wry observations of Yemeni life from a long-time San'a resident

Listen to *Habibi Ta'al* by Ahmed Fathey, a renowned Yemeni oud player and singer

Watch Pier Paolo Pasolini's *Arabian Nights*, a racy adaptation of the age-old collection of stories that includes scenes shot in Yemen; or *A New Day in Old Sanaa'a*, the first-ever Yemeni film by Bader Ben Hirsi

Eat *salta* (a piping-hot meat stew with lentils, beans, coriander and fenugreek)

Drink tea scented with cardamom; or coffee with ginger

IN A WORD
Mumkin ithnayn shay (Two teas please)

TRADEMARKS
Frankincense; Queen of Sheba; mud skyscrapers in the Wadi Hadramawt; Bedouin tribesmen with *jambiyas* (ceremonial daggers); chewing *qat* (an intoxicating plant)

RANDOM FACT
Despite having been unified for centuries, modern Yemen was actually divided into two countries – South Yemen and North Yemen – until 1990

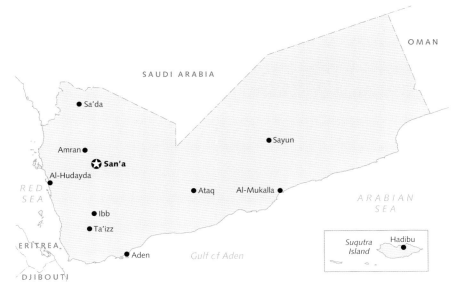

MAP REF **L,25**

1. The mud tower-houses of Habban resemble miniature toy buildings, set at the foot of the mountains
2. Cheeky grins welcome you to Thilla
3. Kick up your heels at a local celebration in Sayun
4. The gorge crossing over the 17th-century Shihara bridge is not for those who suffer from vertigo

2.

3.

1.

Although copper and cobalt run through Zambia's veins, its heart is made of anything but heavy metal. The people, who've long been encouraged to embrace their varied cultural backgrounds and traditions, are perfect examples – they're easy-going, incredibly welcoming and open. The vast swathes of untapped wilderness, many of which are national parks, also stand in contrast to the all-important mining industry. Home to an incredible diversity of wildlife, and some of Africa's best-trained guides, the parks offer some of the most rewarding safari experiences on the continent – visitors don't just see wildlife, they get to know it.

BEST TIME TO VISIT
May to early October, when skies are dry, temperatures are cool and all the safari camps are open

TOP THINGS TO SEE
- Your white-water raft after one of the Zambezi's Class-V rapids
- Eight million fruit bats flocking into Kasanka National Park in late October
- The wildlife of the 'Emerald Season' in Kafue National Park (December to April)
- The Lozi king leading his people's retreat from the annual floods in the Ku'omboka ceremony
- Cheetah chasing puku on the Busanga Plains

TOP THINGS TO DO
- Delicately dodge hippos and crocs while canoeing in Lower Zambezi National Park
- Bungee jump into the abyss from the Zambezi bridge
- Wade across the Luangwa River on a safari walk in South Luangwa National Park
- Venture into the wilderness of Liuwa Plain National Park to witness the other wildebeest migration
- Stand on the cliff facing Victoria Falls and watch sparkling water droplets dance in the updraught

GETTING UNDER THE SKIN
Read *A Point of No Return* by Fawanyanga Mulikita; *Kakuli* by Norman Carr; *The Unheard* by Josh Swiller

Listen to Kalindula music – Ricki Ilonga and Larry Maluma are both great options

Watch *The Death of Tyson*, a short documentary on the life of an AIDS orphan

Eat *nshima* (porridge made from ground maize) with *chibwabwa* (pumpkin leaves) and *nkuku mu chikasu* (village chicken)

Drink the local beer, *chibuku*

IN A WORD
Muzuhile? (How are you? in Bemba)

TRADEMARKS
The Zambezi; Victoria Falls; the Copper Belt; walking safaris; Luangwa leopards

RANDOM FACT
One cheeky monkey relieved himself on President Rupiah Banda during a televised press conference in the State House gardens in 2009 – Banda laughed, looked up at the tree and jokingly scolded: 'You have urinated on my jacket!'; later that year the State House's wild primates were all evicted (coincidence?)

MAP REF **P,22**

1. Home for these girls is Nzunga, in Zambia's Eastern Province
2. Netball skills draw a crowd in Bomakavumbe village near Petuake
3. A taxi boat prepares for its trip on Lake Tanganyika, which borders four countries
4. Are looking at me? A buffalo in Lower Zambezi National Park throws a challenging stare

1.

2.

3.

For anything to steal the limelight from this brilliant nation's unrivalled natural and historical treasures, it has to be something truly staggering in its own right. Tragically for Zimbabweans, their country's dire political leadership since independence has been just that – staggering. It was only the formation of the unity government in 2008 and the subsequent hyperinflation-stopping dollarisation of the economy that finally brought renewed hope to a population longing for progress. For travellers, the welcomes are as warm as they've always been, and the bounteous national parks are still offering some of Africa's most rewarding wildlife encounters. Zimbabwe is ready and waiting. All it's missing is you.

BEST TIME TO VISIT
May to October (the dry season)

TOP THINGS TO SEE
- Endangered African wild dogs hunting en masse in Hwange National Park
- Victoria Falls thundering below from the seat of a microlight aircraft
- The medieval city of Great Zimbabwe, once a religious and political capital
- Fossilised skeletons of dinosaurs while hiking on the Sentinel estate
- The 'wilderness of elephants', otherwise known as Gonarezhou National Park

TOP THINGS TO DO
- Push your canoe into the Zambezi's current and float serenely past hippos, elephants and crocodiles in Mana Pools National Park
- Sense the palpable spirit exuded by the sacred Matobo Hills, a dramatic showroom hosting 3000 ancient rock-art sites
- Fly like a superhero across Batoka Gorge on the 'Zambezi Swing'
- Walk into the Eastern Highlands' mists and wonder how you ended up in Scotland
- Walk with young lions in the wilds of Antelope Park

GETTING UNDER THE SKIN
Read *When a Crocodile Eats the Sun: A Memoir of Africa* by Peter Godwin, a moving story of a father's (and country's) demise

Listen to *Viva Zimbabwe*, a compilation of Zimbabwean musical genres, ranging from catchy political anthems to Sungura guitar melodies

Watch *Mugabe and the White African*, an intimate documentary following a white farmer and his family as they try to save their farm from the 'Land Reform' programme

Eat *sadza ne nyama* (maize-meal porridge with meat gravy)

Drink Bohlinger, a Zimbabwean-brewed lager

IN A WORD
Mhoro (Hello, in Shona)

TRADEMARKS
Victoria Falls and the Zambezi River; Robert Mugabe; internationally unrecognised election results; hyperinflation; Great Zimbabwe; compelling national parks

RANDOM FACT
During Zimbabwe's economic meltdown, inflation peaked at 89.7 sextillion per cent (89,700,000,000,000,000,000,000%), which meant prices were doubling each day; the largest bill printed was a 100 trillion dollar note

MAP REF Q,23

1. Charge! Rhinos make their move in Matobo National Park
2. Dry husks rustle in Harare as a woman picks corn
3. School cases all packed, children wait for the bus in Bulawayo
4. With an astonishing 1.7km-wide precipice, Victoria Falls plummets into the Zambezi River

DEPENDENCIES, OVERSEAS TERRITORIES, DEPARTMENTS & ADMINISTRATIVE DIVISIONS/REGIONS

AUSTRALIA
- » **Ashmore & Cartier Islands** (northwest of Australia in the Indian Ocean)
- » **Christmas Island** (south of Indonesia in the Indian Ocean)
- » **Cocos (Keeling) Islands** (south of Indonesia in the Indian Ocean)
- » **Coral Sea Islands** (northeast of Australia in the Coral Sea)
- » **Heard Island & McDonald Islands** (southwest of Australia in the southern Indian Ocean)
- » **Norfolk Island** (east of Australia in the South Pacific Ocean)

CHINA
- » **Hong Kong** (see p179)
- » **Macau** (see p239)

DENMARK
- » **Faroe Islands** (east of Norway in the North Atlantic Ocean)
- » **Greenland** (see p159)

FRANCE
- » **Bassas da India** (west of Madagascar in the Mozambique Channel)
- » **Clipperton Island** (southwest of Mexico in the North Pacific Ocean)
- » **Europa Island** (west of Madagascar in the Mozambique Channel)
- » **French Guiana** (see p145)
- » **French Polynesia** (east of Tahiti in the Pacific Ocean)
- » **French Southern & Antarctic Lands** (southeast of Africa in the southern Indian Ocean)
- » **Glorioso Islands** (northwest of Madgascar in the Indian Ocean)
- » **Guadeloupe** (see p163)
- » **Juan de Nova Island** (west of Madagascar in the Mozambique Channel)
- » **Martinique** (see p257)
- » **Mayotte** (in the Mozambique Channel in southern Africa, between Mozambique and Madagascar)
- » **New Caledonia** (see p289)
- » **Réunion** (see p445)
- » **Saint Pierre & Miquelon** (in the North Atlantic Ocean, south of east coast of Canada)
- » **Tromelin Island** (east of Madagascar in the Indian Ocean)
- » **Wallis & Futuna** (see p446)

NETHERLANDS
- » **Aruba** (see p444)
- » **Netherlands Antilles** (see p444)

NEW ZEALAND
- » **Cook Islands** (see p97)
- » **Niue** (see p445)
- » **Tokelau** (see p446)

NORWAY
- » **Bouvet Island** (southwest of South Africa in the South Atlantic Ocean)
- » **Jan Mayen** (east of Greenland in the Norwegian Sea)
- » **Svalbard** (see p446)

UK
- » **Anguilla** (see p19)
- » **Bermuda** (see p51)
- » **British Indian Ocean Territory** (see p445)
- » **British Virgin Islands** (see p435)
- » **Cayman Islands** (see p79)
- » **Falkland Islands** (see p137)
- » **Gibraltar** (see p445)
- » **Guernsey** (northwest of France in the English Channel)
- » **Jersey** (northwest of France in the English Channel)
- » **Isle of Man** (Irish Sea)
- » **Montserrat** (see p445)
- » **Pitcairn Islands** (see p319)
- » **Saint Helena** (includes Ascension, Tristan da Cunha, Gough, Inaccessible and the three Nightingale Islands)
- » **South Georgia & the South Sandwich Islands** (see p446)
- » **Turks & Caicos Islands** (see p411)

USA
- » **American Samoa** (see p341)
- » **Baker Island** (North Pacific Ocean)
- » **Guam** (see p165)
- » **Howland Island** (North Pacific Ocean)
- » **Jarvis Island** (South Pacific Ocean)
- » **Johnston Atoll** (southwest of Hawaii in the North Pacific Ocean)
- » **Kingman Reef** (North Pacific Ocean)
- » **Midway Islands** (west of Hawaii in the North Pacific Ocean)
- » **Navassa Island** (west of Haiti in the Caribbean Sea)
- » **Northern Mariana Islands** (see p165)
- » **Palmyra Atoll** (North Pacific Ocean)
- » **Puerto Rico** (see p325)
- » **Virgin Islands** (see p435)
- » **Wake Island** (North Pacific Ocean)

DISPUTED TERRITORIES
- » **Antarctica** (see p21)
- » **Gaza Strip**
- » **Paracel Islands**
- » **Spratly Islands**
- » **West Bank**
- » **Western Sahara**

OTHER PLACES OF INTEREST TO TRAVELLERS

The following destinations don't fit neatly elsewhere in this book. They are officially dependencies of other nations, but they are not large enough or on a road well enough travelled to warrant a full and separate entry. Despite this, at Lonely Planet we believe that these destinations are of special interest, whether that be due to wildlife or history or geography, and they are generally considered to have a strong independent identity and to be quite different from their parent countries. Tony Wheeler, Lonely Planet's founder and perennial explorer, compiled this section.

ARUBA & THE NETHERLANDS ANTILLES

CAPITAL Oranjestad (A), Willemstad (N) | **POPULATION** 103,000 (A), 227,000 (N)
AREA 193 sq km (A), 960 sq km (N) | **OFFICIAL LANGUAGE** Dutch

It's possible that the Dutch Antilles is the most concentrated area of multiculturalism in the world. Papiamento, spoken throughout the Netherlands Antilles, is testament to this fact – the language is derived from every culture that has impacted on the region, including traces of Spanish, Portuguese, Dutch, French and local Indian languages. The islands are diverse: there are the cutesy houses of Curaçao; ruggedly steep Saba; Sint Maarten with its large resorts and casinos; and the delightfully slow pace of Sint Eustatius.

DIEGO GARCIA – BRITISH INDIAN OCEAN TERRITORY (UK)

POPULATION 4000 | **AREA** 60 sq km | **OFFICIAL LANGUAGE** English

Diego Garcia and the islands of the Chagos Archipelago make up the British Indian Ocean Territory. Technically it's uninhabited: in the 1970s the island's British administrators deported the population and most of them now live in less than happy circumstances on Mauritius. They were replaced by military personnel as Diego Garcia became a military base, a stationary aircraft carrier handy for US B52s to set out on bombing missions to Iraq or Afghanistan. It also acts as an Indian Ocean alternative to Guantanamo Bay in Cuba. Don't plan on visiting the territory's islands, atolls and reefs; visitors are definitely not welcome.

GIBRALTAR (UK)

POPULATION 28,000 | **AREA** 7 sq km | **OFFICIAL LANGUAGE** English

Strategically situated guarding the Straits of Gibraltar, the narrow entrance to the Mediterranean from the Atlantic Ocean, the Rock makes an interesting stumbling block for British-Spanish relations. The Spanish want it back and the British would probably be happy to hand it over, but there's no way the citizens of Gibraltar will go. They like their curious little corner of England on the shores of the Mediterranean. Towering over the town, the upper Rock offers spectacular views, and houses the colony of Barbary macaques – Europe's only primates. If they ever depart, so the legend goes, so will the British.

MONTSERRAT (UK)

CAPITAL Plymouth | **POPULATION** 4800 | **AREA** 100 sq km
OFFICIAL LANGUAGE English

In 1997 a volcanic eruption devastated Montserrat. Despite plenty of warning that after 400 sleepy years the Soufrière Hills Volcano was about to wake up, there were still 19 deaths. Today, more than 10 years after the calamity, life is moving forward. But despite the reconstruction, there's a certain magnificent desolation about the place. Montserrat's few visitors come for volcano-related day trips. Those who stay longer will relish the solitude and enjoy the chance to become part of the island's rebirth.

NIUE (NEW ZEALAND)

CAPITAL Alofi | **POPULATION** 1400 | **AREA** 259 sq km
OFFICIAL LANGUAGES Niuean & English

Midway between Tonga and the Cook Islands, which makes it a long way from anywhere, Niue is a classic example of a makatea island, an upthrust coral reef. It rises often vertically out of the ocean so there's very little beach, but in compensation there are amazing chasms, ravines, gullies and caves all around the coast. Some of them extend underwater, giving the island superb scuba-diving sites. Like a number of other Pacific nations, the world's smallest self-governing state has been suffering a population decline: today there are more Niueans in New Zealand than on 'the Rock of Polynesia'.

RÉUNION

CAPITAL St-Denis | **POPULATION** 782,000 | **AREA** 2517 sq km
OFFICIAL LANGUAGE French

Réunion is so sheer and lush, it looks like it has risen dripping wet from the sea – which it effectively has, being the tip of a massive submerged prehistoric volcano. The island is run as an overseas department of France, and French culture dominates every facet of life, from the coffee and croissant in the morning to the bottle of Evian and the carafe of red wine at the dinner table. However, the French atmosphere of the island has a firmly tropical twist, with subtle traces of Indian, African and Chinese cultures.

SOUTH GEORGIA (UK)

CAPITAL Grytviken I **POPULATION** 10–20 I **AREA** 3755 sq km I **OFFICIAL LANGUAGE** English

Aptly described as looking like an Alpine mountain range soaring straight out of the ocean, South Georgia's spectacular topography is matched only by its equally spectacular wildlife. The remote island's human population, scientists of the British Antarctic Survey, may drop as low as 10 during the long Antarctic winter. But there are two to three million seals, a similar number of penguins and 50 million birds, including a large proportion of the world's albatrosses. Add spectacular examples of industrial archaeology in the shape of the island's half a dozen abandoned whaling stations, plus South Georgia's role as the stage for the final act in Sir Ernest Shackleton's epic escape from the ice, and it's no wonder this is one of the most popular destinations for Antarctic tourists.

SVALBARD (NORWAY)

CAPITAL Longyearbyen I **POPULATION** 2100 I **AREA** 61,229 sq km
OFFICIAL LANGUAGE Norwegian

Far to the north of Norway, the archipelago of Svalbard has become a popular destination for Arctic travellers, keen to cruise the ice floes in search of whales, seals, walruses and polar bears. Apart from wildlife there are also some terrific hiking possibilities on the main island where you might encounter reindeer and Arctic foxes. The main town, the engagingly named Longyearbyen, has a long history of coal mining.

TOKELAU (NEW ZEALAND)

POPULATION 1400 I **AREA** 12 sq km I **OFFICIAL LANGUAGES** Tokelaun, English & Samoan

Tokelau consists of three tiny atolls, each of them laid out on classic atoll design principles: a necklace of palm-fringed islands around a central lagoon. Off to the north of Samoa, the islands are not only a long way from anywhere, but also a long way from each other; it's 150km from Atafu past Nukunonu to Fakaofo. They're also very crowded: there may be only 1400 people but they've got very little land to share; none of the islets is more than 200m wide and you've got to climb a coconut tree to get more than 5m above sea level. Getting there is difficult even for yachties, as none of the lagoons has a pass deep enough for a yacht to enter.

TRISTAN DA CUNHA (UK)

CAPITAL Edinburgh I **POPULATION** 260 I **AREA** 98 sq km I **OFFICIAL LANGUAGE** English

Officially a dependency of St Helena, over 2300km to the north, Tristan da Cunha is frequently cited as the most remote populated place in the world. The island is a simple, towering volcano cone, and an eruption in 1961 forced the complete evacuation of the island. The displaced islanders put up with life in England for two years but most of them returned as soon as the island was declared safe in 1963 and went straight back to catching the crawfish that are the island's main export. Nightingale, Inaccessible and two smaller islands lie slightly southeast of the main island.

WALLIS & FUTUNA (FRANCE)

CAPITAL Mata'Utu I **POPULATION** 15,300 I **AREA** 274 sq km
OFFICIAL LANGUAGES Wallisian, Futunan & French

This French Pacific colony is made up of two islands, separated by 230km of open ocean and remarkably dissimilar. Wallis is relatively low lying with a surrounding lagoon fringed by classic sandy *motus* (islets) while Futuna is much more mountainous and paired with smaller Alofi. The populations are equally dissimilar: Futuna has connections to Samoa while the Wallis links were with Tonga. Wallis has one of the Pacific's best archaeological sites at Talietumu and an unusual collection of crater lakes, while both islands are dotted with colourful and often eccentrically designed churches.

THE AUTHORS

CAROLYN BAIN

AREA OF EXPERTISE Scandinavia and Baltic Europe | **YEARS AS AN LP AUTHOR** 10
NUMBER OF COUNTRIES VISITED 41 | **FAVOURITE COUNTRY** Denmark

Melbourne-based Carolyn was raised on a steady diet of ABBA and first travelled around Scandinavia as a teenager, while living and studying in Denmark. That experience left her with a love of all that Scandinavia has to offer: open, egalitarian societies populated by unfairly attractive people; long summer nights and cosy winters; superb design; unpronounceable vowels. It seemed only natural that from Scandinavia, she branched out to the Baltic countries. For Lonely Planet she has covered, among other destinations, Denmark, Sweden and Estonia.

JOE BINDLOSS

AREA OF EXPERTISE Asia | **YEARS AS AN LP AUTHOR** 10 | **NUMBER OF COUNTRIES VISITED** 50 | **FAVOURITE COUNTRY** India

Joe has worked on more than 30 guidebooks for Lonely Planet. This has taken him all over Asia – from India and Nepal to Myanmar, Malaysia, Thailand and the Philippines – with the odd detour to Australia, Africa and the Indian Ocean. When not writing for Lonely Planet, Joe works as a journalist and restaurant critic in London, writing for a broad sweep of magazines, newspapers, websites and travel publishers.

CELESTE BRASH

AREA OF EXPERTISE The Pacific | **YEARS AS AN LP AUTHOR** 5 | **NUMBER OF COUNTRIES VISITED** 37 | **FAVOURITE COUNTRY** French Polynesia

Celeste's first five years in French Polynesia were spent living on a remote atoll but for the last 10 years she has called Tahiti home. In the meantime she has travelled the breadth of the Pacific and explored much of the rest of the world. Her award-winning travel stories have been published in Travelers' Tales books and her articles in publications including the *LA Times* and *Islands* magazine. Coconut Radio (www.coconutradio.blogspot.com) is her blog about travel and Polynesia.

PAUL CLAMMER

AREA OF EXPERTISE the Islamic world | **YEARS AS AN LP AUTHOR** 6 | **NUMBER OF COUNTRIES VISITED** 37 | **FAVOURITE COUNTRY** Afghanistan

Once a molecular biologist, Paul has long since traded his test tubes for a rucksack and the vicarious life of a travel writer. Overlanding in Africa was his first significant travel experience, but since then he's danced until dawn in Port-au-Prince's nightclubs; narrowly avoided being tear-gassed in Peru; broken bread with the Taliban a fortnight before the 9/11 attacks; and learned how to argue with taxi drivers in half a dozen new languages. It beats working behind a desk.

MARY FITZPATRICK

AREA OF EXPERTISE Southern and East Africa | **YEARS AS AN LP AUTHOR** 14 | **NUMBER OF COUNTRIES VISITED** over 70 | **FAVOURITE COUNTRIES** Mozambique, Tanzania and South Africa

Mary first arrived in Africa almost two decades ago, and immediately fell in love with the continent. She has spent most of the intervening time working in, travelling around and writing about many of its countries. Among her most cherished southern Africa moments: witnessing South Africa's first multiracial elections; hiking in the snow in Lesotho; sailing in a dhow past remote Indian Ocean islands; and being on the receiving end of the wonderful hospitality of so many residents.

WILL GOURLAY

AREA OF EXPERTISE Southeastern Europe | **YEARS AS AN LP AUTHOR** 7 | **NUMBER OF COUNTRIES VISITED** 48 | **FAVOURITE COUNTRIES** Greece, Turkey and Iran

Will first arrived in Europe as a wet-behind-the-ears backpacker just after the Wall came down, and was immediately smitten. He has since studied in Spain, taught in Turkey, worked as a writer and editor in London and his native Melbourne, and travelled extensively, often with other generations of Gourlays. In the process he has become a bit obsessed with Persian bazaars, Balkan cinema, Georgian architecture, Kurdish culture, Greek mountain lore, Turkish history, post-rock guitar music and books about all of the above.

ANTHONY HAM

AREA OF EXPERTISE North Africa, West Africa and Middle East | **YEARS AS AN LP AUTHOR** 11 | **NUMBER OF COUNTRIES VISITED** 52 | **FAVOURITE COUNTRIES** Mali and Spain

Anthony is a Madrid-based Australian writer and photographer who has written more than 40 guidebooks for Lonely Planet, as well as articles on current affairs and the environment for magazines and newspapers around the world. He was once a refugee lawyer and has a Masters degree in Middle Eastern politics, but has learned far more listening to storytellers in Damascus or staring into the embers of a campfire deep in the Sahara Desert.

BRADLEY MAYHEW

AREA OF EXPERTISE Central Asia and the Himalayas | **YEARS AS AN LP AUTHOR** 12 **NUMBER OF COUNTRIES VISITED** 43 | **FAVOURITE COUNTRY** Tibet

Bradley is Lonely Planet's main expert on landlocked mountainous countries, Chinese sleeper buses and mutton-based cuisine. It's taken him years to scramble to such lofty heights. Bradley has lectured on Central Asia to the Royal Geographical Society, is the co-author of the *Odyssey* guide to Uzbekistan and has written Lonely Planet guides to Central Asia, Bhutan, Tibet and Nepal, among others. A graduate of Oriental Studies from Oxford University, he also specialises in Silk Road history and the more remote corners of China.

CAROLYN MCCARTHY

AREA OF EXPERTISE Latin America | **YEARS AS AN LP AUTHOR** 7 | **NUMBER OF COUNTRIES VISITED** 18 | **FAVOURITE COUNTRY** Chile

Author of 10 travel guides, Carolyn has been writing about the Americas since 1998. No stranger to tough travel, she has explored the Amazon Basin via dugout canoe and solo hiked Patagonia. Her work seeks out original destinations, explores environmental issues and forges meaningful connections with local cultures. A former Fulbright scholar and Banff Mountain Culture grantee, Carolyn's writing has appeared in *National Geographic,* the *Boston Globe, Sherman's Travel* and other publications. Follow her Americas blog at www.carolynswildblueyonder.blogspot.com.

MATT PHILLIPS

AREA OF EXPERTISE Africa | **YEARS AS AN LP AUTHOR** 6 | **NUMBER OF COUNTRIES VISITED** 51 | **FAVOURITE COUNTRY** Ethiopia

Matt has shared campfires with hyenas in Zimbabwe, crossed the Sahara in a couple of directions, dodged Mauritanian landmines, skydived over the Namib Desert and wept for joy when an Ethiopian highlander successfully gave birth in his 4WD. His extensive African experiences never seem to be anything less than extraordinary, and that's why he's covered over two dozen of its nations for Lonely Planet. He's penned numerous guidebooks, coordinated Lonely Planet's *Africa Book,* and is currently the editor of *Travel Africa* magazine.

ROBERT REID

AREA OF EXPERTISE Vietnam and New York City | **YEARS AS AN LP AUTHOR** 8 **NUMBER OF COUNTRIES VISITED** 34 | **FAVOURITE COUNTRY** Home, after a long trip

Robert is Lonely Planet's US travel editor and an author of a couple dozen Lonely Planet guidebooks (including Central America, Trans-Siberian Railway and New York City). He has lived in London, Melbourne, San Francisco, Ho Chi Minh City and New York City, but still occasionally pulls out his Oklahoma accent. He blogs on the Lonely Planet website and runs the '76-Second Travel Show' at www.reidontravel.com.

REGIS ST LOUIS

AREA OF EXPERTISE South America, Russia and Eastern Europe | **YEARS AS AN LP AUTHOR** 7 | **NUMBER OF COUNTRIES VISITED** 41 | **FAVOURITE COUNTRIES** Brazil and Russia

Regis grew up in a small Indiana town and dreamed of big adventures in faraway lands. His obsession with foreign languages and world cultures led him to extensive travels in the former Soviet Union and Latin America, where he hiked the Andes, boated up the Amazon and logged thousands of miles on dodgy roads – often on assignment for Lonely Planet. He speaks Russian, Spanish, Portuguese and French and has contributed to dozens of Lonely Planet titles. He lives in New York City.

RYAN VER BERKMOES

AREA OF EXPERTISE North America, Caribbean, Western Europe | **YEARS AS AN LP AUTHOR** 12 | **NUMBER OF COUNTRIES VISITED** 87 | **FAVOURITE COUNTRY** France

Ryan has been travelling since he was carried aboard a flight at the tender age of one month. During a long career as a journalist he covered everything from wars to bars worldwide and definitely prefers the latter. Although he remains profoundly moved by time spent in places like Afghanistan and feels that no year is complete without a trip to the Yukon, these days Ryan feels most at home in places where he can don his favoured uniform of shorts, sandals and a T-shirt.

NICOLA WILLIAMS

AREA OF EXPERTISE Western Europe | **YEARS AS AN LP AUTHOR** 13 | **NUMBER OF COUNTRIES VISITED** 42 | **FAVOURITE COUNTRY** Italy

Living on the French side of Lake Geneva, Nicola has adopted border-hopping as a way of life. She started out as a singleton living the high life in Vilnius, clocking up months of night trains as features editor of the *Baltic Times* and subsequent editor for publisher In Your Pocket. Three kids later, as independent writer and editorial consultant, she pours her professional energy into more gourmet French, Swiss and Italian travel. Nicola blogs at www.tripalong.wordpress.com and tweets @tripalong.

THE TRAVEL BOOK
A JOURNEY THROUGH EVERY COUNTRY IN THE WORLD

2nd Edition
Published September 2010
First Published October 2004

PUBLISHER Chris Rennie
ASSOCIATE PUBLISHER Ben Handicott
COMMISSIONING EDITOR Janine Eberle
PROJECT MANAGER Jane Atkin
COORDINATING EDITOR Alison Ridgway
MANAGING EDITORS Liz Heynes, Katie Lynch, Laura Stansfeld
ASSISTING EDITORS Trent Holden, Erin Richards, Louisa Syme, Kate Whitfield
ART DIRECTION AND DESIGN Mark Adams
LAYOUT DESIGNER Jim Hsu
ASSISTING LAYOUT DESIGNERS Carol Jackson, Nicholas Colicchia, Wibowo Rusli, Carlos Solarte
MANAGING LAYOUT DESIGNER Sally Darmody
IMAGE RESEARCH Sabrina Dalbesio, Jane Hart, Naomi Parker, Aude Vauconsant
CARTOGRAPHERS Hunor Csutoros, Wayne Murphy
PRE-PRESS PRODUCTION Ryan Evans
PRINT PRODUCTION MANAGER Graham Imeson
THANKS Glenn Beanland, Ellen Burrows, Chris Girdler, Brendan Dempsey, Martin Heng, Laura Jane, Indra Kilfoyle, Yvonne Kirk, Chris Lee Ack, Nic Lehman, Charity Mackinnon, Kate Morgan, Jacqui Saunders, Dianne Schallmeiner, Tony Wheeler, Celia Wood

PUBLISHED BY
Lonely Planet Pty Ltd ABN 36 005 607 983
90 Maribyrnong St, Footscray, Victoria 3011, Australia

ISBN 978 1 74179 211 9
Text & maps © Lonely Planet Pty Ltd 2010
Photos © as indicated 2010

PHOTOGRAPHS
Many of the images in this guide are available for licensing from **Lonely Planet Images** www.lonelyplanetimages.com.

Printed by Colorcraft Ltd, Hong Kong
Printed in Hong Kong

LONELY PLANET OFFICES

AUSTRALIA (HEAD OFFICE)
90 Maribyrnong St, Footscray, Victoria, 3011
Phone 03 8379 8000 **Fax** 03 8379 8111
Email talk2us@lonelyplanet.com.au

USA
150 Linden St, Oakland, CA 94607
Phone 510 250 6400 **Toll free** 800 275 8555
Fax 510 893 8572 **Email** info@lonelyplanet.com

UK
2nd Floor, 186 City Rd, London, EC1V 2NT
Phone 020 7106 2100 **Fax** 020 7106 2101
Email go@lonelyplanet.co.uk

FRONT COVER IMAGES (FROM LEFT TO RIGHT) Mother carrying daughter swathed in hand-woven fabrics (Richard I'Anson / Lonely Planet Images); Female lion moving cubs to new den (Dave Hamman / Lonely Planet Images); Baobabs on Avenue du Baobab at sunset (Anders Blomqvist / Lonely Planet Images); Long Horn Miao girls in traditional costume to celebrate Flower Dance Festival (Keren Su / Lonely Planet Images); Staircase at Vatican Museum (Tony Burns / Lonely Planet Images). **INSIDE FRONT COVER IMAGES** (FROM LEFT TO RIGHT) Goldfields region: "Balanced Rock", a giant granite boulder is part of a collection of large stones near Kookynie, Western Australia (Ross Barnett / Lonely Planet Images); Vegetable sellers crossing Yamuna River at sunrise in front of Taj Mahal (Michael Gebicki / Lonely Planet Images).

SPINE IMAGE Girl wearing bakit kebaya at temple ceremony at Sengkidu (Gregory Adams / Lonely Planet Images). **BACK COVER IMAGES** (CLOCKWISE FROM TOP LEFT) St Paul's Cathedral and Millennium Bridge (Doug McKinlay / Lonely Planet Images); Performer playing cymbals at parade on Tonhwamunno St, Nagwon-dong (Jeff Yates / Lonely Planet Images); People in traditional costume dancing Sevillana inside *caseta* (marquee) during Feria de Abril fiesta (Bruce Yuan-Yue Bi / Lonely Planet Images); Boy from the Maasai tribe near the Ngorongoro Crater, Ngorongoro Conservation Area (David Wall / Lonely Planet Images); Workers harvesting spring onions (Nicholas Reuss / Lonely Planet Images); Pow Wow – Ojicree (Emily Riddell / Lonely Planet Images); Puffins, Breidavik, Latrabjarg Peninsula, (Frans Lemmens / Lonely Planet Images); Skeleton as folk art for sale (Richard I'Anson / Lonely Planet Images); Nordenskjold Glacier and medial moraine (Graeme Cornwallis / Lonely Planet Images); Young dancer and musician in City Palace Cafe (Brent Winebrenner / Lonely Planet Images); Cuban musician playing double bass at restaurant in Vieja district (Christian Aslund / Lonely Planet Images); Mountain gorilla in Volcanoes National Park, Ruhengeri, Rwanda (Ariadne Van Zandbergen/ Lonely Planet Images); Nyatapola Temple and surrounding buildings of Taumadhi Tole at sunset (Ryan Fox / Lonely Planet Images); Sculpture of face on Roman ruins, Leptis Magna (Frans Lemmens / Lonely Planet Images); Buskers performing on street corner, St Michel, Latin Quarter (Kevin Clogstoun / Lonely Planet Images); Neon sign at Flamingo Hotel (Oliver Strewe / Lonely Planet Images); Rocky outcrops rising behind the sand dunes of the Sahara Desert, Akakus (Acacus) National Park (Frans Lemmens / Lonely Planet Images); Tattooed dancer with headdress (Oliver Strewe / Lonely Planet Images); Young monks, Wat Si Saket temple (Jerry Galea / Lonely Planet Images); Campsite at Patriot Hills, Ellsworth Mountains (David Tipling / Lonely Planet Images); Four young smiling trainee sumos (Martin Moos / Lonely Planet Images); Interior of Reichstag dome (Nicholas Pavloff / Lonely Planet Images); People climbing on Monument to the Discoveries (Jean-Pierre Lescourret / Lonely Planet Images); Changing of presidential guard in front of Parliament Building, Syntagma Square (Krzysztof Dydynski / Lonely Planet Images); Tango dancers at Sunday market in Plaza Dorrego (Michael Taylor / Lonely Planet Images); Marsaxlokk harbor (Jean-Pierre Lescourret / Lonely Planet Images); Portrait of sadhu (Hindu holy man) outside Kasthamandap temple in Durbar Square (Nicholas Reuss / Lonely Planet Images); Cheetah and cubs, Masai Mara National Reserve (Alex Dissanayake / Lonely Planet Images). **INSIDE BACK COVER IMAGES** (FROM LEFT TO RIGHT) Rain falling on Buddhist monks preparing to participate in Tamshing Goemba monastery Tsechu festival (Gavin Gough / Lonely Planet Images); Girls perparing to perform an Indian dance (Felix Hug / Lonely Planet Images).

PAGE 1 Young Touareg woman and baby at festival in Gao (Frans Lemmens / Lonely Planet Images). **PAGES 2–3** Sufi dancing from Egyptian Heritage Dance Troupe (Becca Posterino / Lonely Planet Images). **PAGE 4** (CLOCKWISE FROM TOP LEFT) Portrait of woman of Rendille tribe (Ariadne Van Zandbergen / Lonely Planet Images); Visitors viewing Glacier Perito Moreno from catwalk (Douglas Steakley / Lonely Planet Images); Men embracing at Pushkar Fair (Dan Gair / Lonely Planet Images); Dancers performing at Wangdue Phodrang Dzong Tsechu festival (Gavin Gough / Lonely Planet Images). **PAGE 5** (CLOCKWISE FROM TOP LEFT) Steamed dumplings on boat on river (Richard I'Anson / Lonely Planet Images); Lioness in tall grass (Andrew Parkinson / Lonely Planet Images); Rio city garbage men in front of their Copacabana headquarters (John Maier Jr / Lonely Planet Images); Brooklyn Bridge cables from pedestrian walkway (Jeff Greenberg / Lonely Planet Images).